MINE
YOSHIZAKI

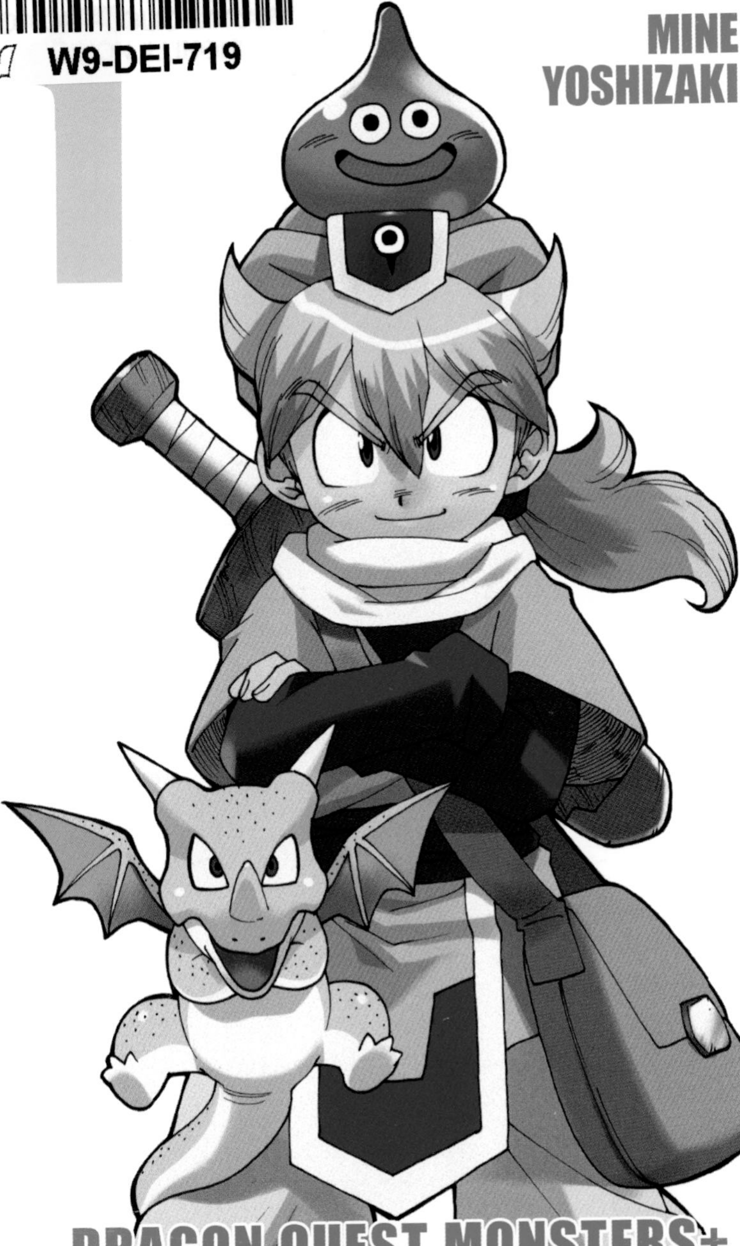

DRAGON QUEST MONSTERS+

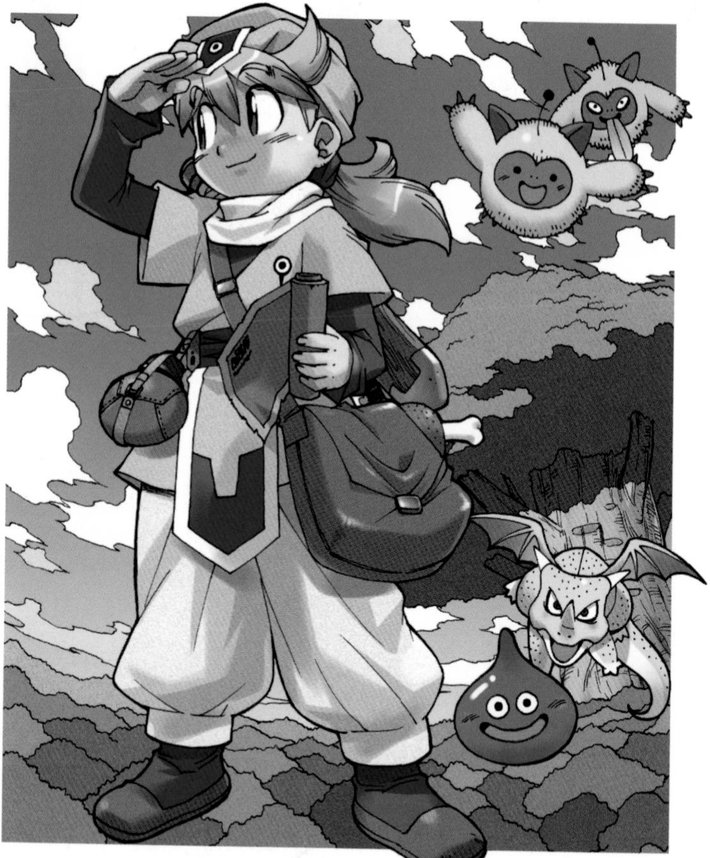

DQM+ 1
DRAGON QUEST MONSTERS

CONTENTS

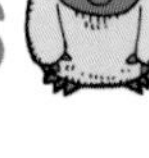

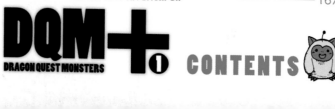

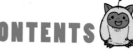

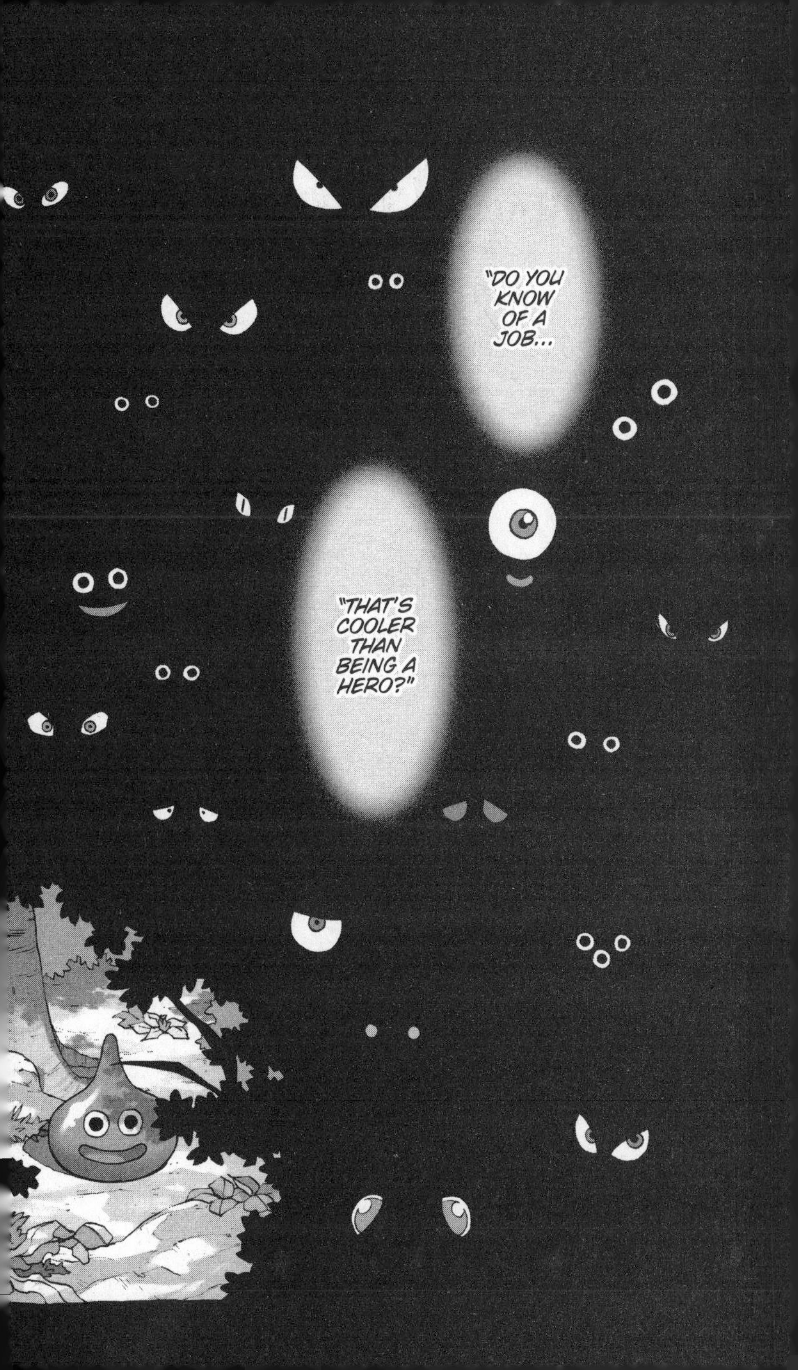
"DO YOU KNOW OF A JOB...
"THAT'S COOLER THAN BEING A HERO?"

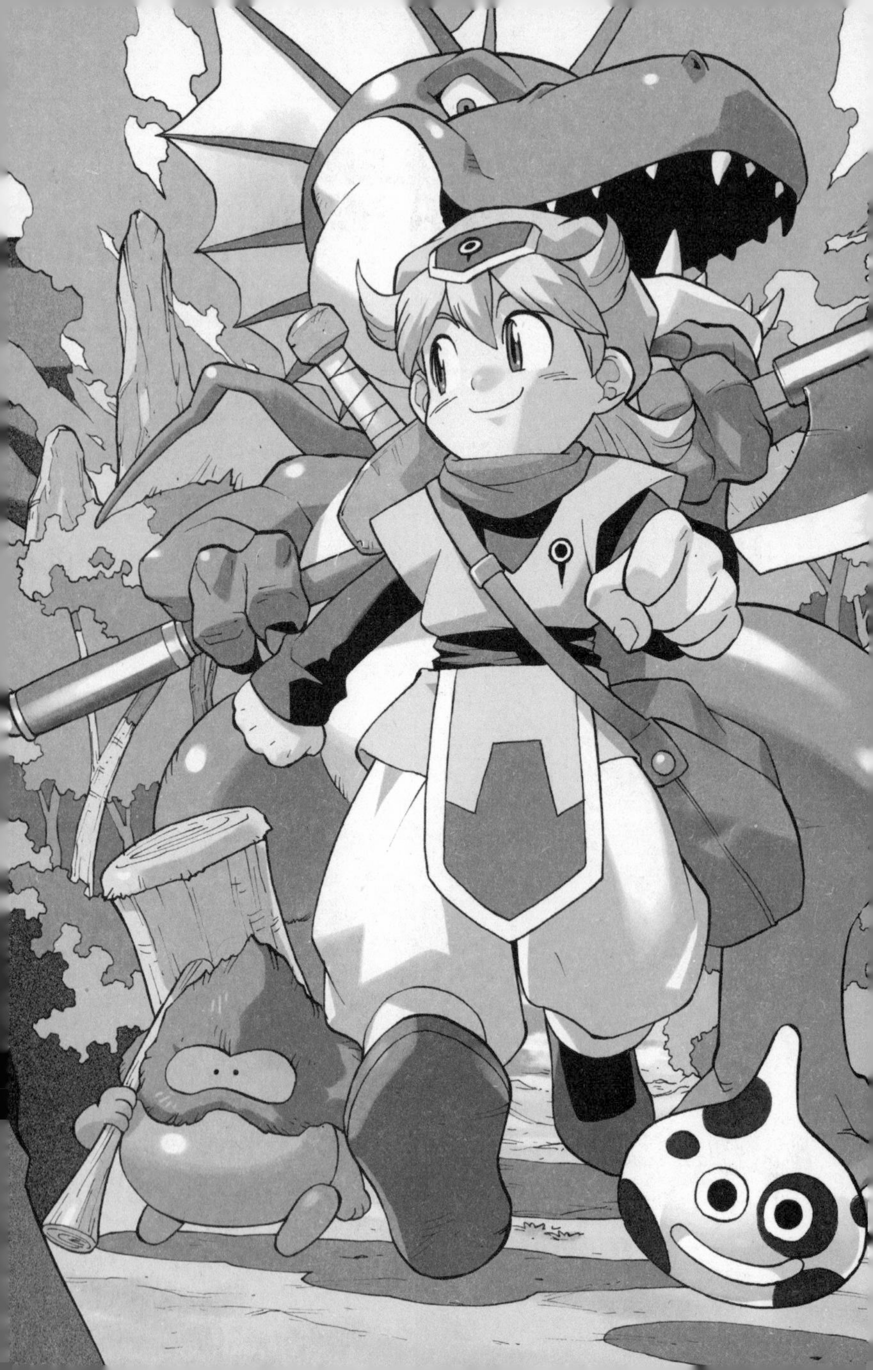

The 1st Night

IT'S WAY COOLER THAN BEING A HERO, YOU KNOW...!!

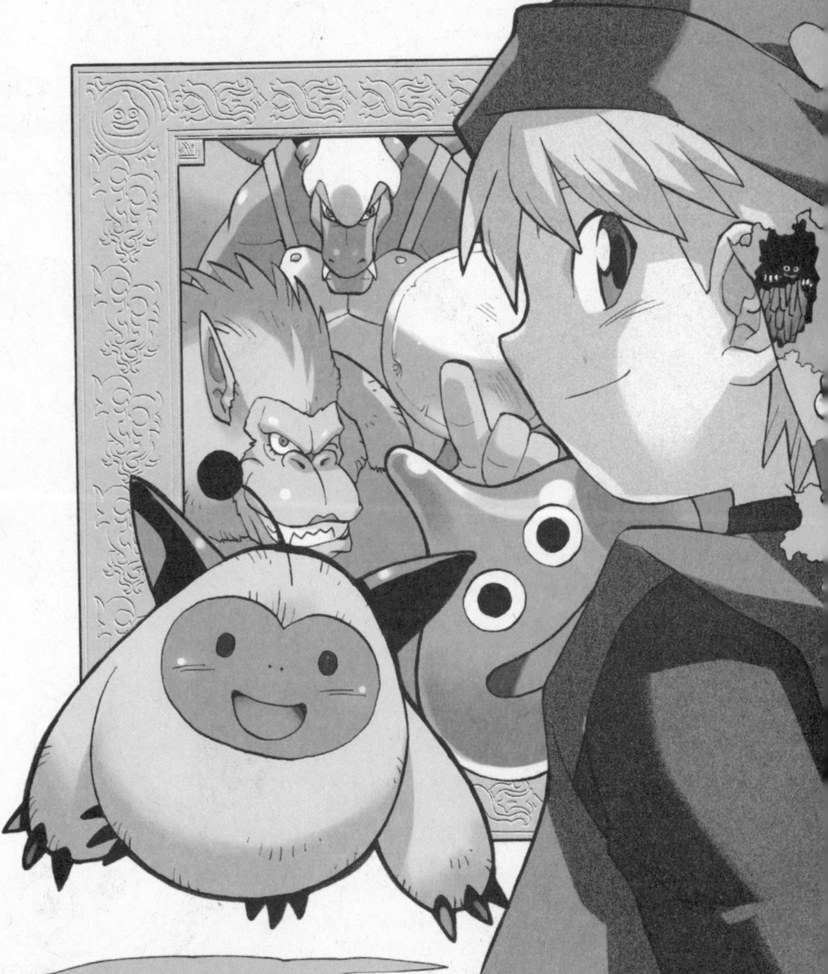

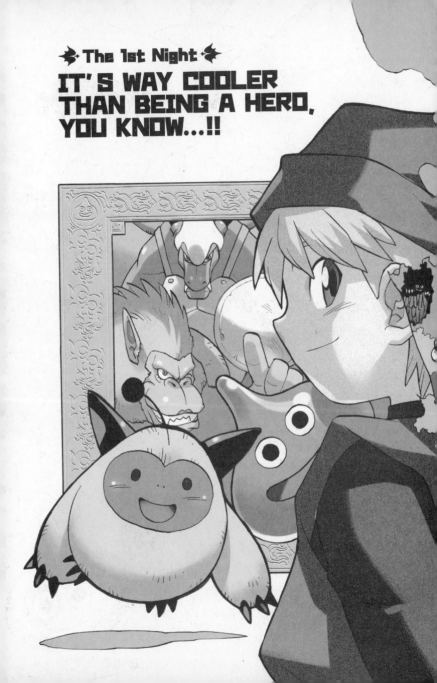

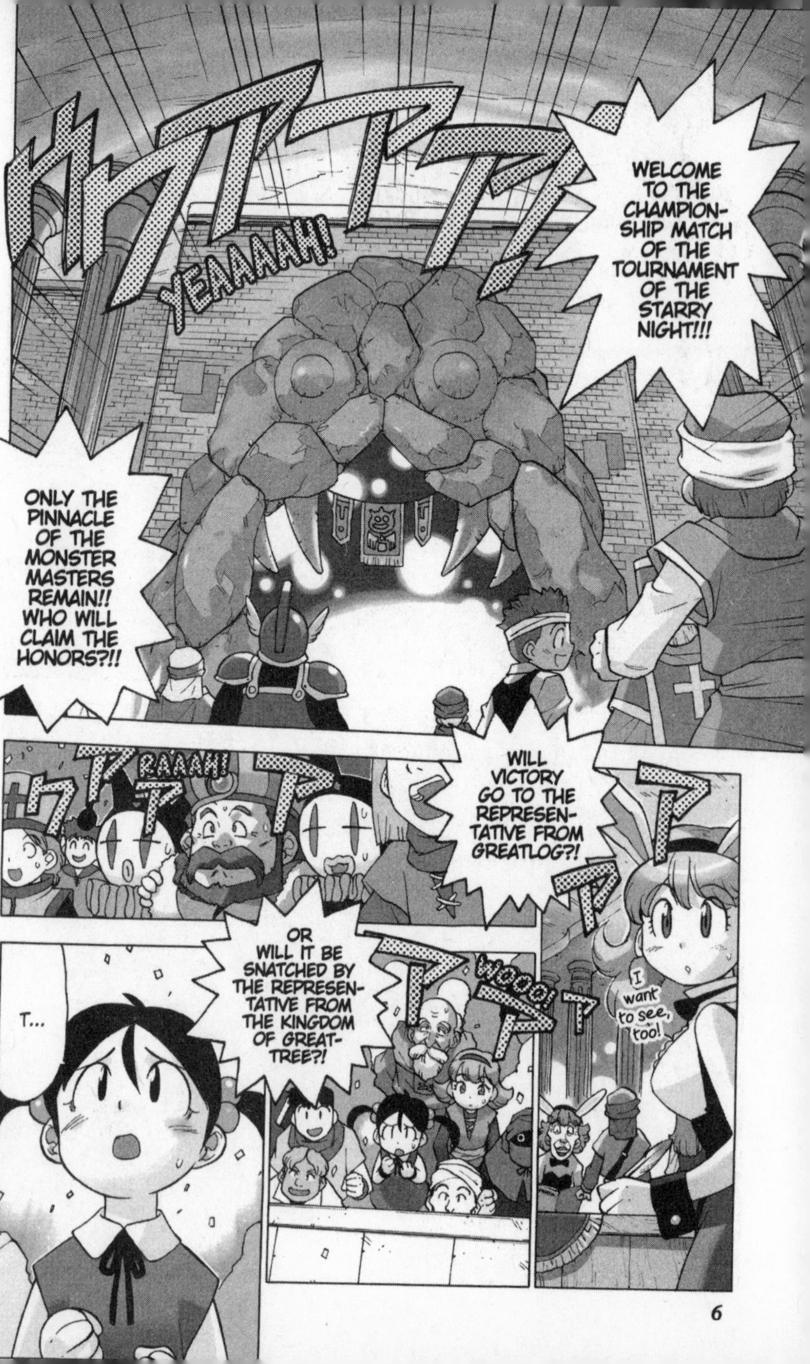
WELCOME TO THE CHAMPIONSHIP MATCH OF THE TOURNAMENT OF THE STARRY NIGHT!!!
YEAAAAH!
ONLY THE PINNACLE OF THE MONSTER MASTERS REMAIN!! WHO WILL CLAIM THE HONORS?!!
WILL VICTORY GO TO THE REPRESENTATIVE FROM GREATLOG?!
I want to see, too!
RAAAH!
OR WILL IT BE SNATCHED BY THE REPRESENTATIVE FROM THE KINGDOM OF GREAT-TREE?!
WOOO!
T...

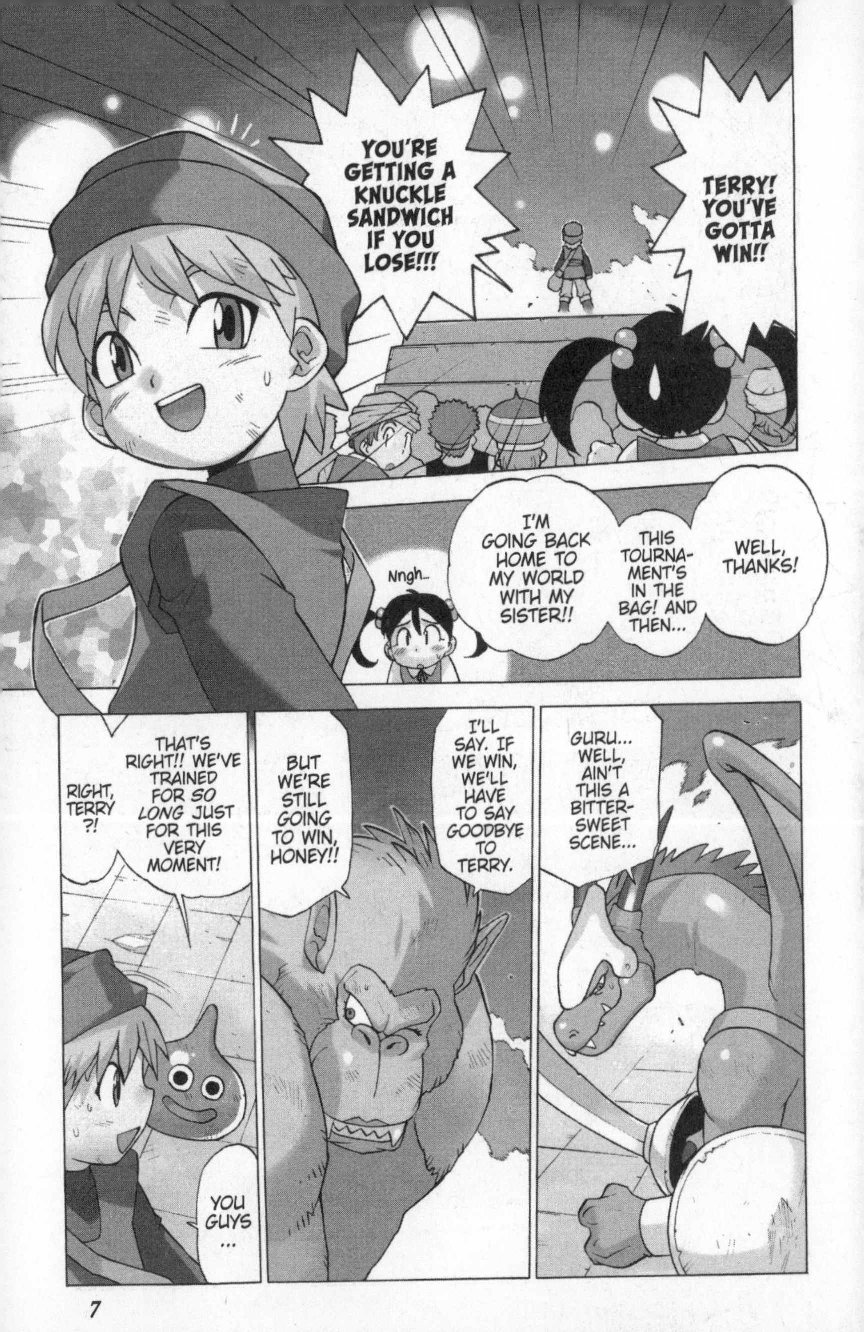
TERRY! YOU'VE GOTTA WIN!!
YOU'RE GETTING A KNUCKLE SANDWICH IF YOU LOSE!!!
WELL, THANKS!
THIS TOURNAMENT'S IN THE BAG! AND THEN...
I'M GOING BACK HOME TO MY WORLD WITH MY SISTER!!
Nngh..
GURU... WELL, AIN'T THIS A BITTER-SWEET SCENE...
I'LL SAY. IF WE WIN, WE'LL HAVE TO SAY GOODBYE TO TERRY.
BUT WE'RE STILL GOING TO WIN, HONEY!!
THAT'S RIGHT!! WE'VE TRAINED FOR SO *LONG* JUST FOR THIS VERY MOMENT!
RIGHT, TERRY?!
YOU GUYS ...

DQM +

DRAGON QUEST MONSTERS

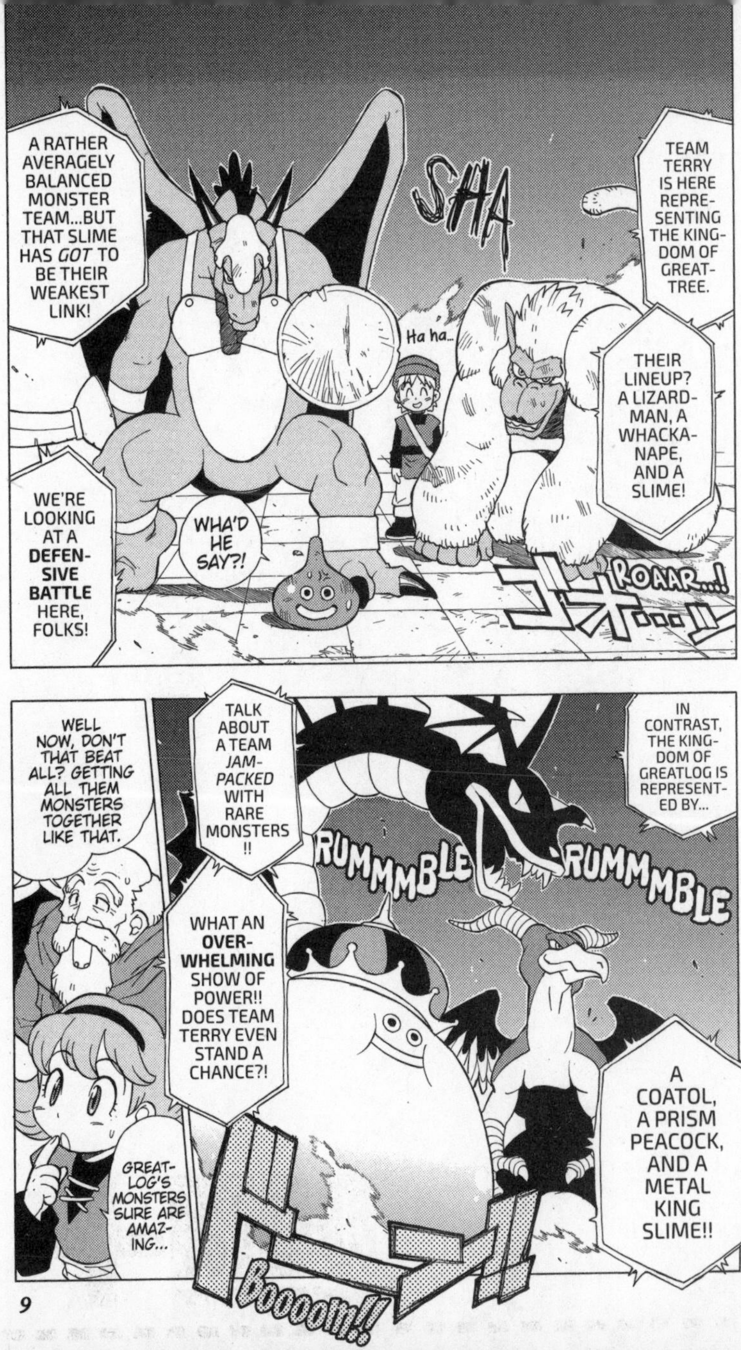

TEAM TERRY IS HERE REPRESENTING THE KINGDOM OF GREATTREE.
SHA
Ha ha...
THEIR LINEUP? A LIZARDMAN, A WHACKANAPE, AND A SLIME!
A RATHER AVERAGELY BALANCED MONSTER TEAM...BUT THAT SLIME HAS *GOT* TO BE THEIR WEAKEST LINK!
WHA'D HE SAY?!
WE'RE LOOKING AT A **DEFENSIVE BATTLE** HERE, FOLKS!
ROAAR...!
IN CONTRAST, THE KINGDOM OF GREATLOG IS REPRESENTED BY...
RUMMMBLE RUMMMBLE
TALK ABOUT A TEAM *JAM-PACKED* WITH RARE MONSTERS!!
WELL NOW, DON'T THAT BEAT ALL? GETTING ALL THEM MONSTERS TOGETHER LIKE THAT.
A COATOL, A PRISM PEACOCK, AND A METAL KING SLIME!!
WHAT AN **OVERWHELMING** SHOW OF POWER!! DOES TEAM TERRY EVEN STAND A CHANCE?!
GREATLOG'S MONSTERS SURE ARE AMAZING...
boooom!!

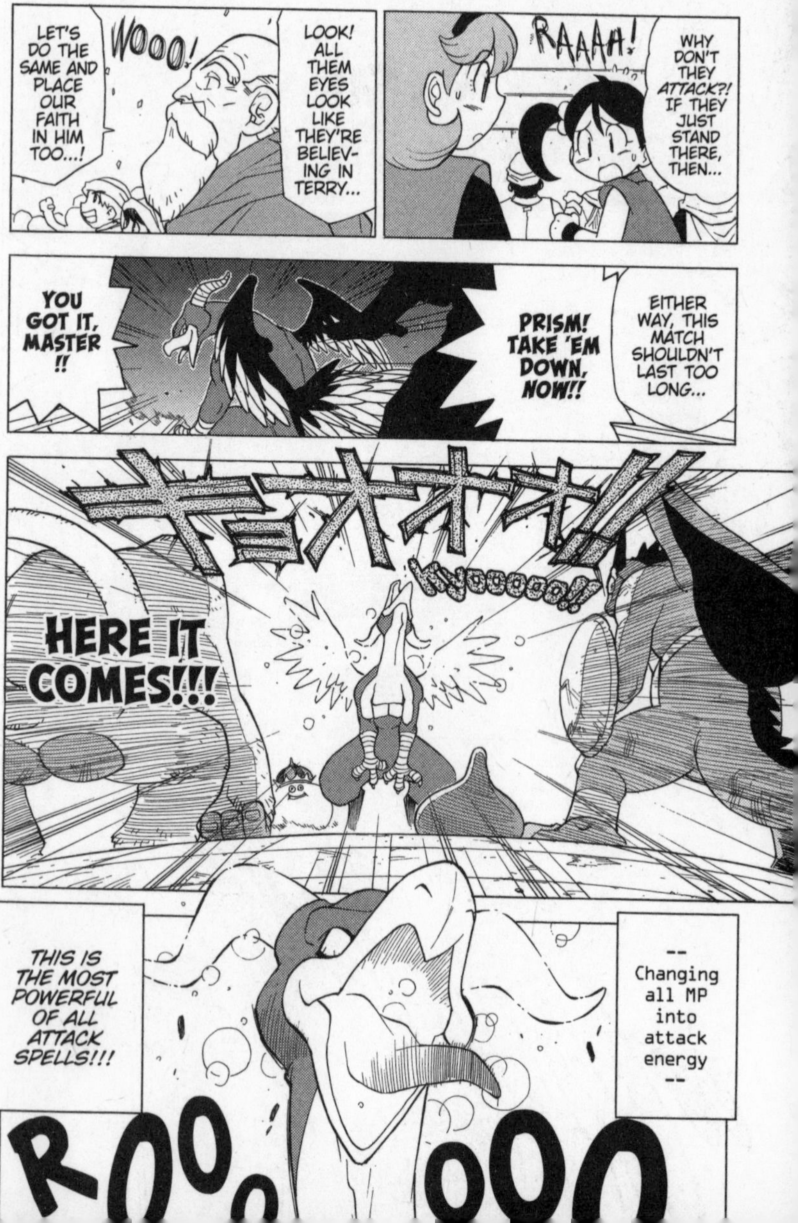
RAAAH!
WHY DON'T THEY ATTACK?! IF THEY JUST STAND THERE, THEN...
LOOK! ALL THEM EYES LOOK LIKE THEY'RE BELIEV-ING IN TERRY...
WOOO!
LET'S DO THE SAME AND PLACE OUR FAITH IN HIM TOO...!
EITHER WAY, THIS MATCH SHOULDN'T LAST TOO LONG...
PRISM! TAKE 'EM DOWN, NOW!!
YOU GOT IT, MASTER!!
キョオオオ!!
KYOOOOOO!!
HERE IT COMES!!!
-- Changing all MP into attack energy --
THIS IS THE MOST POWERFUL OF ALL ATTACK SPELLS!!!
ROOO OOO

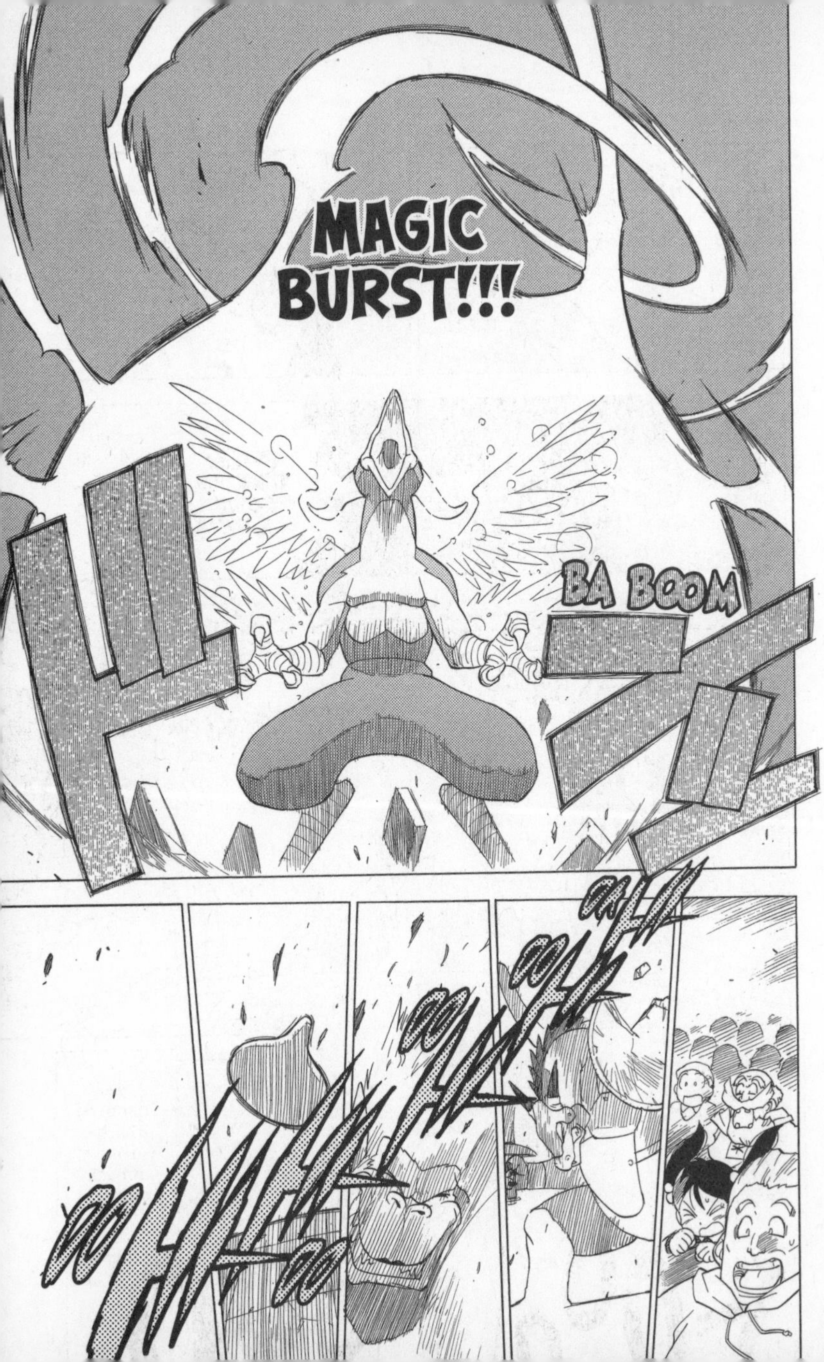
MAGIC BURST!!!
BA BOOM

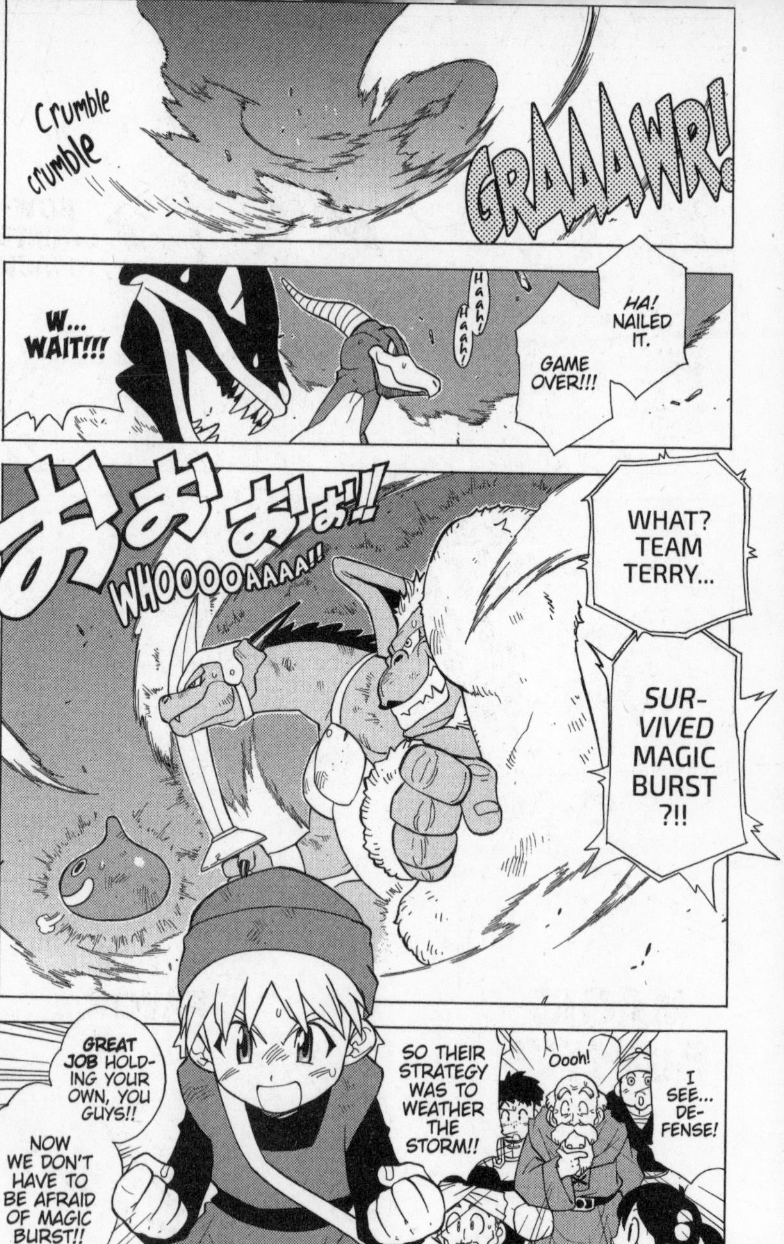
GRAAAWR!
Crumble crumble
HA! NAILED IT.
GAME OVER!!!
Haah! Haah!
W... WAIT!!!
WHAT? TEAM TERRY...
SUR-VIVED MAGIC BURST?!!
おおおぉ!!
WHOOOOAAAA!!
I SEE... DE-FENSE!
Oooh!
SO THEIR STRATEGY WAS TO WEATHER THE STORM!!
GREAT JOB HOLD-ING YOUR OWN, YOU GUYS!!
NOW WE DON'T HAVE TO BE AFRAID OF MAGIC BURST!!

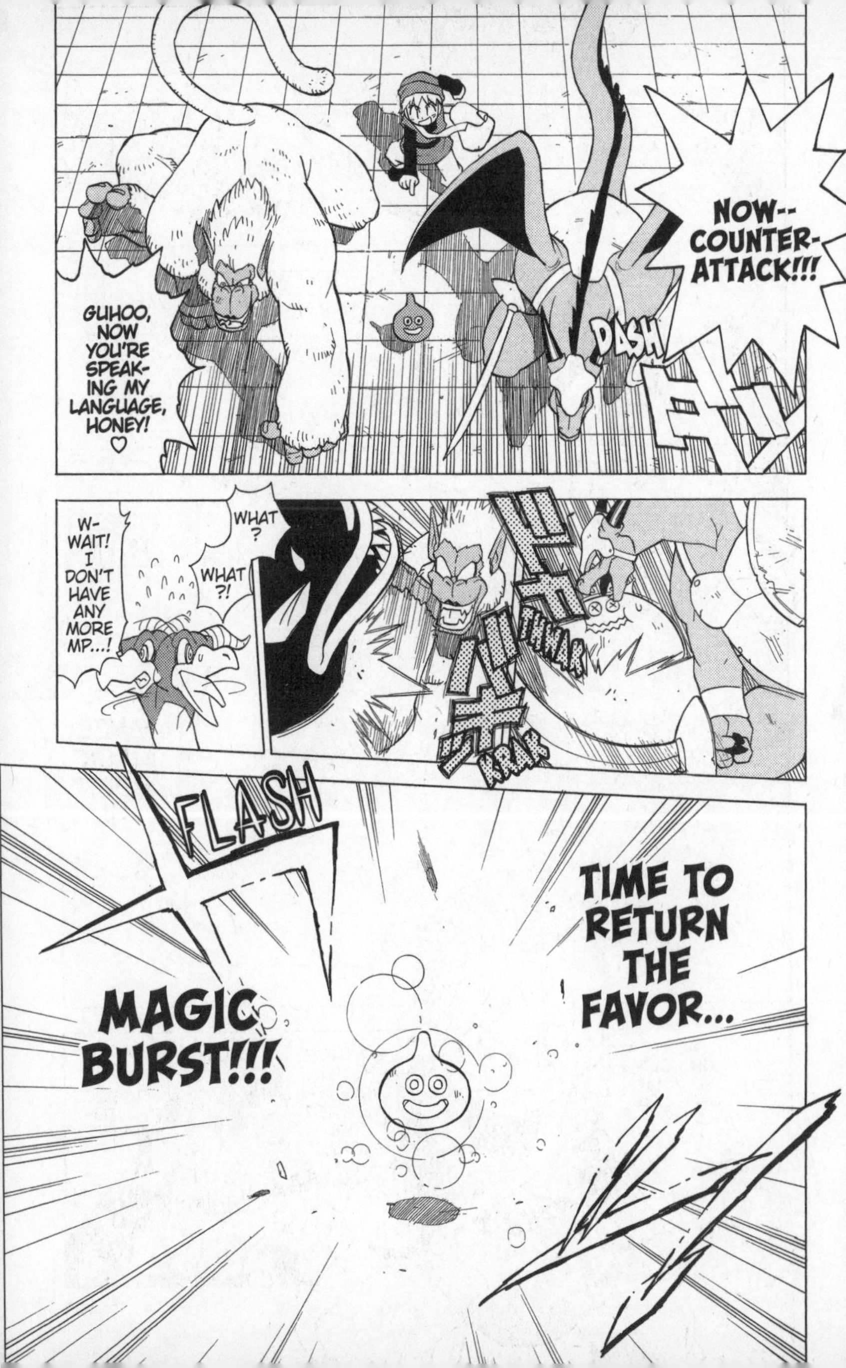
NOW-- COUNTER-ATTACK!!!
DASH
GUHOO, NOW YOU'RE SPEAK-ING MY LANGUAGE, HONEY! ♡
THWAK
KRAK
WHAT?
WHAT?!
W-WAIT! I DON'T HAVE ANY MORE MP...!
FLASH
TIME TO RETURN THE FAVOR...
MAGIC BURST!!!

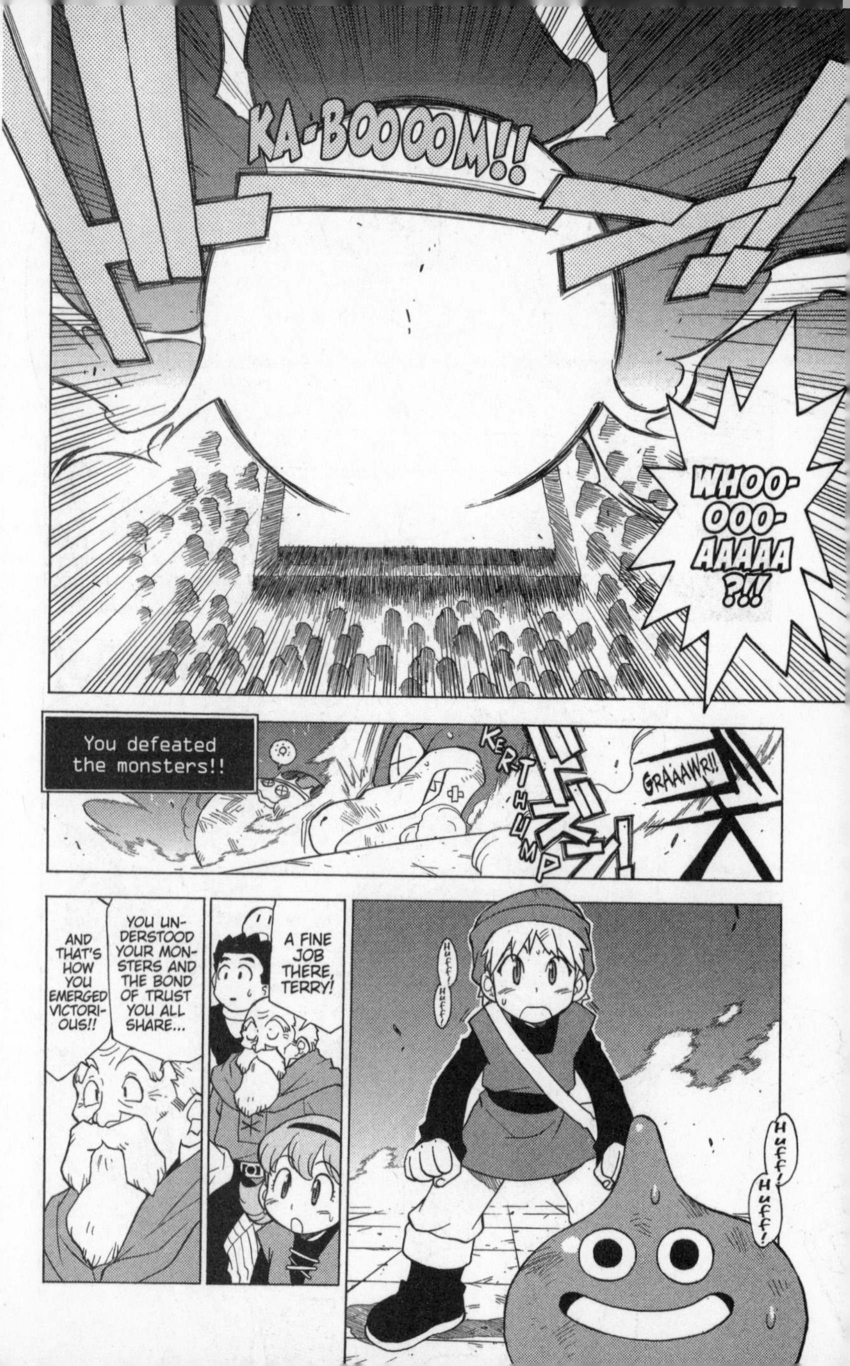
KA-BOOOOM!!
WHOOO-OOO-AAAAA?!!
GRAAAWR!!
KER-THUMP
You defeated the monsters!!
Huff! Huff!
Huff! Huff!
A FINE JOB THERE, TERRY!
YOU UNDERSTOOD YOUR MONSTERS AND THE BOND OF TRUST YOU ALL SHARE...
AND THAT'S HOW YOU EMERGED VICTORIOUS!!

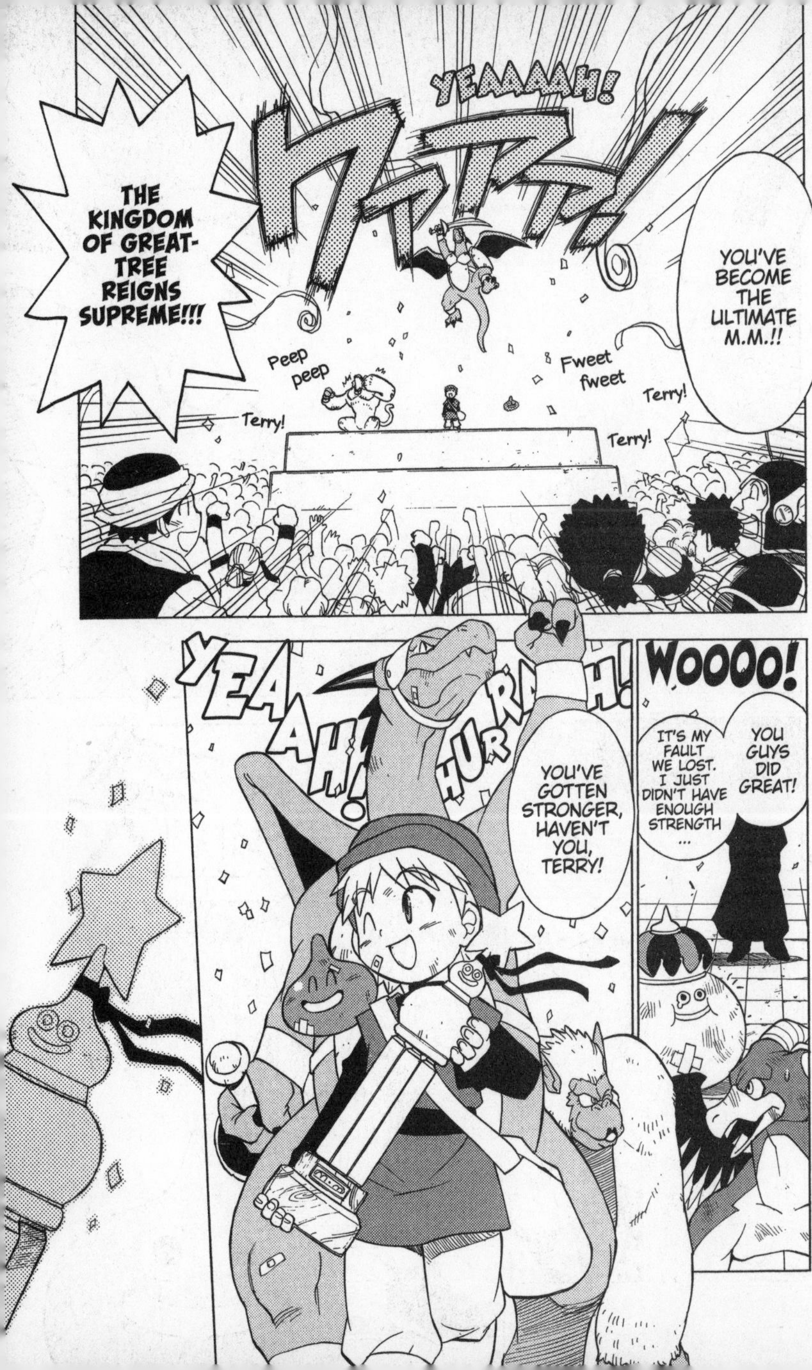
YOU'VE BECOME THE ULTIMATE M.M.!!
YEAAAAH!
THE KINGDOM OF GREAT-TREE REIGNS SUPREME!!!
Terry!
Fweet fweet
Terry!
Peep peep
Terry!
WOOOO!
YOU GUYS DID GREAT!
IT'S MY FAULT WE LOST. I JUST DIDN'T HAVE ENOUGH STRENGTH ...
HURRAH!
YOU'VE GOTTEN STRONGER, HAVEN'T YOU, TERRY!
YEAAAH!

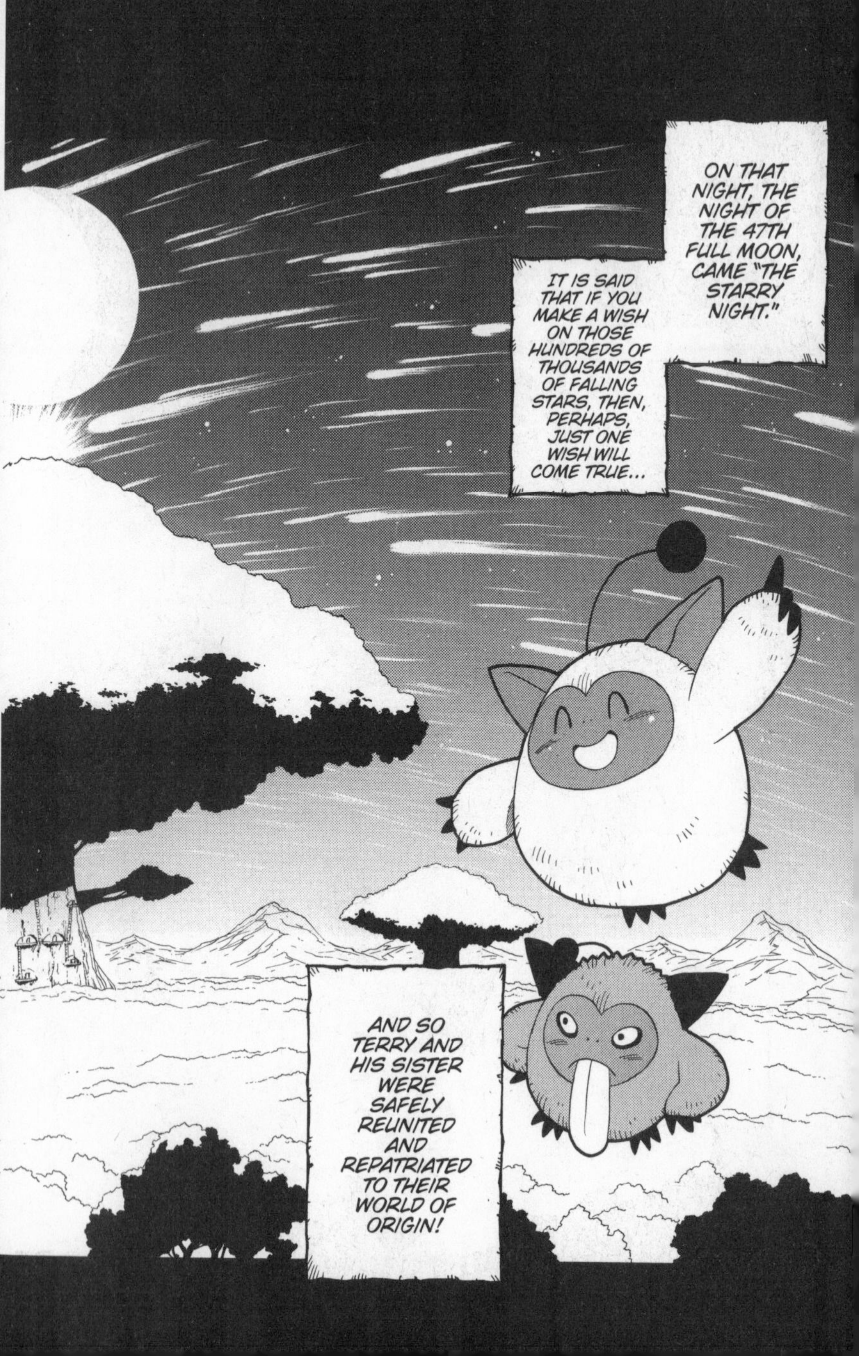
ON THAT NIGHT, THE NIGHT OF THE 47TH FULL MOON, CAME "THE STARRY NIGHT."
IT IS SAID THAT IF YOU MAKE A WISH ON THOSE HUNDREDS OF THOUSANDS OF FALLING STARS, THEN, PERHAPS, JUST ONE WISH WILL COME TRUE...
AND SO TERRY AND HIS SISTER WERE SAFELY REUNITED AND REPATRIATED TO THEIR WORLD OF ORIGIN!

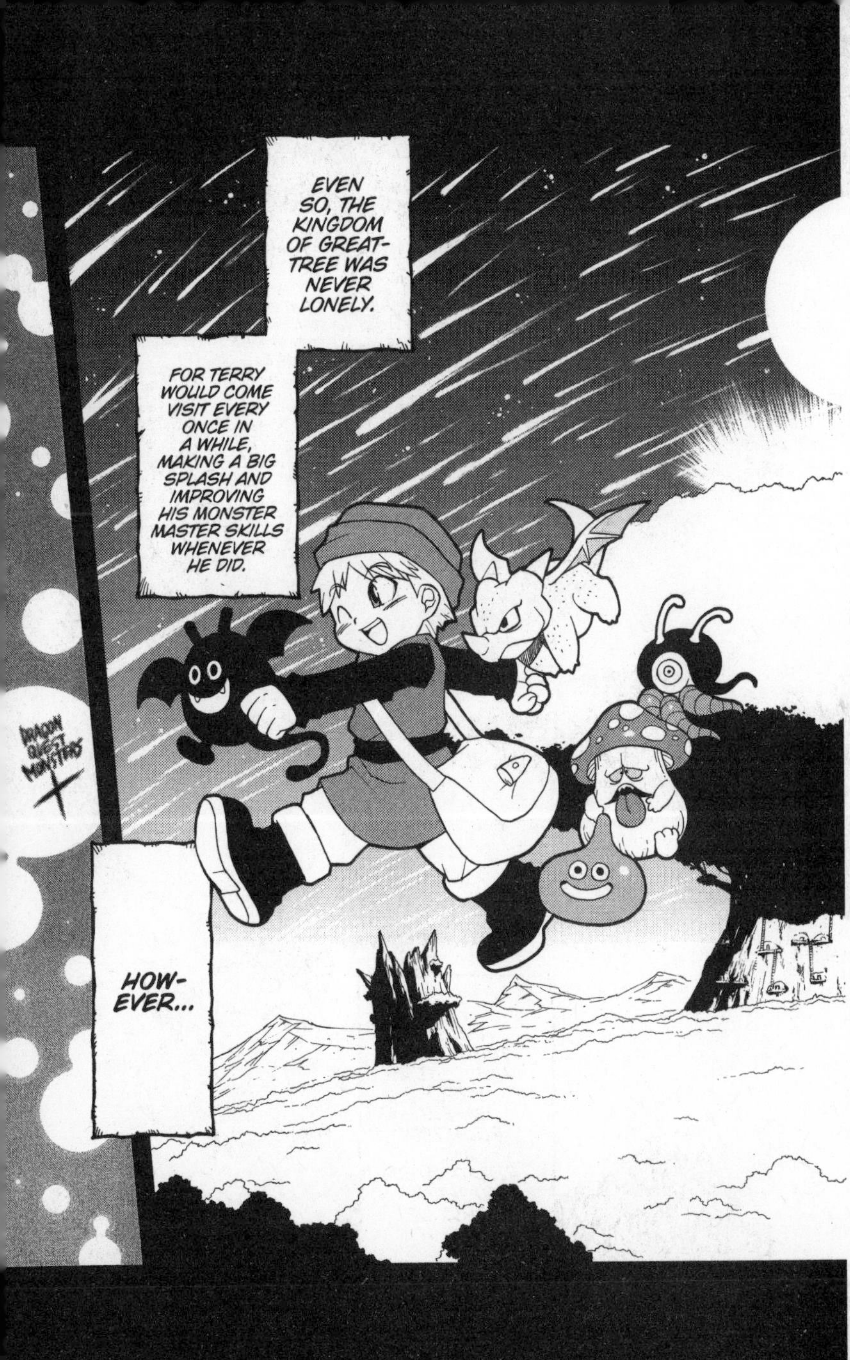
EVEN SO, THE KINGDOM OF GREAT-TREE WAS NEVER LONELY.
FOR TERRY WOULD COME VISIT EVERY ONCE IN A WHILE, MAKING A BIG SPLASH AND IMPROVING HIS MONSTER MASTER SKILLS WHENEVER HE DID.
HOW-EVER...
DRAGON QUEST MONSTERS +

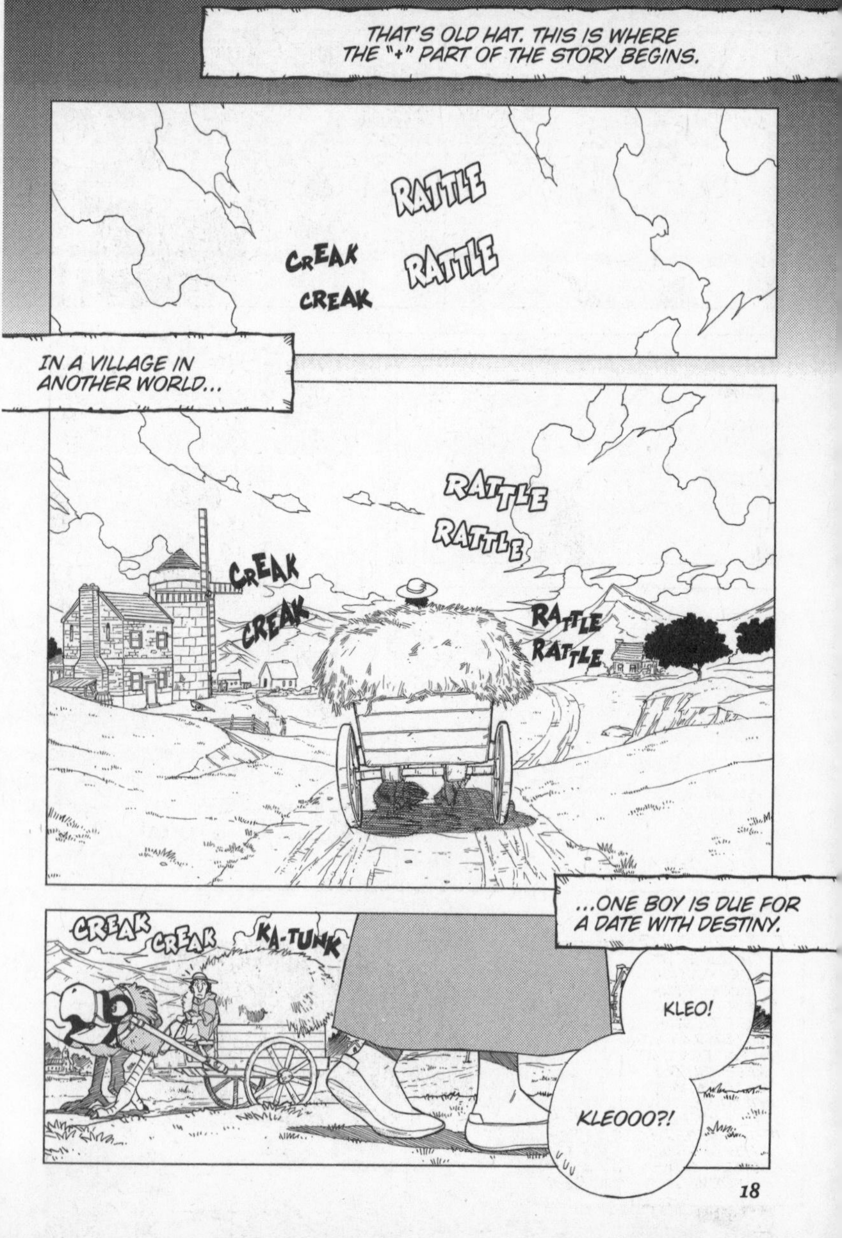
THAT'S OLD HAT. THIS IS WHERE THE "+" PART OF THE STORY BEGINS.
RATTLE
RATTLE
CREAK
CREAK
IN A VILLAGE IN ANOTHER WORLD...
RATTLE
RATTLE
RATTLE
RATTLE
CREAK
CREAK
...ONE BOY IS DUE FOR A DATE WITH DESTINY.
KLEO!
KLEOOO?!
KA-TUNK
CREAK
CREAK

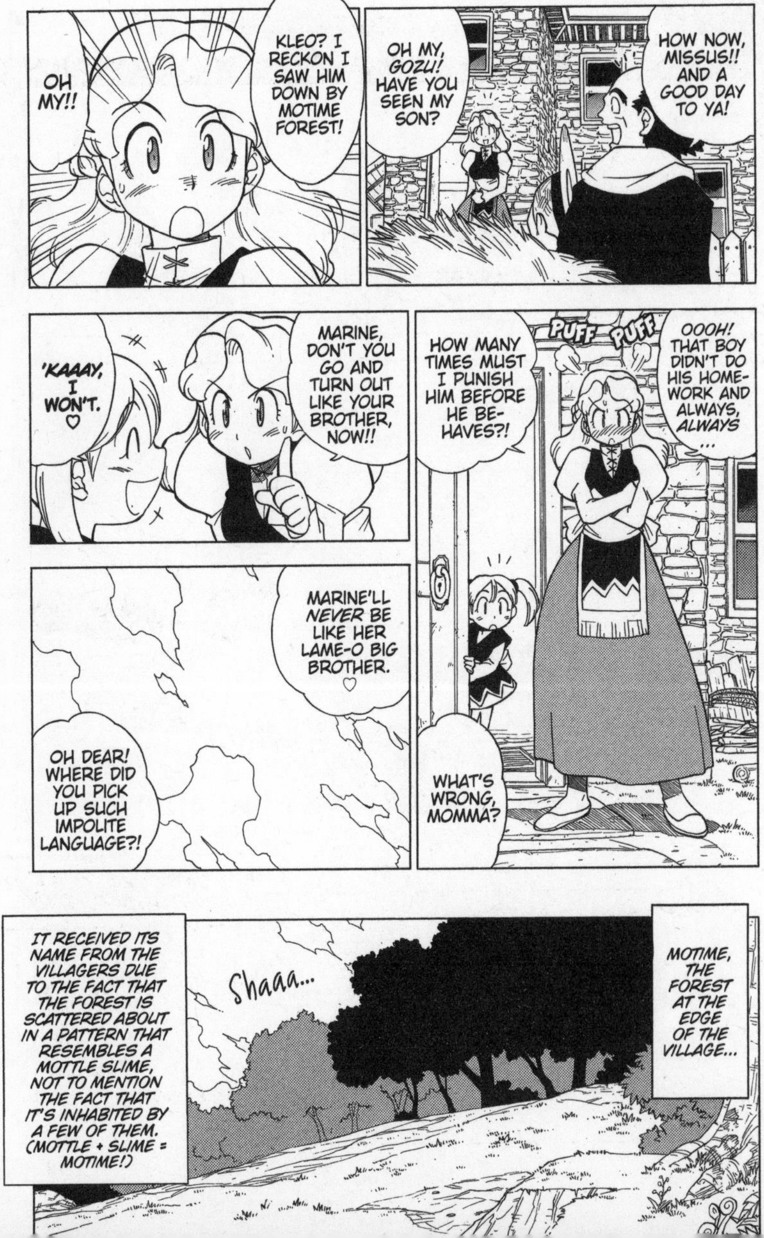
HOW NOW, MISSUS!! AND A GOOD DAY TO YA!
OH MY, GOZU! HAVE YOU SEEN MY SON?
KLEO? I RECKON I SAW HIM DOWN BY MOTIME FOREST!
OH MY!!
PUFF PUFF
OOOH! THAT BOY DIDN'T DO HIS HOME-WORK AND ALWAYS, ALWAYS ...
HOW MANY TIMES MUST I PUNISH HIM BEFORE HE BE-HAVES?!
WHAT'S WRONG, MOMMA?
MARINE, DON'T YOU GO AND TURN OUT LIKE YOUR BROTHER, NOW!!
'KAAAY, I WON'T. ♡
MARINE'LL NEVER BE LIKE HER LAME-O BIG BROTHER. ♡
OH DEAR! WHERE DID YOU PICK UP SUCH IMPOLITE LANGUAGE?!
MOTIME, THE FOREST AT THE EDGE OF THE VILLAGE...
Shaaa...
IT RECEIVED ITS NAME FROM THE VILLAGERS DUE TO THE FACT THAT THE FOREST IS SCATTERED ABOUT IN A PATTERN THAT RESEMBLES A MOTTLE SLIME, NOT TO MENTION THE FACT THAT IT'S INHABITED BY A FEW OF THEM. (MOTTLE + SLIME = MOTIME!)

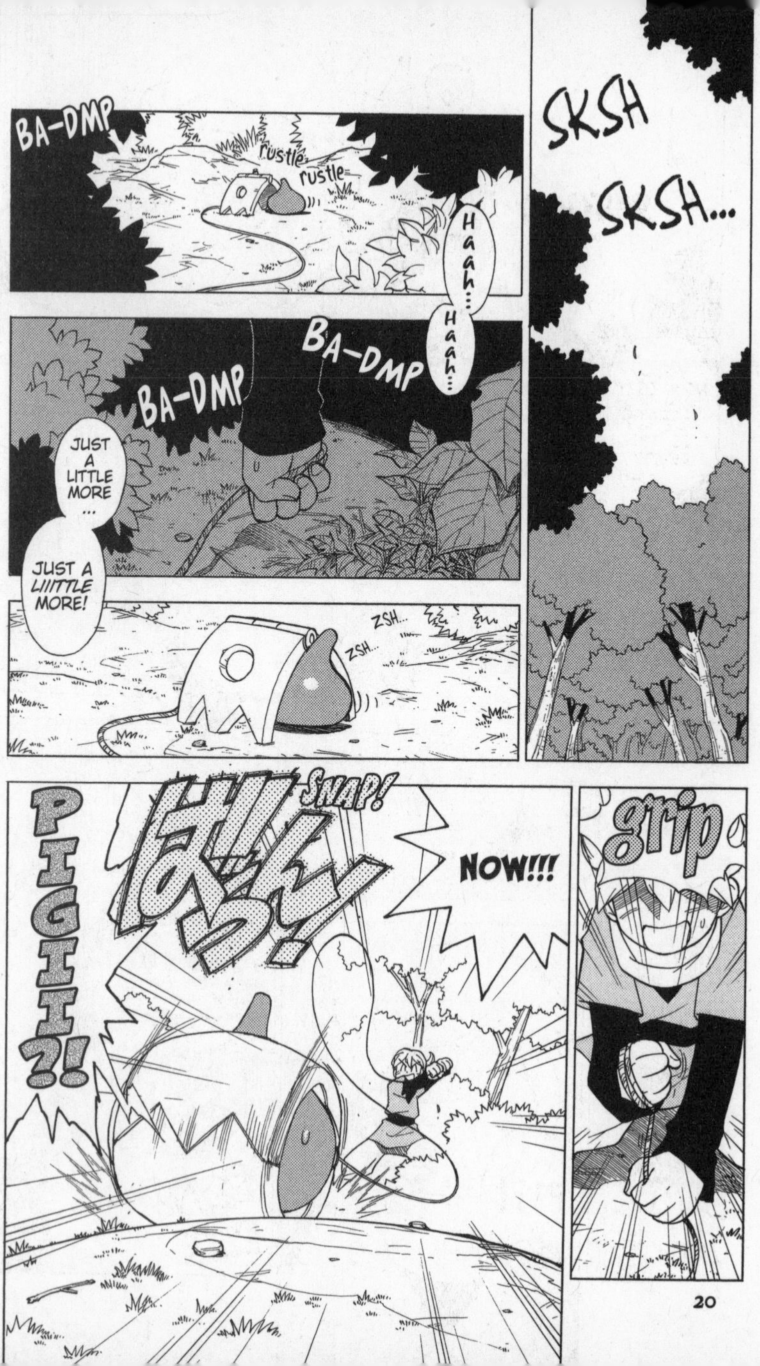
SKSH
SKSH...
BA-DMP
rustle
rustle
Haah...
Haah...
BA-DMP
BA-DMP
JUST A LITTLE MORE...
JUST A LIIITTLE MORE!
ZSH...
ZSH...
grip
SNAP!
NOW!!!
PIGII?!

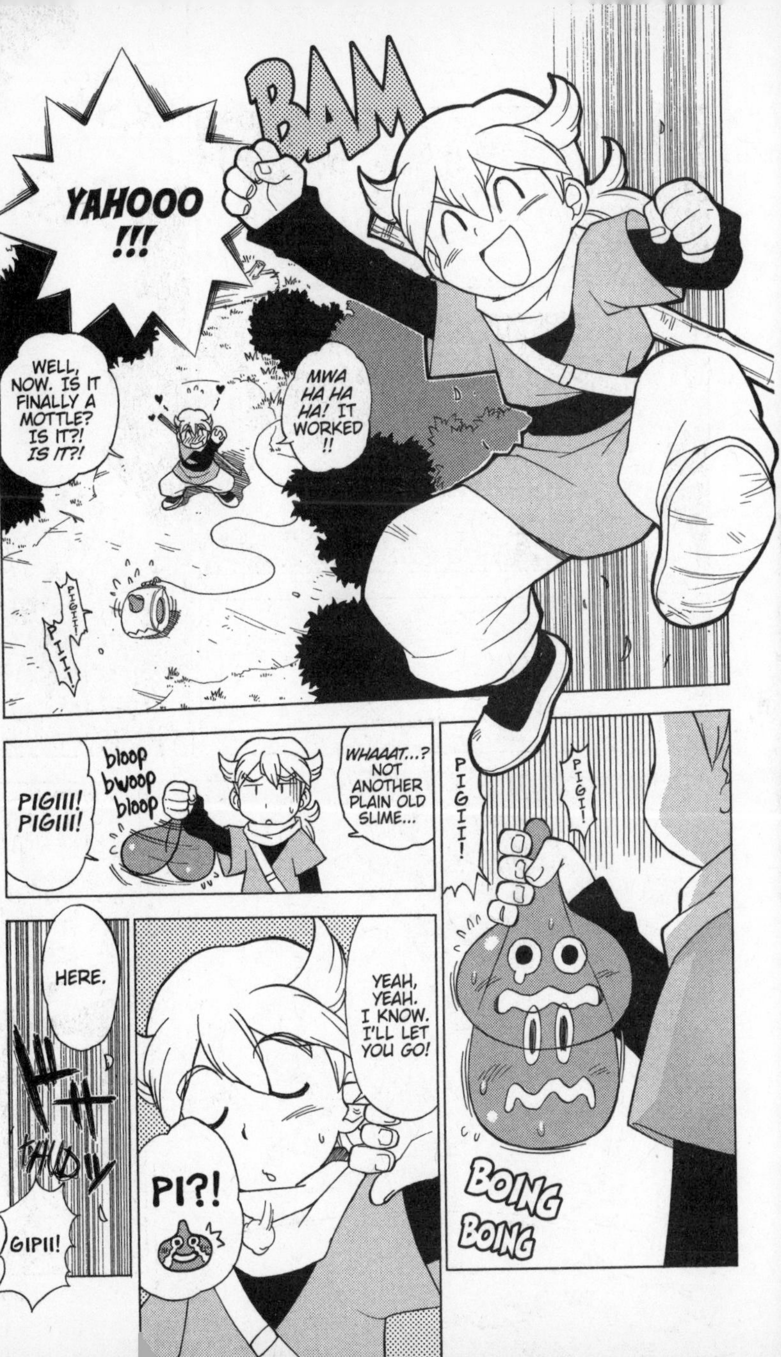
BAM
MWA HA HA HA! IT WORKED!!
YAHOOO!!!
WELL, NOW. IS IT FINALLY A MOTTLE? IS IT?! IS IT?!
PIGIII
PIII!
PIGII!
PIGIII!
BOING
BOING
WHAAAT...? NOT ANOTHER PLAIN OLD SLIME...
bloop bwoop bloop
PIGIII! PIGIII!
YEAH, YEAH. I KNOW. I'LL LET YOU GO!
PI?!
HERE.
THUD
GIPII!

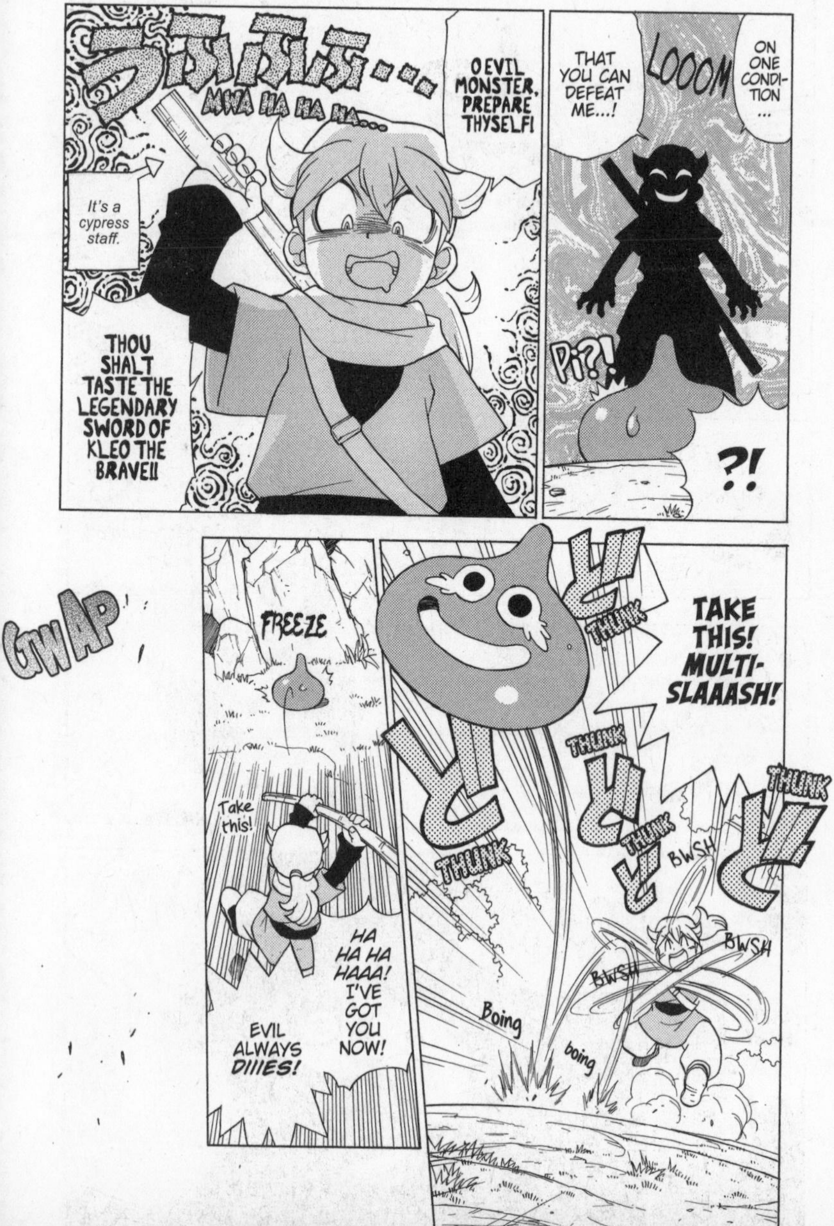

ON ONE CONDITION...
LOOOM
THAT YOU CAN DEFEAT ME...!
Pi?!
?!
O EVIL MONSTER, PREPARE THYSELF!
うふふふ…
MWA HA HA HA...
It's a cypress staff.
THOU SHALT TASTE THE LEGENDARY SWORD OF KLEO THE BRAVE!!
TAKE THIS! MULTI-SLAAASH!
ど
THUNK
ど
THUNK
ど
THUNK
ど
THUNK
ど
THUNK
BWSH
BWSH
BWSH
Boing
boing
GWAP
FREEZE
Take this!
HA HA HA HAAA! I'VE GOT YOU NOW!
EVIL ALWAYS DIIIES!

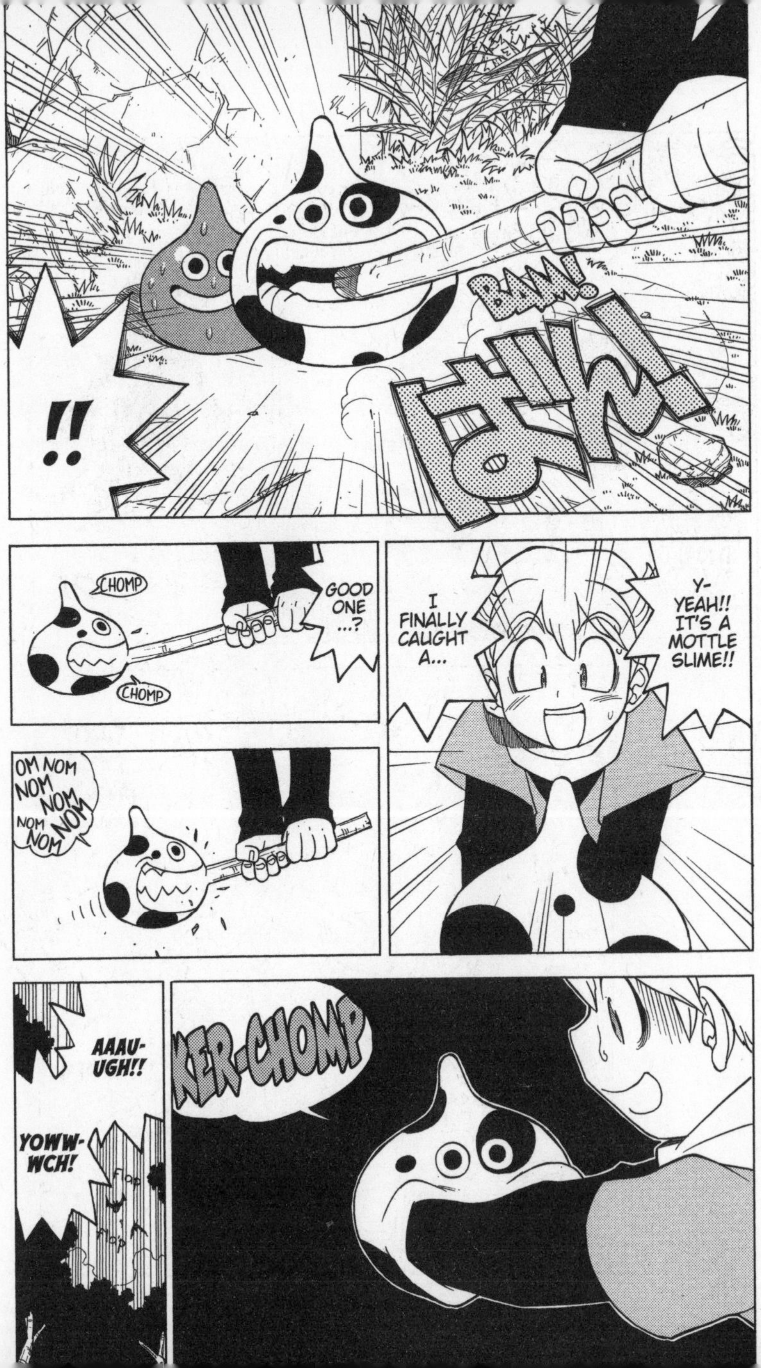
BAM!
!!
Y-YEAH!! IT'S A MOTTLE SLIME!!
I FINALLY CAUGHT A...
GOOD ONE ...?
CHOMP
CHOMP
OM NOM NOM NOM NOM NOM
KER-CHOMP
AAAU-UGH!!
YOWW-WCH!
flop
flop

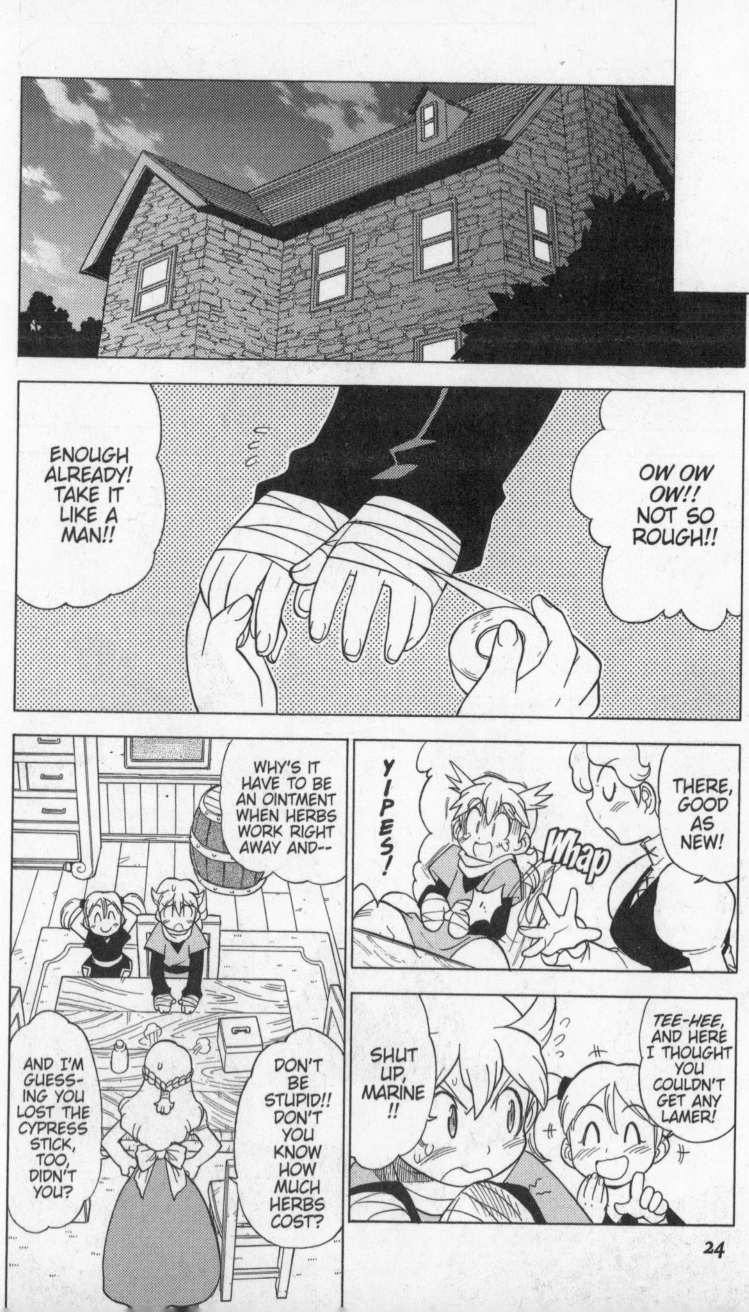

OW OW OW!! NOT SO ROUGH!!
ENOUGH ALREADY! TAKE IT LIKE A MAN!!
THERE, GOOD AS NEW!
Whap
YIPES!
TEE-HEE, AND HERE I THOUGHT YOU COULDN'T GET ANY LAMER!
SHUT UP, MARINE!!
WHY'S IT HAVE TO BE AN OINTMENT WHEN HERBS WORK RIGHT AWAY AND--
DON'T BE STUPID!! DON'T YOU KNOW HOW MUCH HERBS COST?
AND I'M GUESSING YOU LOST THE CYPRESS STICK, TOO, DIDN'T YOU?

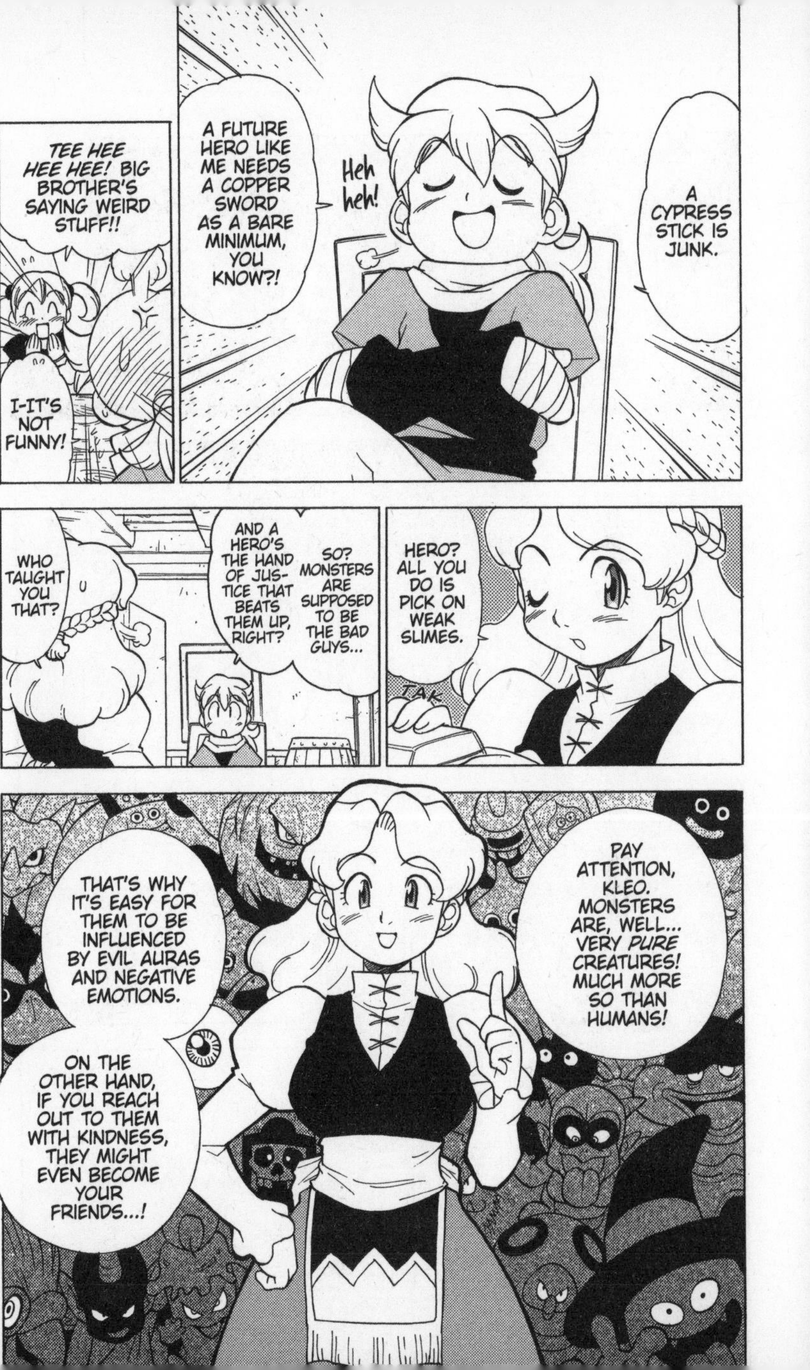
A CYPRESS STICK IS JUNK.
A FUTURE HERO LIKE ME NEEDS A COPPER SWORD AS A BARE MINIMUM, YOU KNOW?!
Heh heh!
TEE HEE HEE HEE! BIG BROTHER'S SAYING WEIRD STUFF!!
I-IT'S NOT FUNNY!
HERO? ALL YOU DO IS PICK ON WEAK SLIMES.
TAK
SO? MONSTERS ARE SUPPOSED TO BE THE BAD GUYS...
AND A HERO'S THE HAND OF JUS-TICE THAT BEATS THEM UP, RIGHT?
WHO TAUGHT YOU THAT?
PAY ATTENTION, KLEO. MONSTERS ARE, WELL... VERY *PURE* CREATURES! MUCH MORE SO THAN HUMANS!
THAT'S WHY IT'S EASY FOR THEM TO BE INFLUENCED BY EVIL AURAS AND NEGATIVE EMOTIONS.
ON THE OTHER HAND, IF YOU REACH OUT TO THEM WITH KINDNESS, THEY MIGHT EVEN BECOME YOUR FRIENDS...!

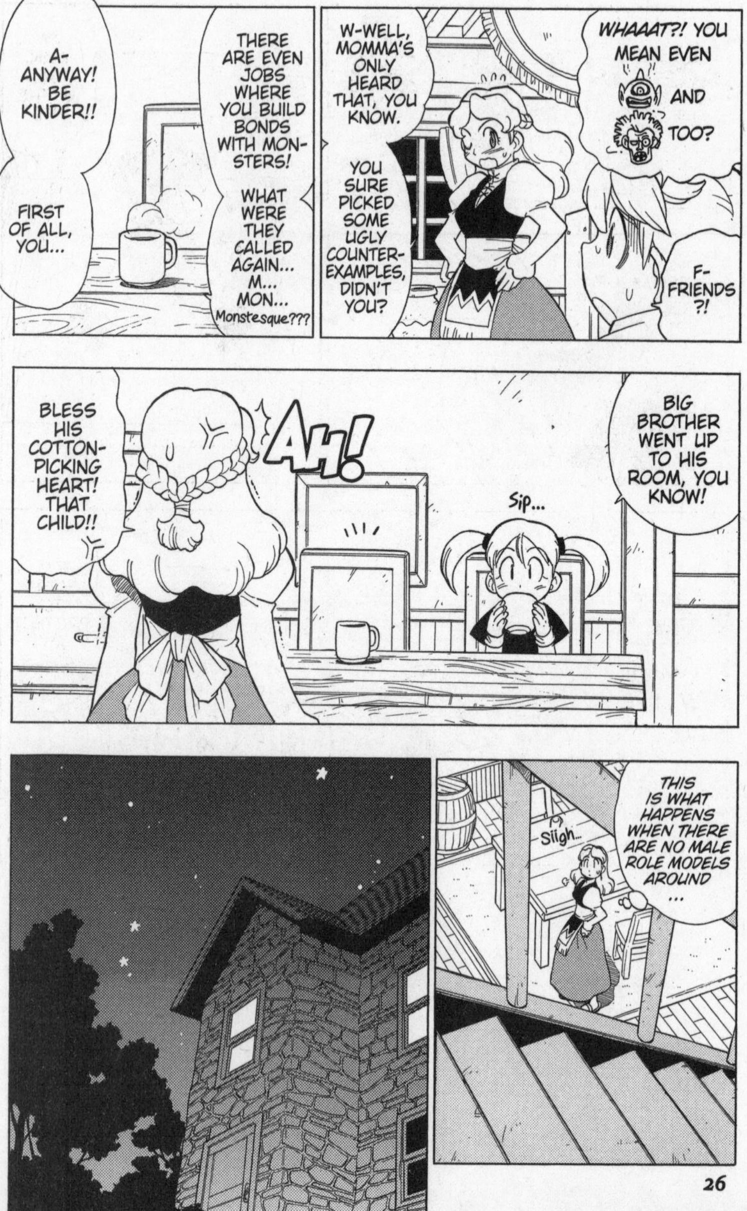
WHAAAT?! YOU MEAN EVEN
AND
TOO?
F-FRIENDS?!
W-WELL, MOMMA'S ONLY HEARD THAT, YOU KNOW.
YOU SURE PICKED SOME UGLY COUNTER-EXAMPLES, DIDN'T YOU?
THERE ARE EVEN JOBS WHERE YOU BUILD BONDS WITH MON-STERS!
WHAT WERE THEY CALLED AGAIN... M... MON... Monstesque???
A-ANYWAY! BE KINDER!!
FIRST OF ALL, YOU...
BIG BROTHER WENT UP TO HIS ROOM, YOU KNOW!
Sip...
AH!
BLESS HIS COTTON-PICKING HEART! THAT CHILD!!
THIS IS WHAT HAPPENS WHEN THERE ARE NO MALE ROLE MODELS AROUND...
Siigh...

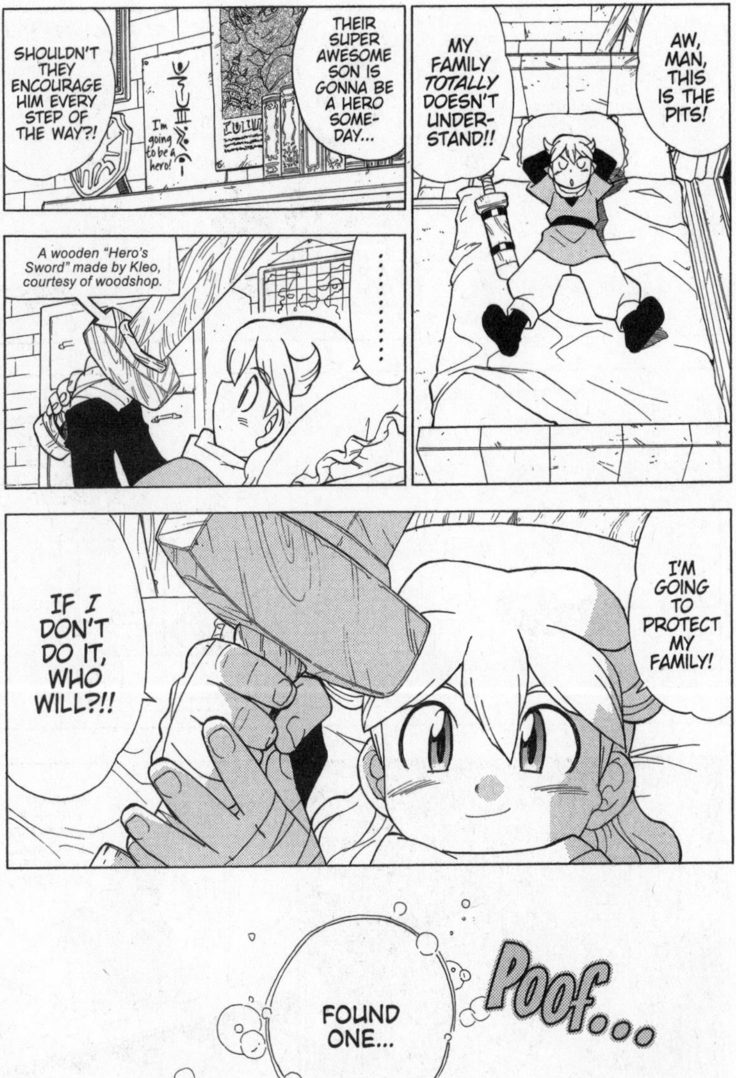
AW, MAN, THIS IS THE PITS!
MY FAMILY *TOTALLY* DOESN'T UNDER-STAND!!
THEIR SUPER AWESOME SON IS GONNA BE A HERO SOME-DAY...
I'm going to be a hero!
SHOULDN'T THEY ENCOURAGE HIM EVERY STEP OF THE WAY?!
......
A wooden "Hero's Sword" made by Kleo, courtesy of woodshop.
I'M GOING TO PROTECT MY FAMILY!
IF *I* DON'T DO IT, WHO WILL?!!
Poof...
FOUND ONE...

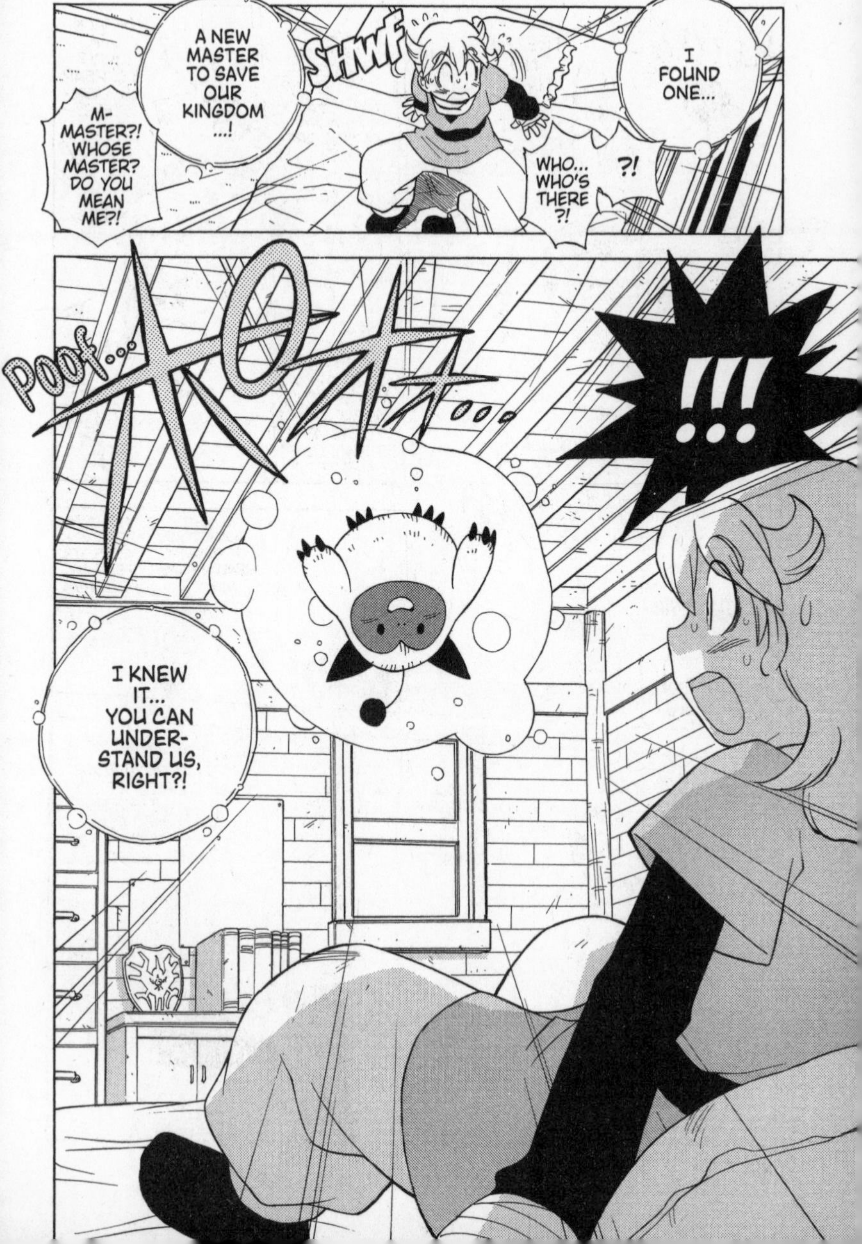
I FOUND ONE...
?!
WHO... WHO'S THERE ?!
SHWF
A NEW MASTER TO SAVE OUR KINGDOM ...!
M-MASTER?! WHOSE MASTER? DO YOU MEAN ME?!
!!! ...
POOF...
I KNEW IT... YOU CAN UNDER-STAND US, RIGHT?!

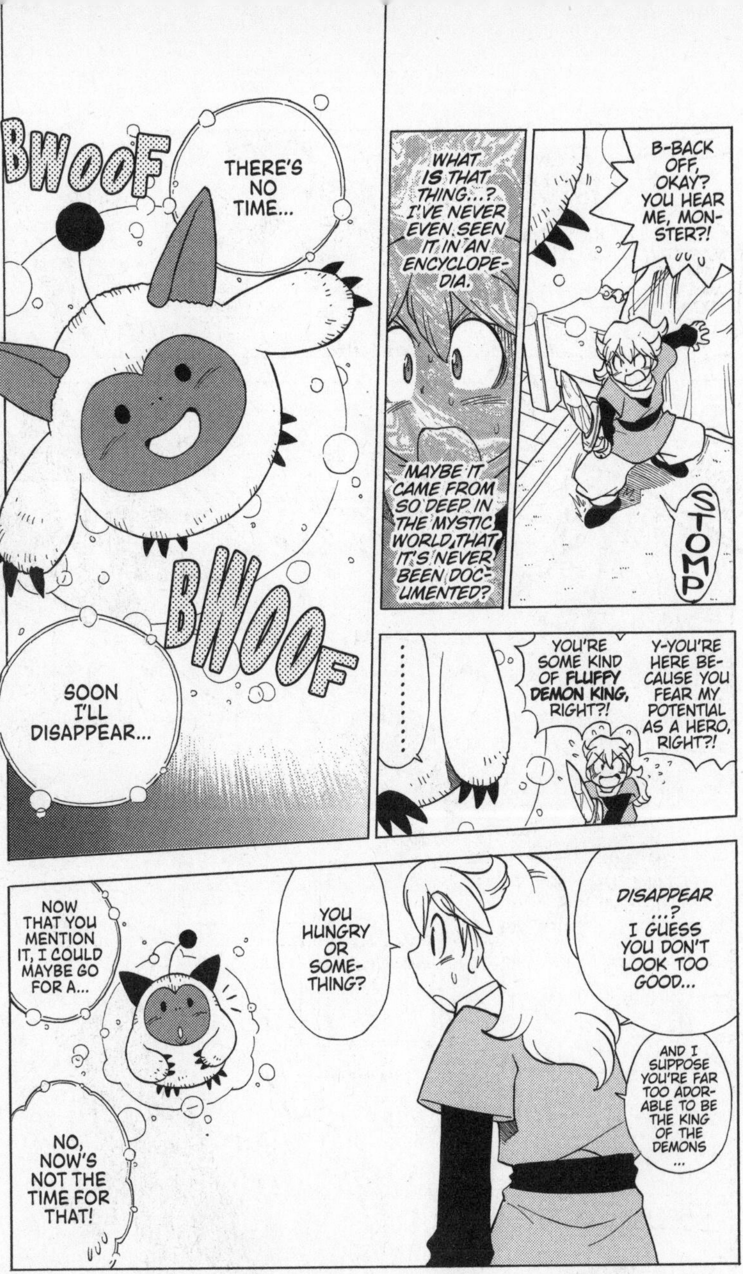
B-BACK OFF, OKAY? YOU HEAR ME, MONSTER?!
STOMP
WHAT IS THAT THING...? I'VE NEVER EVEN SEEN IT IN AN ENCYCLOPEDIA.
MAYBE IT CAME FROM SO DEEP IN THE MYSTIC WORLD THAT IT'S NEVER BEEN DOCUMENTED?
Y-YOU'RE HERE BECAUSE YOU FEAR MY POTENTIAL AS A HERO, RIGHT?!
YOU'RE SOME KIND OF FLUFFY DEMON KING, RIGHT?!
......
BWOOF
THERE'S NO TIME...
BWOOF
SOON I'LL DISAPPEAR...
DISAPPEAR...? I GUESS YOU DON'T LOOK TOO GOOD...
AND I SUPPOSE YOU'RE FAR TOO ADORABLE TO BE THE KING OF THE DEMONS...
YOU HUNGRY OR SOMETHING?
NOW THAT YOU MENTION IT, I COULD MAYBE GO FOR A...
NO, NOW'S NOT THE TIME FOR THAT!

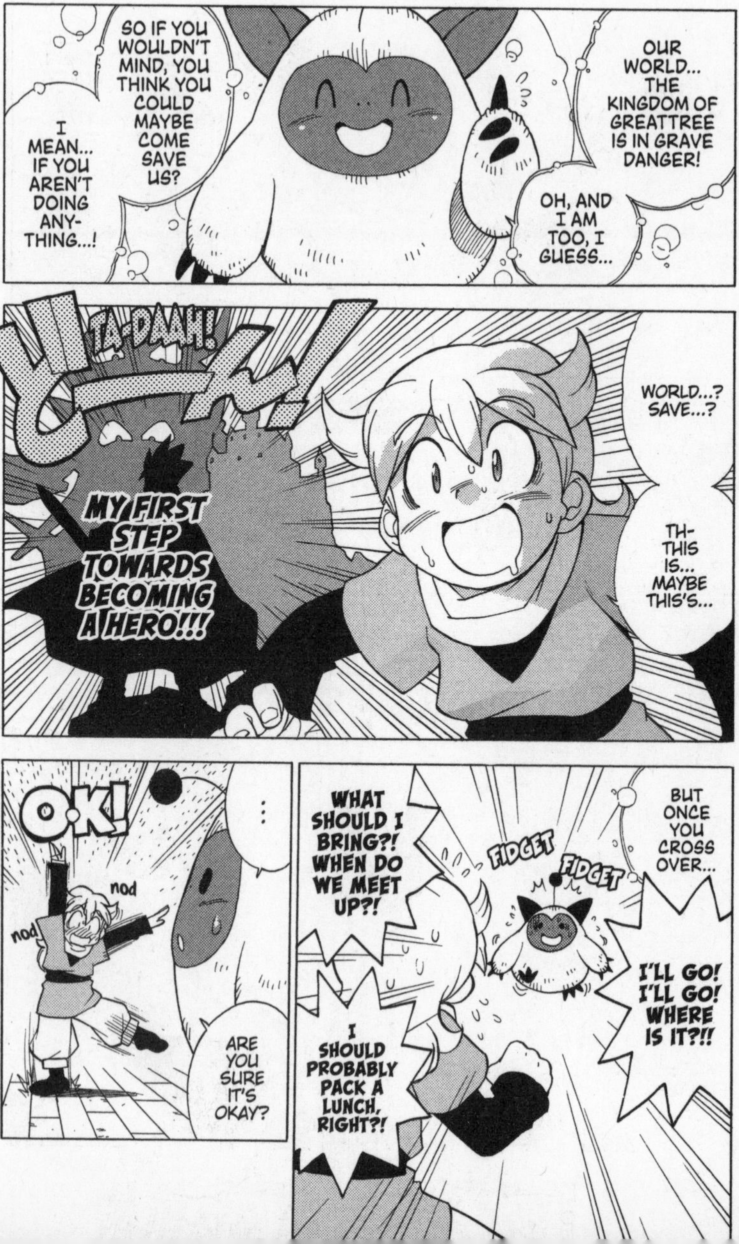
OUR WORLD... THE KINGDOM OF GREATTREE IS IN GRAVE DANGER!
OH, AND I AM TOO, I GUESS...
SO IF YOU WOULDN'T MIND, YOU THINK YOU COULD MAYBE COME SAVE US?
I MEAN... IF YOU AREN'T DOING ANY-THING...!
WORLD...? SAVE...?
TH-THIS IS... MAYBE THIS'S...
TA-DAAH!
MY FIRST STEP TOWARDS BECOMING A HERO!!!
BUT ONCE YOU CROSS OVER...
FIDGET
FIDGET
I'LL GO! I'LL GO! WHERE IS IT?!!
WHAT SHOULD I BRING?! WHEN DO WE MEET UP?!
I SHOULD PROBABLY PACK A LUNCH, RIGHT?!
...
O.K!
nod
nod
ARE YOU SURE IT'S OKAY?

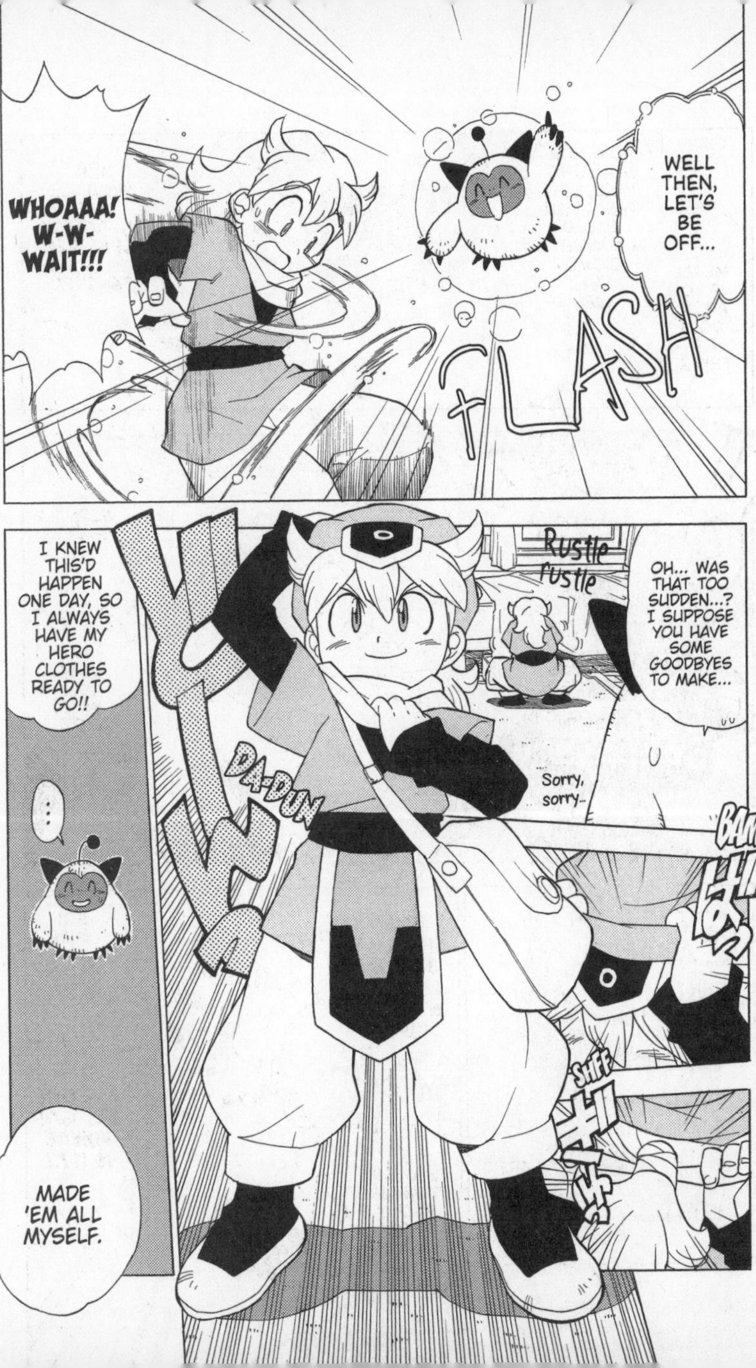
WELL THEN, LET'S BE OFF...
FLASH
WHOAAA! W-W-WAIT!!!
OH... WAS THAT TOO SUDDEN...? I SUPPOSE YOU HAVE SOME GOODBYES TO MAKE...
Rustle rustle
...Sorry, sorry...
BAM
SHFF
DA-DUN
I KNEW THIS'D HAPPEN ONE DAY, SO I ALWAYS HAVE MY HERO CLOTHES READY TO GO!!
...
MADE 'EM ALL MYSELF.

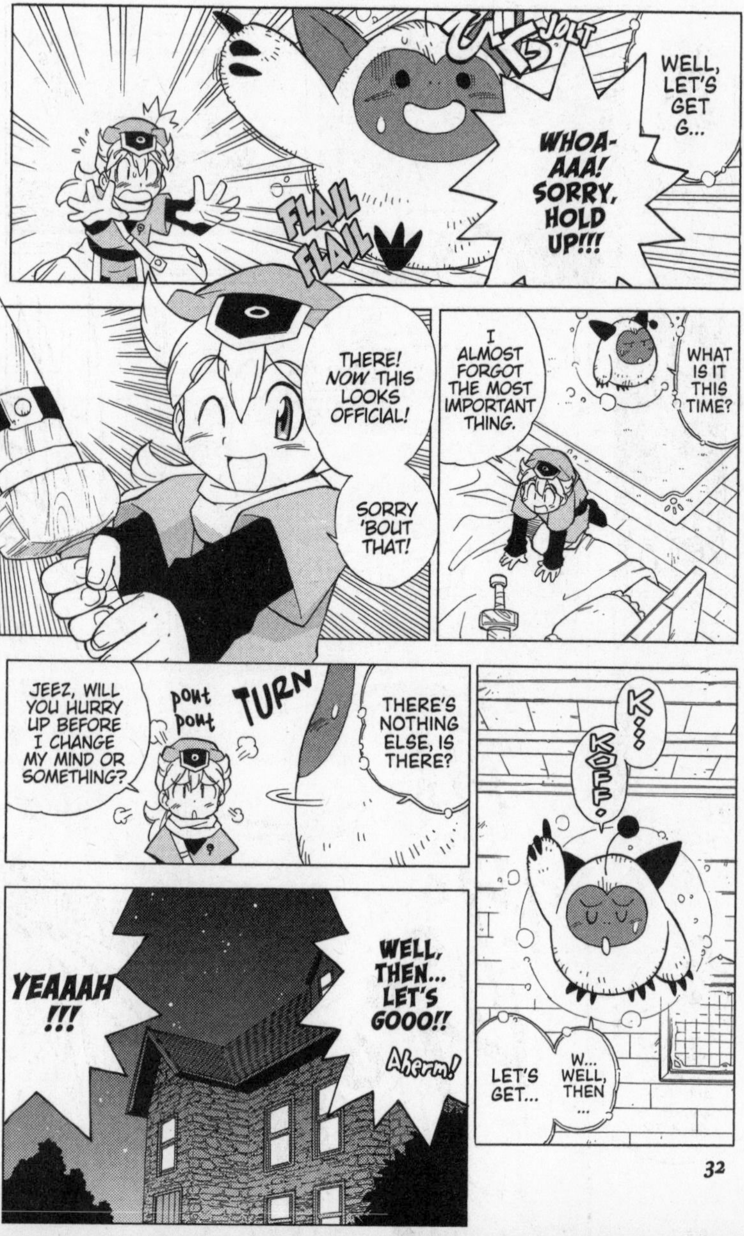
JOLT
WELL, LET'S GET G...
WHOA-AAA! SORRY, HOLD UP!!!
FLAIL FLAIL
WHAT IS IT THIS TIME?
I ALMOST FORGOT THE MOST IMPORTANT THING.
THERE! *NOW* THIS LOOKS OFFICIAL!
SORRY 'BOUT THAT!
K... KOFF.
W... WELL, THEN ...
LET'S GET...
TURN
THERE'S NOTHING ELSE, IS THERE?
pout pout
JEEZ, WILL YOU HURRY UP BEFORE I CHANGE MY MIND OR SOMETHING?
WELL, THEN... LET'S GOOO!!
Aherm!
YEAAAH!!!

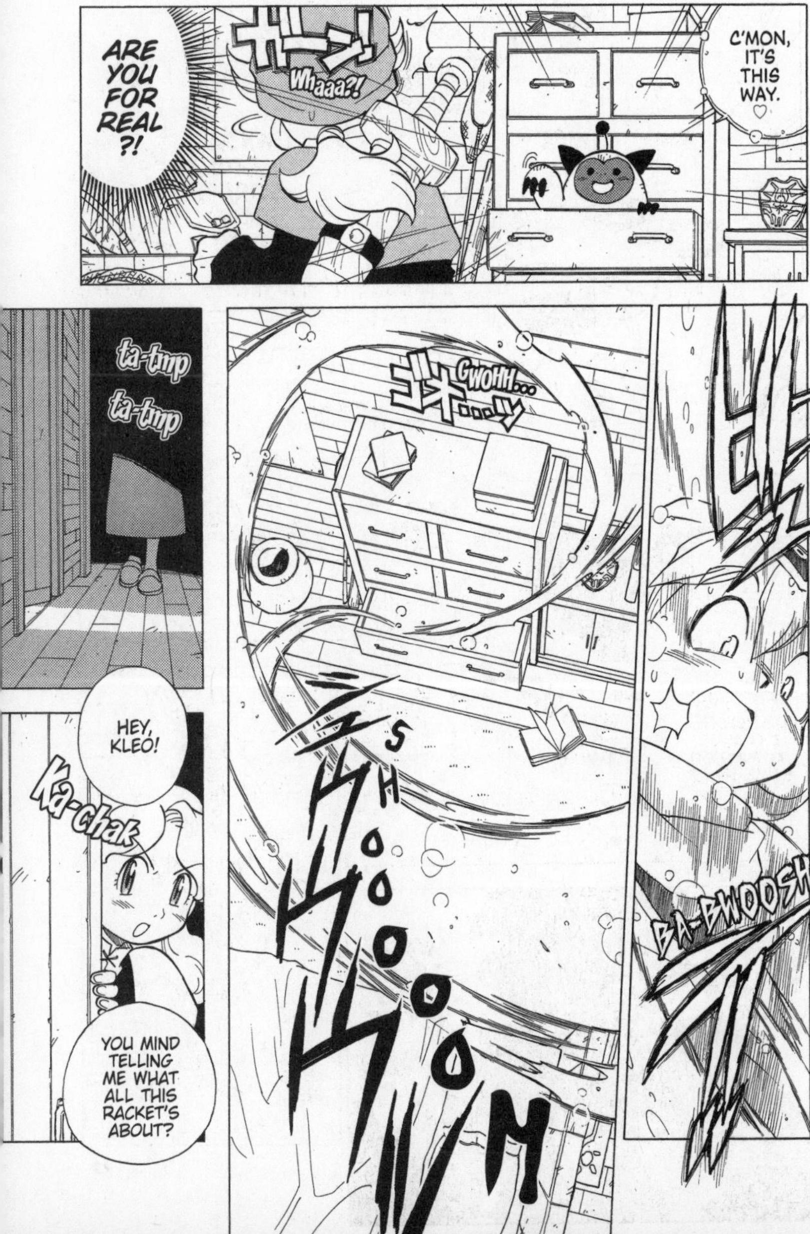
C'MON, IT'S THIS WAY. ♡
Whaaa?!
ARE YOU FOR REAL?!
BA-BWOOSH!!
GWOHH...
SHOOOOOM
ta-tmp
ta-tmp
HEY, KLEO!
Ka-chak
YOU MIND TELLING ME WHAT ALL THIS RACKET'S ABOUT?

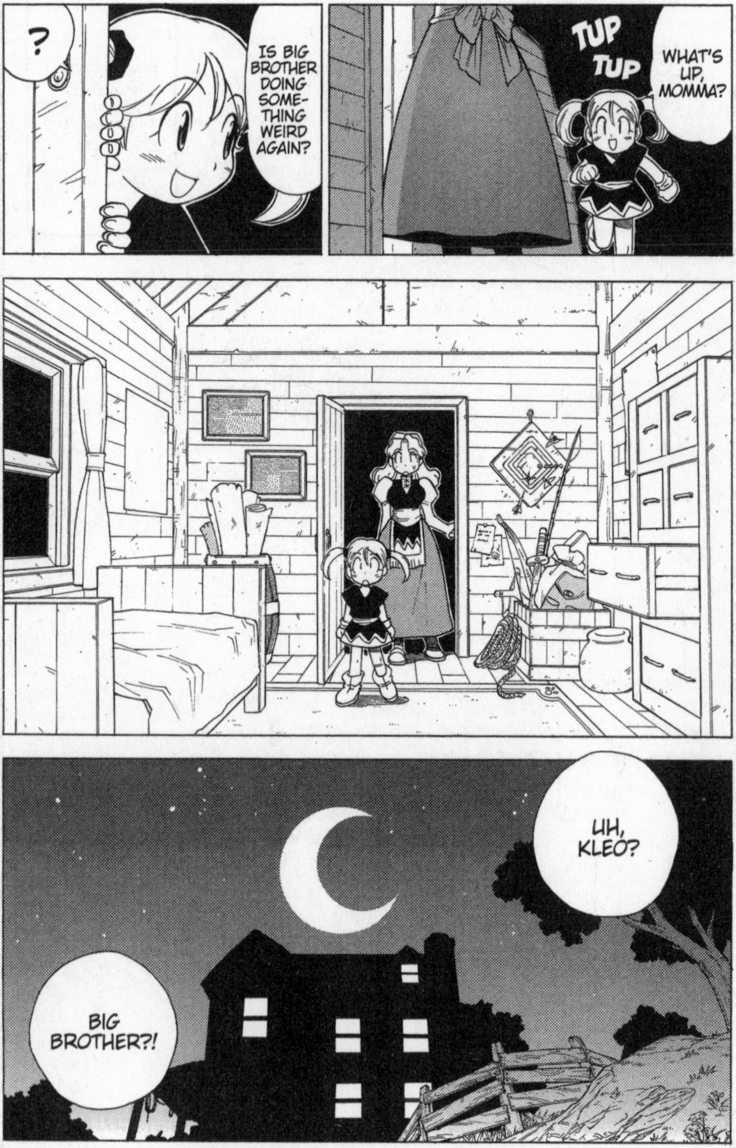
TUP
TUP
WHAT'S UP, MOMMA?
?
IS BIG BROTHER DOING SOME-THING WEIRD AGAIN?
UH, KLEO?
BIG BROTHER?!

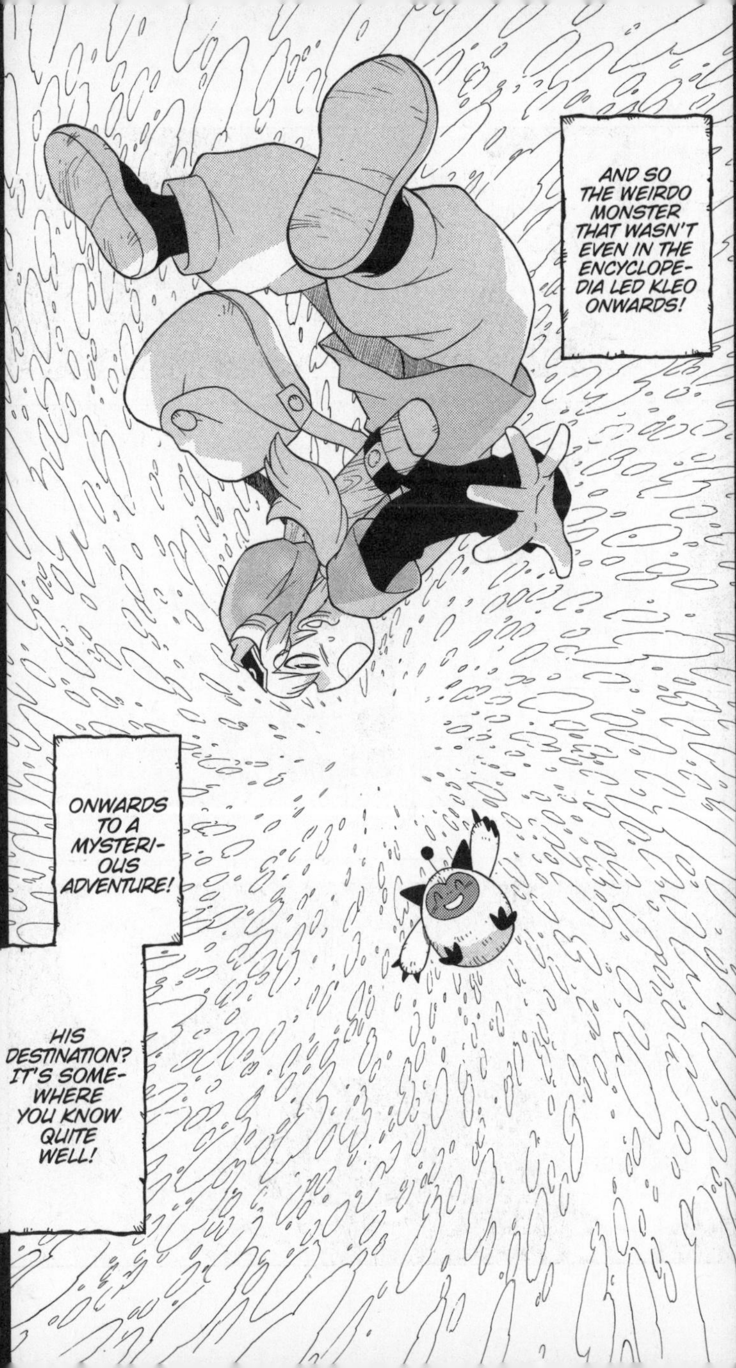
AND SO THE WEIRDO MONSTER THAT WASN'T EVEN IN THE ENCYCLOPE-DIA LED KLEO ONWARDS!
ONWARDS TO A MYSTERI-OUS ADVENTURE!
HIS DESTINATION? IT'S SOME-WHERE YOU KNOW QUITE WELL!

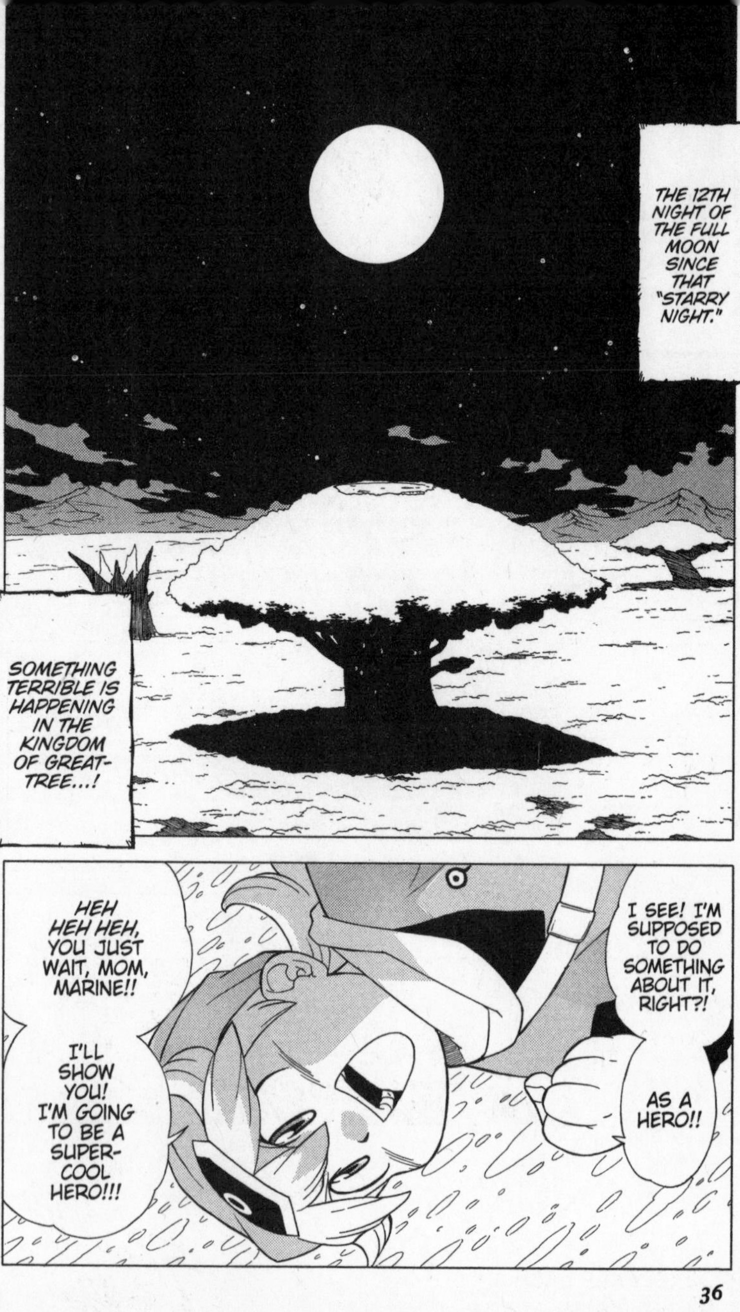
THE 12TH NIGHT OF THE FULL MOON SINCE THAT "STARRY NIGHT."
SOMETHING TERRIBLE IS HAPPENING IN THE KINGDOM OF GREAT-TREE...!
I SEE! I'M SUPPOSED TO DO SOMETHING ABOUT IT, RIGHT?!
AS A HERO!!
HEH HEH HEH, YOU JUST WAIT, MOM, MARINE!!
I'LL SHOW YOU! I'M GOING TO BE A SUPER-COOL HERO!!!

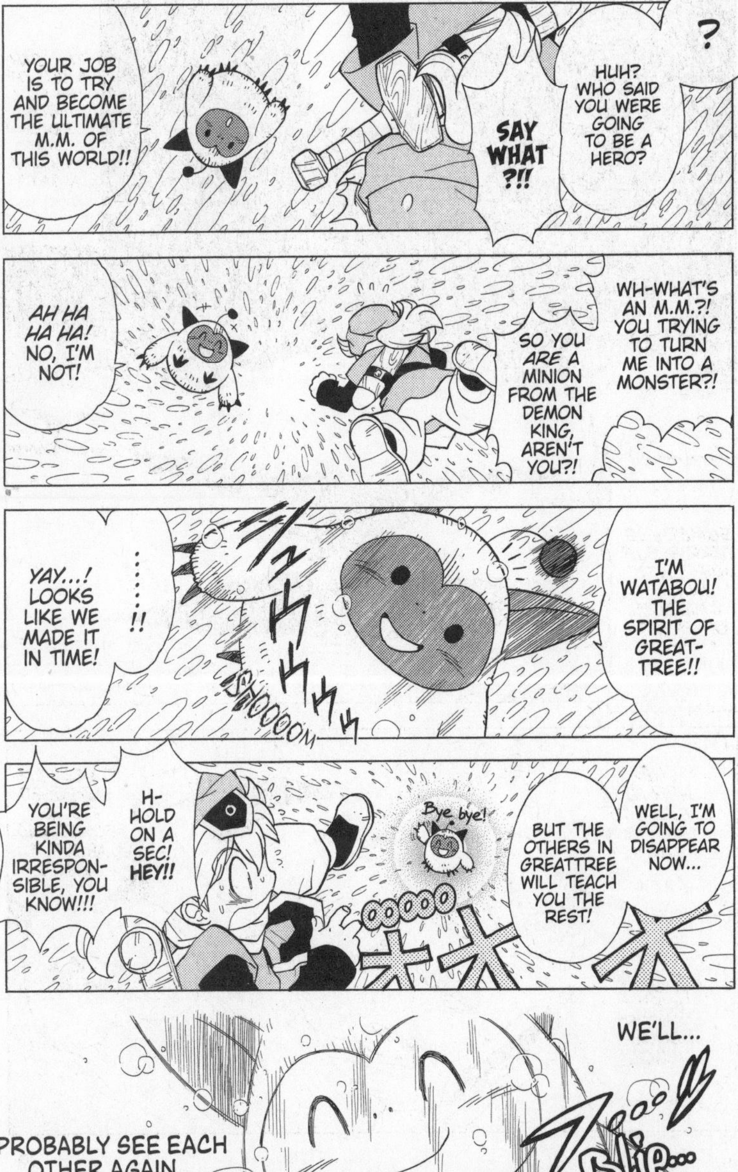
?
HUH? WHO SAID YOU WERE GOING TO BE A HERO?
SAY WHAT?!!
YOUR JOB IS TO TRY AND BECOME THE ULTIMATE M.M. OF THIS WORLD!!
WH-WHAT'S AN M.M.?! YOU TRYING TO TURN ME INTO A MONSTER?!
SO YOU *ARE* A MINION FROM THE DEMON KING, AREN'T YOU?!
AH HA HA HA! NO, I'M NOT!
I'M WATABOU! THE SPIRIT OF GREAT-TREE!!
SHOOOOM
......!!
YAY...! LOOKS LIKE WE MADE IT IN TIME!
WELL, I'M GOING TO DISAPPEAR NOW...
BUT THE OTHERS IN GREATTREE WILL TEACH YOU THE REST!
Bye bye!
H-HOLD ON A SEC! **HEY!!**
YOU'RE BEING KINDA IRRESPON-SIBLE, YOU KNOW!!!
WE'LL...
Blip...
PROBABLY SEE EACH OTHER AGAIN...

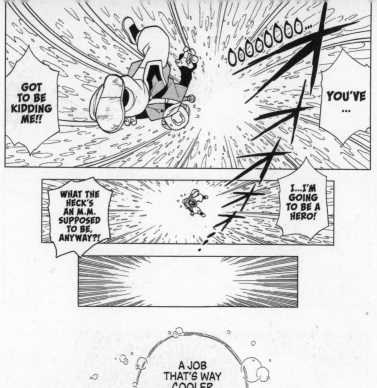

OOOOOOOO...
YOU'VE ...
GOT TO BE KIDDING ME!!
I...I'M GOING TO BE A HERO!
WHAT THE HECK'S AN M.M. SUPPOSED TO BE, ANYWAY?!
A JOB THAT'S WAY COOLER THAN BEING A HERO, YOU KNOW...!!
Fsshh...

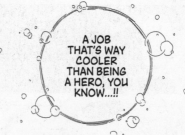

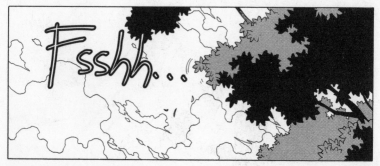

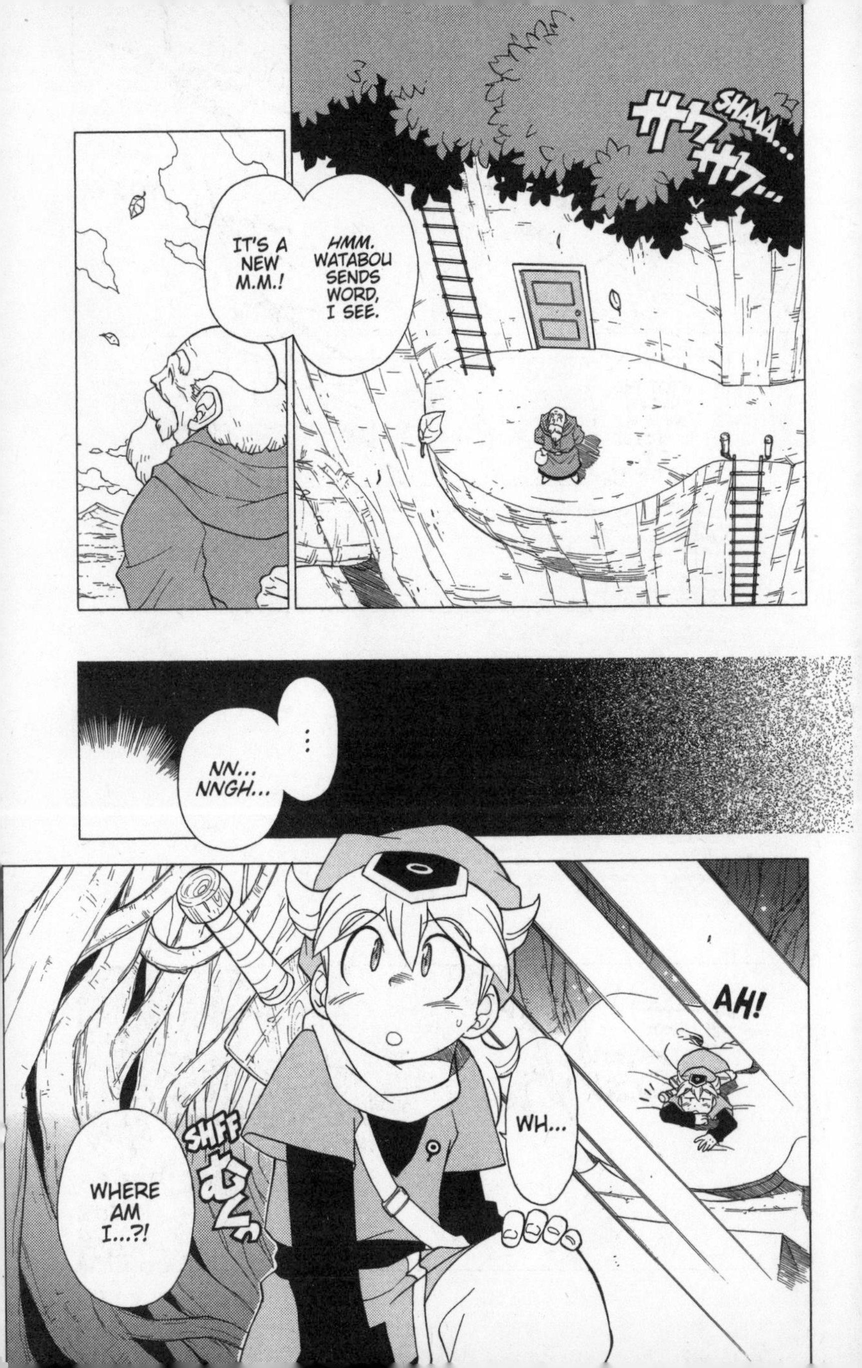
SHAAA...
サワサワ...
HMM. WATABOU SENDS WORD, I SEE.
IT'S A NEW M.M.!
...
NN... NNGH...
AH!
WH...
SHFF
むくっ
WHERE AM I...?!

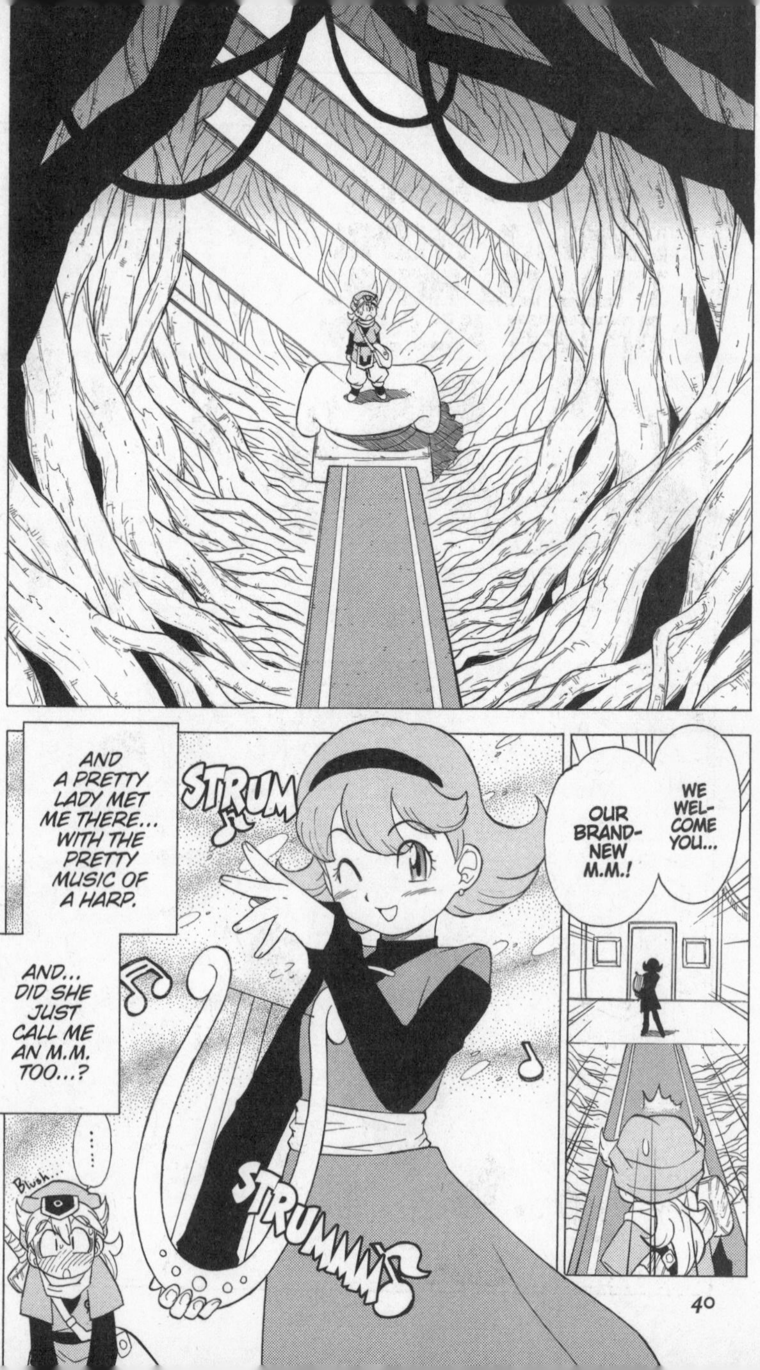
WE WEL-COME YOU...
OUR BRAND-NEW M.M.!
AND A PRETTY LADY MET ME THERE... WITH THE PRETTY MUSIC OF A HARP.
STRUM
AND... DID SHE JUST CALL ME AN M.M. TOO...?
STRUMMM
Blush...
......

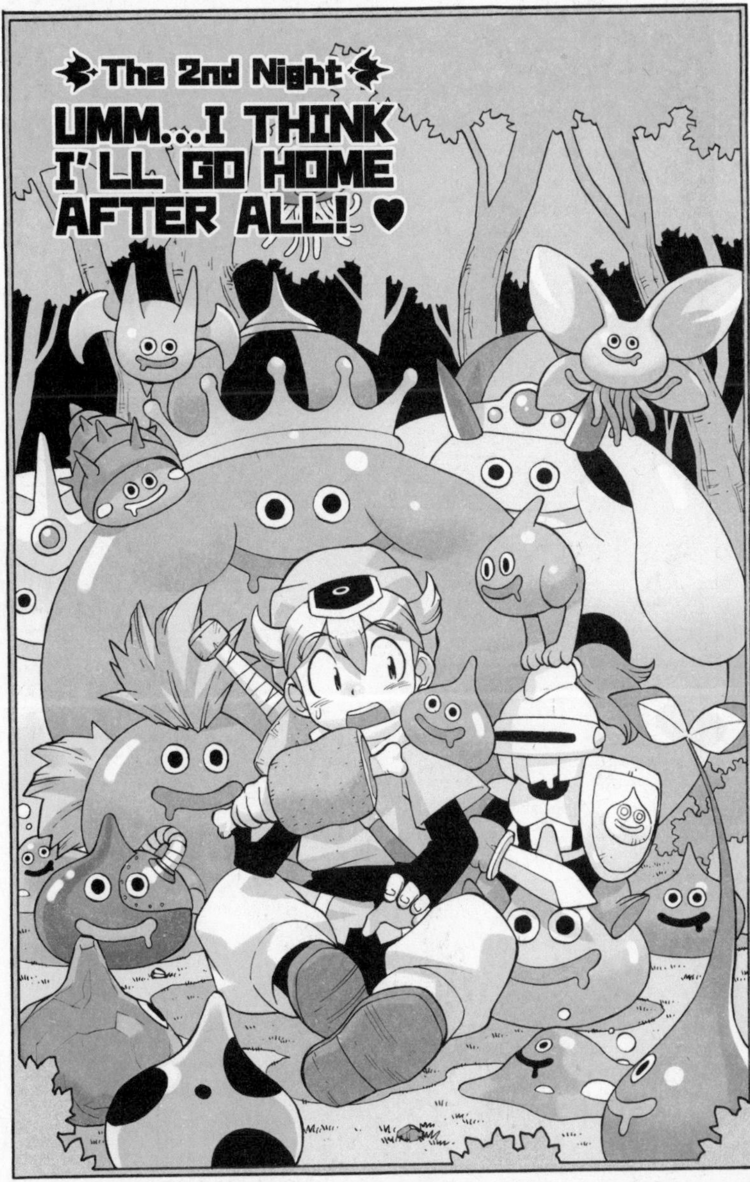
The 2nd Night
UMM...I THINK I'LL GO HOME AFTER ALL! ♥

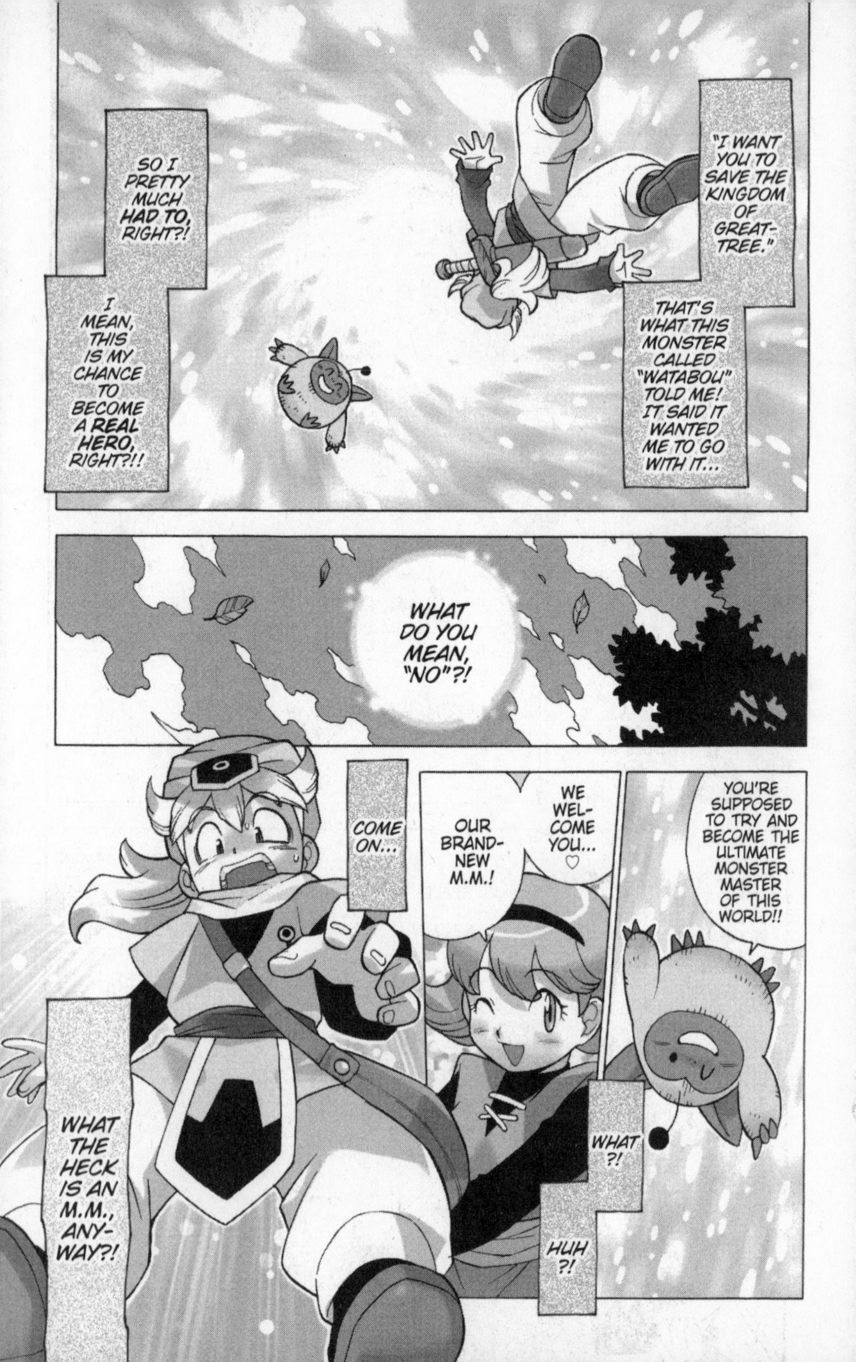
"I WANT YOU TO SAVE THE KINGDOM OF GREAT-TREE."
THAT'S WHAT THIS MONSTER CALLED "WATABOU" TOLD ME! IT SAID IT WANTED ME TO GO WITH IT...
SO I PRETTY MUCH **HAD TO**, RIGHT?!
I MEAN, THIS IS MY CHANCE TO BECOME A **REAL HERO**, RIGHT?!!
WHAT DO YOU MEAN, "NO"?!
YOU'RE SUPPOSED TO TRY AND BECOME THE ULTIMATE MONSTER MASTER OF THIS WORLD!!
WE WEL-COME YOU...♡
OUR BRAND-NEW M.M.!
WHAT?!
HUH?!
COME ON...
WHAT THE HECK IS AN M.M., ANY-WAY?!

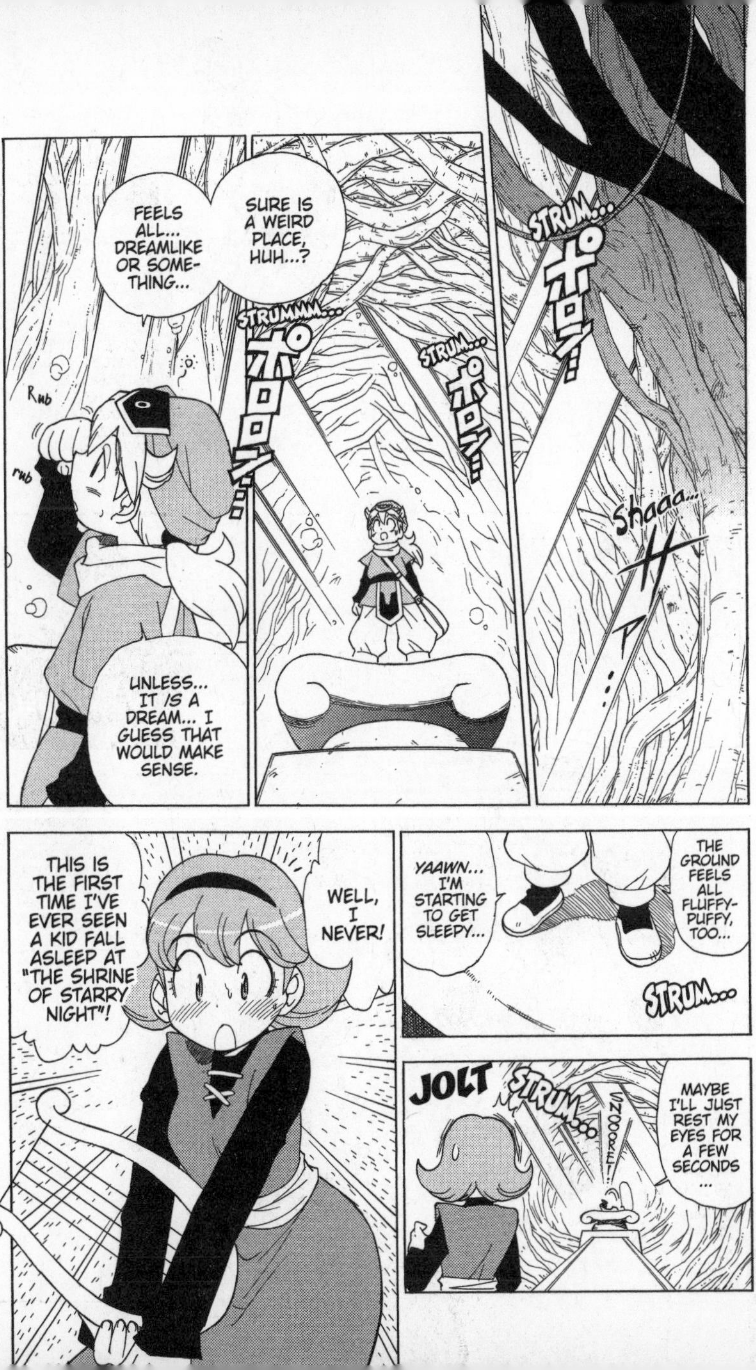
STRUM...
ポロン!!
Shaaa...
SURE IS A WEIRD PLACE, HUH...?
STRUMMM...
ポロロン!!...
STRUM...
ポロン...
FEELS ALL... DREAMLIKE OR SOME-THING...
Rub
rub
UNLESS... IT IS A DREAM... I GUESS THAT WOULD MAKE SENSE.
THE GROUND FEELS ALL FLUFFY-PUFFY, TOO...
YAAWN... I'M STARTING TO GET SLEEPY...
STRUM...
MAYBE I'LL JUST REST MY EYES FOR A FEW SECONDS ...
SNOOORE!!
STRUM...
JOLT
WELL, I NEVER!
THIS IS THE FIRST TIME I'VE EVER SEEN A KID FALL ASLEEP AT "THE SHRINE OF STARRY NIGHT"!

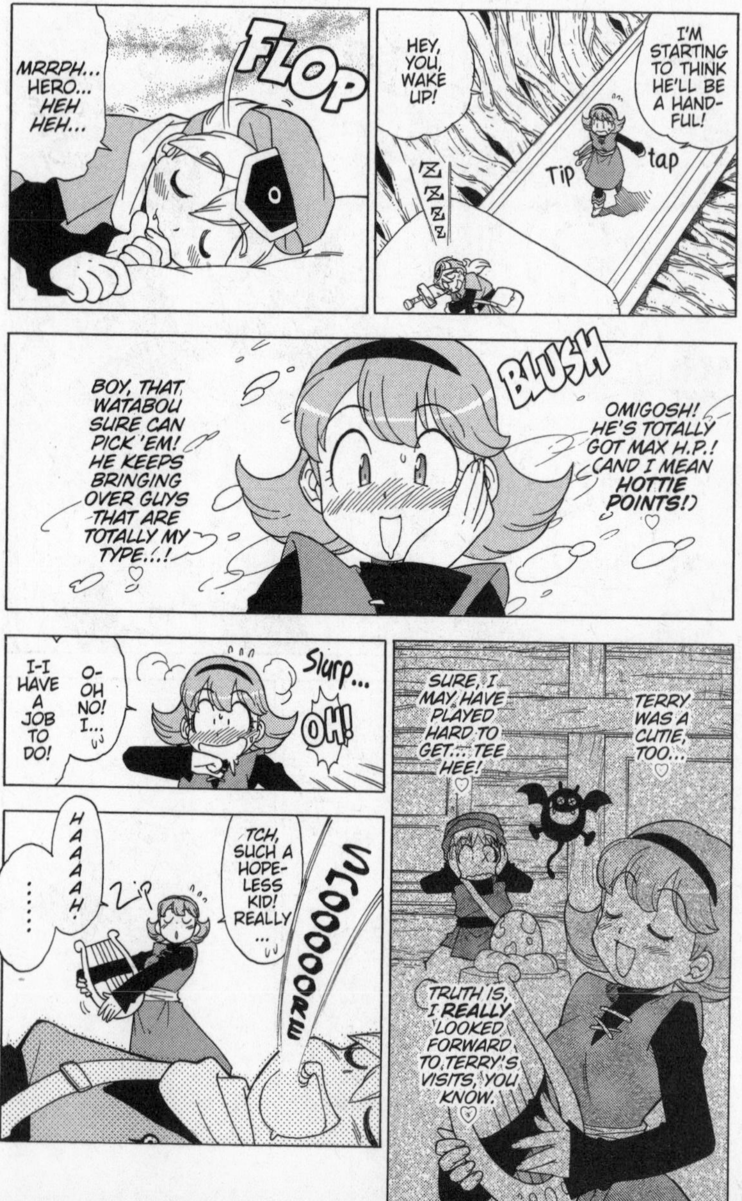

I'M STARTING TO THINK HE'LL BE A HANDFUL!
HEY, YOU, WAKE UP!
tap
Tip
ZZZZZ
FLOP
MRRPH... HERO... HEH HEH...
BLUSH
OMIGOSH! HE'S TOTALLY GOT MAX H.P.! (AND I MEAN HOTTIE POINTS!)
BOY, THAT WATABOU SURE CAN PICK 'EM! HE KEEPS BRINGING OVER GUYS THAT ARE TOTALLY MY TYPE...!
TERRY WAS A CUTIE, TOO...
SURE, I MAY HAVE PLAYED HARD TO GET... TEE HEE!
TRUTH IS, I REALLY LOOKED FORWARD TO TERRY'S VISITS, YOU KNOW.
Slurp...
OH!
O-OH NO! I...
I-I HAVE A JOB TO DO!
SJOOOOOORE
TCH, SUCH A HOPE-LESS KID! REALLY...
HAAAAAH!
ZIP
......

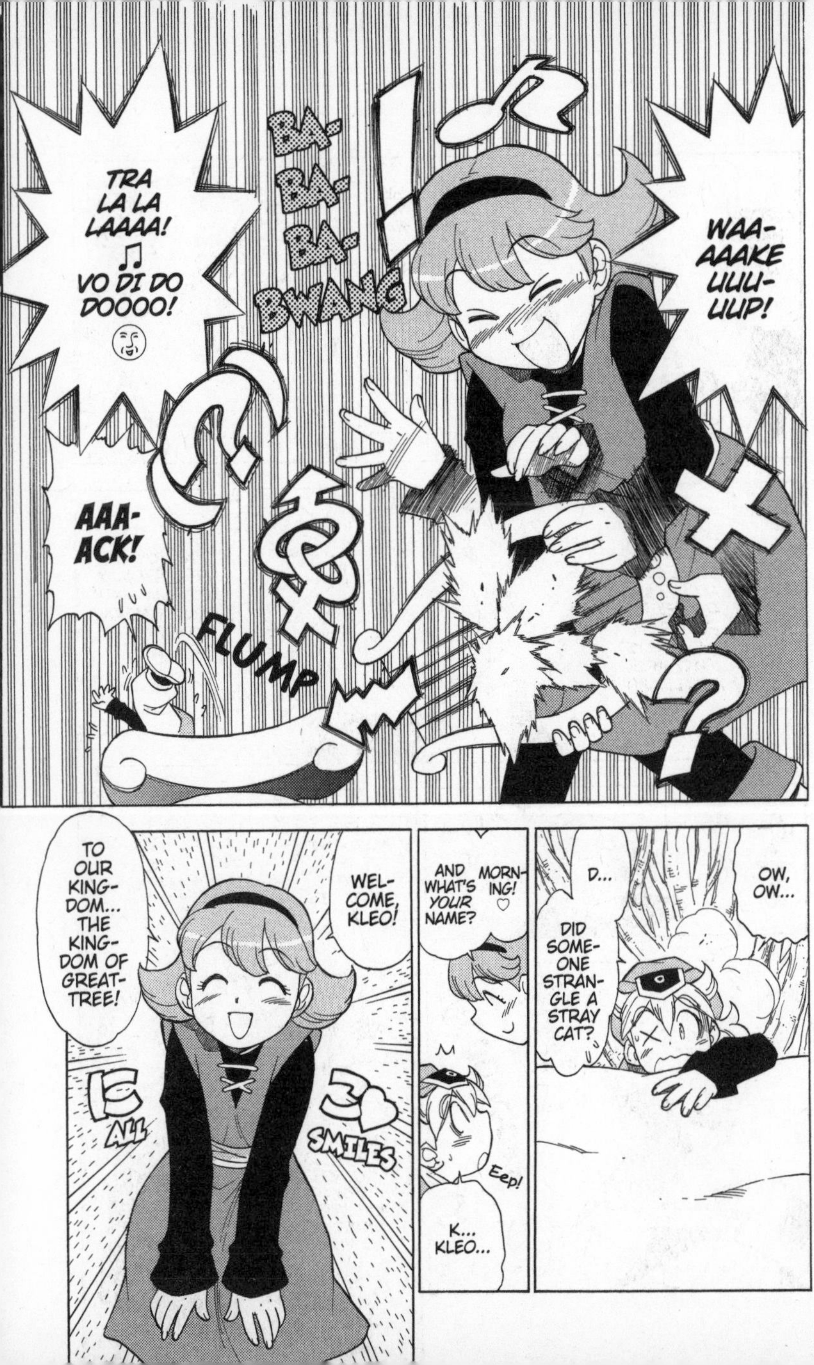
WAA-AAAKE UUU-UUUP!
BA-BA-BA-BWANG
TRA LA LA LAAAA! ♫ VO DI DO DOOOO!
AAA-ACK!
FLUMP
OW, OW...
D...
DID SOME-ONE STRAN-GLE A STRAY CAT?
MORN-ING! ♡
AND WHAT'S *YOUR* NAME?
Eep!
K... KLEO...
WEL-COME, KLEO!
TO OUR KING-DOM... THE KING-DOM OF GREAT-TREE!
ALL SMILES

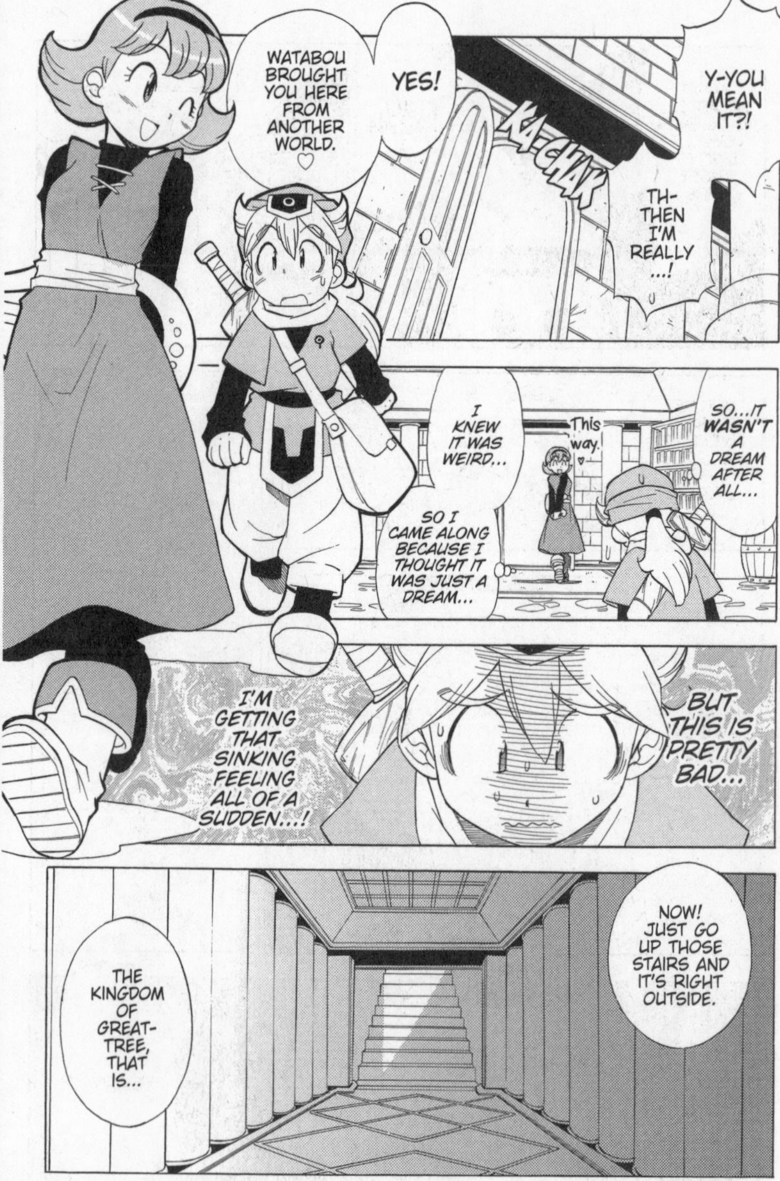
Y-YOU MEAN IT?!
KA-CHAK
TH-THEN I'M REALLY ...!
YES!
WATABOU BROUGHT YOU HERE FROM ANOTHER WORLD. ♡
SO...IT WASN'T A DREAM AFTER ALL...
This way. ♡
I KNEW IT WAS WEIRD...
SO I CAME ALONG BECAUSE I THOUGHT IT WAS JUST A DREAM...
BUT THIS IS PRETTY BAD...
I'M GETTING THAT SINKING FEELING ALL OF A SUDDEN...!
NOW! JUST GO UP THOSE STAIRS AND IT'S RIGHT OUTSIDE.
THE KINGDOM OF GREAT-TREE, THAT IS...

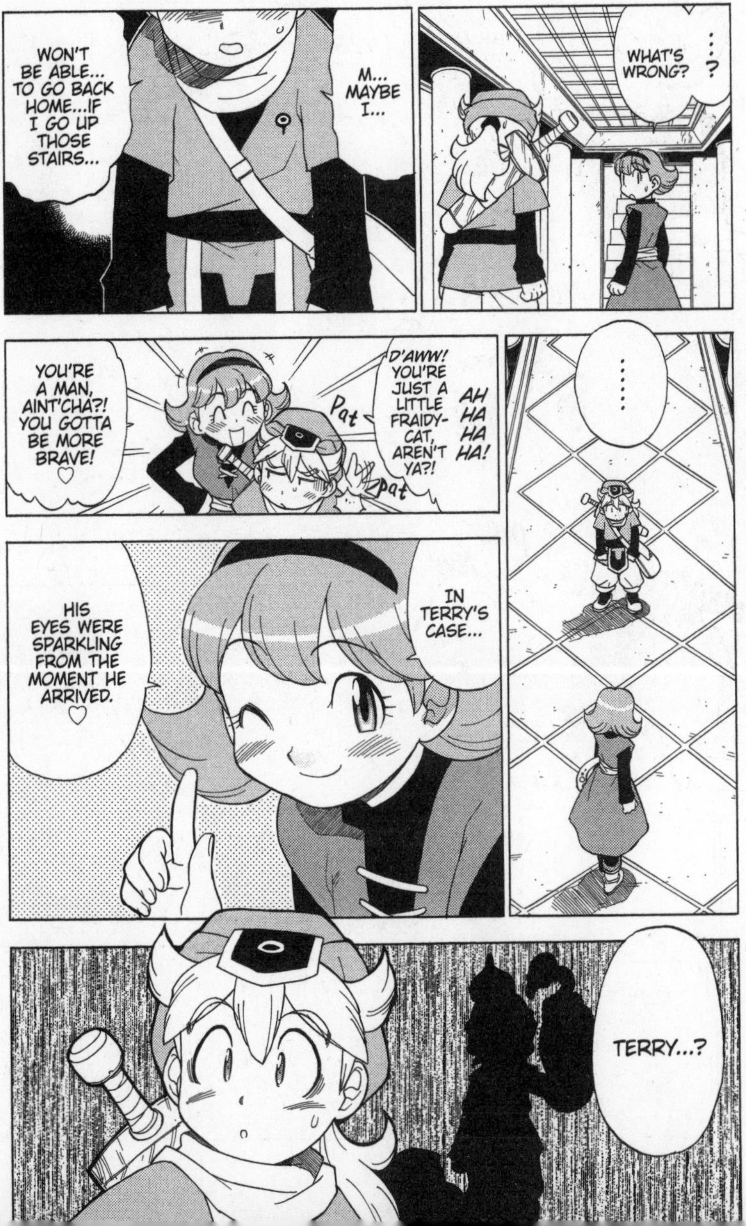
...?
WHAT'S WRONG?
M... MAYBE I...
WON'T BE ABLE... TO GO BACK HOME...IF I GO UP THOSE STAIRS...
......
D'AWW! YOU'RE JUST A LITTLE FRAIDY-CAT, AREN'T YA?!
AH HA HA HA!
Pat
pat
YOU'RE A MAN, AINT'CHA?! YOU GOTTA BE MORE BRAVE! ♡
IN TERRY'S CASE...
HIS EYES WERE SPARKLING FROM THE MOMENT HE ARRIVED. ♡
TERRY...?

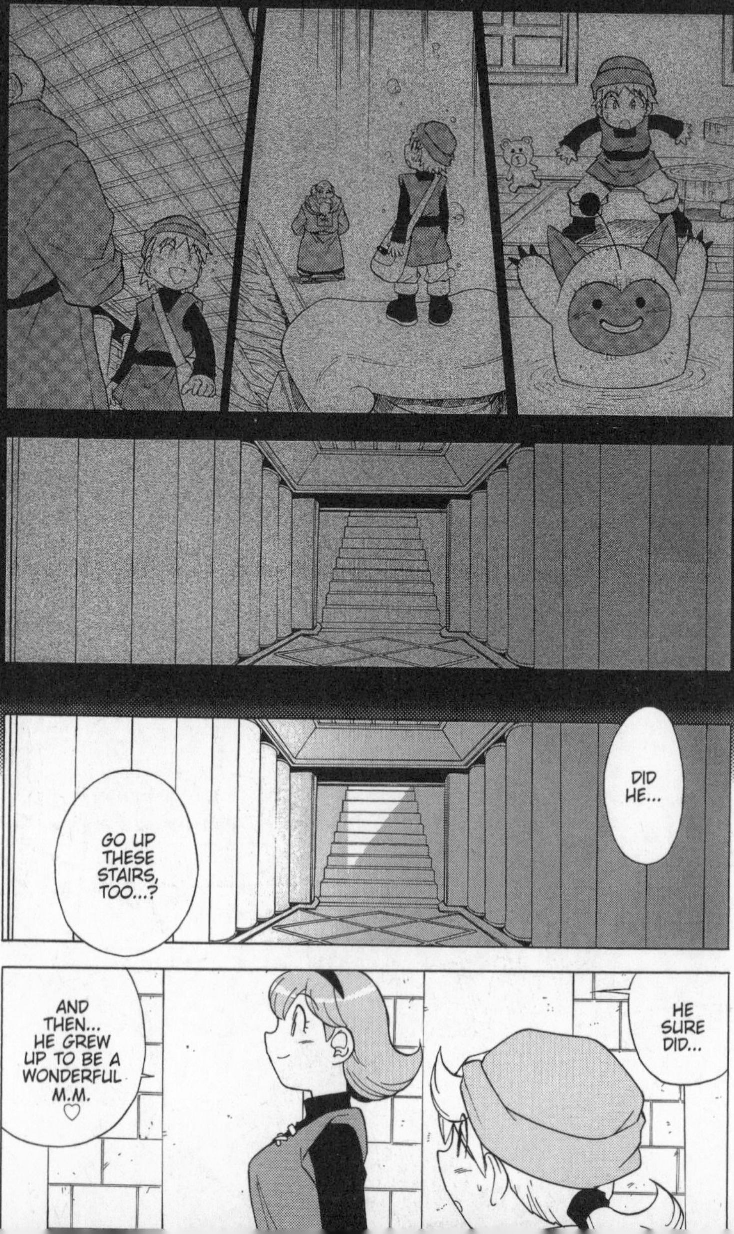
DID HE...
GO UP THESE STAIRS, TOO...?
HE SURE DID...
AND THEN... HE GREW UP TO BE A WONDERFUL M.M. ♡

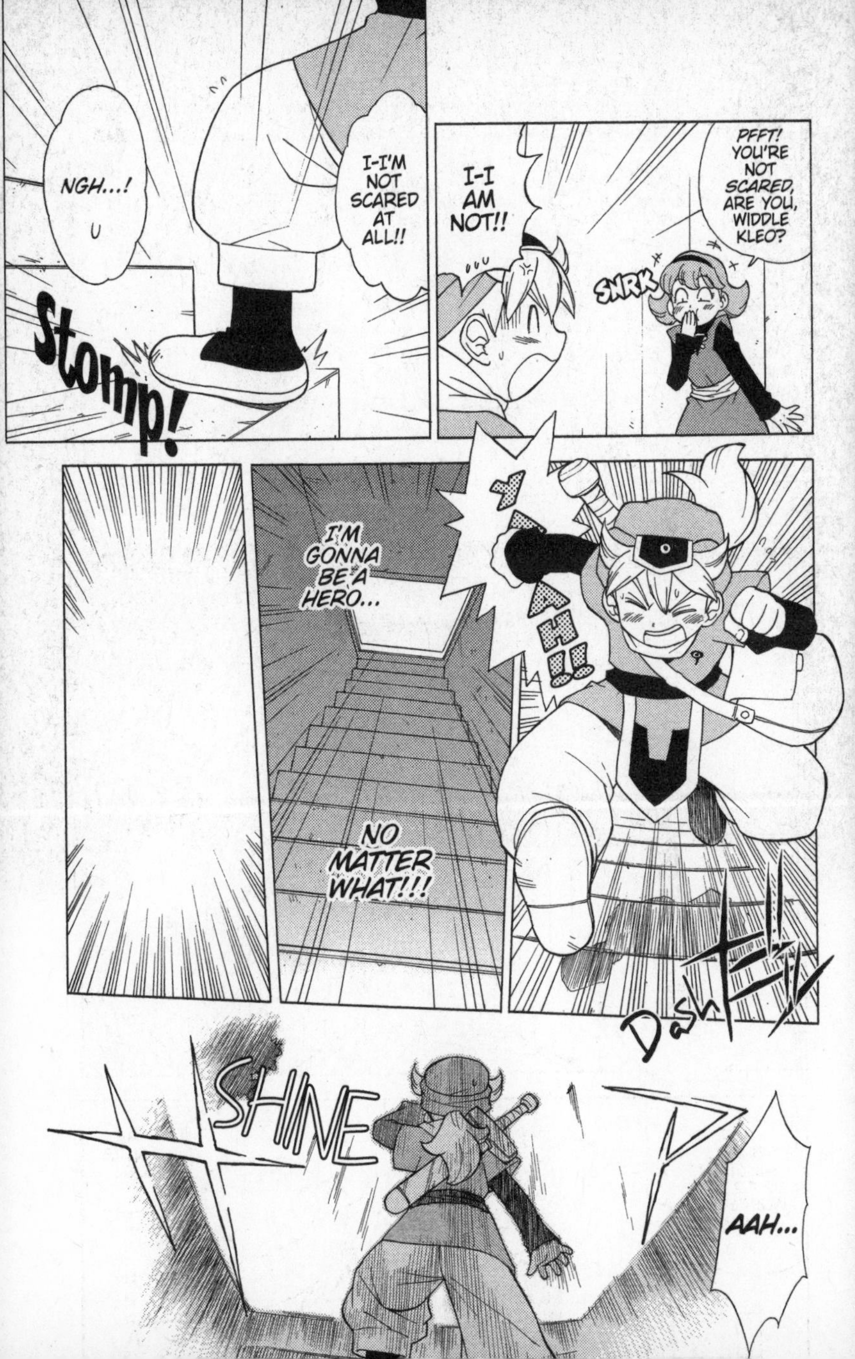
PFFT! YOU'RE NOT SCARED, ARE YOU, WIDDLE KLEO?
I-I AM NOT!!
SNRK
I-I'M NOT SCARED AT ALL!!
NGH...!
Stomp!
YAAH!!
Dash
I'M GONNA BE A HERO...
NO MATTER WHAT!!!
AAH...
SHINE

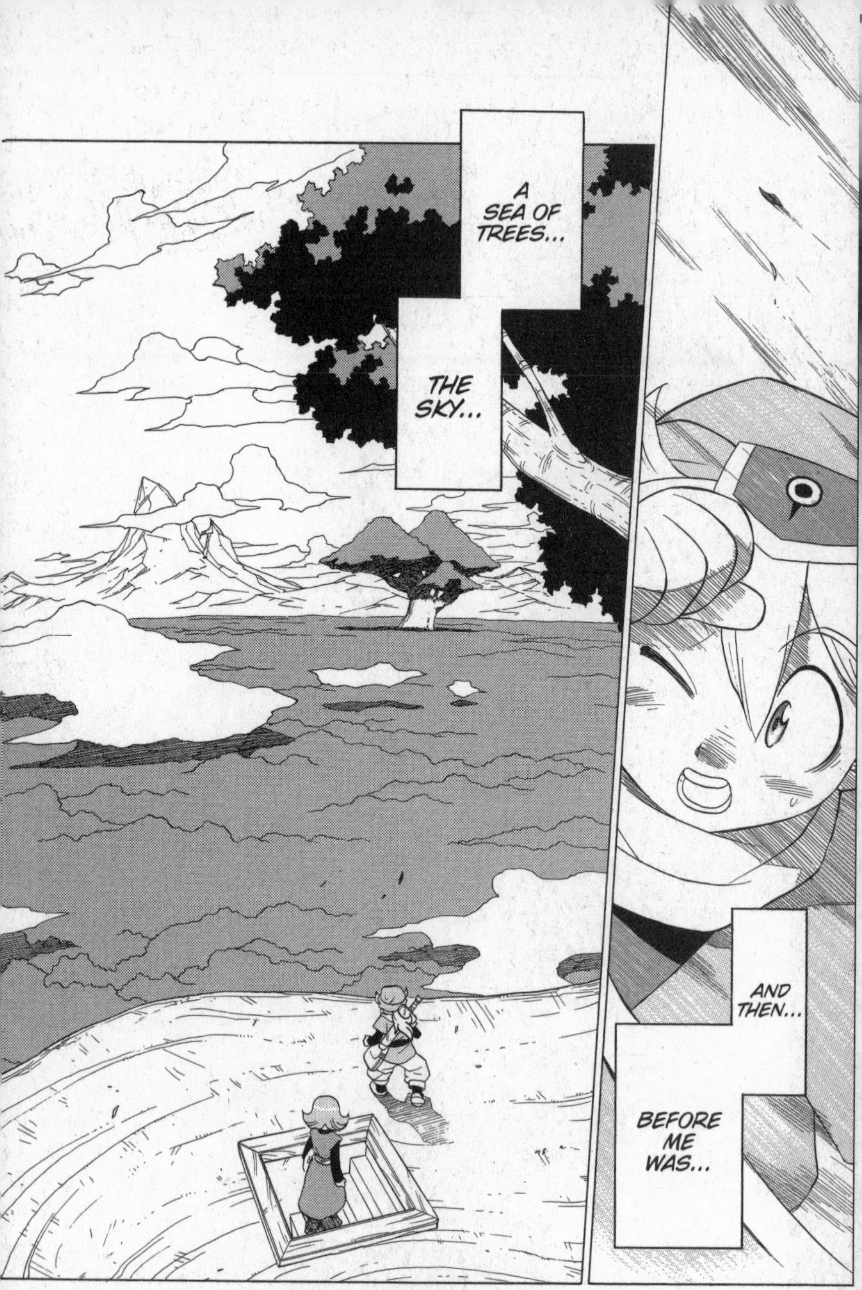
AND THEN...
BEFORE ME WAS...
A SEA OF TREES...
THE SKY...

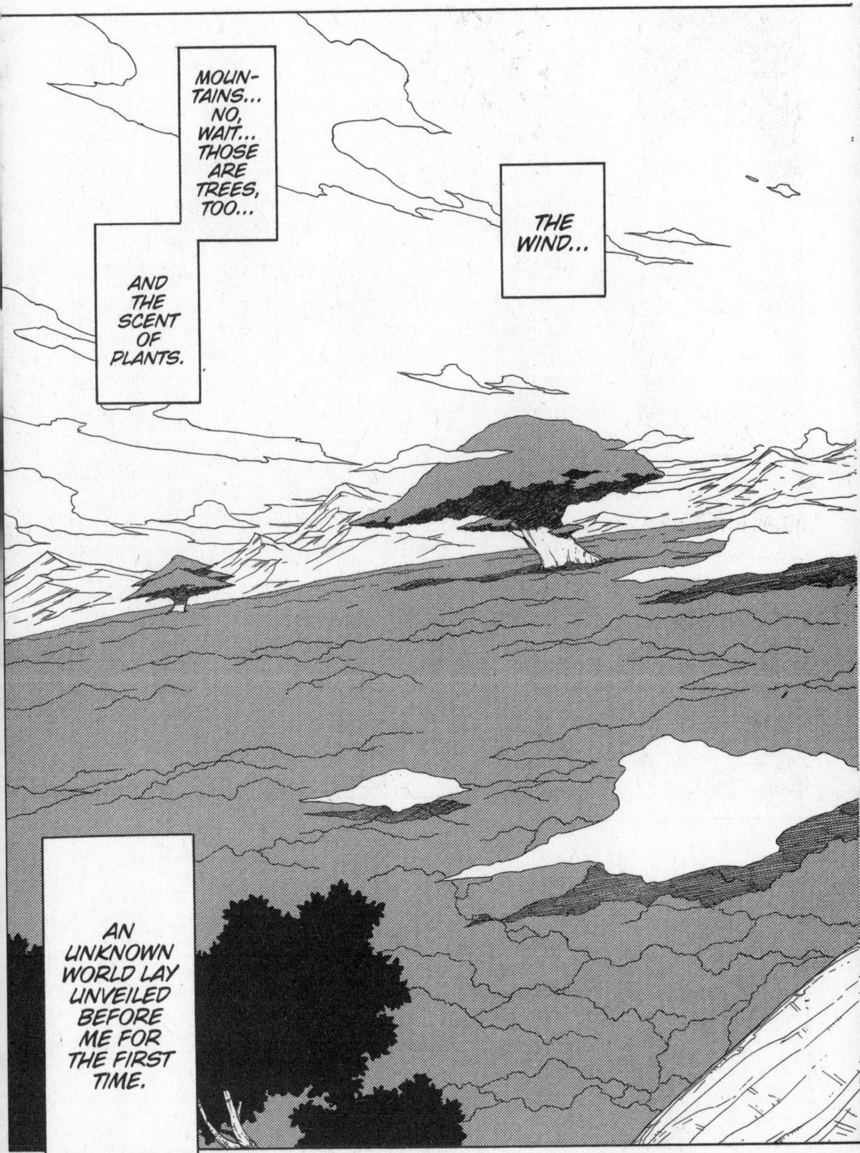
THE WIND...
MOUNTAINS... NO, WAIT... THOSE ARE TREES, TOO...
AND THE SCENT OF PLANTS.
AN UNKNOWN WORLD LAY UNVEILED BEFORE ME FOR THE FIRST TIME.

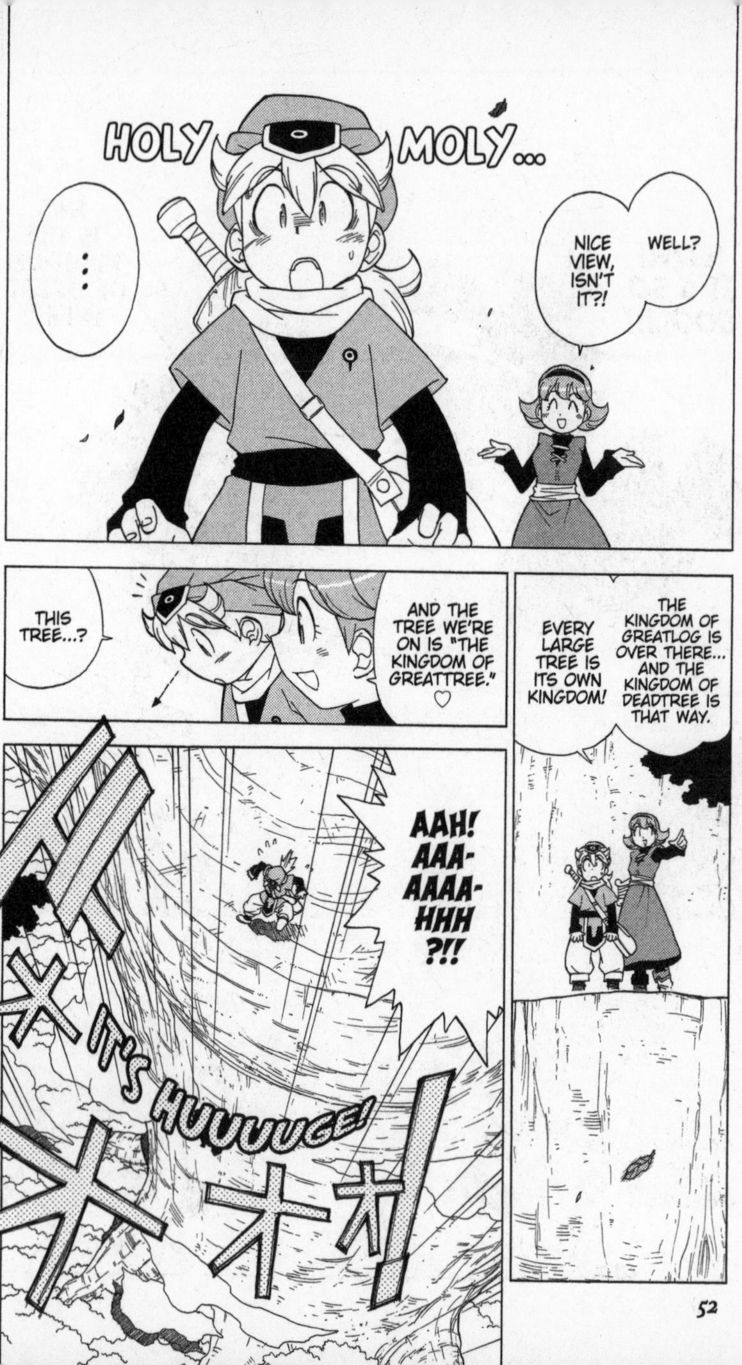
WELL?
NICE VIEW, ISN'T IT?!
HOLY MOLY...
...
THE KINGDOM OF GREATLOG IS OVER THERE... AND THE KINGDOM OF DEADTREE IS THAT WAY.
EVERY LARGE TREE IS ITS OWN KINGDOM!
AND THE TREE WE'RE ON IS "THE KINGDOM OF GREATTREE." ♡
THIS TREE...?
AAH! AAA-AAAA-HHH?!!
IT'S HUUUUGE!

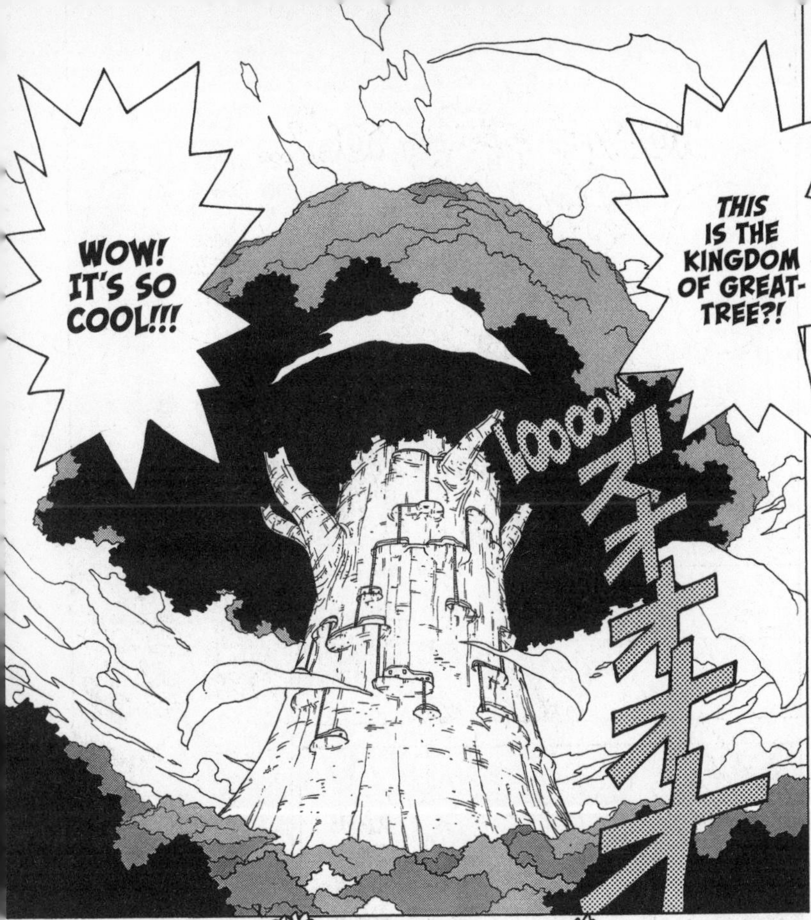
THIS IS THE KINGDOM OF GREAT-TREE?!
WOW! IT'S SO COOL!!!
LOOOOM

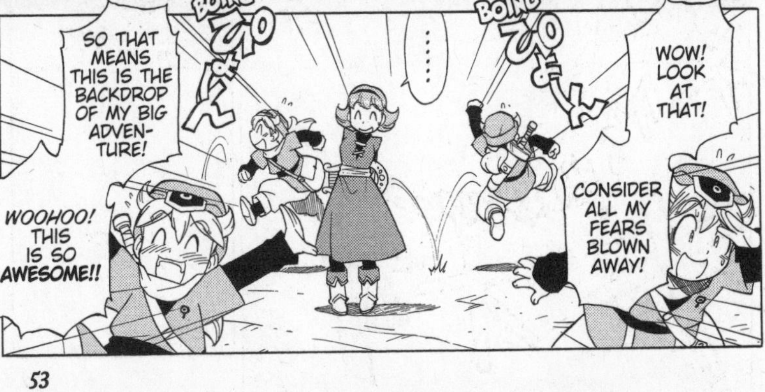
WOW! LOOK AT THAT!
BOING
......
BOING
SO THAT MEANS THIS IS THE BACKDROP OF MY BIG ADVEN-TURE!
CONSIDER ALL MY FEARS BLOWN AWAY!
WOOHOO! THIS IS SO AWESOME!!

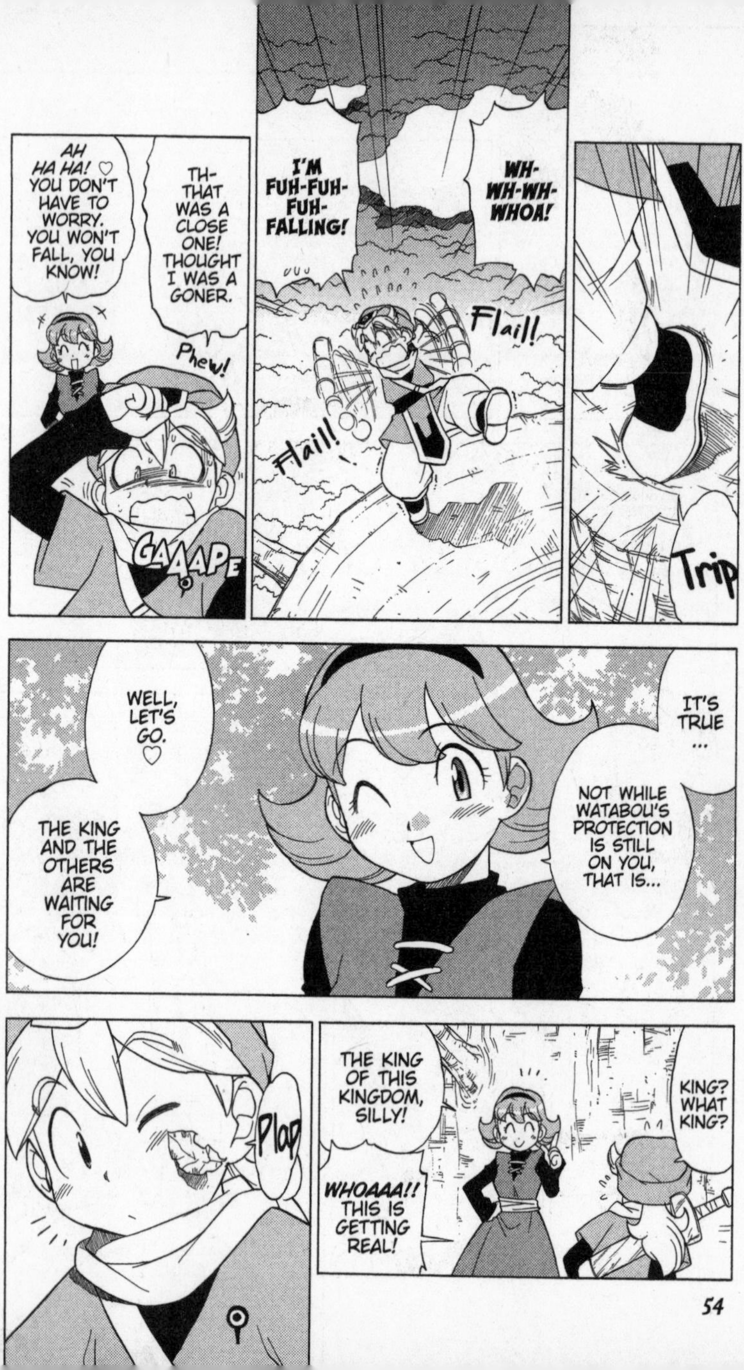

Trip
WH-WH-WH-WHOA!
I'M FUH-FUH-FUH-FALLING!
Flail!
Flail!
TH-THAT WAS A CLOSE ONE! THOUGHT I WAS A GONER.
Phew!
AH HA HA! ♡ YOU DON'T HAVE TO WORRY. YOU WON'T FALL, YOU KNOW!
GAAAPE
IT'S TRUE...
NOT WHILE WATABOU'S PROTECTION IS STILL ON YOU, THAT IS...
WELL, LET'S GO. ♡
THE KING AND THE OTHERS ARE WAITING FOR YOU!
KING? WHAT KING?
THE KING OF THIS KINGDOM, SILLY!
WHOAAA!! THIS IS GETTING REAL!
Plap

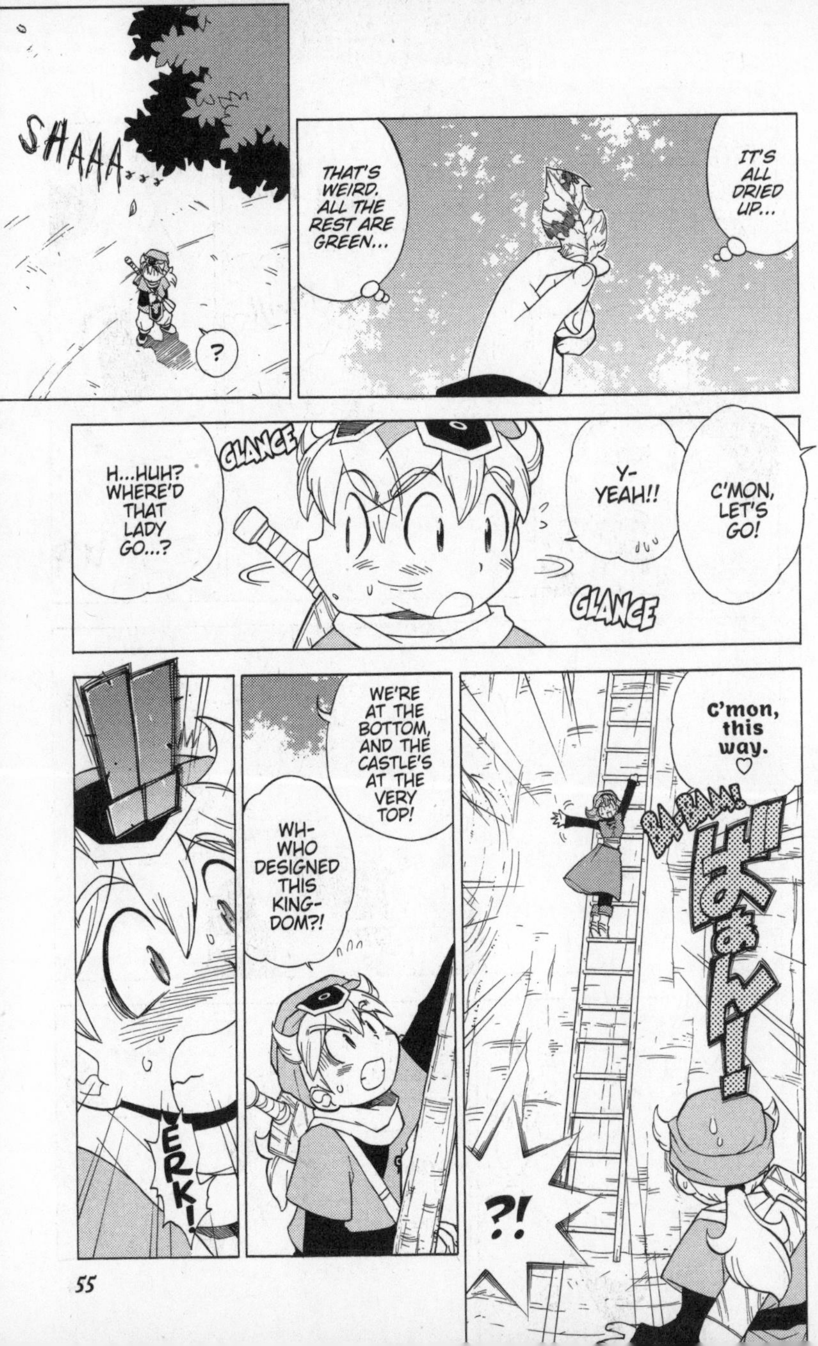
IT'S ALL DRIED UP...
THAT'S WEIRD. ALL THE REST ARE GREEN...
SHAAA
?
C'MON, LET'S GO!
Y-YEAH!!
GLANCE
GLANCE
H...HUH? WHERE'D THAT LADY GO...?
C'mon, this way. ♡
BA-BAM!
?!
WE'RE AT THE BOTTOM, AND THE CASTLE'S AT THE VERY TOP!
WH-WHO DESIGNED THIS KING-DOM?!
ERK!

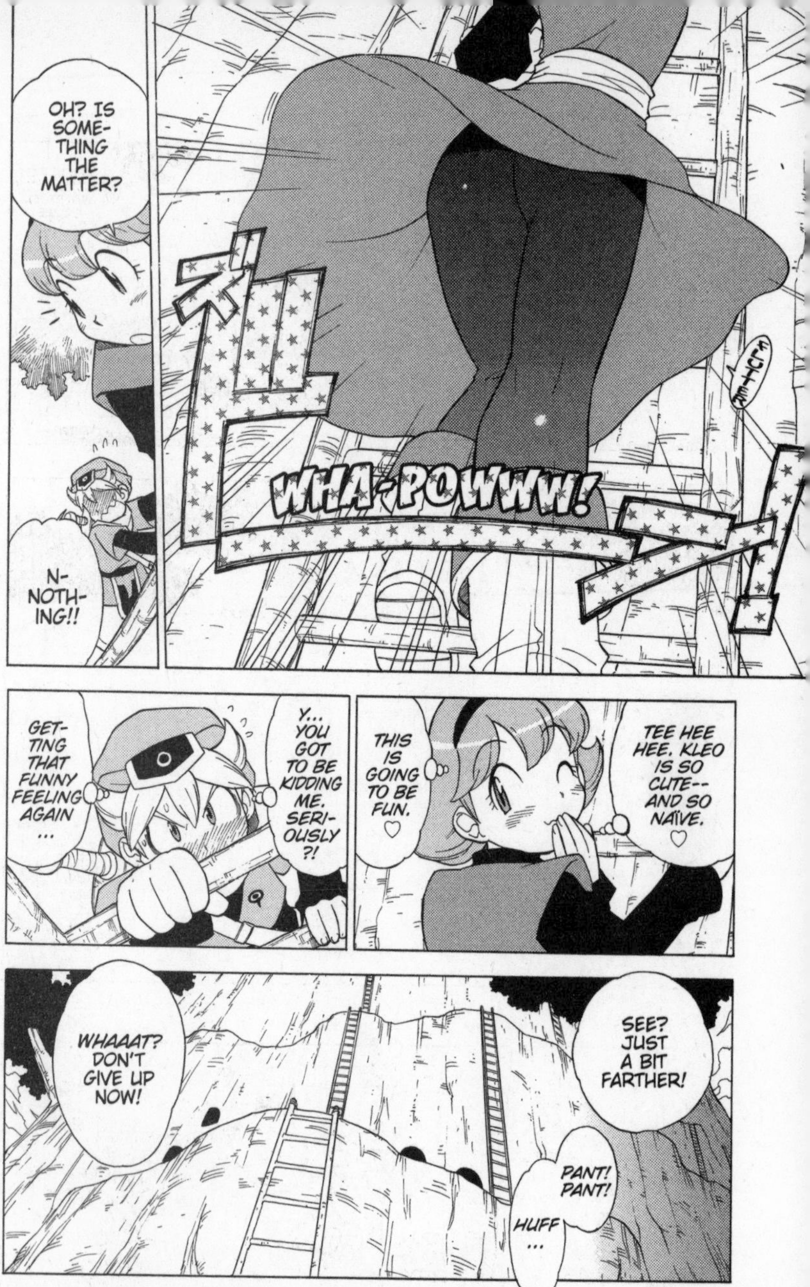
FLUTTER
WHA-POWWW!
OH? IS SOMETHING THE MATTER?
N-NOTHING!!
TEE HEE HEE. KLEO IS SO CUTE--AND SO NAÏVE. ♡
THIS IS GOING TO BE FUN. ♡
Y... YOU GOT TO BE KIDDING ME. SERIOUSLY?!
GETTING THAT FUNNY FEELING AGAIN...
SEE? JUST A BIT FARTHER!
WHAAAT? DON'T GIVE UP NOW!
PANT! PANT!
HUFF...

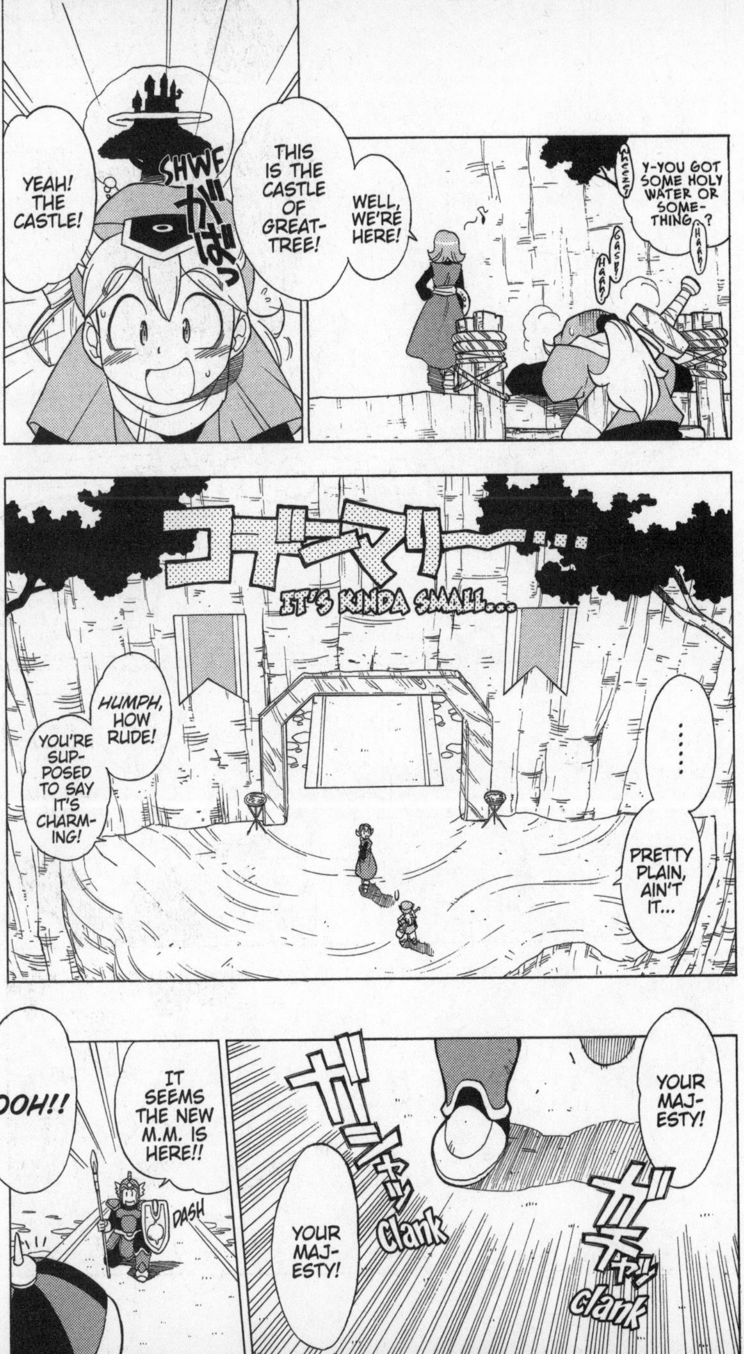
WHEEZE!
Y-YOU GOT SOME HOLY WATER OR SOME-THING...?
HAAH!
GASP!
HAAH!
WELL, WE'RE HERE!
THIS IS THE CASTLE OF GREAT-TREE!
SHWF
がばっ
YEAH! THE CASTLE!
コヂンマリ～…
IT'S KINDA SMALL...
......
PRETTY PLAIN, AIN'T IT...
HUMPH, HOW RUDE!
YOU'RE SUP-POSED TO SAY IT'S CHARM-ING!
YOUR MAJ-ESTY!
ガチャッ
clank
ガチャッ
Clank
YOUR MAJ-ESTY!
IT SEEMS THE NEW M.M. IS HERE!!
OOH!!
DASH

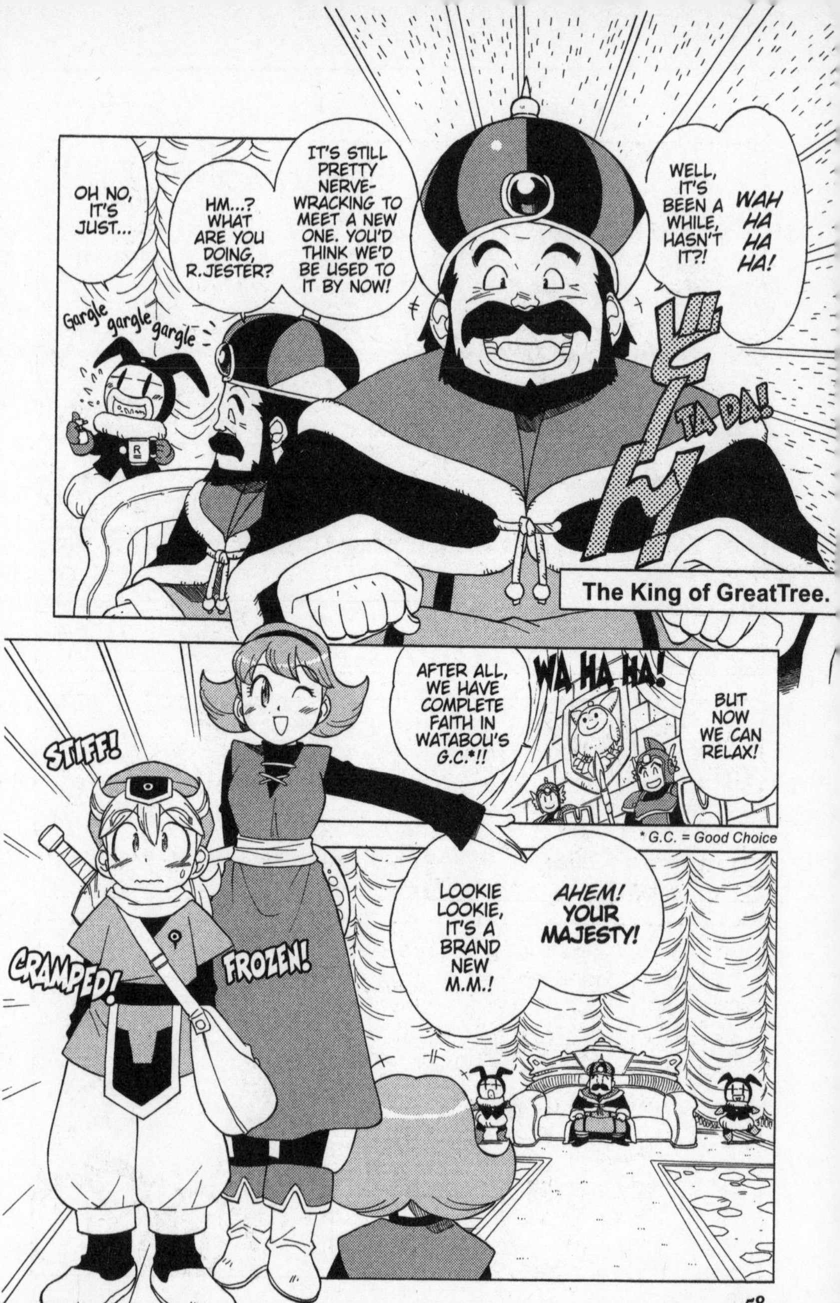
WELL, IT'S BEEN A WHILE, HASN'T IT?!
WAH HA HA HA!
IT'S STILL PRETTY NERVE-WRACKING TO MEET A NEW ONE. YOU'D THINK WE'D BE USED TO IT BY NOW!
HM...? WHAT ARE YOU DOING, R.JESTER?
OH NO, IT'S JUST...
Gargle gargle gargle
TA DA!
The King of GreatTree.
BUT NOW WE CAN RELAX!
WA HA HA!
AFTER ALL, WE HAVE COMPLETE FAITH IN WATABOU'S G.C.*!!
* G.C. = Good Choice
AHEM! YOUR MAJESTY!
LOOKIE LOOKIE, IT'S A BRAND NEW M.M.!
FROZEN!
STIFF!
CRAMPED!

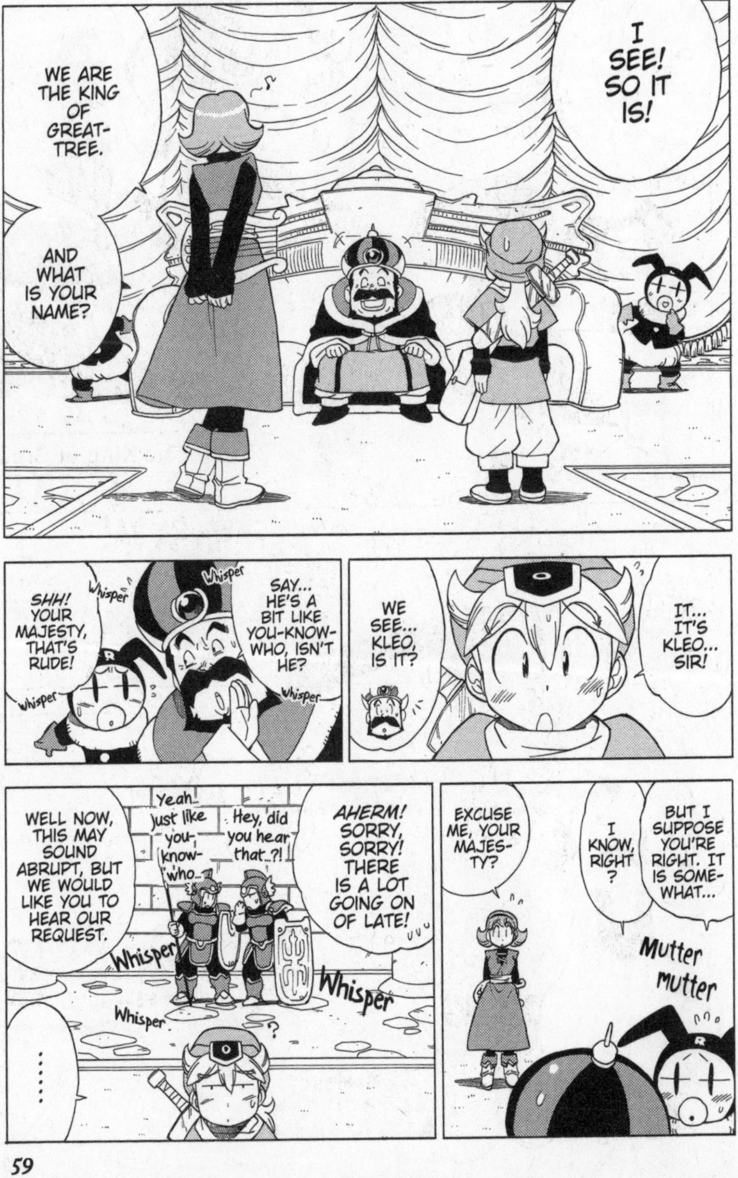
I SEE! SO IT IS!
WE ARE THE KING OF GREAT-TREE.
AND WHAT IS YOUR NAME?
IT... IT'S KLEO... SIR!
WE SEE... KLEO, IS IT?
Whisper
SAY... HE'S A BIT LIKE YOU-KNOW-WHO, ISN'T HE?
Whisper
SHH! YOUR MAJESTY, THAT'S RUDE!
Whisper
Whisper
BUT I SUPPOSE YOU'RE RIGHT. IT IS SOME-WHAT...
I KNOW, RIGHT?
EXCUSE ME, YOUR MAJES-TY?
Mutter mutter
AHERM! SORRY, SORRY! THERE IS A LOT GOING ON OF LATE!
Hey, did you hear that..?!
Yeah.. Just like you-know-who...
WELL NOW, THIS MAY SOUND ABRUPT, BUT WE WOULD LIKE YOU TO HEAR OUR REQUEST.
Whisper
Whisper
Whisper
......

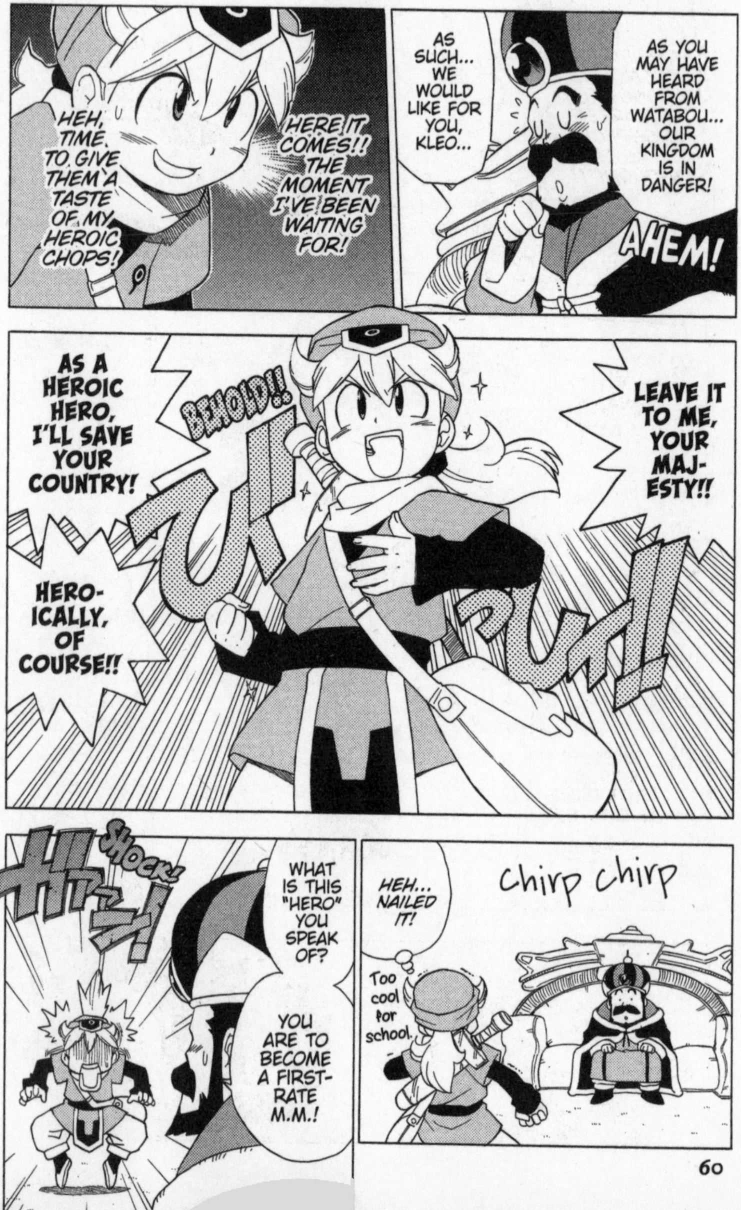
AS YOU MAY HAVE HEARD FROM WATABOU... OUR KINGDOM IS IN DANGER!
AHEM!
AS SUCH... WE WOULD LIKE FOR YOU, KLEO...
HERE IT COMES!! THE MOMENT I'VE BEEN WAITING FOR!
HEH, TIME TO GIVE THEM A TASTE OF MY HEROIC CHOPS!
LEAVE IT TO ME, YOUR MAJ-ESTY!!
BEHOLD!!
AS A HEROIC HERO, I'LL SAVE YOUR COUNTRY!
HERO-ICALLY, OF COURSE!!
Chirp chirp
HEH... NAILED IT!
Too cool for school.
WHAT IS THIS "HERO" YOU SPEAK OF?
YOU ARE TO BECOME A FIRST-RATE M.M.!
SHOCK!

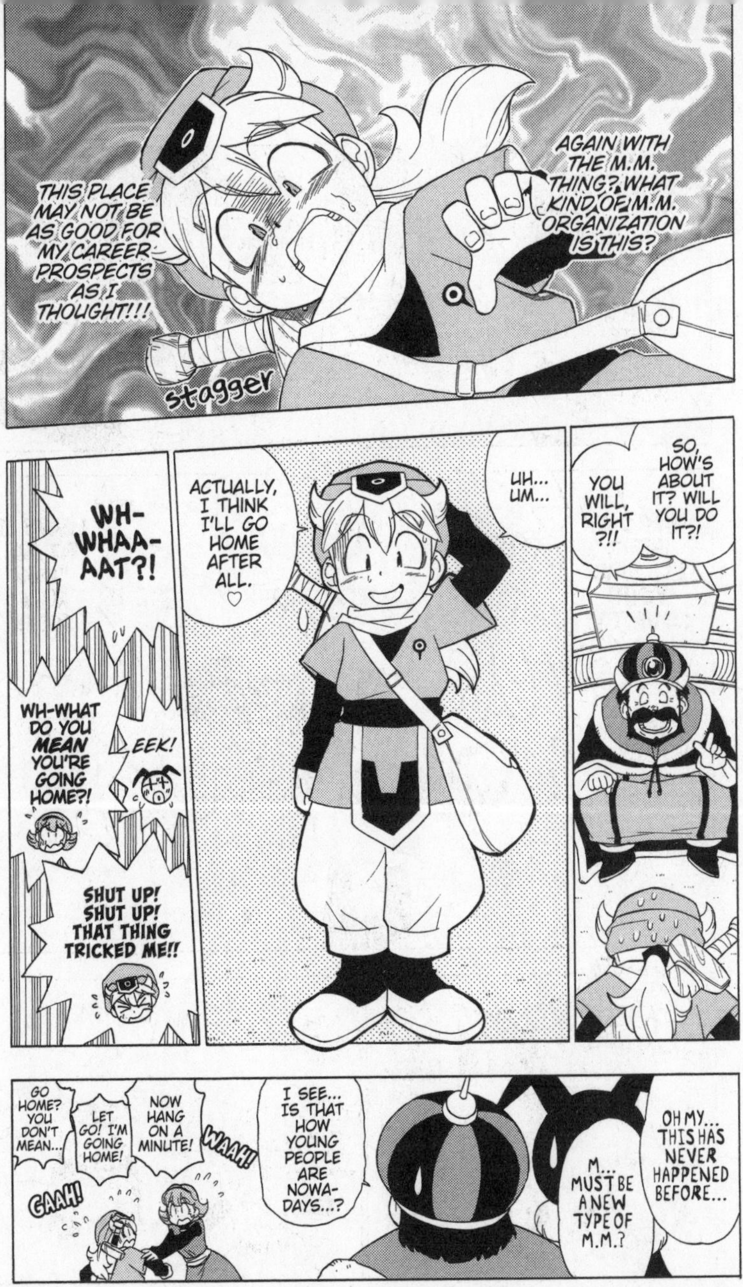
AGAIN WITH THE M.M. THING? WHAT KIND OF M.M. ORGANIZATION IS THIS?
THIS PLACE MAY NOT BE AS GOOD FOR MY CAREER PROSPECTS AS I THOUGHT!!!
stagger
SO, HOW'S ABOUT IT? WILL YOU DO IT?!
YOU WILL, RIGHT?!!
UH... UM...
ACTUALLY, I THINK I'LL GO HOME AFTER ALL. ♡
WH-WHAAA-AAT?!
EEK!
WH-WHAT DO YOU MEAN YOU'RE GOING HOME?!
SHUT UP! SHUT UP! THAT THING TRICKED ME!!
OH MY... THIS HAS NEVER HAPPENED BEFORE...
M... MUST BE A NEW TYPE OF M.M.?
I SEE... IS THAT HOW YOUNG PEOPLE ARE NOWADAYS...?
WAAH!
NOW HANG ON A MINUTE!
LET GO! I'M GOING HOME!
GO HOME? YOU DON'T MEAN...
GAAH!

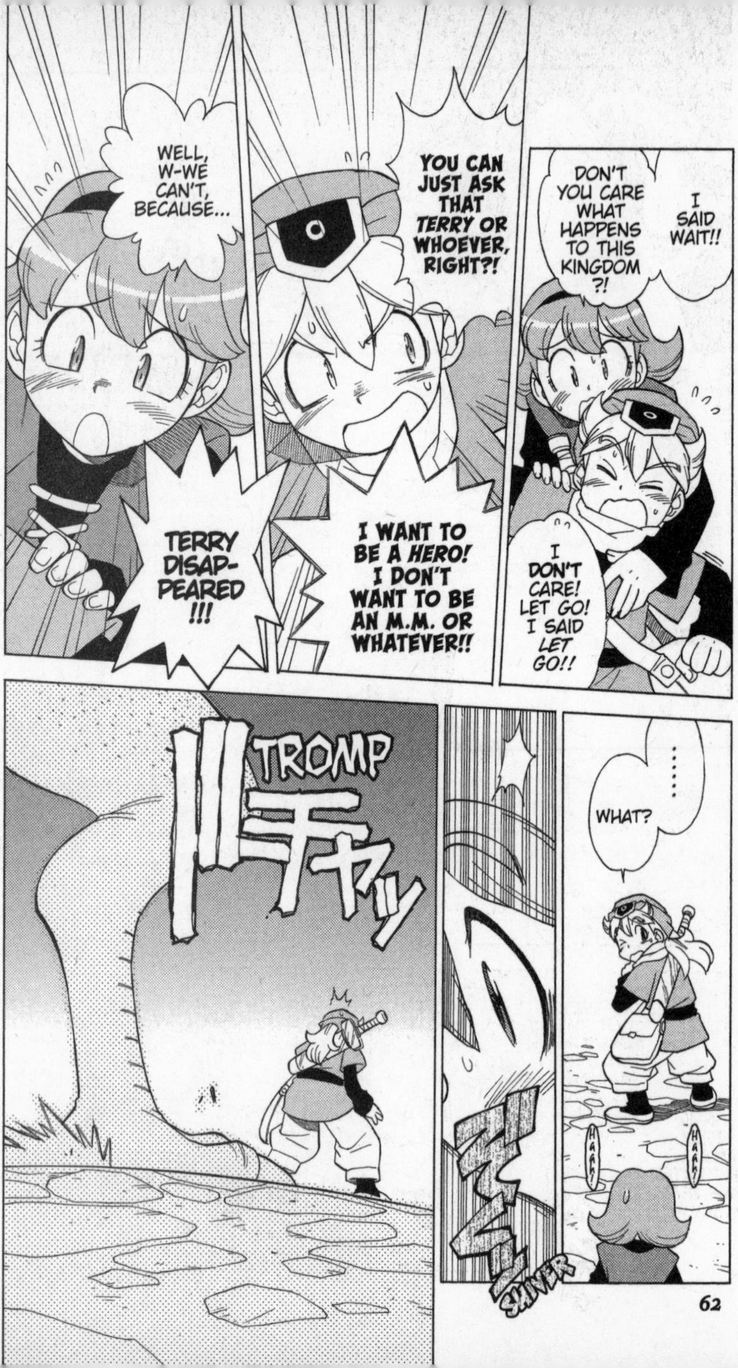

I SAID WAIT!!
DON'T YOU CARE WHAT HAPPENS TO THIS KINGDOM?!
I DON'T CARE! LET GO! I SAID *LET* GO!!
YOU CAN JUST ASK THAT *TERRY* OR WHOEVER, RIGHT?!
I WANT TO BE A *HERO!* I DON'T WANT TO BE AN M.M. OR WHATEVER!!
WELL, W-WE CAN'T, BECAUSE...
TERRY DISAPPEARED!!!
......
WHAT?
HAH
HAH
SHIVER
TROMP

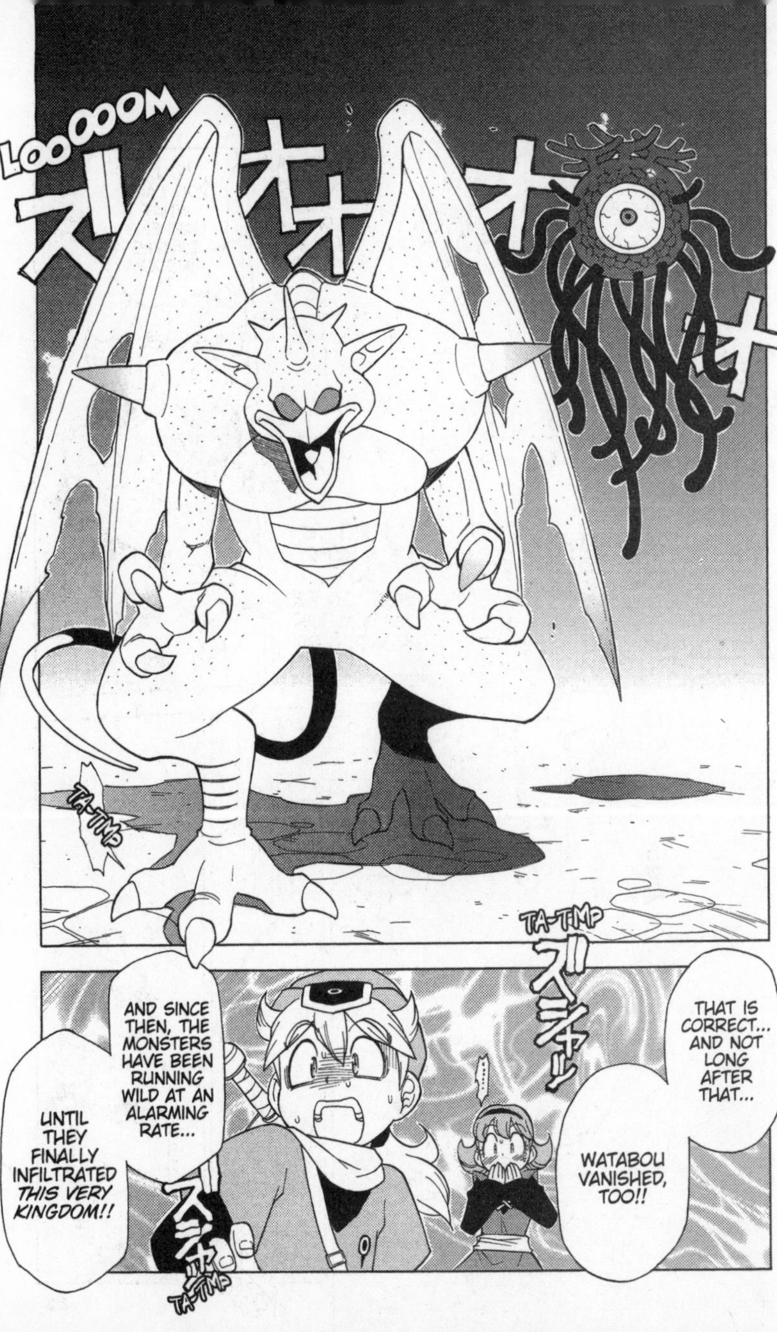
LOOOOOM
TA-TMP
TA-TMP
THAT IS CORRECT... AND NOT LONG AFTER THAT...
WATABOU VANISHED, TOO!!
AND SINCE THEN, THE MONSTERS HAVE BEEN RUNNING WILD AT AN ALARMING RATE...
UNTIL THEY FINALLY INFILTRATED *THIS VERY KINGDOM!!*
TA-TMP

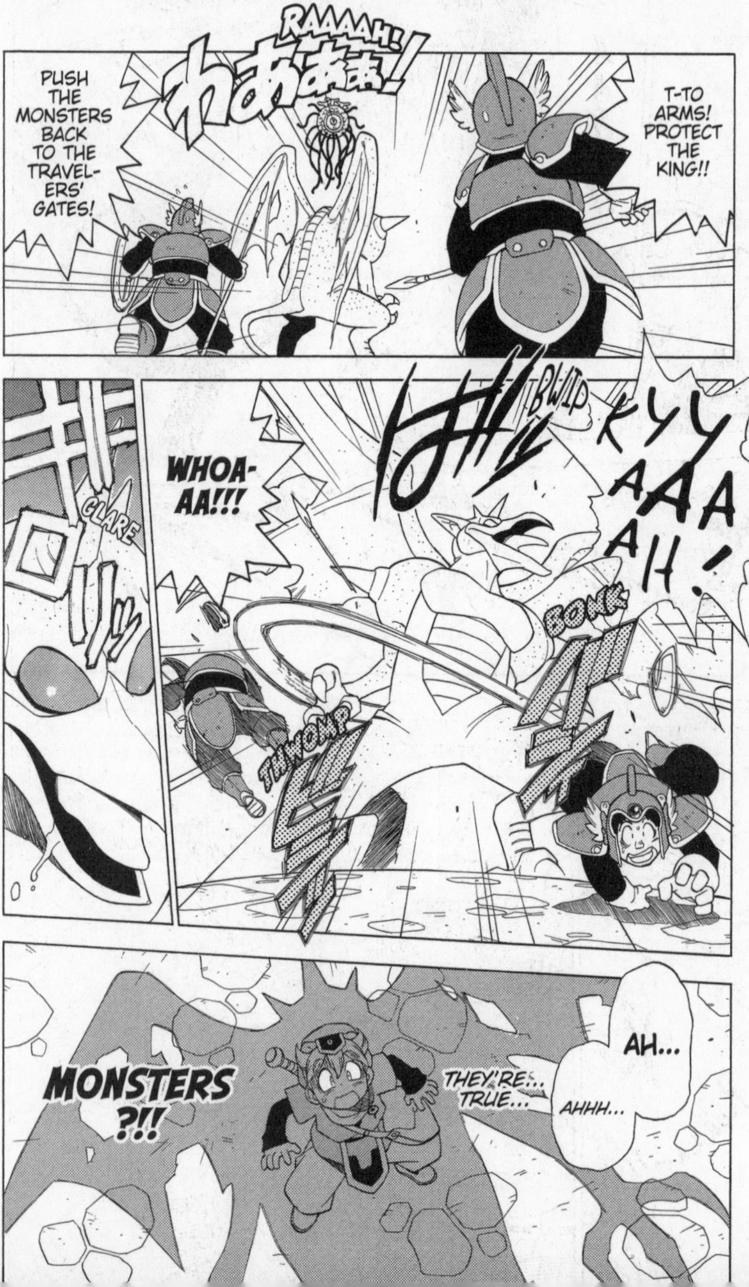
T-TO ARMS! PROTECT THE KING!!
RAAAAH!!
わあああ!
PUSH THE MONSTERS BACK TO THE TRAVELERS' GATES!
KYYAAAAAH!
BWIP
WHOA-AA!!!
BONK
THWOMP
GLARE
AH...
AHHH...
THEY'RE... TRUE...
MONSTERS?!!

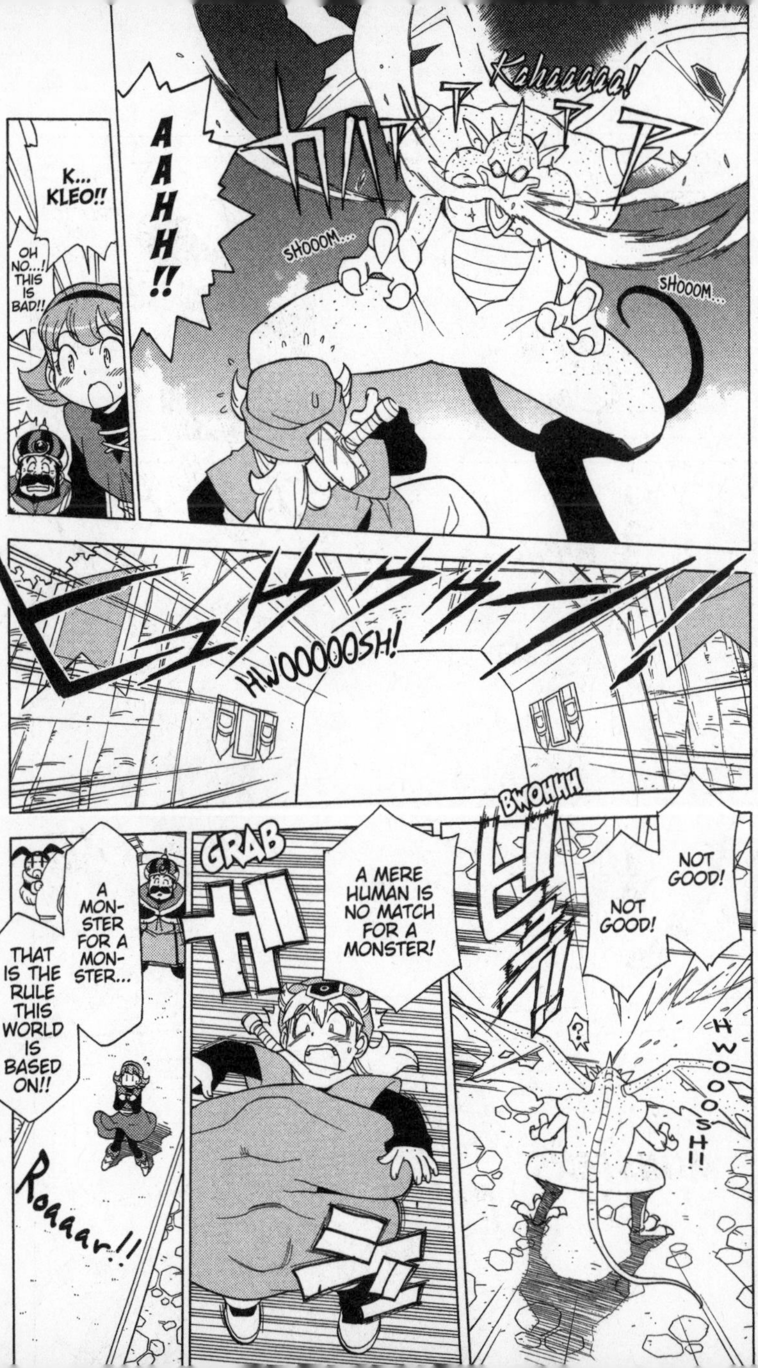
Kahaaaaa!
SHOOOM...
SHOOOM...
AAAHH!!
K... KLEO!!
OH NO...! THIS IS BAD!!
HWOOOOOSH!
BWOHHH
NOT GOOD!
NOT GOOD!
HWOOOOSH!!
A MERE HUMAN IS NO MATCH FOR A MONSTER!
GRAB
A MONSTER FOR A MONSTER...
THAT IS THE RULE THIS WORLD IS BASED ON!!
Roaaaar!!

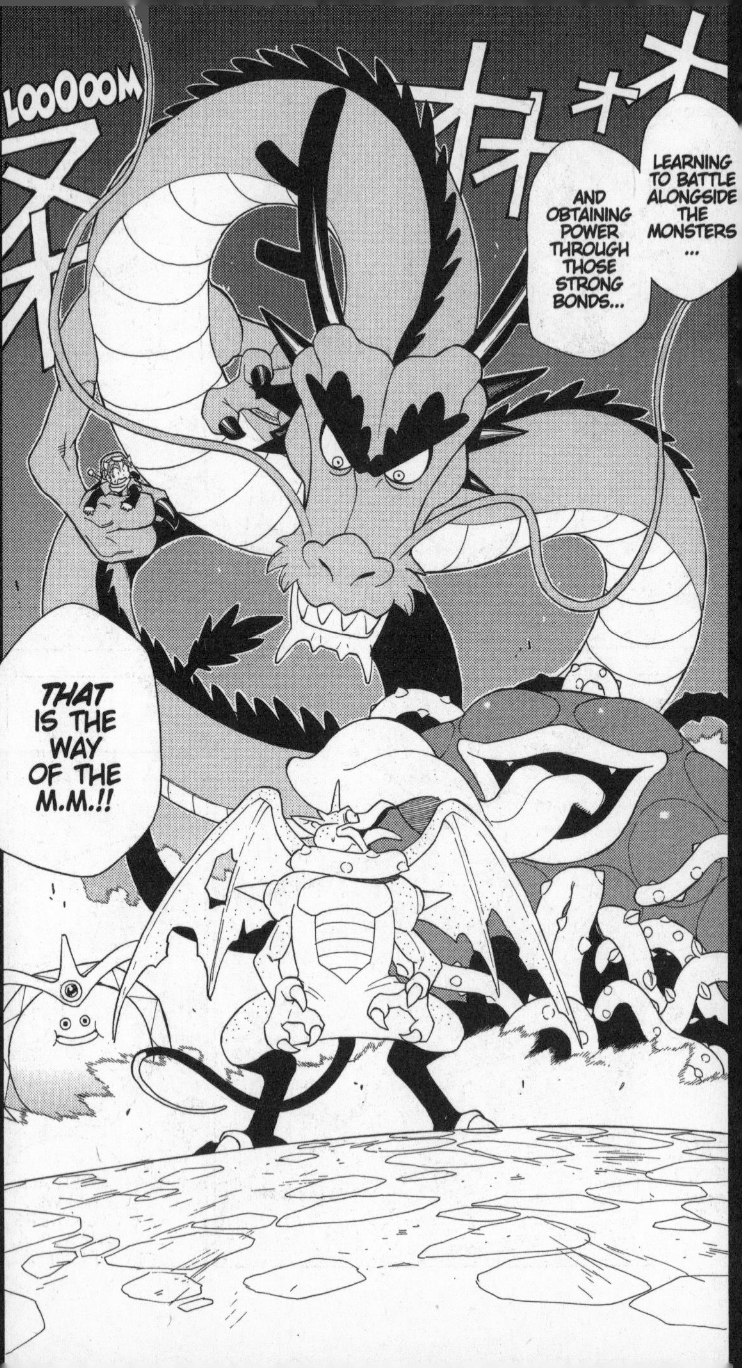
LOOOOOM
LEARNING TO BATTLE ALONGSIDE THE MONSTERS ...
AND OBTAINING POWER THROUGH THOSE STRONG BONDS...
THAT IS THE WAY OF THE M.M.!!

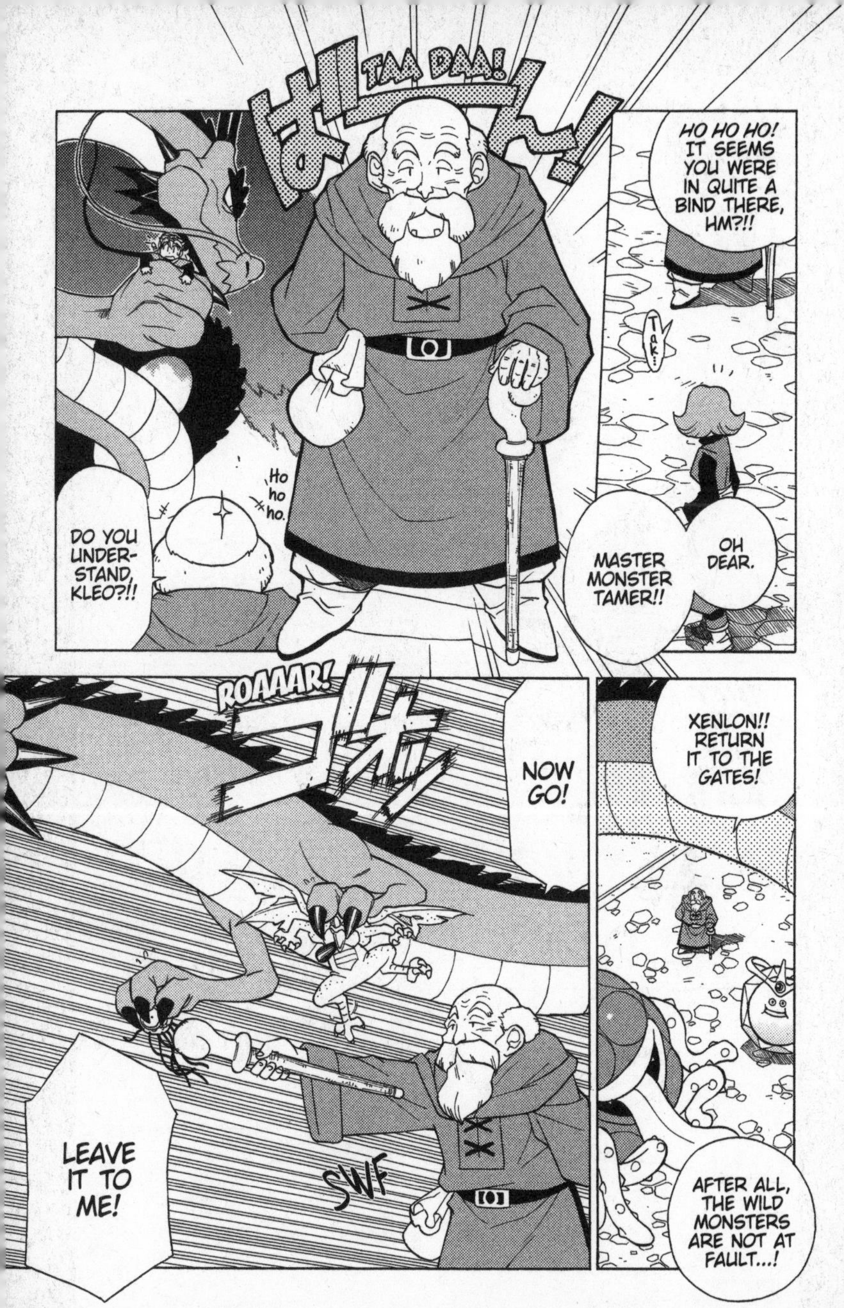
HO HO HO! IT SEEMS YOU WERE IN QUITE A BIND THERE, HM?!!
Tak..
OH DEAR.
MASTER MONSTER TAMER!!
TAA DAA!
Ho ho ho.
DO YOU UNDER-STAND, KLEO?!!
XENLON!! RETURN IT TO THE GATES!
AFTER ALL, THE WILD MONSTERS ARE NOT AT FAULT...!
ROAAAR!
NOW GO!
SWF
LEAVE IT TO ME!

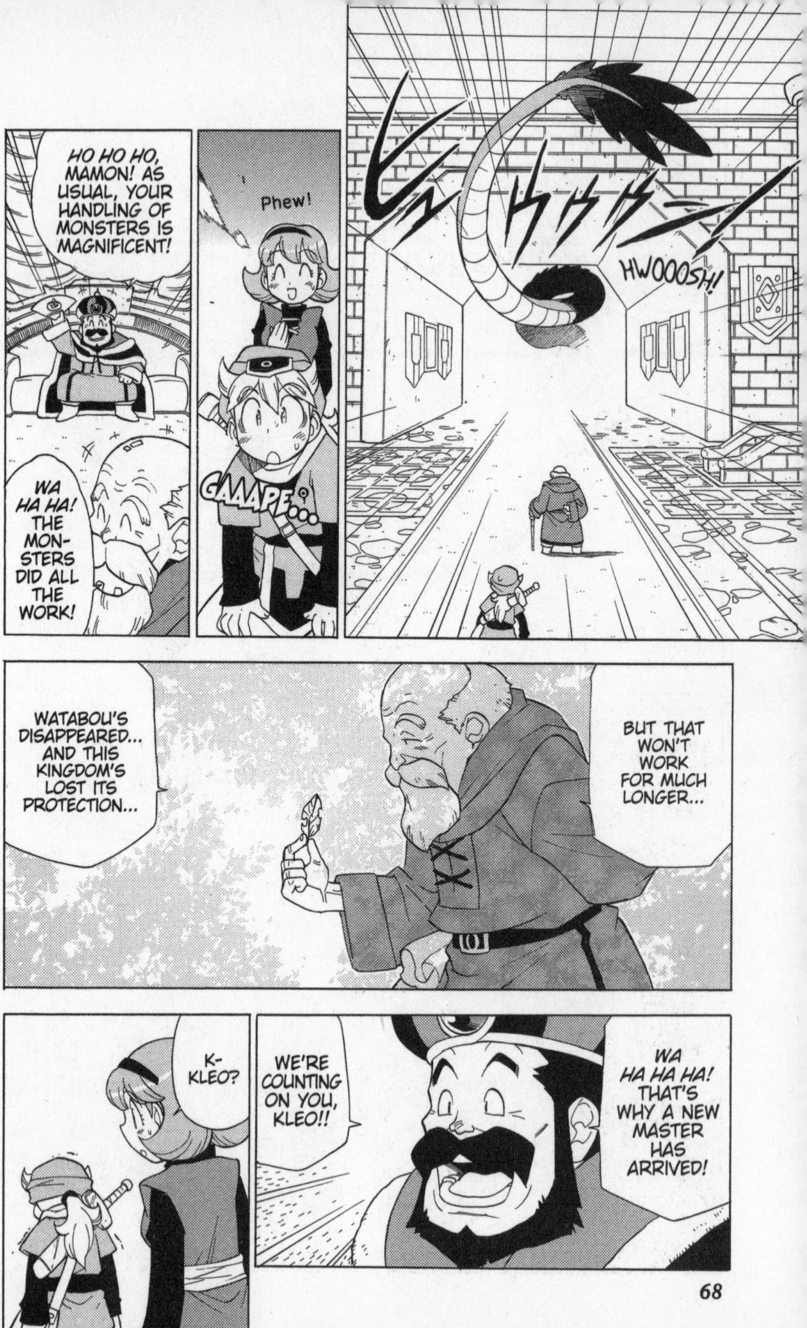
HWOOOSH!
Phew!
GAAAPE...
HO HO HO, MAMON! AS USUAL, YOUR HANDLING OF MONSTERS IS MAGNIFICENT!
WA HA HA! THE MON-STERS DID ALL THE WORK!
WATABOU'S DISAPPEARED... AND THIS KINGDOM'S LOST ITS PROTECTION...
BUT THAT WON'T WORK FOR MUCH LONGER...
WA HA HA HA! THAT'S WHY A NEW MASTER HAS ARRIVED!
WE'RE COUNTING ON YOU, KLEO!!
K-KLEO?

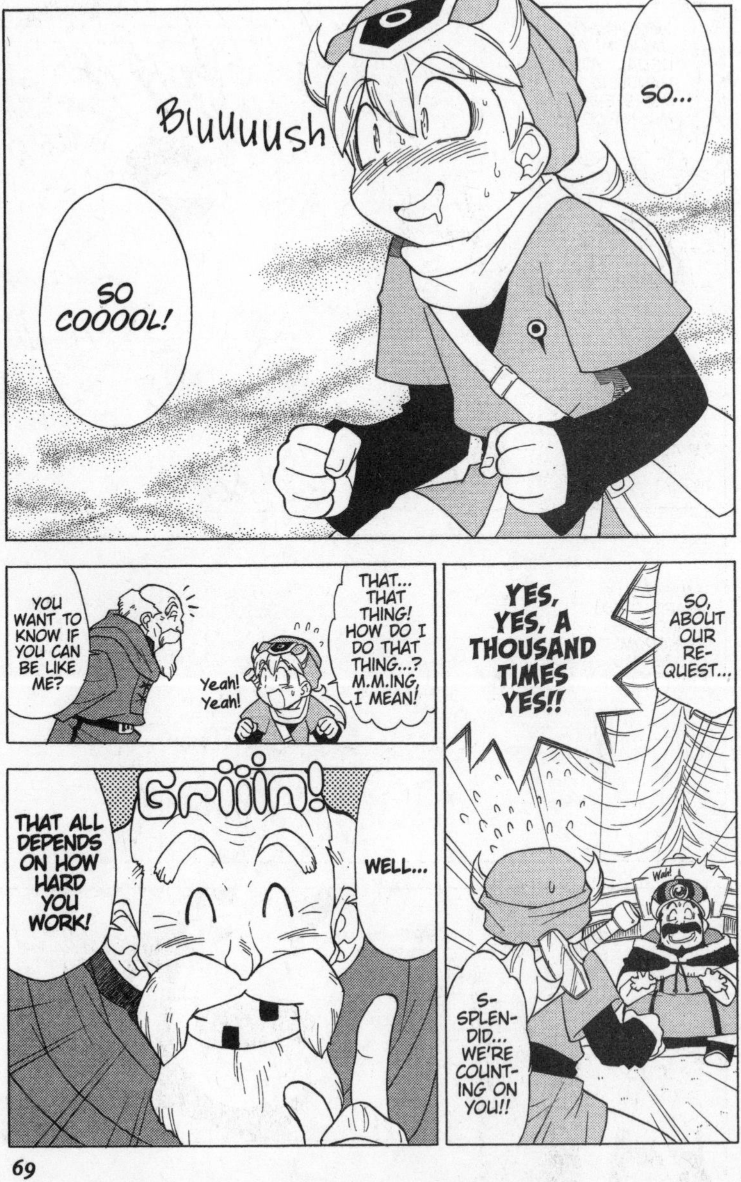
SO...
Bluuuush
SO COOOOL!
SO, ABOUT OUR REQUEST...
YES, YES, A THOUSAND TIMES YES!!
Wah!
S-SPLENDID... WE'RE COUNTING ON YOU!!
THAT... THAT THING! HOW DO I DO THAT THING...? M.M.ING, I MEAN!
Yeah! Yeah!
YOU WANT TO KNOW IF YOU CAN BE LIKE ME?
Griiin!
WELL...
THAT ALL DEPENDS ON HOW HARD YOU WORK!

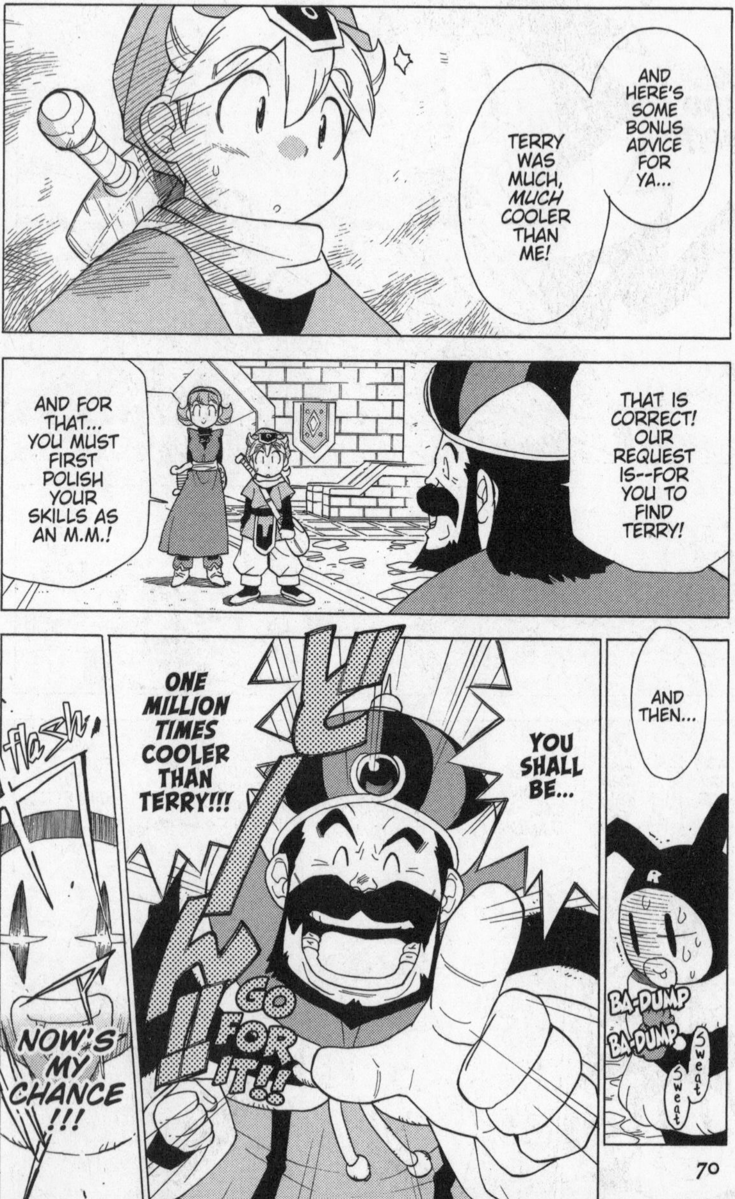
AND HERE'S SOME BONUS ADVICE FOR YA...
TERRY WAS MUCH, *MUCH* COOLER THAN ME!
THAT IS CORRECT! OUR REQUEST IS--FOR YOU TO FIND TERRY!
AND FOR THAT... YOU MUST FIRST POLISH YOUR SKILLS AS AN M.M.!
AND THEN...
BA-DUMP
BA-DUMP
Sweat
Sweat
YOU SHALL BE...
ONE MILLION TIMES COOLER THAN TERRY!!!
GO FOR IT!!
flash
NOW'S MY CHANCE!!!

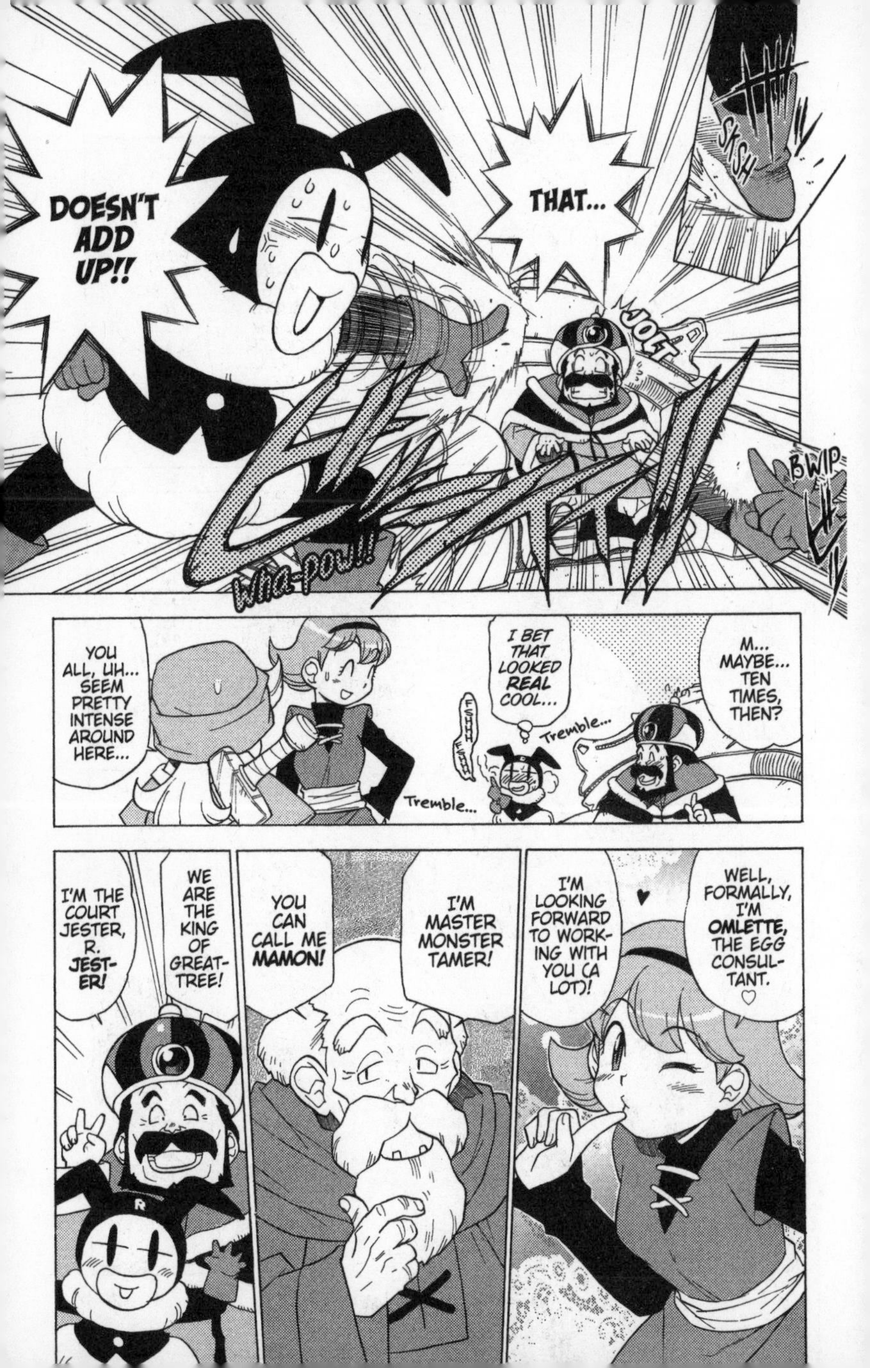
SKSH
THAT...
DOESN'T ADD UP!!
JOLT
BWIP
Wha-pow!!
M... MAYBE... TEN TIMES, THEN?
I BET THAT LOOKED REAL COOL...
FSHHH FSHHH
Tremble...
YOU ALL, UH... SEEM PRETTY INTENSE AROUND HERE...
Tremble...
WELL, FORMALLY, I'M OMLETTE, THE EGG CONSULTANT. ♡
I'M LOOKING FORWARD TO WORKING WITH YOU (A LOT)!
I'M MASTER MONSTER TAMER!
YOU CAN CALL ME MAMON!
WE ARE THE KING OF GREAT-TREE!
I'M THE COURT JESTER, R. JESTER!

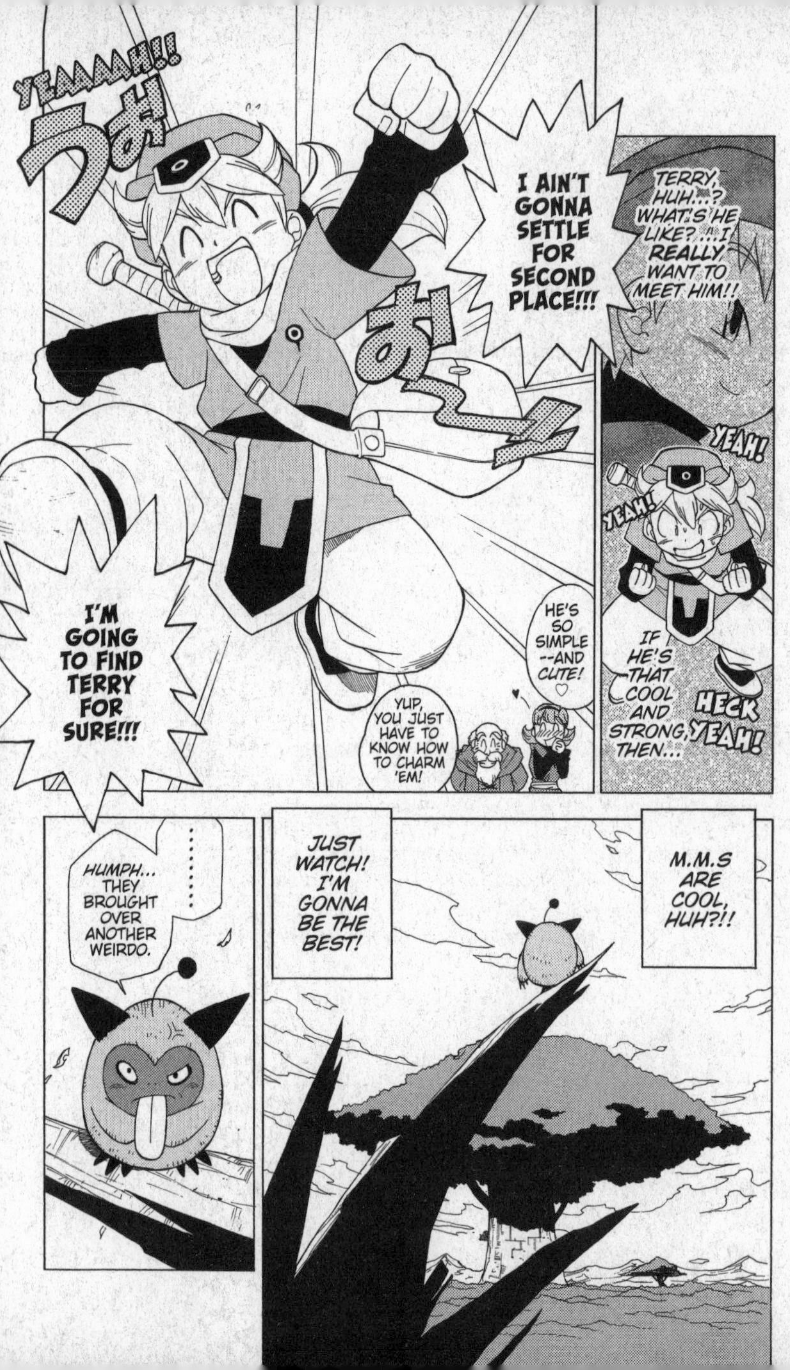

TERRY, HUH...? WHAT'S HE LIKE? ...I REALLY WANT TO MEET HIM!!
YEAH!
YEAH!
IF HE'S THAT COOL AND STRONG, THEN...
HECK YEAH!
YEAAAAH!!
うお
I AIN'T GONNA SETTLE FOR SECOND PLACE!!!
お
HE'S SO SIMPLE --AND CUTE! ♡
YUP, YOU JUST HAVE TO KNOW HOW TO CHARM 'EM!
I'M GOING TO FIND TERRY FOR SURE!!!
M.M.S ARE COOL, HUH?!!
JUST WATCH! I'M GONNA BE THE BEST!
......
HUMPH... THEY BROUGHT OVER ANOTHER WEIRDO.

DRAGON
QUEST
MONSTERS +

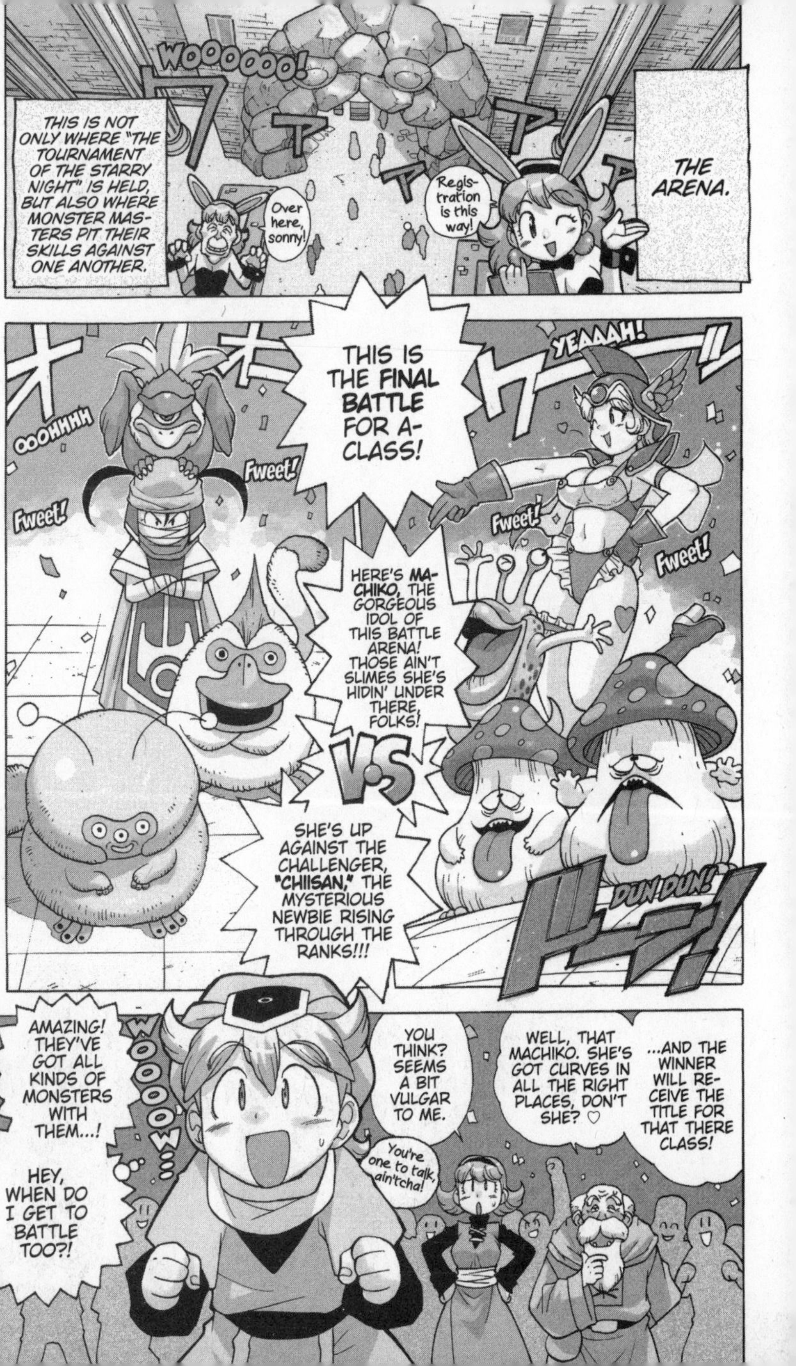
THE ARENA.
WOOOOOO!
Regis-tration is this way!
Over here, sonny!
THIS IS NOT ONLY WHERE "THE TOURNAMENT OF THE STARRY NIGHT" IS HELD, BUT ALSO WHERE MONSTER MASTERS PIT THEIR SKILLS AGAINST ONE ANOTHER.
YEAAAH!
THIS IS THE FINAL BATTLE FOR A-CLASS!
OOOHHHH
Fweet!
Fweet!
Fweet!
Fweet!
HERE'S MACHIKO, THE GORGEOUS IDOL OF THIS BATTLE ARENA! THOSE AIN'T SLIMES SHE'S HIDIN' UNDER THERE, FOLKS!
VS
SHE'S UP AGAINST THE CHALLENGER, "CHIISAN," THE MYSTERIOUS NEWBIE RISING THROUGH THE RANKS!!!
DUN DUN!
...AND THE WINNER WILL RECEIVE THE TITLE FOR THAT THERE CLASS!
WELL, THAT MACHIKO. SHE'S GOT CURVES IN ALL THE RIGHT PLACES, DON'T SHE? ♡
YOU THINK? SEEMS A BIT VULGAR TO ME.
You're one to talk, ain'tcha!
WOOOOOW...
AMAZING! THEY'VE GOT ALL KINDS OF MONSTERS WITH THEM...!
HEY, WHEN DO I GET TO BATTLE TOO?!

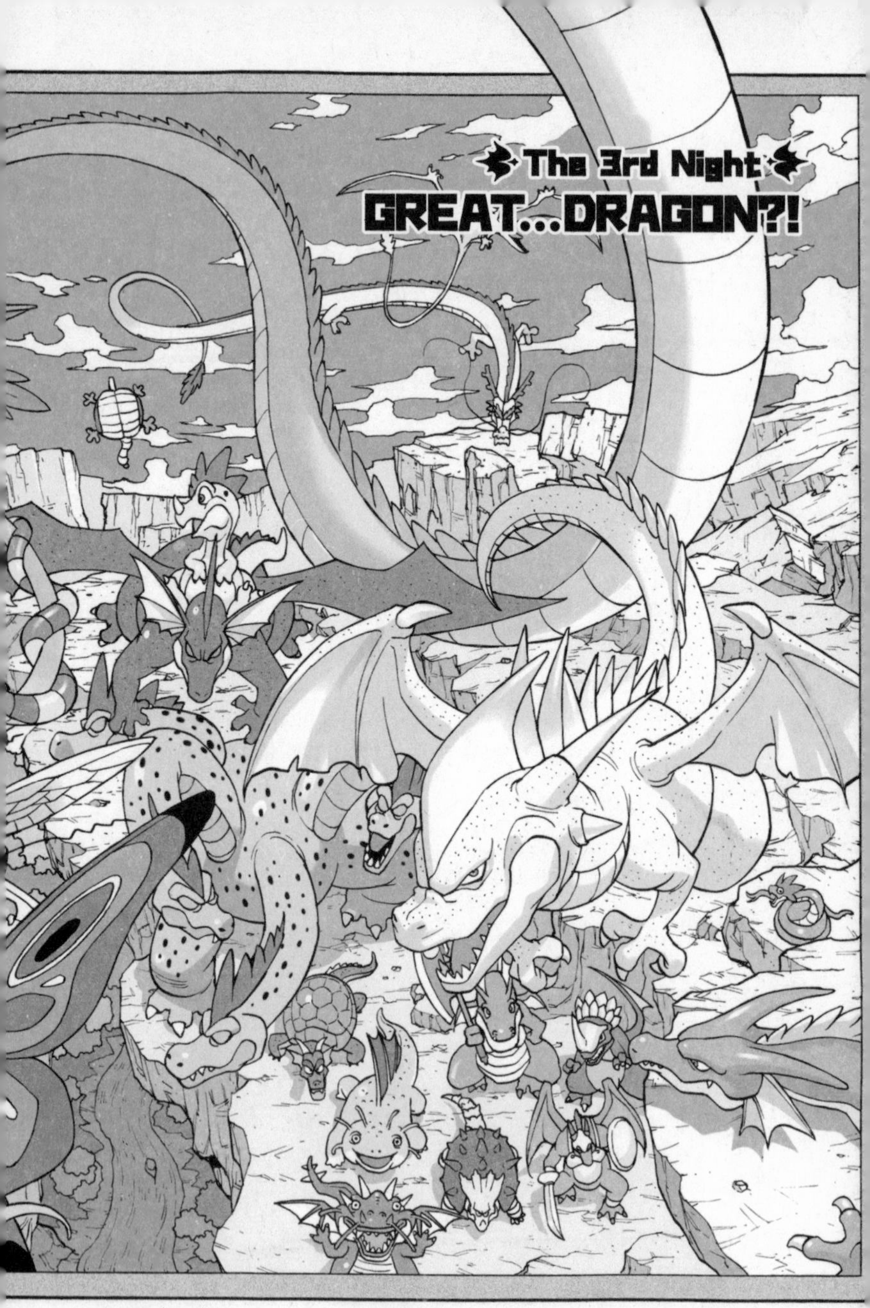
The 3rd Night
GREAT...DRAGON?!

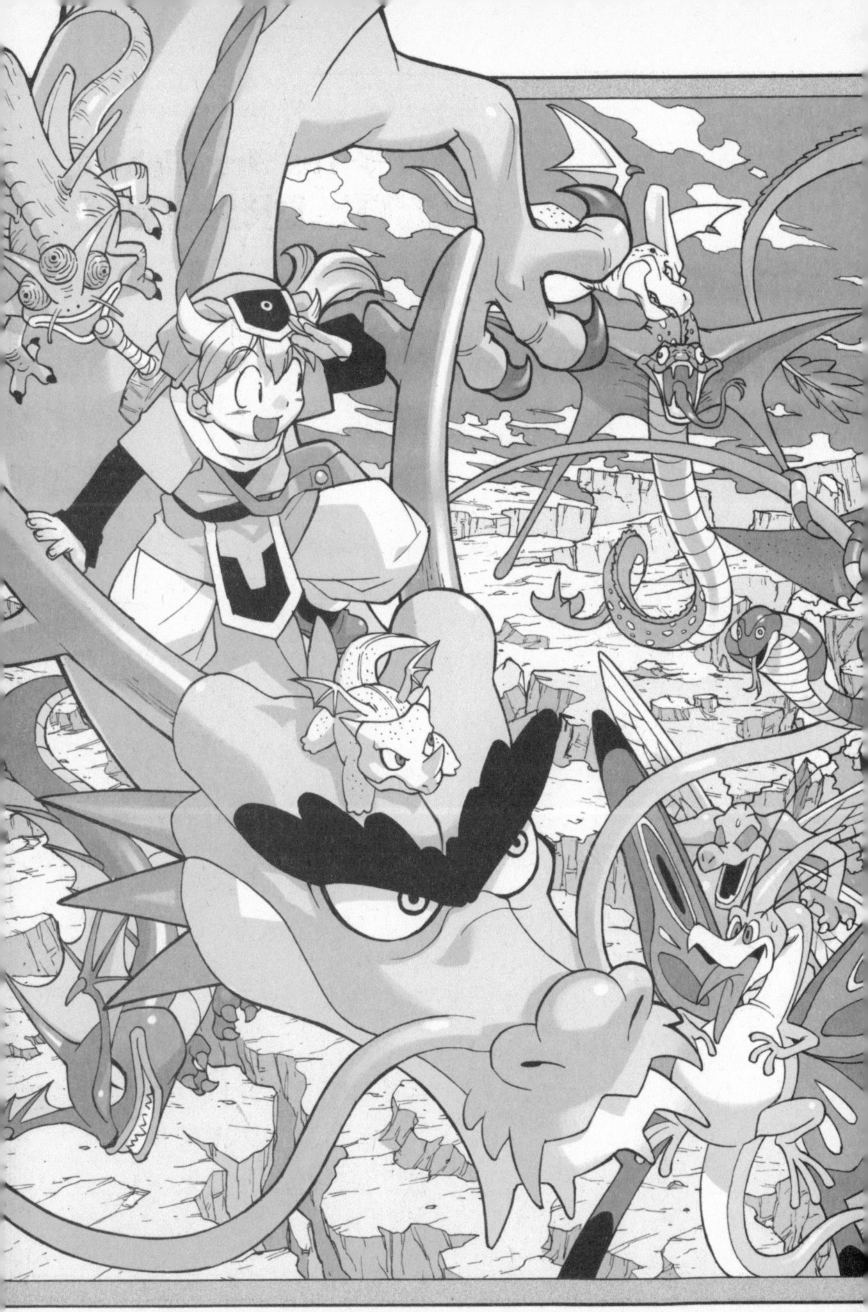

DRAGON
QUEST
MONSTERS

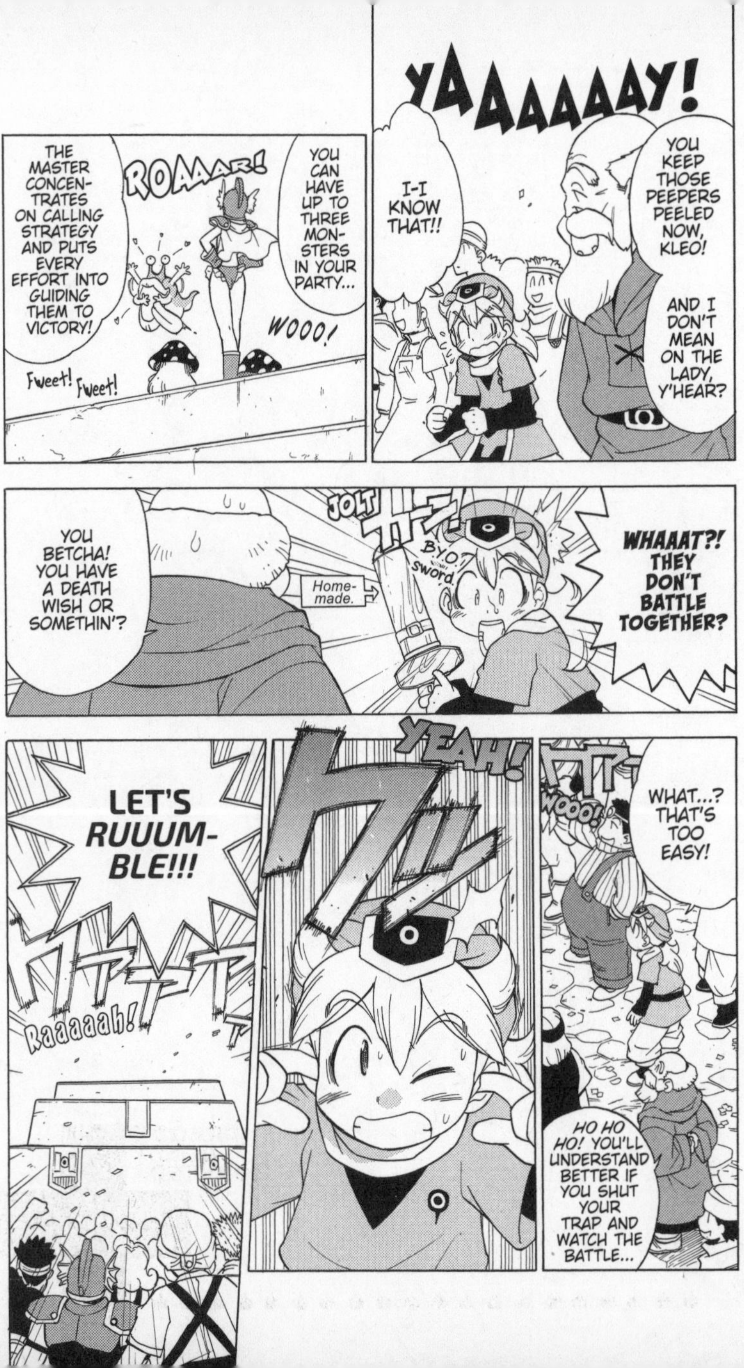
YAAAAAAY!
YOU KEEP THOSE PEEPERS PEELED NOW, KLEO!
AND I DON'T MEAN ON THE LADY, Y'HEAR?
I-I KNOW THAT!!
YOU CAN HAVE UP TO THREE MON-STERS IN YOUR PARTY...
ROAAAR!
THE MASTER CONCEN-TRATES ON CALLING STRATEGY AND PUTS EVERY EFFORT INTO GUIDING THEM TO VICTORY!
WOOO!
Fweet! Fweet!
JOLT
WHAAAT?! THEY DON'T BATTLE TOGETHER?
B.Y.O. sword.
Home-made.
YOU BETCHA! YOU HAVE A DEATH WISH OR SOMETHIN'?
WOOO!
WHAT...? THAT'S TOO EASY!
HO HO HO! YOU'LL UNDERSTAND BETTER IF YOU SHUT YOUR TRAP AND WATCH THE BATTLE...
YEAH!
LET'S RUUUM-BLE!!!
Raaaaah!

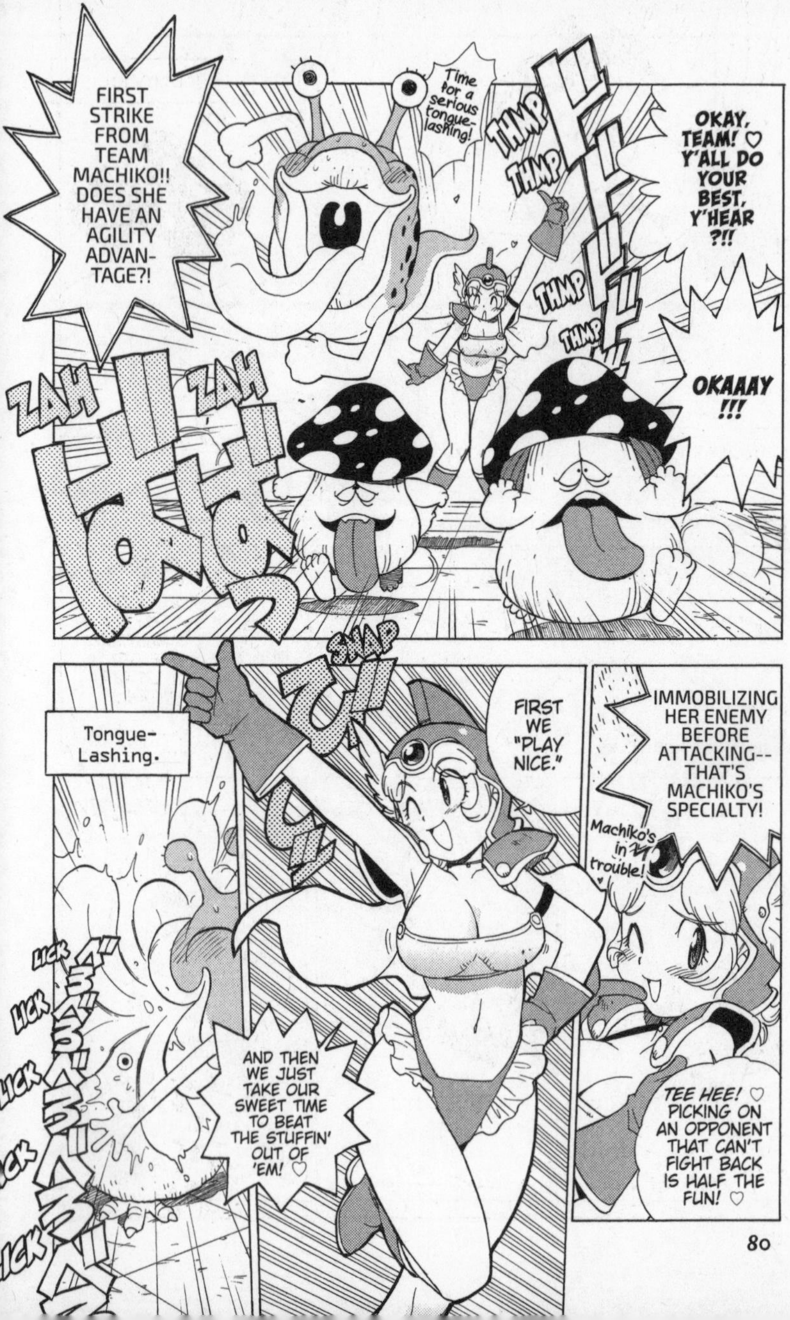
OKAY, TEAM! ♡ Y'ALL DO YOUR BEST, Y'HEAR?!!
THMP
THMP
THMP
THMP
Time for a serious tongue-lashing!
FIRST STRIKE FROM TEAM MACHIKO!! DOES SHE HAVE AN AGILITY ADVANTAGE?!
OKAAAY!!!
ZAH
ZAH
IMMOBILIZING HER ENEMY BEFORE ATTACKING-- THAT'S MACHIKO'S SPECIALTY!
Machiko's in trouble!
TEE HEE! ♡ PICKING ON AN OPPONENT THAT CAN'T FIGHT BACK IS HALF THE FUN! ♡
FIRST WE "PLAY NICE."
SNAP
Tongue-Lashing.
AND THEN WE JUST TAKE OUR SWEET TIME TO BEAT THE STUFFIN' OUT OF 'EM! ♡
LICK
LICK
LICK

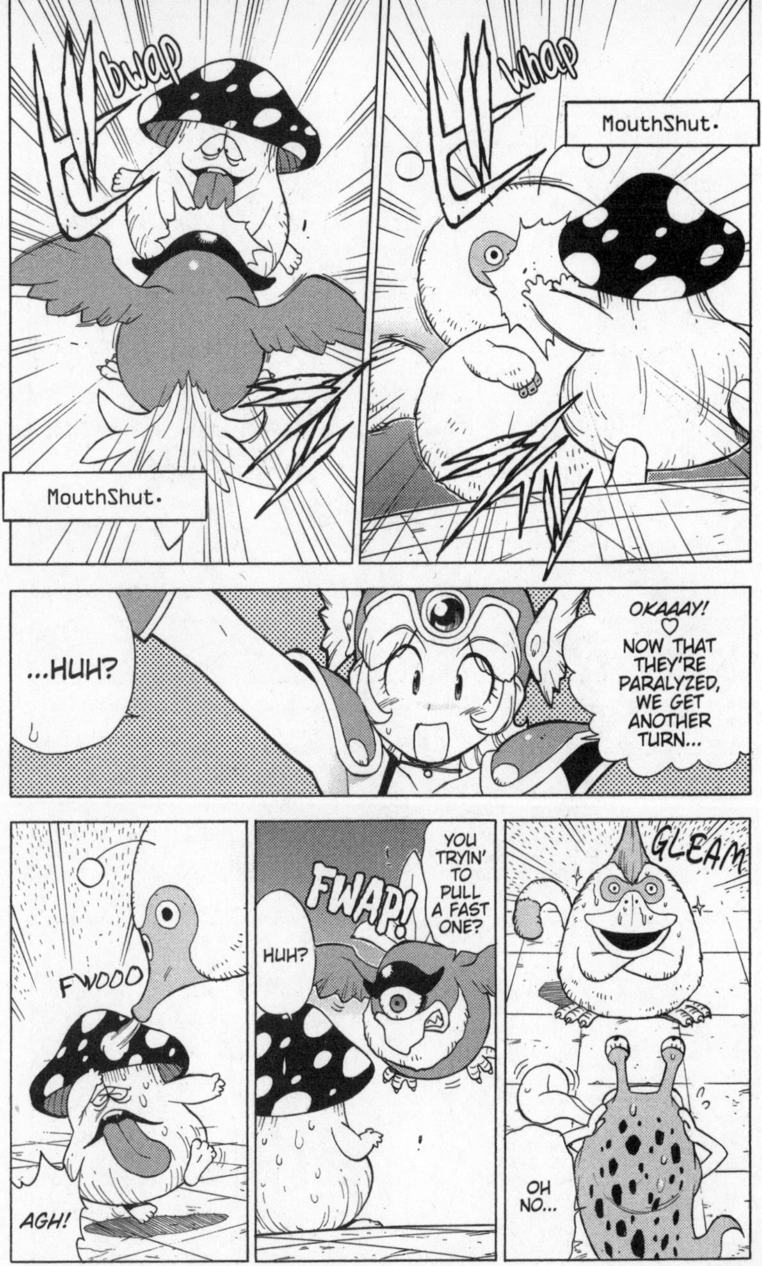
whap
MouthShut.
bwap
MouthShut.
OKAAAY! ♡ NOW THAT THEY'RE PARALYZED, WE GET ANOTHER TURN...
...HUH?
GLEAM
OH NO...
YOU TRYIN' TO PULL A FAST ONE?
FWAP!
HUH?
FWOOO
AGH!

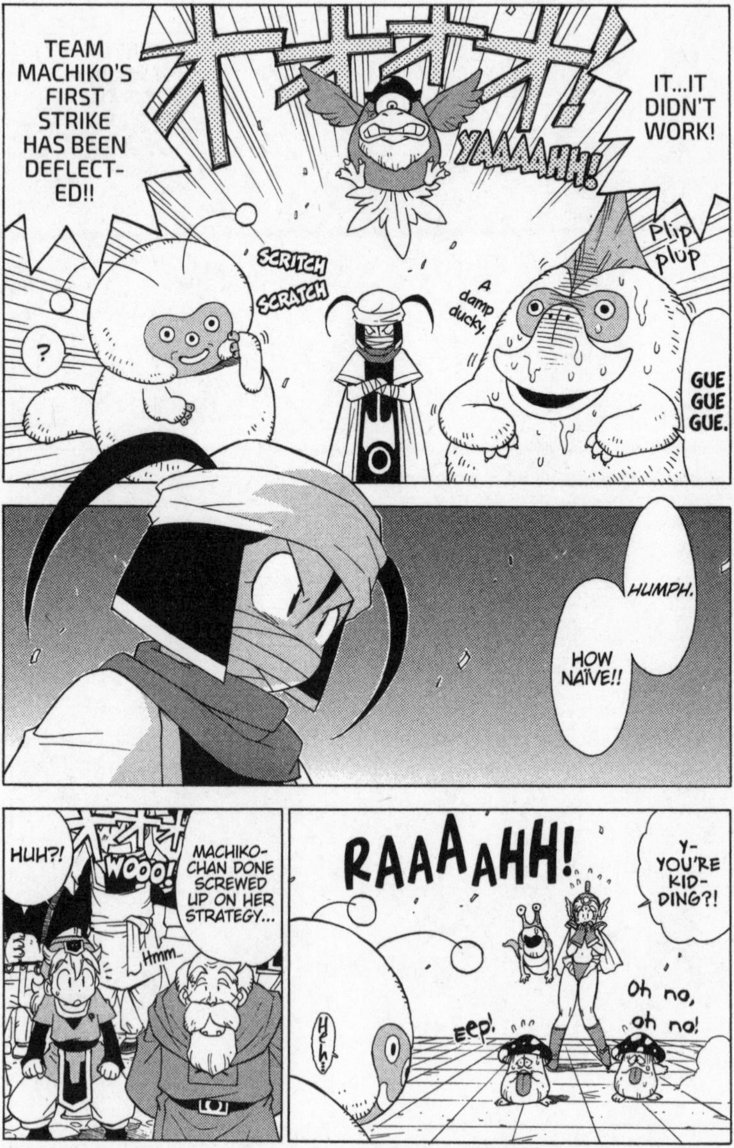
IT...IT DIDN'T WORK!
オオオオ!
YAAAAHH!
TEAM MACHIKO'S FIRST STRIKE HAS BEEN DEFLECTED!!
Plip plup
A damp ducky.
SCRITCH
SCRATCH
GUE GUE GUE.
?
HUMPH.
HOW NAÏVE!!
Y-YOU'RE KIDDING?!
RAAAAHH!
Oh no, oh no!
Eep!
Heh...
MACHIKO-CHAN DONE SCREWED UP ON HER STRATEGY...
オオオ
WOOO!
HUH?!
Hmm..

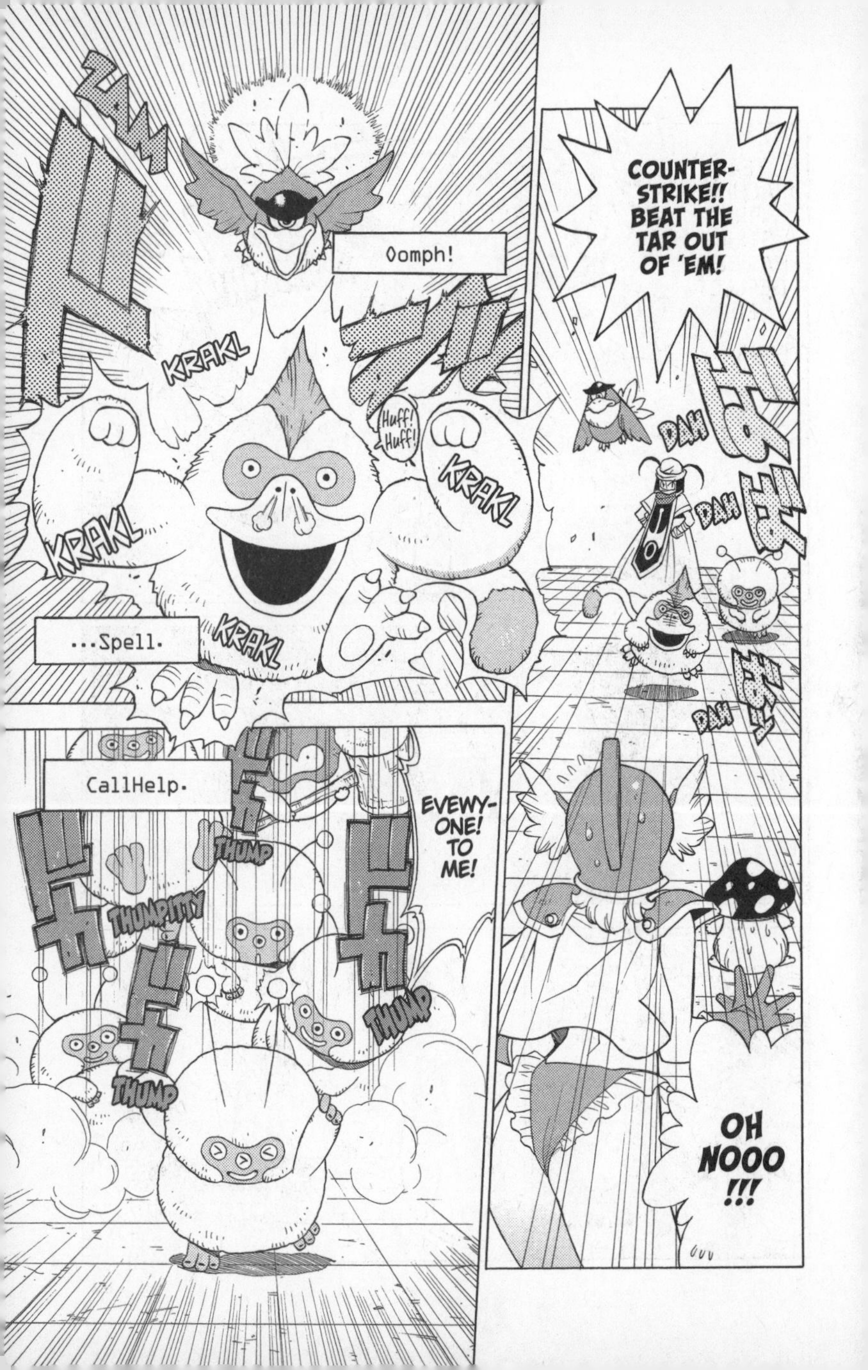
COUNTER-STRIKE!! BEAT THE TAR OUT OF 'EM!
DAH
DAH
DAH
OH NOOO !!!
ZAAM
Oomph!
KRAKL
Huff! Huff!
KRAKL
KRAKL
KRAKL
...Spell.
CallHelp.
EVEWY-ONE! TO ME!
THUMP
THUMPITTY
THUMP
THUMP

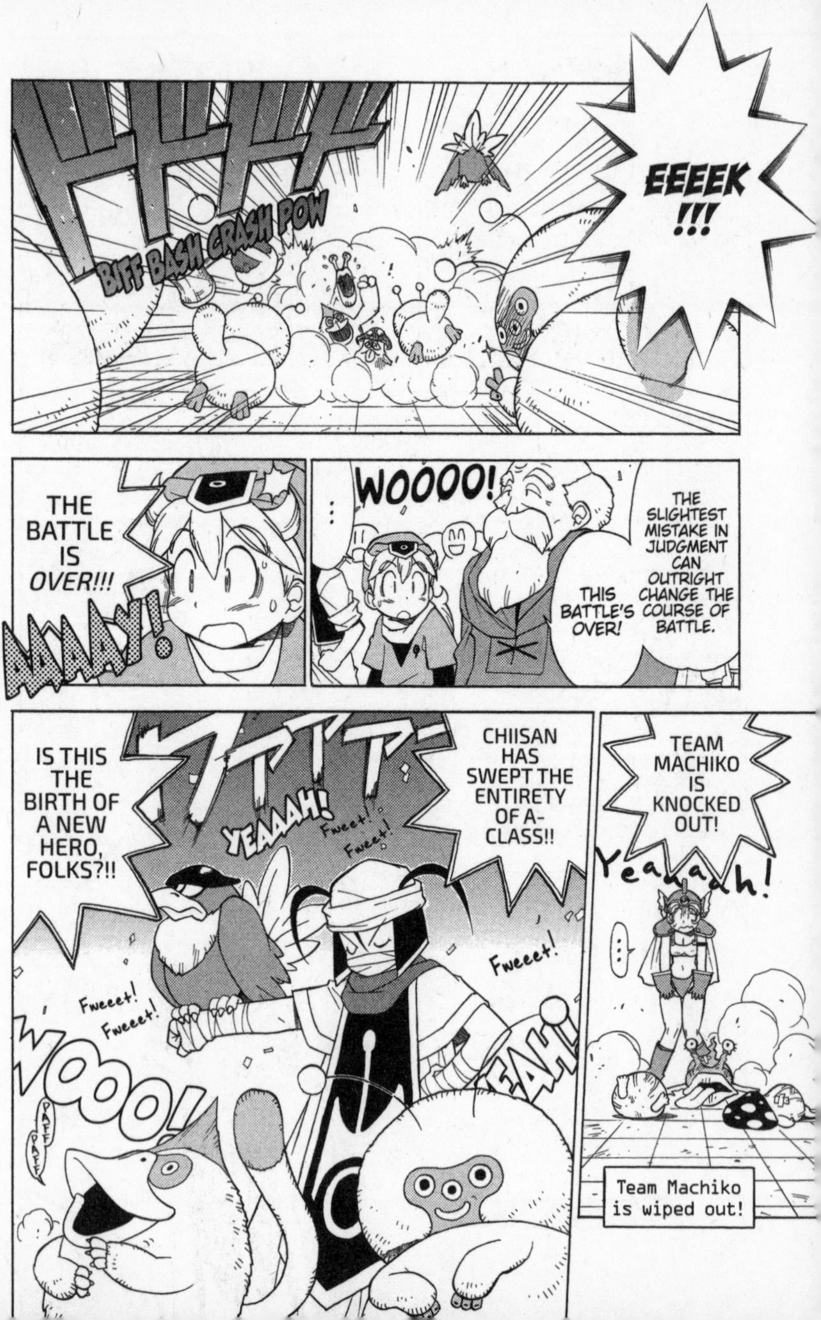
EEEEK!!!
BIFF BASH CRASH POW
THE SLIGHTEST MISTAKE IN JUDGMENT CAN OUTRIGHT CHANGE THE COURSE OF BATTLE.
WOOOO!
...
THIS BATTLE'S OVER!
THE BATTLE IS *OVER!!!*
YAAAAY!
TEAM MACHIKO IS KNOCKED OUT!
Yeaaaah!
...
Team Machiko is wiped out!
CHIISAN HAS SWEPT THE ENTIRETY OF A-CLASS!!
YEAAAH!
Fweet! Fweet!
IS THIS THE BIRTH OF A NEW HERO, FOLKS?!!
Fweeet!
EAH!
Fweeet! Fweeet!
WOOOO!
PAFF PAFF

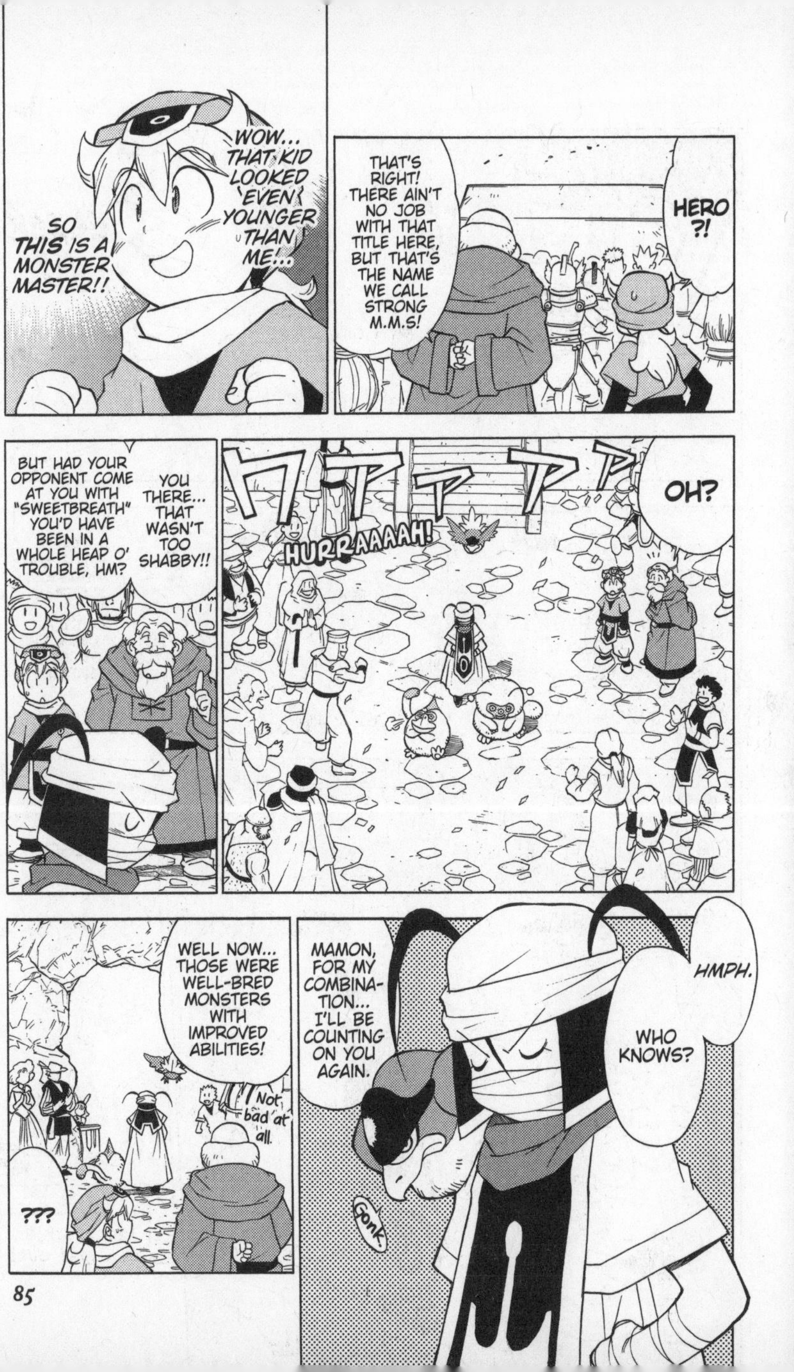
HERO ?!
THAT'S RIGHT! THERE AIN'T NO JOB WITH THAT TITLE HERE, BUT THAT'S THE NAME WE CALL STRONG M.M.S!
WOW... THAT KID LOOKED EVEN YOUNGER THAN ME...
SO THIS IS A MONSTER MASTER!!
OH?
ワァァァァ
HURRAAAAH!
YOU THERE... THAT WASN'T TOO SHABBY!!
BUT HAD YOUR OPPONENT COME AT YOU WITH "SWEETBREATH" YOU'D HAVE BEEN IN A WHOLE HEAP O' TROUBLE, HM?
HMPH.
WHO KNOWS?
MAMON, FOR MY COMBINA-TION... I'LL BE COUNTING ON YOU AGAIN.
Gonk
WELL NOW... THOSE WERE WELL-BRED MONSTERS WITH IMPROVED ABILITIES!
Not bad at all.
???

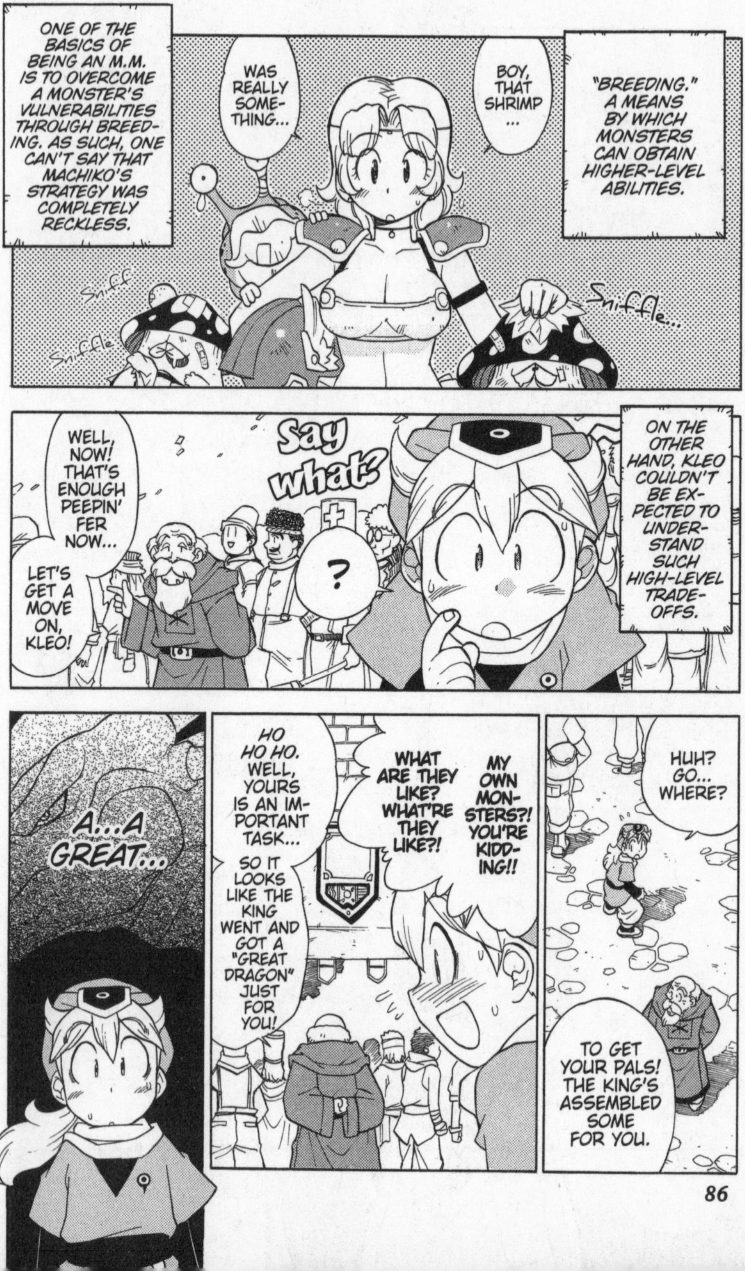
"BREEDING." A MEANS BY WHICH MONSTERS CAN OBTAIN HIGHER-LEVEL ABILITIES.
BOY, THAT SHRIMP...
WAS REALLY SOME-THING...
ONE OF THE BASICS OF BEING AN M.M. IS TO OVERCOME A MONSTER'S VULNERABILITIES THROUGH BREED-ING. AS SUCH, ONE CAN'T SAY THAT MACHIKO'S STRATEGY WAS COMPLETELY RECKLESS.
Sniffle...
Sniff
Sniffle
ON THE OTHER HAND, KLEO COULDN'T BE EX-PECTED TO UNDER-STAND SUCH HIGH-LEVEL TRADE-OFFS.
Say what?
?
WELL, NOW! THAT'S ENOUGH PEEPIN' FER NOW...
LET'S GET A MOVE ON, KLEO!
HUH? GO... WHERE?
TO GET YOUR PALS! THE KING'S ASSEMBLED SOME FOR YOU.
MY OWN MON-STERS?! YOU'RE KIDD-ING!!
WHAT ARE THEY LIKE? WHAT'RE THEY LIKE?!
HO HO HO. WELL, YOURS IS AN IM-PORTANT TASK...
SO IT LOOKS LIKE THE KING WENT AND GOT A "GREAT DRAGON" JUST FOR YOU!
A...A GREAT...

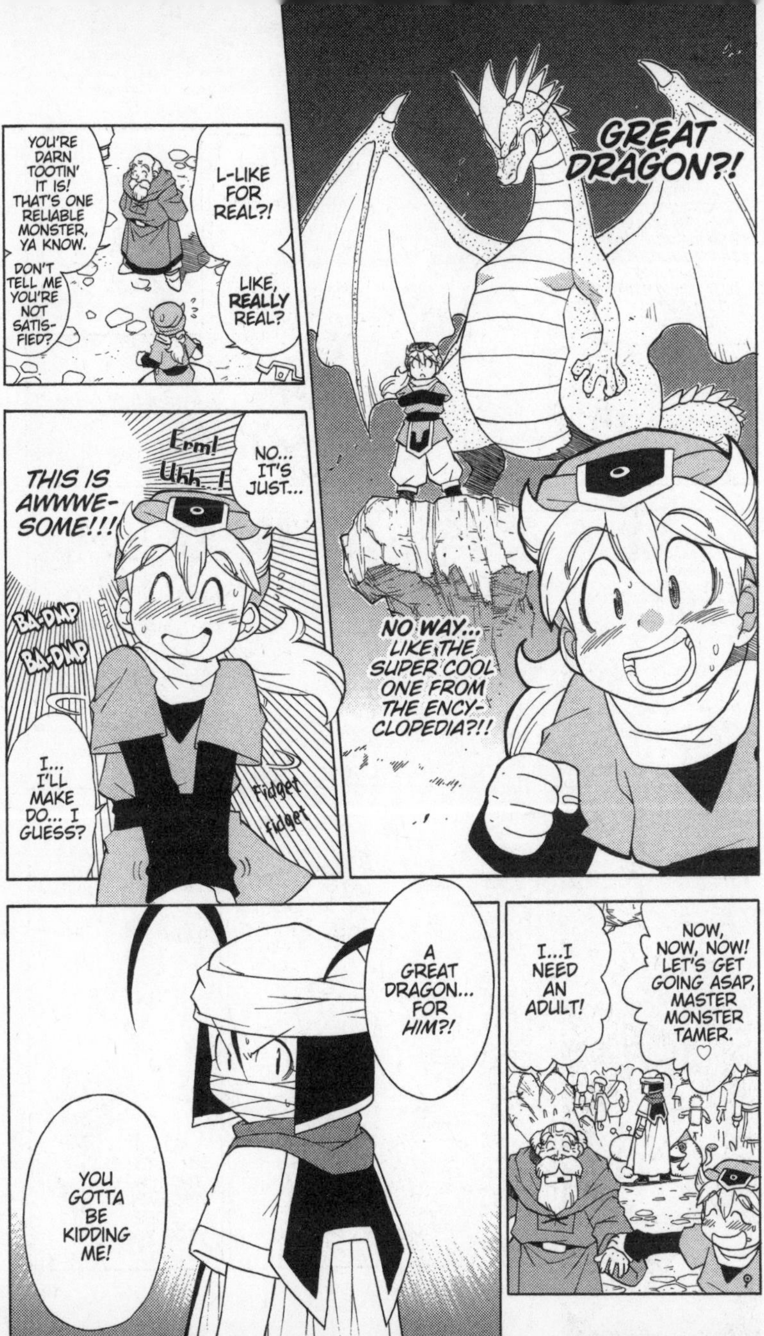
GREAT DRAGON?!
NO WAY... LIKE THE SUPER COOL ONE FROM THE ENCY-CLOPEDIA?!!
L-LIKE FOR REAL?!
LIKE, REALLY REAL?
YOU'RE DARN TOOTIN' IT IS! THAT'S ONE RELIABLE MONSTER, YA KNOW.
DON'T TELL ME YOU'RE NOT SATIS-FIED?
NO... IT'S JUST...
Erm! Uhh...!
THIS IS AWWWE-SOME!!!
BA-DMP
BA-DMP
Fidget fidget
I... I'LL MAKE DO... I GUESS?
NOW, NOW, NOW! LET'S GET GOING ASAP, MASTER MONSTER TAMER. ♡
I...I NEED AN ADULT!
A GREAT DRAGON... FOR HIM?!
YOU GOTTA BE KIDDING ME!

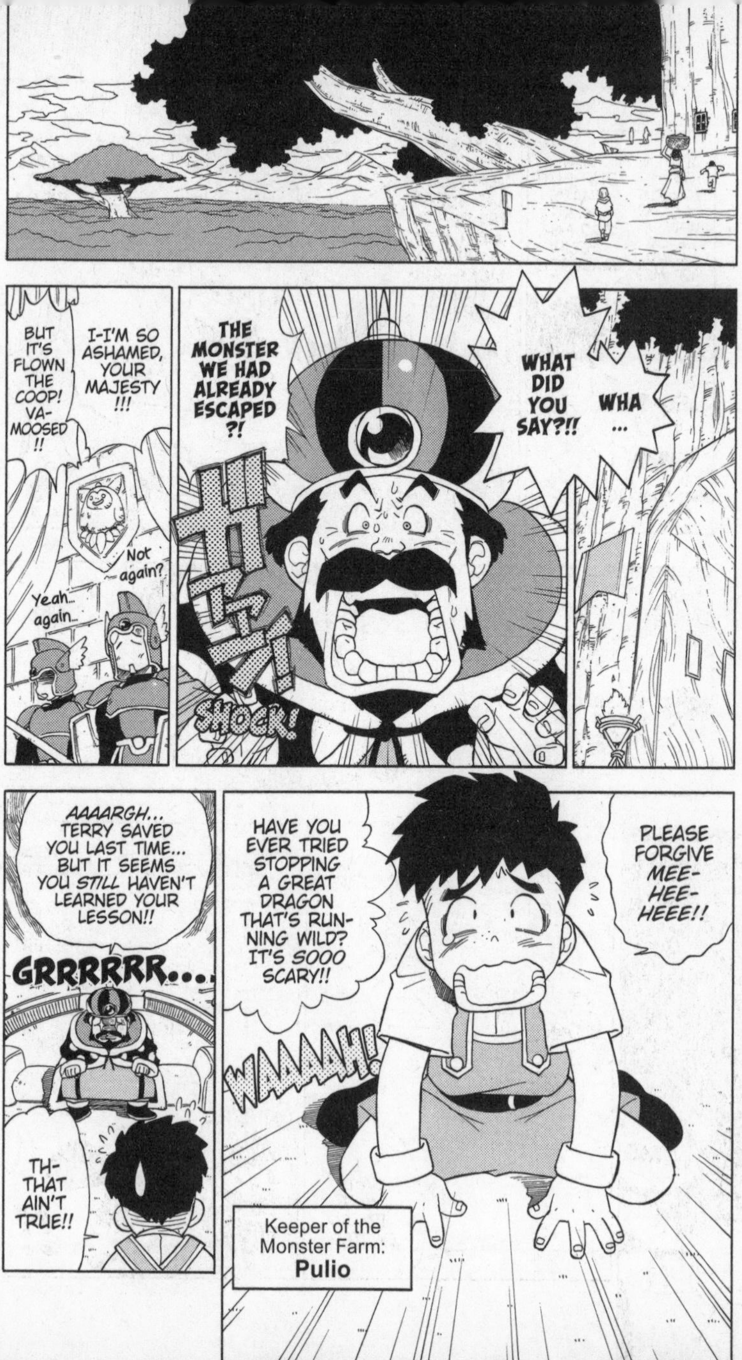
WHA...
WHAT DID YOU SAY?!!
THE MONSTER WE HAD ALREADY ESCAPED?!
SHOCK!
I-I'M SO ASHAMED, YOUR MAJESTY!!!
BUT IT'S FLOWN THE COOP! VA-MOOSED!!
Not again?
Yeah... again...
PLEASE FORGIVE MEE-HEE-HEEE!!
HAVE YOU EVER TRIED STOPPING A GREAT DRAGON THAT'S RUN-NING WILD? IT'S SOOO SCARY!!
WAAAAH!
Keeper of the Monster Farm: Pulio
AAAARGH... TERRY SAVED YOU LAST TIME... BUT IT SEEMS YOU STILL HAVEN'T LEARNED YOUR LESSON!!
GRRRRRR...
TH-THAT AIN'T TRUE!!

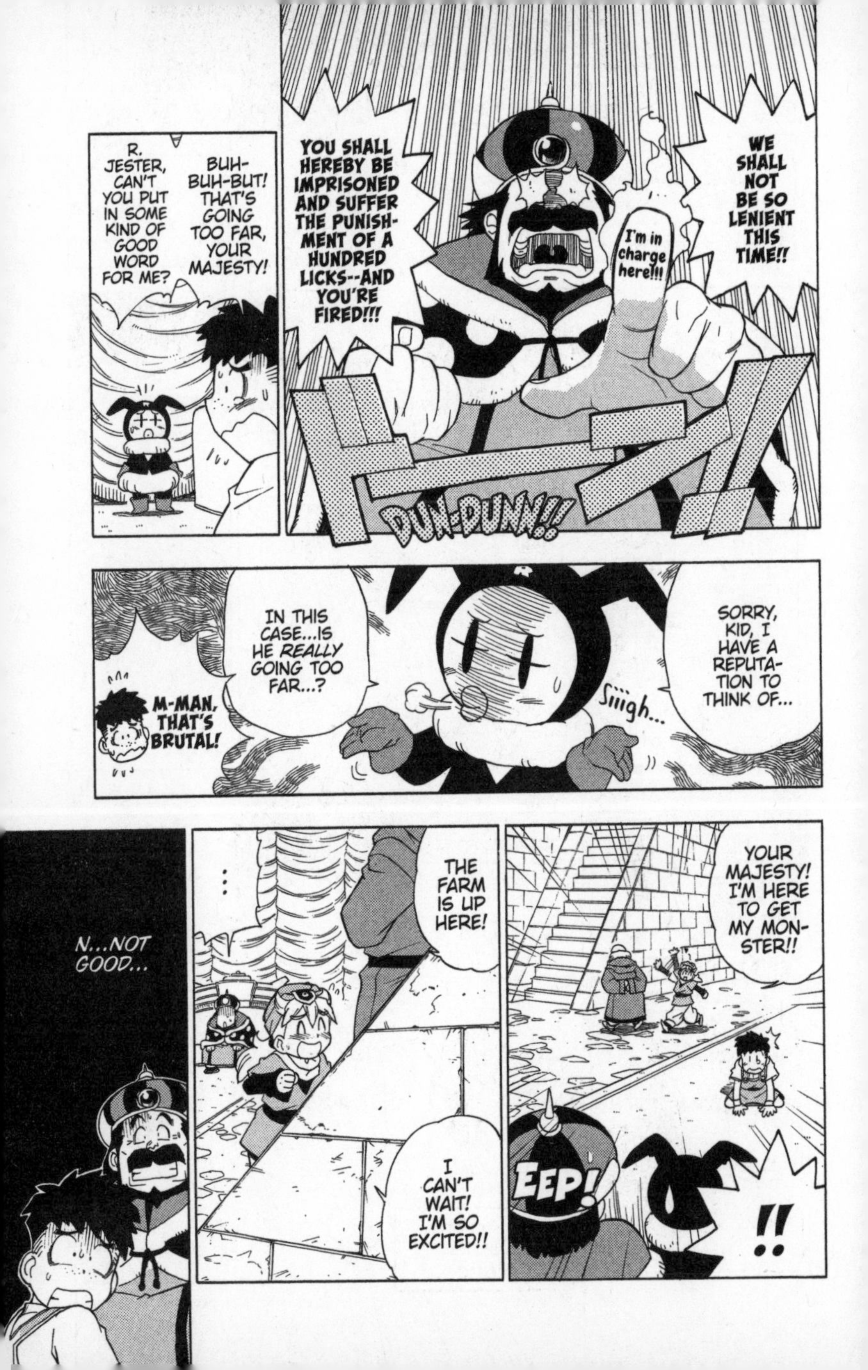
WE SHALL NOT BE SO LENIENT THIS TIME!!
I'm in charge here!!!
YOU SHALL HEREBY BE IMPRISONED AND SUFFER THE PUNISHMENT OF A HUNDRED LICKS--AND YOU'RE FIRED!!!
DUN-DUNN!!
BUH-BUH-BUT! THAT'S GOING TOO FAR, YOUR MAJESTY!
R. JESTER, CAN'T YOU PUT IN SOME KIND OF GOOD WORD FOR ME?
SORRY, KID, I HAVE A REPUTATION TO THINK OF...
Siiigh...
IN THIS CASE...IS HE *REALLY* GOING TOO FAR...?
M-MAN, THAT'S BRUTAL!
YOUR MAJESTY! I'M HERE TO GET MY MONSTER!!
!!
EEP!
THE FARM IS UP HERE!
...
I CAN'T WAIT! I'M SO EXCITED!!
N...NOT GOOD...

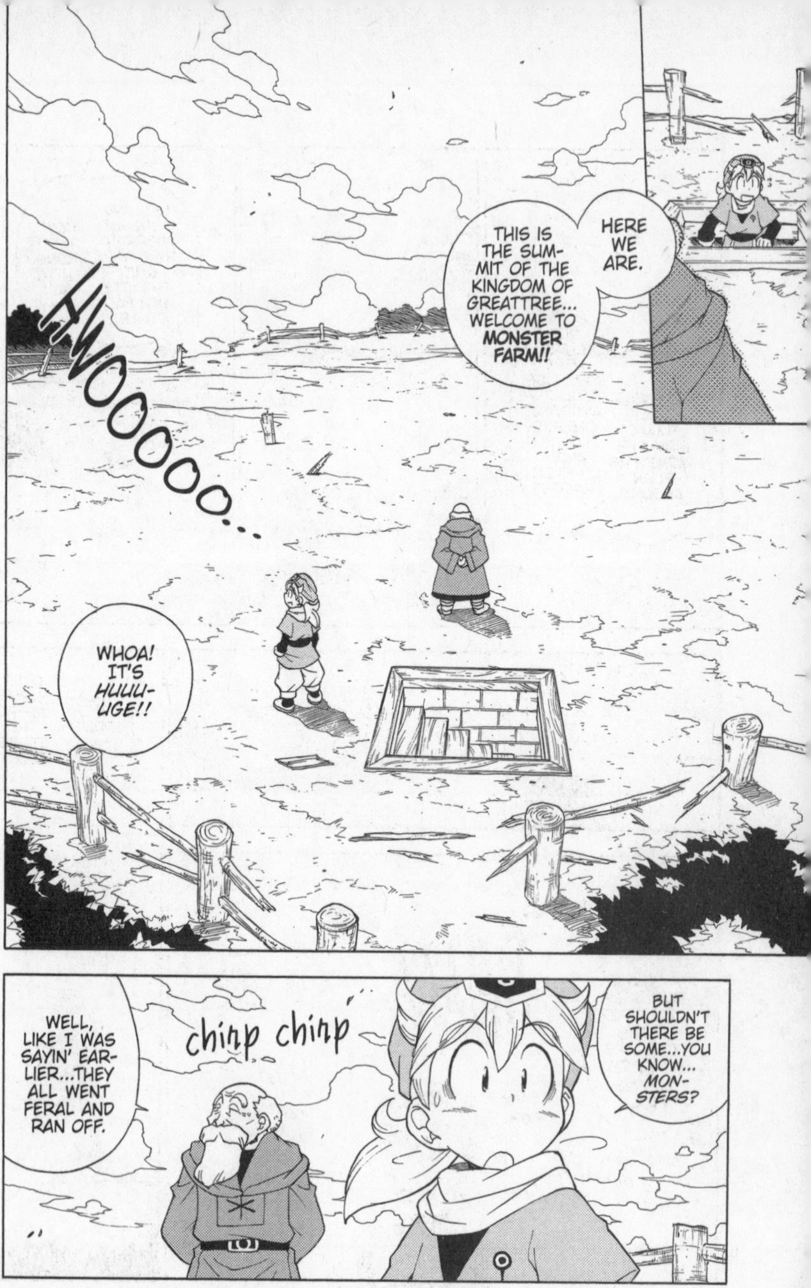
HERE WE ARE.
THIS IS THE SUMMIT OF THE KINGDOM OF GREATTREE... WELCOME TO **MONSTER FARM!!**
HWOOOOO...
WHOA! IT'S *HUUUU-UGE!!*
BUT SHOULDN'T THERE BE SOME...YOU KNOW... *MONSTERS?*
chirp chirp
WELL, LIKE I WAS SAYIN' EARLIER...THEY ALL WENT FERAL AND RAN OFF.

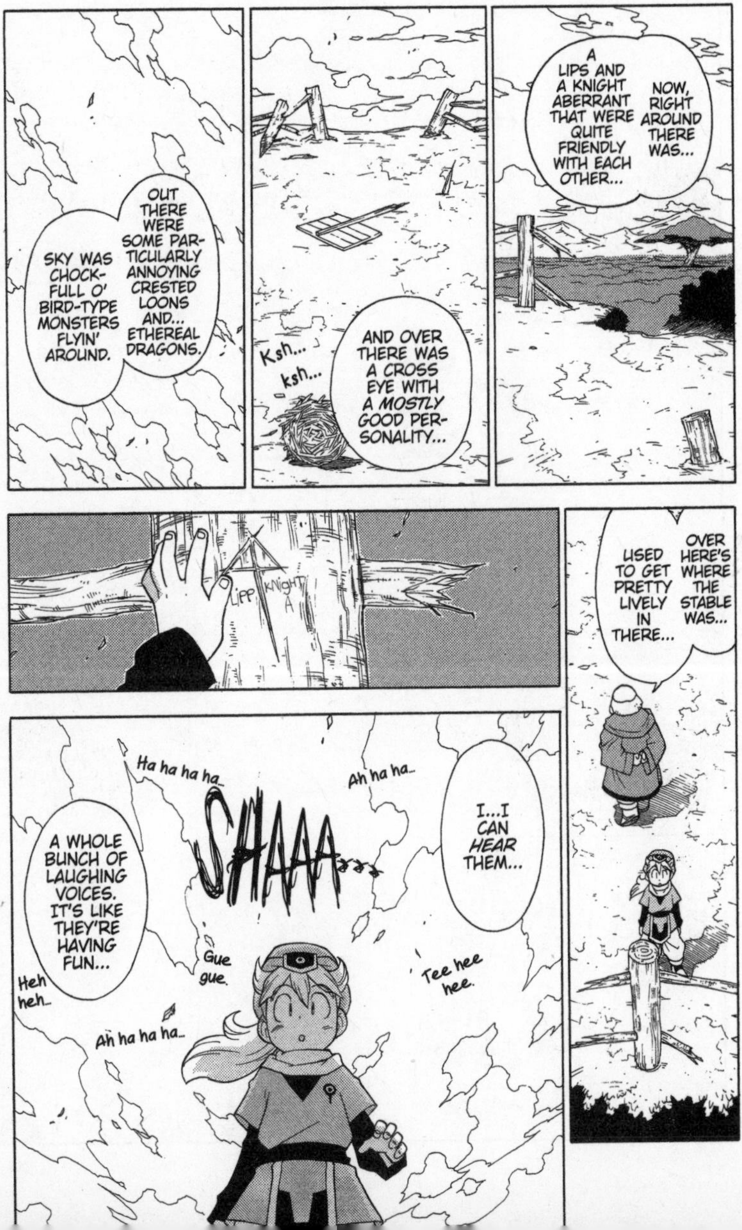
NOW, RIGHT AROUND THERE WAS... A LIPS AND A KNIGHT ABERRANT THAT WERE QUITE FRIENDLY WITH EACH OTHER...
AND OVER THERE WAS A CROSS EYE WITH A *MOSTLY* GOOD PERSONALITY...
Ksh... ksh...
OUT THERE WERE SOME PARTICULARLY ANNOYING CRESTED LOONS AND... ETHEREAL DRAGONS. SKY WAS CHOCK-FULL O' BIRD-TYPE MONSTERS FLYIN' AROUND.
OVER HERE'S WHERE THE STABLE WAS... USED TO GET PRETTY LIVELY IN THERE...
LIPP
KNIGHT A
I...I CAN *HEAR* THEM...
Ah ha ha..
SHAAA...
Ha ha ha ha..
A WHOLE BUNCH OF LAUGHING VOICES. IT'S LIKE THEY'RE HAVING FUN...
Tee hee hee.
Gue gue.
Heh heh..
Ah ha ha ha..

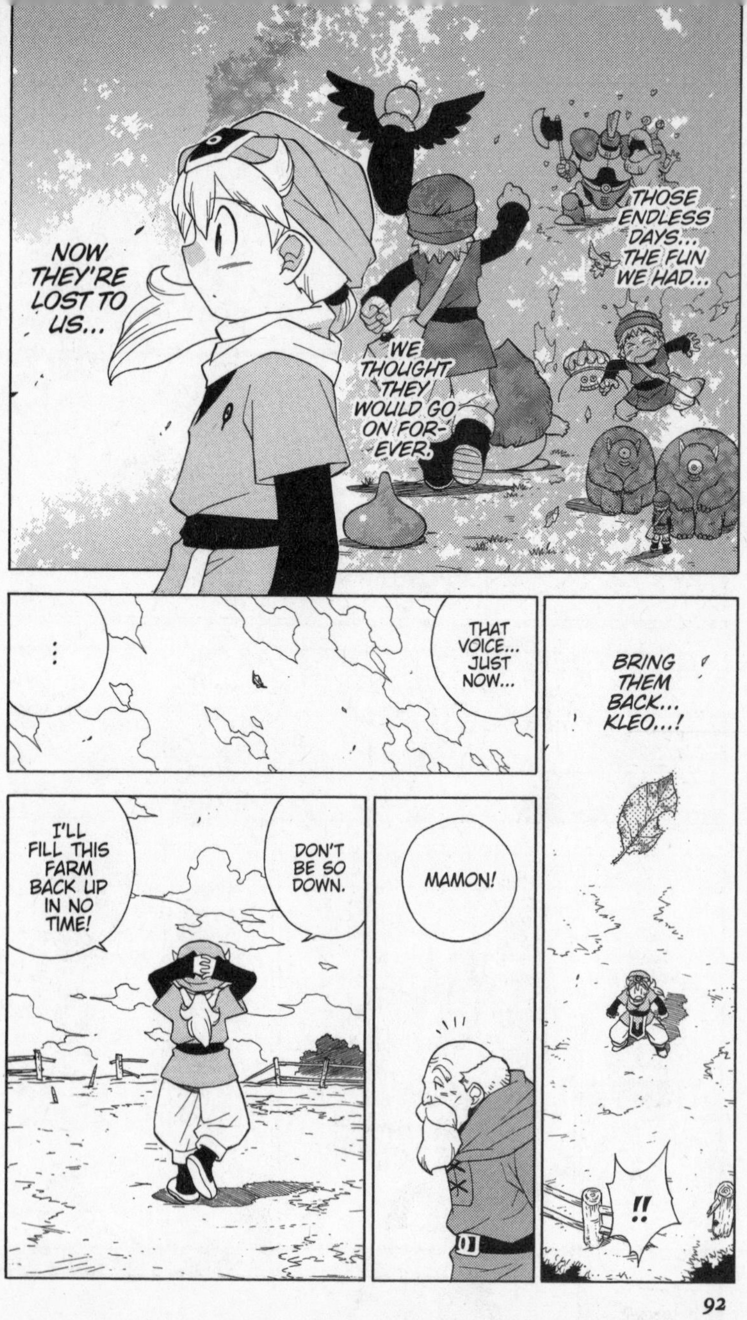
THOSE ENDLESS DAYS... THE FUN WE HAD...
WE THOUGHT THEY WOULD GO ON FOR-EVER.
NOW THEY'RE LOST TO US...
BRING THEM BACK... KLEO...!
!!
THAT VOICE... JUST NOW...
...
MAMON!
DON'T BE SO DOWN.
I'LL FILL THIS FARM BACK UP IN NO TIME!

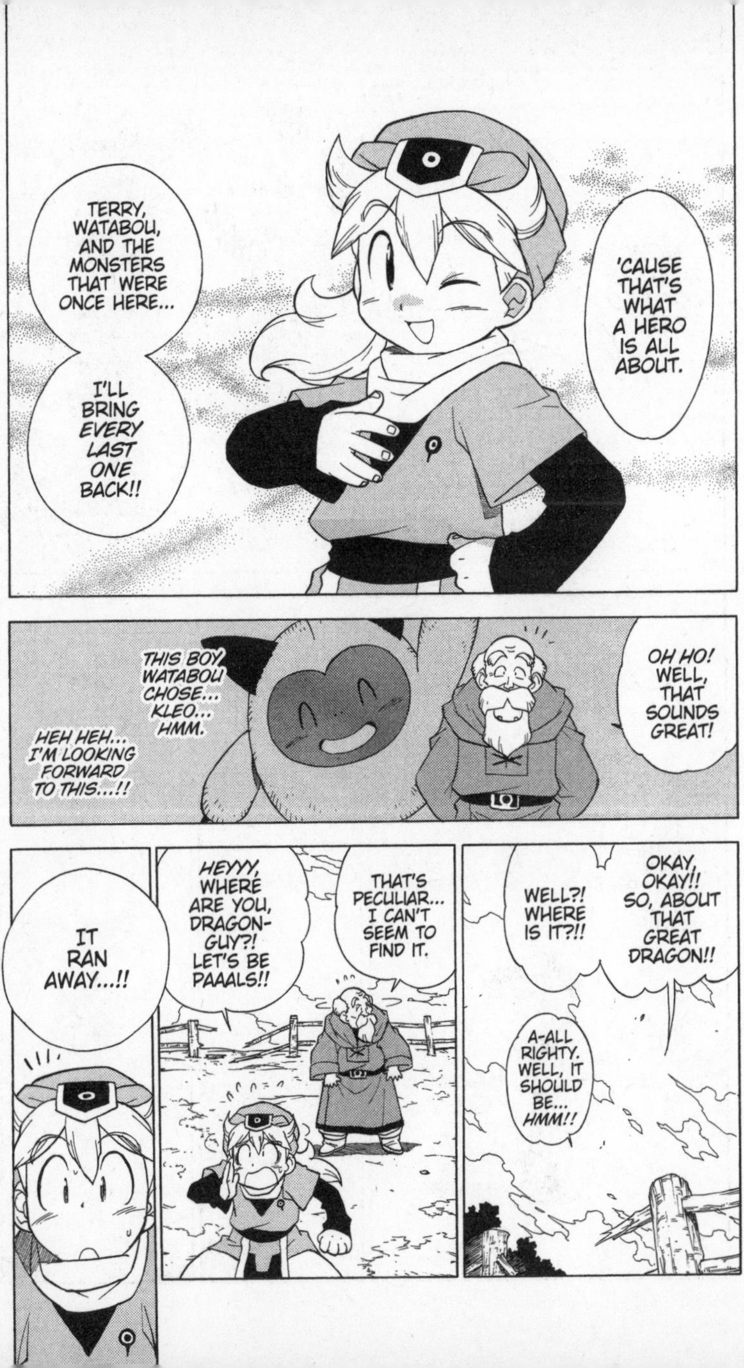
TERRY, WATABOU, AND THE MONSTERS THAT WERE ONCE HERE...
I'LL BRING EVERY LAST ONE BACK!!
'CAUSE THAT'S WHAT A HERO IS ALL ABOUT.
OH HO! WELL, THAT SOUNDS GREAT!
THIS BOY WATABOU CHOSE... KLEO... HMM.
HEH HEH... I'M LOOKING FORWARD TO THIS...!!
OKAY, OKAY!! SO, ABOUT THAT GREAT DRAGON!!
WELL?! WHERE IS IT?!!
A-ALL RIGHTY. WELL, IT SHOULD BE... HMM!!
THAT'S PECULIAR... I CAN'T SEEM TO FIND IT.
HEYYY, WHERE ARE YOU, DRAGON-GUY?! LET'S BE PAAALS!!
IT RAN AWAY...!!

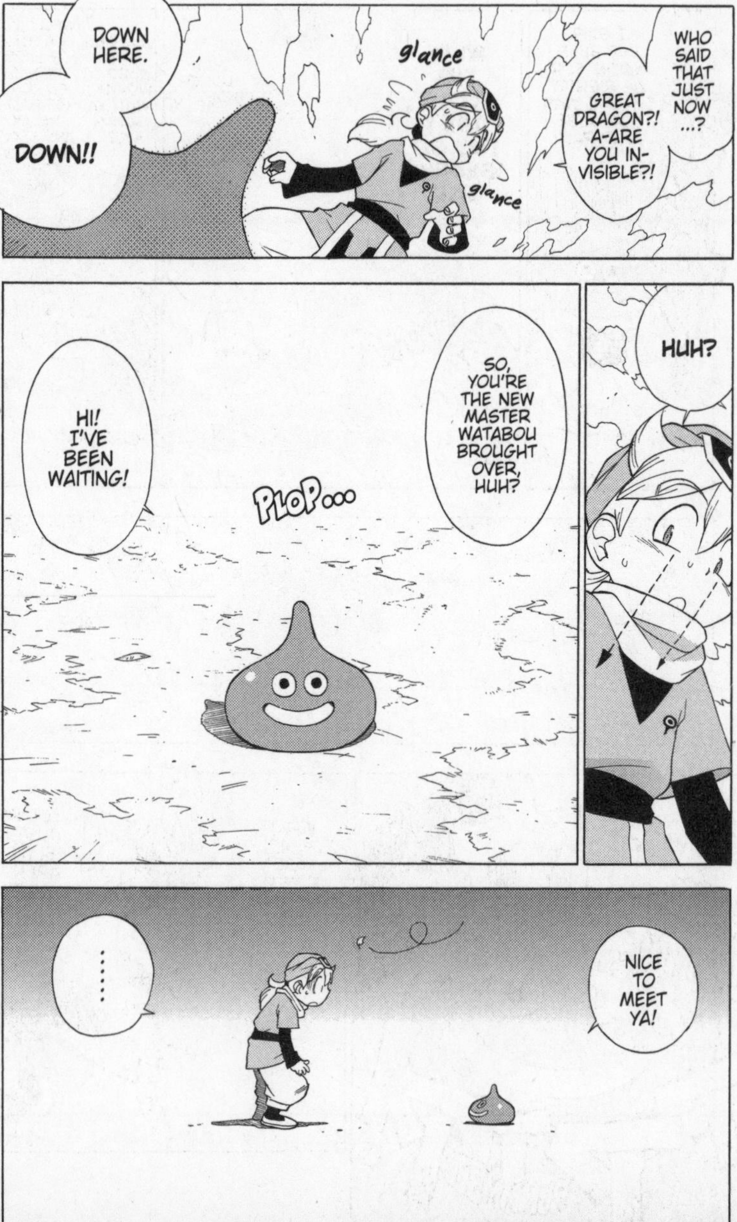
WHO SAID THAT JUST NOW ...?
GREAT DRAGON?! A-ARE YOU IN-VISIBLE?!
glance
DOWN HERE.
DOWN!!
glance
HUH?
SO, YOU'RE THE NEW MASTER WATABOU BROUGHT OVER, HUH?
HI! I'VE BEEN WAITING!
PLOP...
NICE TO MEET YA!
......

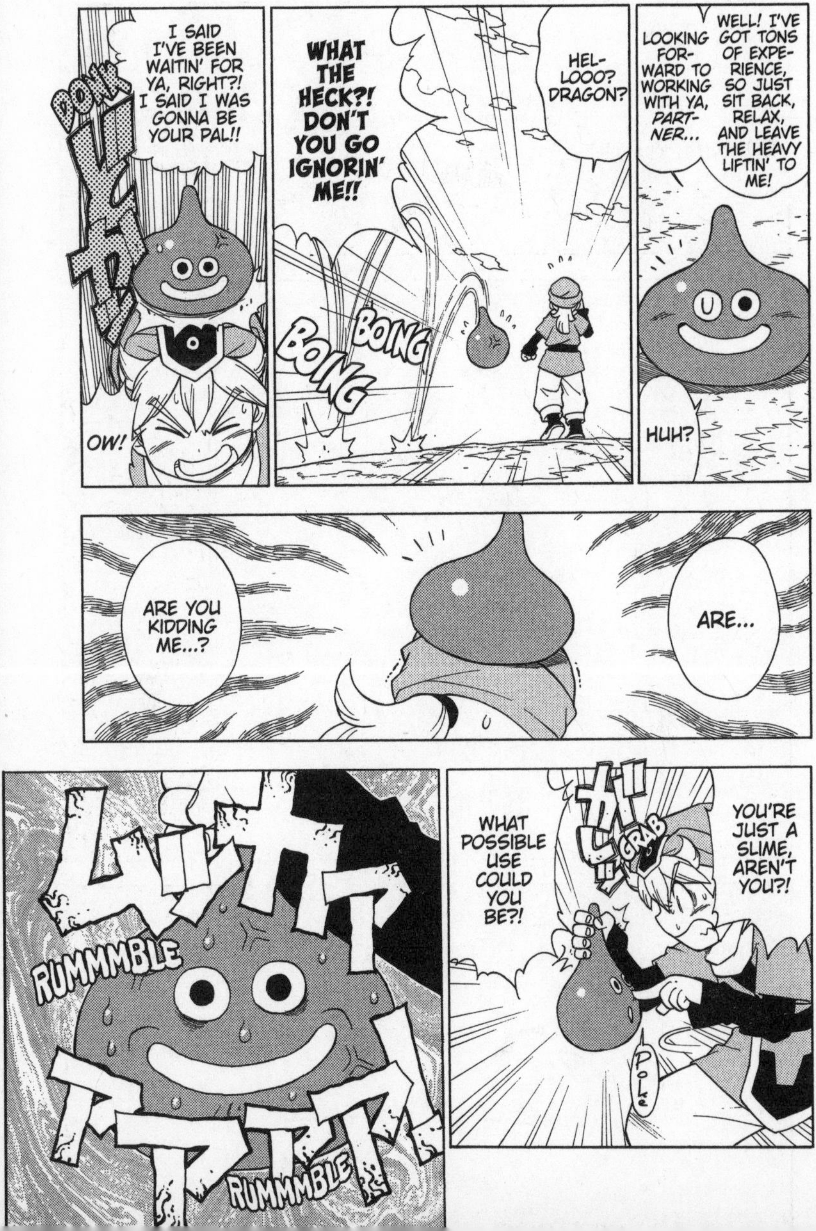
WELL! I'VE GOT TONS OF EXPE-RIENCE, SO JUST SIT BACK, RELAX, AND LEAVE THE HEAVY LIFTIN' TO ME!
LOOKING FOR-WARD TO WORKING WITH YA, PART-NER...
HUH?
HEL-LOOO? DRAGON?
WHAT THE HECK?! DON'T YOU GO IGNORIN' ME!!
BOING
BOING
I SAID I'VE BEEN WAITIN' FOR YA, RIGHT?! I SAID I WAS GONNA BE YOUR PAL!!
DONK
OW!
ARE...
ARE YOU KIDDING ME...?
YOU'RE JUST A SLIME, AREN'T YOU?!
GRAB
WHAT POSSIBLE USE COULD YOU BE?!
Poke
RUMMMBLE
RUMMMBLE

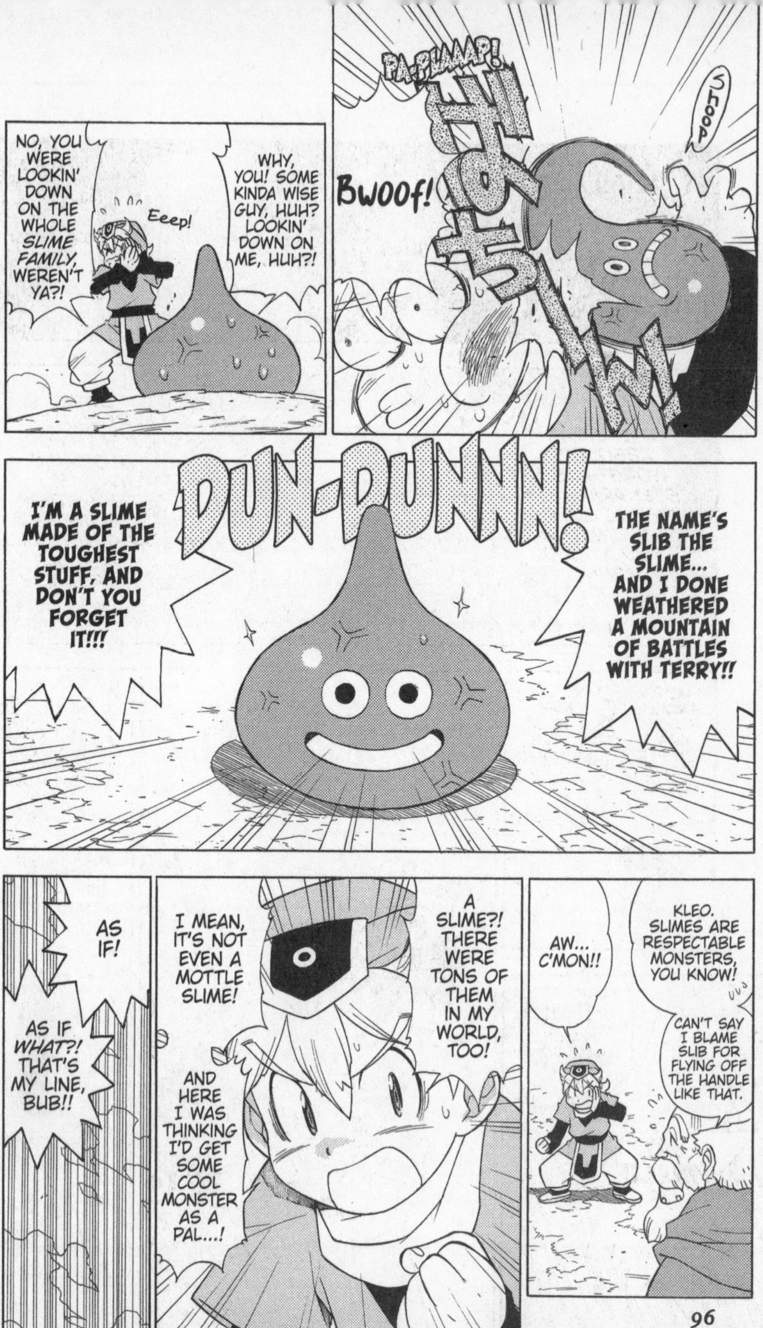
PA-PLAAAP!
SHOOP
Bwoof!
WHY, YOU! SOME KINDA WISE GUY, HUH? LOOKIN' DOWN ON ME, HUH?!
Eeep!
NO, YOU WERE LOOKIN' DOWN ON THE WHOLE *SLIME FAMILY,* WEREN'T YA?!
DUN-DUNNN!
THE NAME'S SLIB THE SLIME... AND I DONE WEATHERED A MOUNTAIN OF BATTLES WITH TERRY!!
I'M A SLIME MADE OF THE TOUGHEST STUFF, AND DON'T YOU FORGET IT!!!
KLEO. SLIMES ARE RESPECTABLE MONSTERS, YOU KNOW!
AW... C'MON!!
CAN'T SAY I BLAME SLIB FOR FLYING OFF THE HANDLE LIKE THAT.
A SLIME?! THERE WERE TONS OF THEM IN MY WORLD, TOO!
I MEAN, IT'S NOT EVEN A MOTTLE SLIME!
AND HERE I WAS THINKING I'D GET SOME COOL MONSTER AS A PAL...!
AS IF!
AS IF *WHAT?!* THAT'S MY LINE, BUB!!

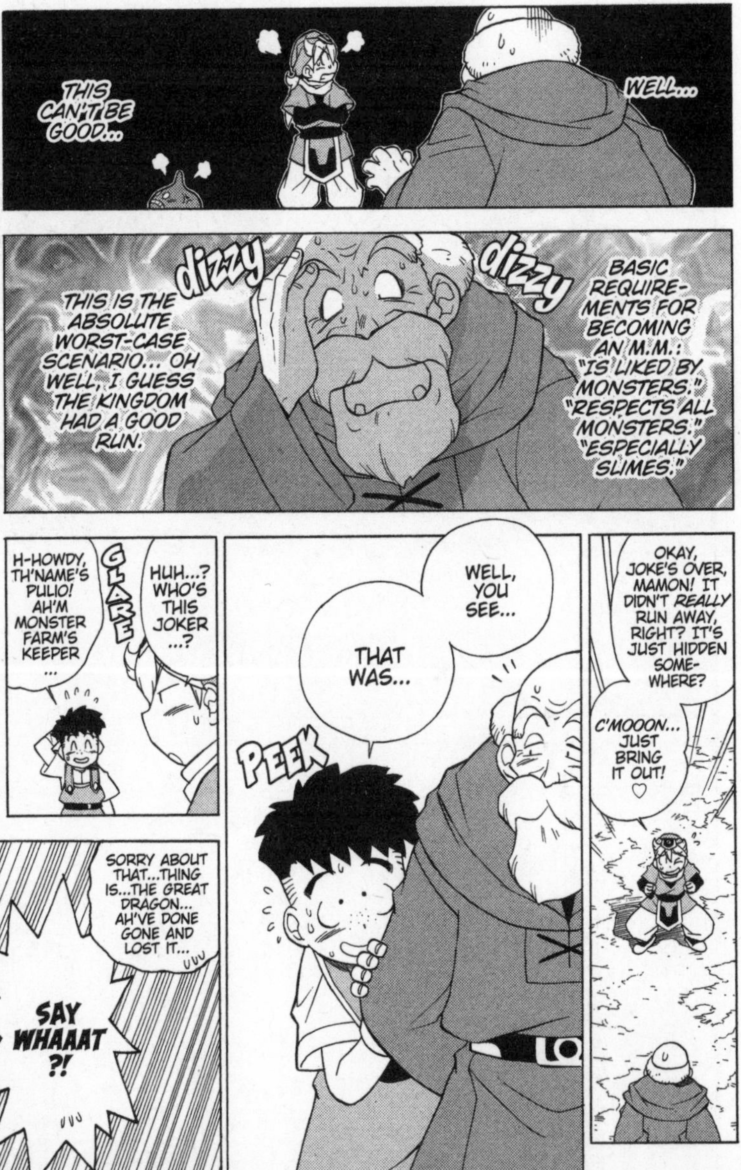
WELL...
THIS CAN'T BE GOOD...
dizzy
dizzy
BASIC REQUIREMENTS FOR BECOMING AN M.M.: "IS LIKED BY MONSTERS." "RESPECTS ALL MONSTERS." "ESPECIALLY SLIMES."
THIS IS THE ABSOLUTE WORST-CASE SCENARIO... OH WELL, I GUESS THE KINGDOM HAD A GOOD RUN.
OKAY, JOKE'S OVER, MAMON! IT DIDN'T *REALLY* RUN AWAY, RIGHT? IT'S JUST HIDDEN SOMEWHERE?
C'MOOON... JUST BRING IT OUT! ♡
WELL, YOU SEE...
THAT WAS...
PEEK
HUH...? WHO'S THIS JOKER...?
GLARE
H-HOWDY, TH'NAME'S PULIO! AH'M MONSTER FARM'S KEEPER...
SORRY ABOUT THAT...THING IS...THE GREAT DRAGON... AH'VE DONE GONE AND LOST IT...
SAY WHAAAT?!

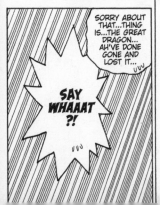

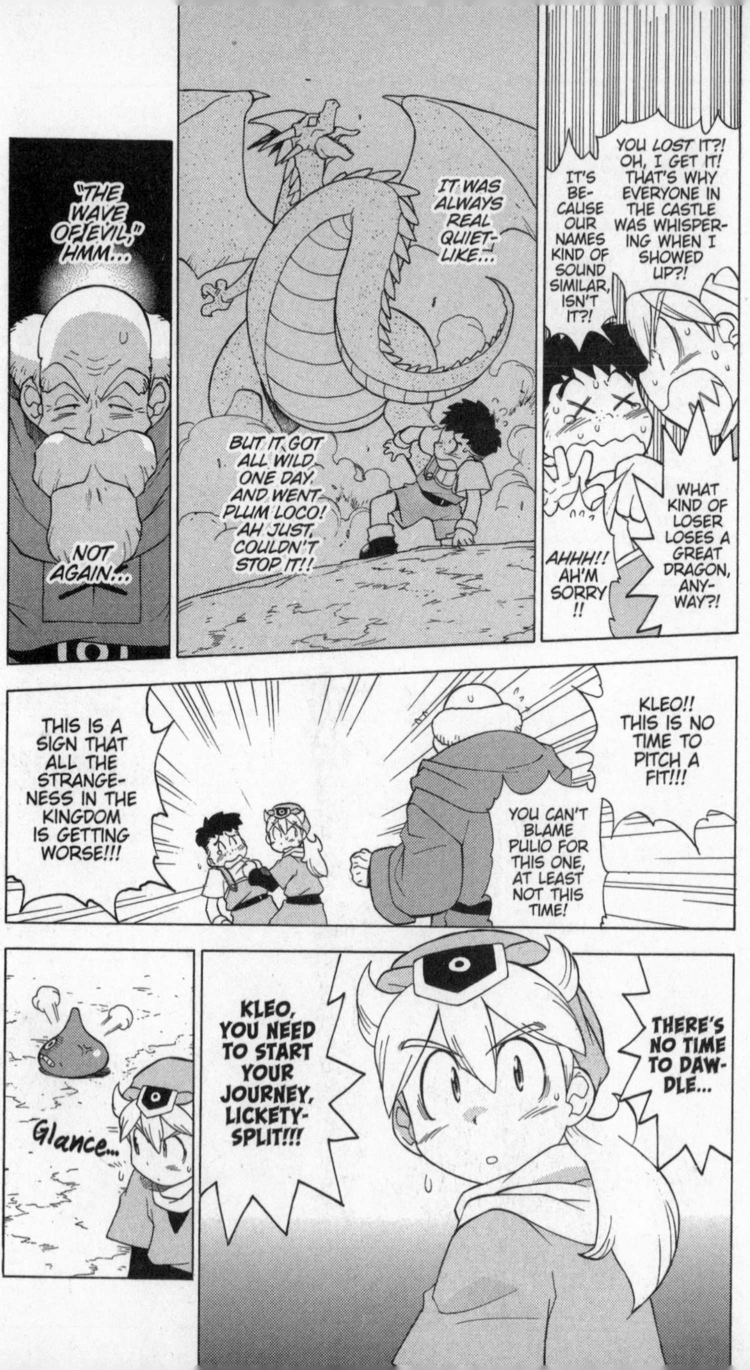
YOU LOST IT?! OH, I GET IT! THAT'S WHY EVERYONE IN THE CASTLE WAS WHISPERING WHEN I SHOWED UP?!
IT'S BECAUSE OUR NAMES KIND OF SOUND SIMILAR, ISN'T IT?!
WHAT KIND OF LOSER LOSES A GREAT DRAGON, ANYWAY?!
AHHH!! AH'M SORRY!!
IT WAS ALWAYS REAL QUIET-LIKE...
BUT IT GOT ALL WILD ONE DAY AND WENT PLUM LOCO! AH JUST COULDN'T STOP IT!!
"THE WAVE OF EVIL," HMM...
NOT AGAIN...
KLEO!! THIS IS NO TIME TO PITCH A FIT!!!
YOU CAN'T BLAME PULIO FOR THIS ONE, AT LEAST NOT THIS TIME!
THIS IS A SIGN THAT ALL THE STRANGENESS IN THE KINGDOM IS GETTING WORSE!!!
THERE'S NO TIME TO DAWDLE...
KLEO, YOU NEED TO START YOUR JOURNEY, LICKETY-SPLIT!!!
Glance...

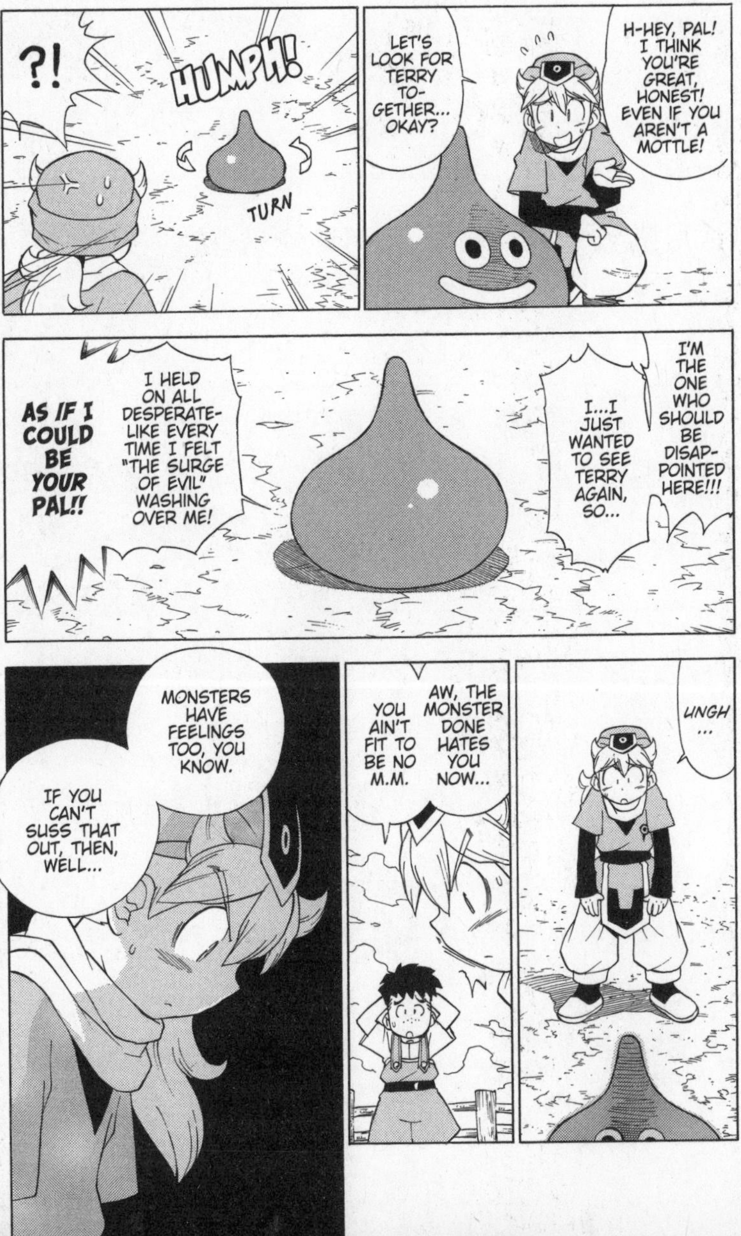
H-HEY, PAL! I THINK YOU'RE GREAT, HONEST! EVEN IF YOU AREN'T A MOTTLE!
LET'S LOOK FOR TERRY TOGETHER... OKAY?
HUMPH!
TURN
?!
I'M THE ONE WHO SHOULD BE DISAPPOINTED HERE!!!
I...I JUST WANTED TO SEE TERRY AGAIN, SO...
I HELD ON ALL DESPERATE-LIKE EVERY TIME I FELT "THE SURGE OF EVIL" WASHING OVER ME!
AS IF I COULD BE YOUR PAL!!
UNGH ...
AW, THE MONSTER DONE HATES YOU NOW...
YOU AIN'T FIT TO BE NO M.M.
MONSTERS HAVE FEELINGS TOO, YOU KNOW.
IF YOU CAN'T SUSS THAT OUT, THEN, WELL...

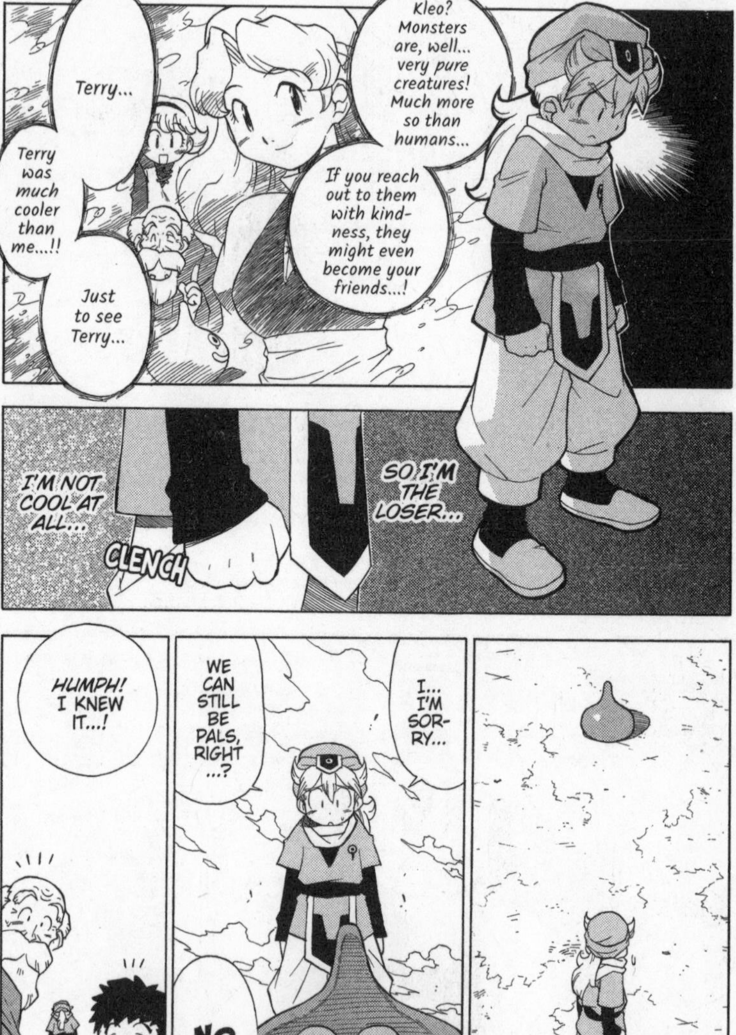

Kleo? Monsters are, well... very pure creatures! Much more so than humans...
If you reach out to them with kind-ness, they might even become your friends...!
Terry...
Terry was much cooler than me...!!
Just to see Terry...
SO I'M THE LOSER...
I'M NOT COOL AT ALL...
CLENCH
I... I'M SOR-RY...
WE CAN STILL BE PALS, RIGHT ...?
NO WAY.
HUMPH! I KNEW IT...!

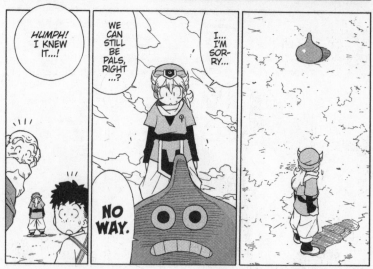

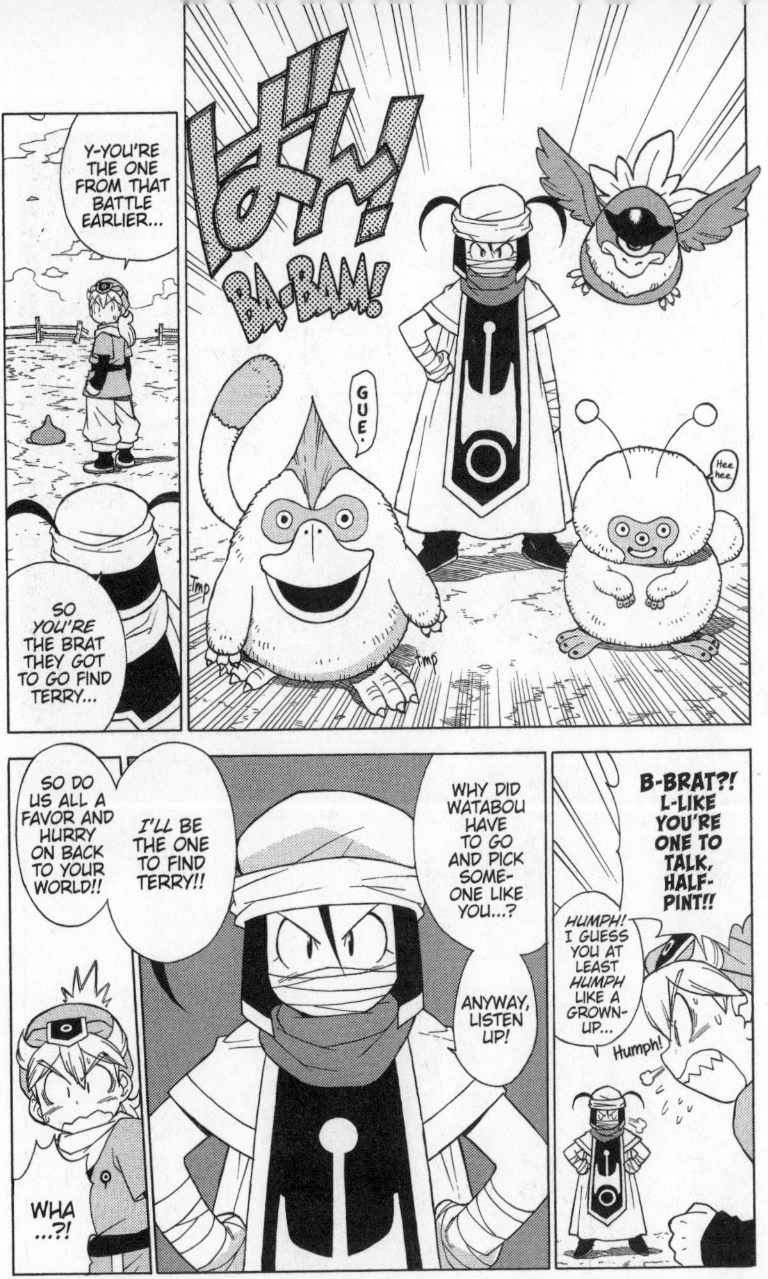
ばん!
BA-BAM!
GUE.
Hee hee.
Y-YOU'RE THE ONE FROM THAT BATTLE EARLIER...
SO *YOU'RE* THE BRAT THEY GOT TO GO FIND TERRY...
B-BRAT?! L-LIKE YOU'RE ONE TO TALK, HALF-PINT!!
HUMPH! I GUESS YOU AT LEAST *HUMPH* LIKE A GROWN-UP...
Humph!
WHY DID WATABOU HAVE TO GO AND PICK SOME-ONE LIKE YOU...?
ANYWAY, LISTEN UP!
I'LL BE THE ONE TO FIND TERRY!!
SO DO US ALL A FAVOR AND HURRY ON BACK TO YOUR WORLD!!
WHA ...?!

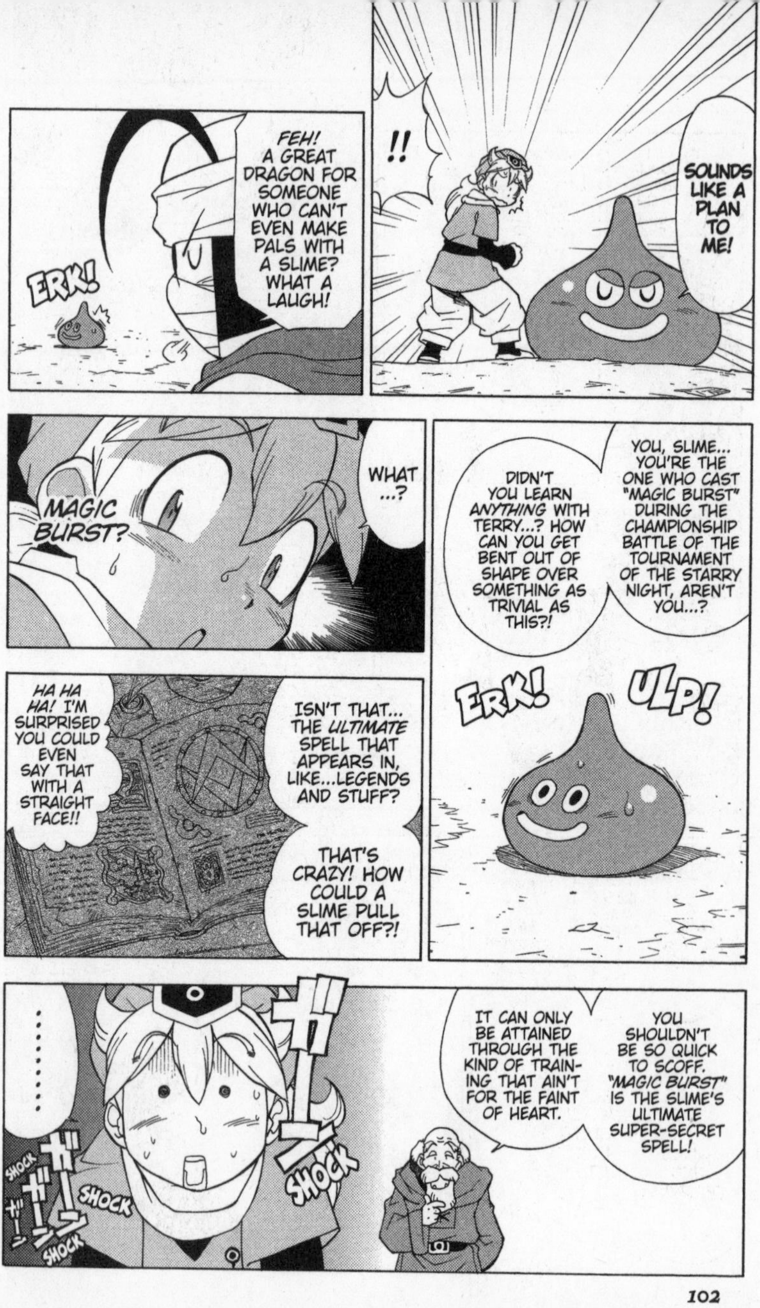
SOUNDS LIKE A PLAN TO ME!
!!
FEH! A GREAT DRAGON FOR SOMEONE WHO CAN'T EVEN MAKE PALS WITH A SLIME? WHAT A LAUGH!
ERK!
YOU, SLIME... YOU'RE THE ONE WHO CAST "MAGIC BURST" DURING THE CHAMPIONSHIP BATTLE OF THE TOURNAMENT OF THE STARRY NIGHT, AREN'T YOU...?
DIDN'T YOU LEARN ANYTHING WITH TERRY...? HOW CAN YOU GET BENT OUT OF SHAPE OVER SOMETHING AS TRIVIAL AS THIS?!
ULP!
ERK!
WHAT ...?
MAGIC BURST?
ISN'T THAT... THE ULTIMATE SPELL THAT APPEARS IN, LIKE...LEGENDS AND STUFF?
THAT'S CRAZY! HOW COULD A SLIME PULL THAT OFF?!
HA HA HA! I'M SURPRISED YOU COULD EVEN SAY THAT WITH A STRAIGHT FACE!!
YOU SHOULDN'T BE SO QUICK TO SCOFF. "MAGIC BURST" IS THE SLIME'S ULTIMATE SUPER-SECRET SPELL!
IT CAN ONLY BE ATTAINED THROUGH THE KIND OF TRAIN-ING THAT AIN'T FOR THE FAINT OF HEART.
SHOCK
SHOCK
SHOCK
SHOCK
....

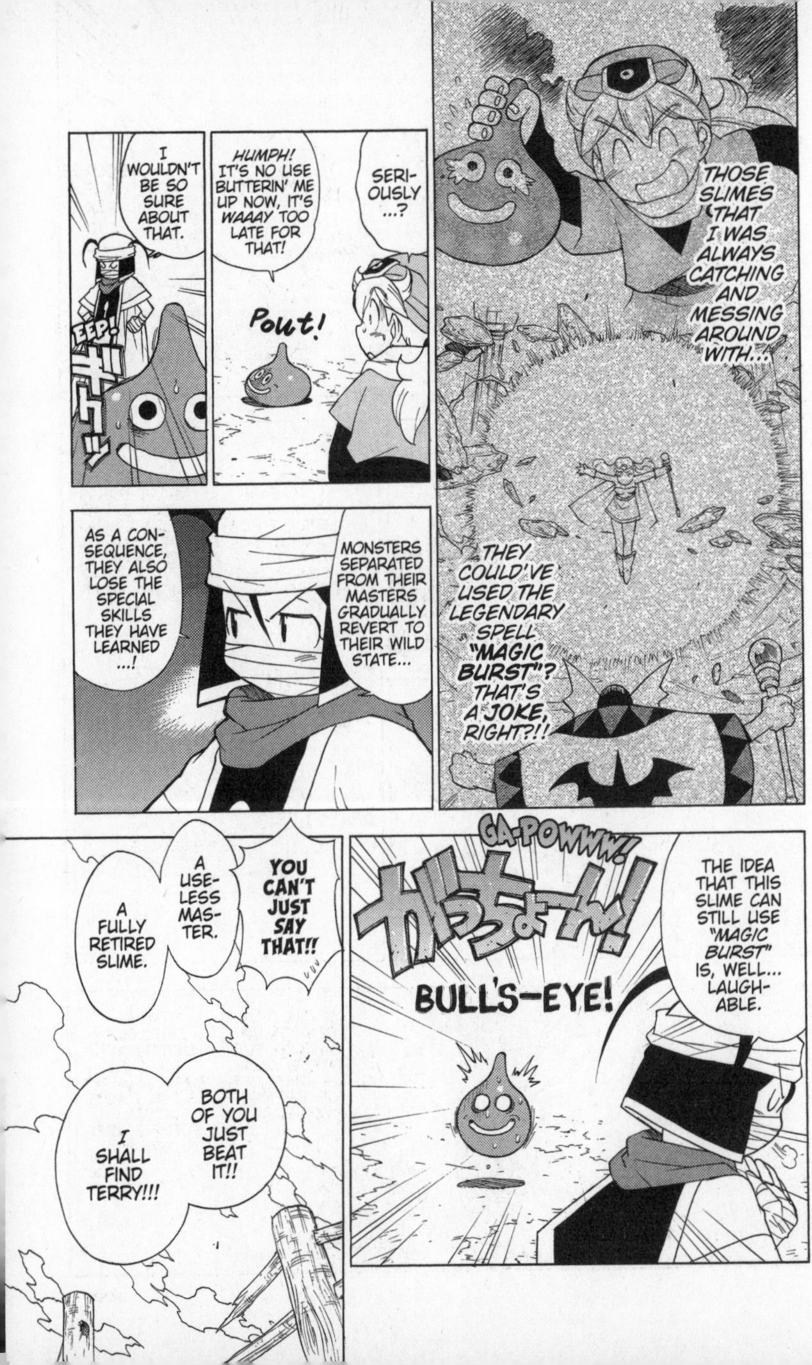
THOSE SLIMES THAT I WAS ALWAYS CATCHING AND MESSING AROUND WITH...
THEY COULD'VE USED THE LEGENDARY SPELL "MAGIC BURST"? THAT'S A JOKE, RIGHT?!!
SERI-OUSLY ...?
HUMPH! IT'S NO USE BUTTERIN' ME UP NOW, IT'S WAAAY TOO LATE FOR THAT!
Pout!
I WOULDN'T BE SO SURE ABOUT THAT.
EEP!
ギクッ
MONSTERS SEPARATED FROM THEIR MASTERS GRADUALLY REVERT TO THEIR WILD STATE...
AS A CON-SEQUENCE, THEY ALSO LOSE THE SPECIAL SKILLS THEY HAVE LEARNED ...!
GA-POWWW!
BULL'S-EYE!
THE IDEA THAT THIS SLIME CAN STILL USE "MAGIC BURST" IS, WELL... LAUGH-ABLE.
YOU CAN'T JUST SAY THAT!!
A USE-LESS MAS-TER.
A FULLY RETIRED SLIME.
BOTH OF YOU JUST BEAT IT!!
I SHALL FIND TERRY!!!

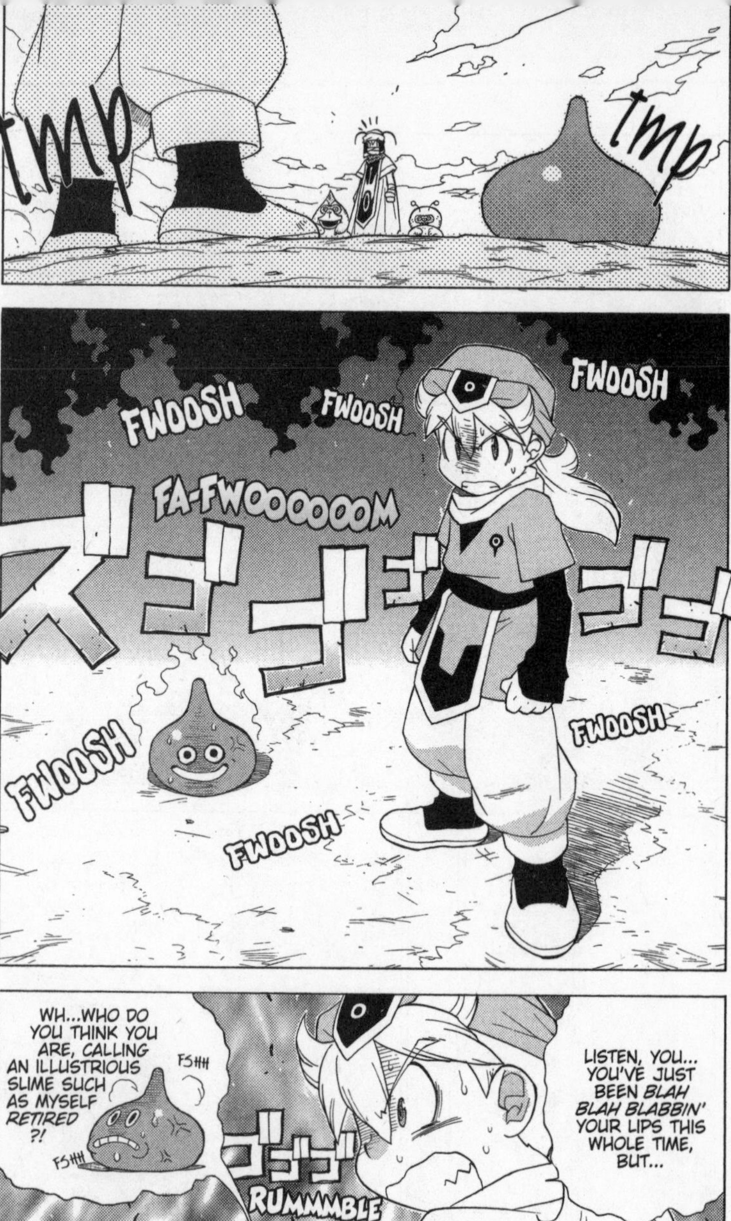
tmp
tmp
FWOOSH
FWOOSH
FWOOSH
FA-FWOOOOOOM
FWOOSH
FWOOSH
FWOOSH
LISTEN, YOU... YOU'VE JUST BEEN *BLAH BLAH BLABBIN'* YOUR LIPS THIS WHOLE TIME, BUT...
RUMMMBLE
FSHH
WH...WHO DO YOU THINK YOU ARE, CALLING AN ILLUSTRIOUS SLIME SUCH AS MYSELF *RETIRED* ?!
FSHH

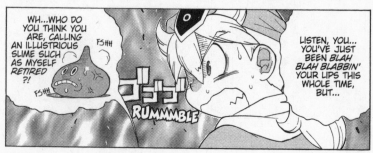

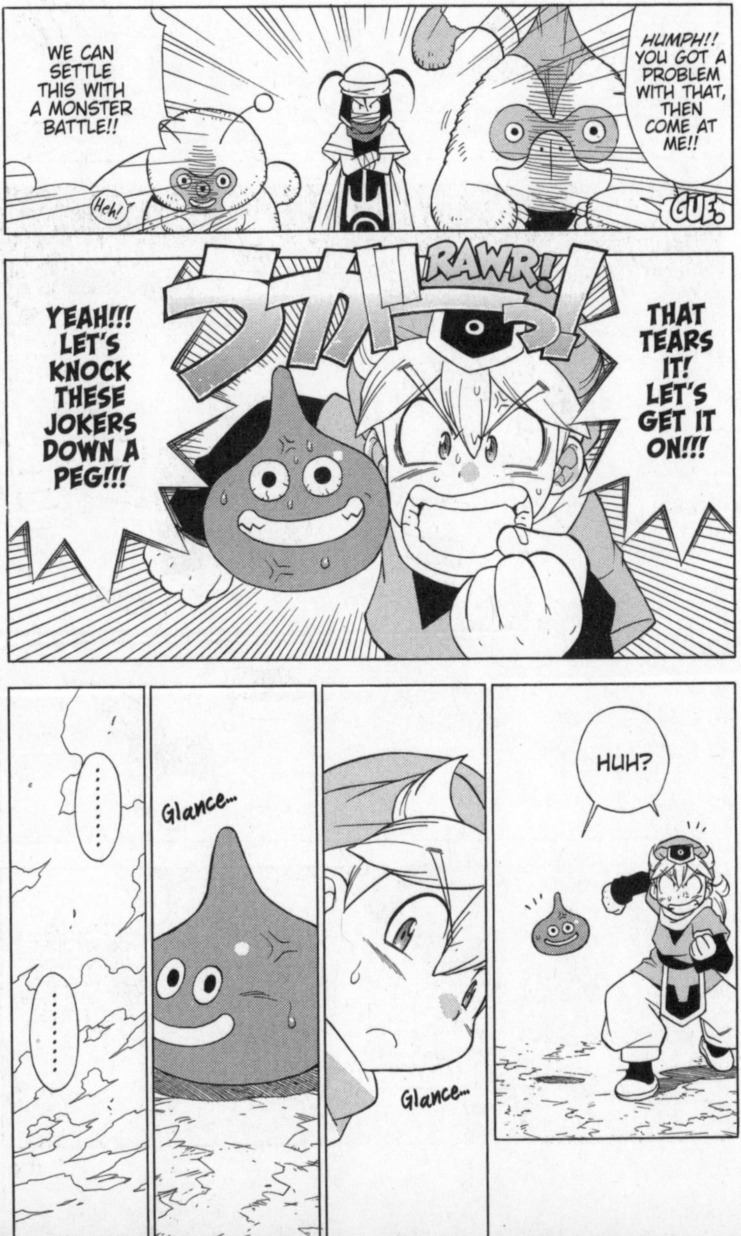
HUMPH!! YOU GOT A PROBLEM WITH THAT, THEN COME AT ME!!
GUE.
WE CAN SETTLE THIS WITH A MONSTER BATTLE!!
Heh!
RAWR!
THAT TEARS IT! LET'S GET IT ON!!!
YEAH!!! LET'S KNOCK THESE JOKERS DOWN A PEG!!!
HUH?
Glance...
Glance...
......
......

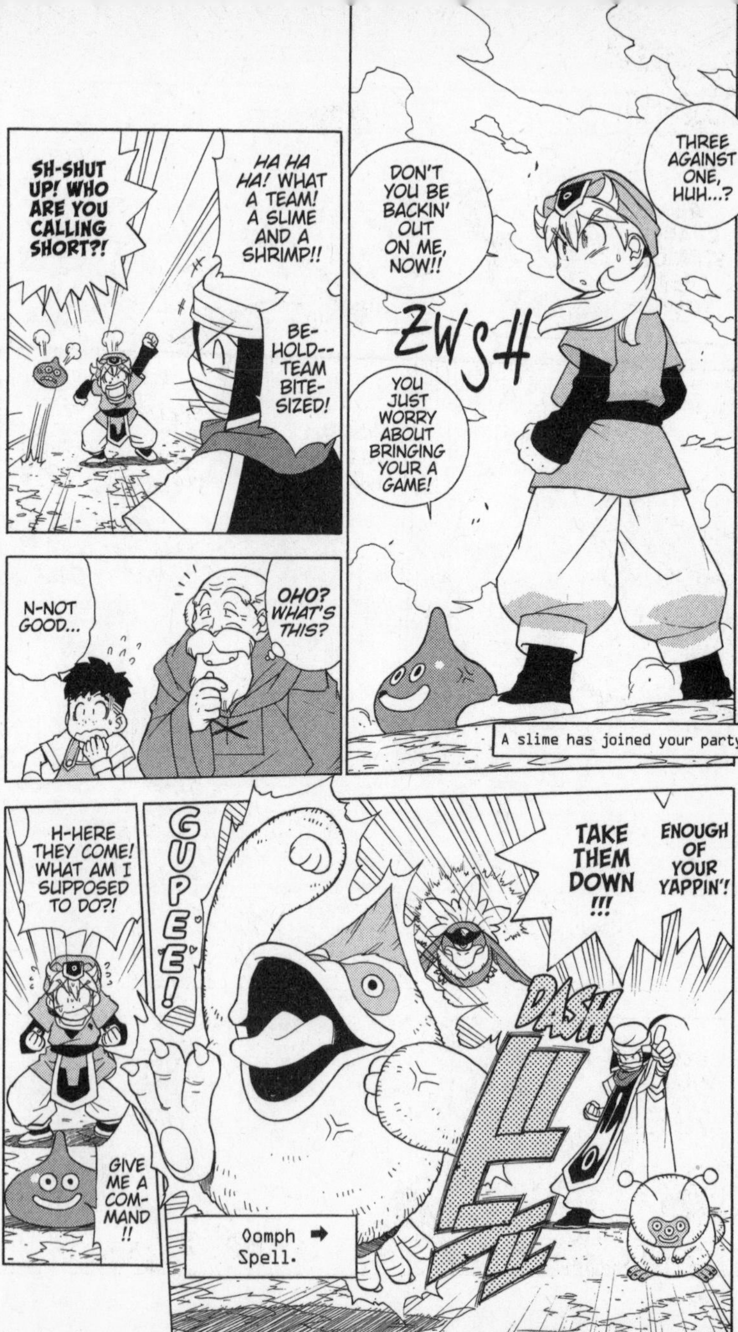
THREE AGAINST ONE, HUH...?
DON'T YOU BE BACKIN' OUT ON ME, NOW!!
ZWSH
YOU JUST WORRY ABOUT BRINGING YOUR A GAME!
A slime has joined your party!
HA HA HA! WHAT A TEAM! A SLIME AND A SHRIMP!!
SH-SHUT UP! WHO ARE YOU CALLING SHORT?!
BE-HOLD--TEAM BITE-SIZED!
OHO? WHAT'S THIS?
N-NOT GOOD...
ENOUGH OF YOUR YAPPIN'!
TAKE THEM DOWN!!!
DASH
GUPEE!
Oomph ➡ Spell.
H-HERE THEY COME! WHAT AM I SUPPOSED TO DO?!
GIVE ME A COM-MAND!!

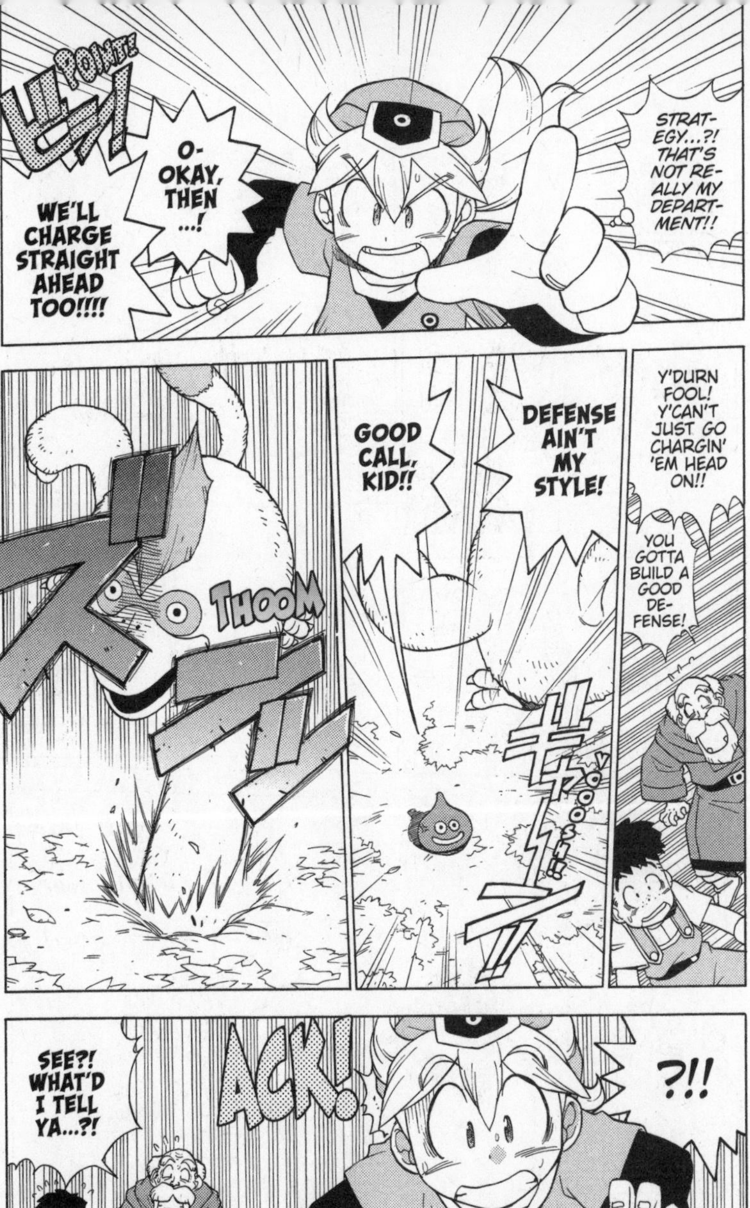
STRAT-EGY...?! THAT'S NOT RE-ALLY MY DEPART-MENT!!
O-OKAY, THEN ...!
LIL' POINTE
WE'LL CHARGE STRAIGHT AHEAD TOO!!!!
Y'DURN FOOL! Y'CAN'T JUST GO CHARGIN' 'EM HEAD ON!!
YOU GOTTA BUILD A GOOD DE-FENSE!
DEFENSE AIN'T MY STYLE!
GOOD CALL, KID!!
VOOOSH!!
THOOM
?!!
ACK!
SEE?! WHAT'D I TELL YA...?!

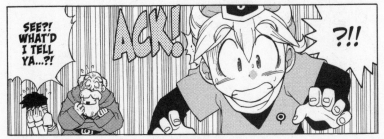

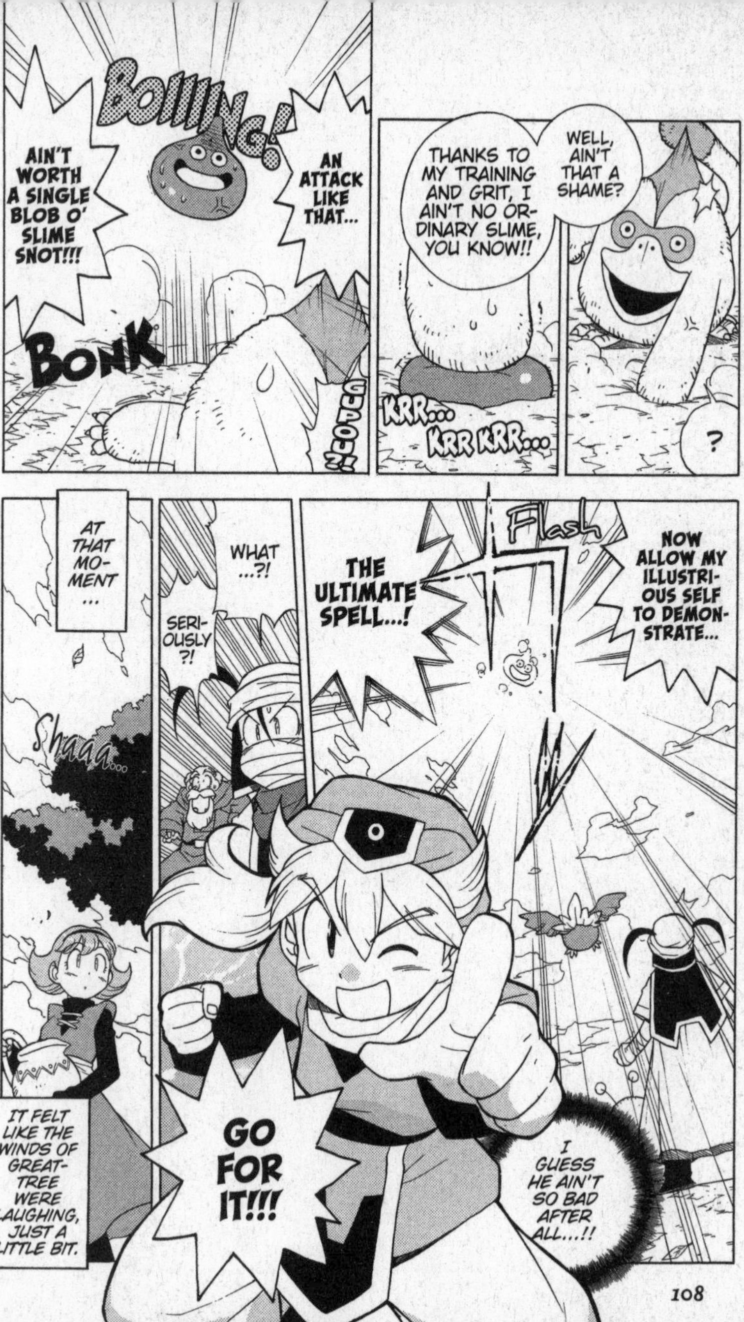
WELL, AIN'T THAT A SHAME?
?
THANKS TO MY TRAINING AND GRIT, I AIN'T NO ORDINARY SLIME, YOU KNOW!!
KRR... KRR KRR...
BOIIING!
AN ATTACK LIKE THAT...
AIN'T WORTH A SINGLE BLOB O' SLIME SNOT!!!
BONK
GUPOU?!
Flash
NOW ALLOW MY ILLUSTRIOUS SELF TO DEMONSTRATE...
THE ULTIMATE SPELL...!
WHAT...?!
SERIOUSLY?!
GO FOR IT!!!
I GUESS HE AIN'T SO BAD AFTER ALL...!!
AT THAT MOMENT...
Shaaa...
IT FELT LIKE THE WINDS OF GREAT-TREE WERE LAUGHING, JUST A LITTLE BIT.

DQM +
DRACON QUEST MONSTERS

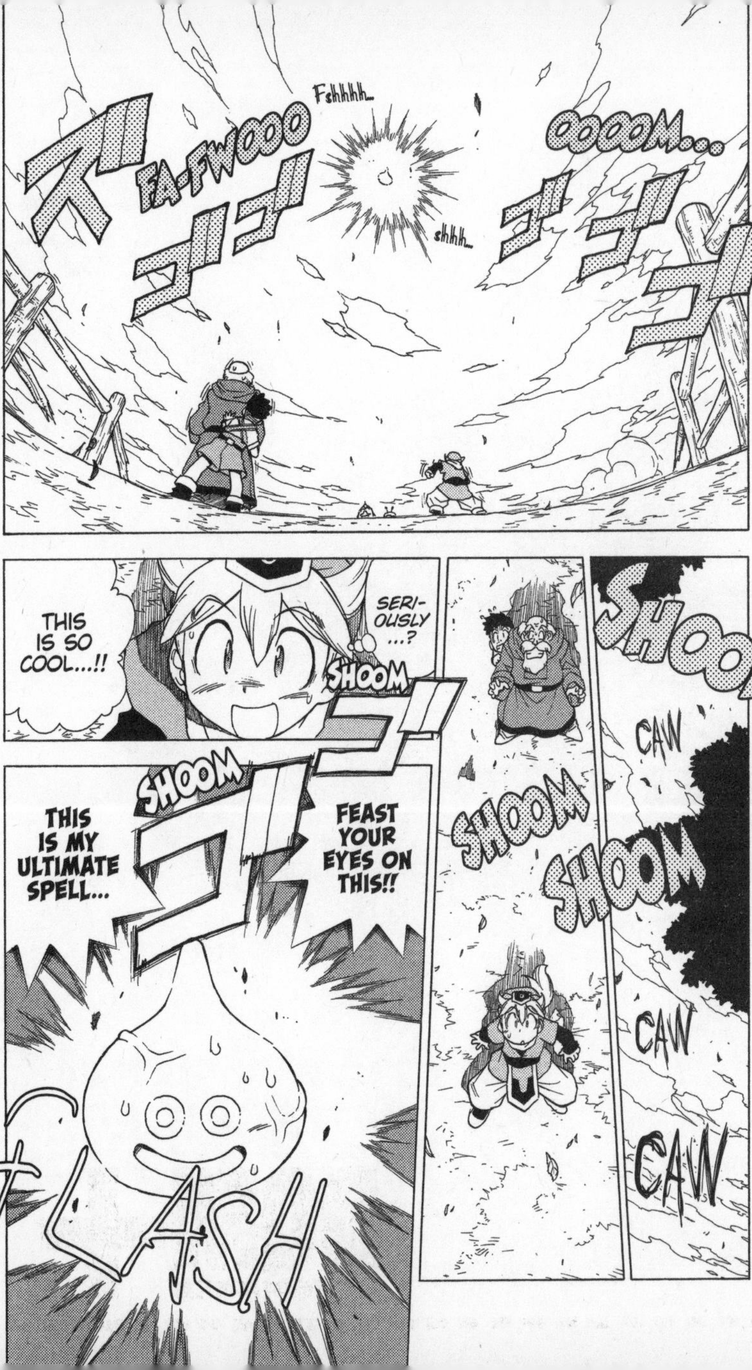

OOOOM...
Fshhhhh...
FA-FWOOO
shhhh...
SHOOM
CAW
CAW
CAW
SHOOM
SHOOM
SERI-OUSLY ...?
SHOOM
THIS IS SO COOL...!!
SHOOM
FEAST YOUR EYES ON THIS!!
THIS IS MY ULTIMATE SPELL...
FLASH

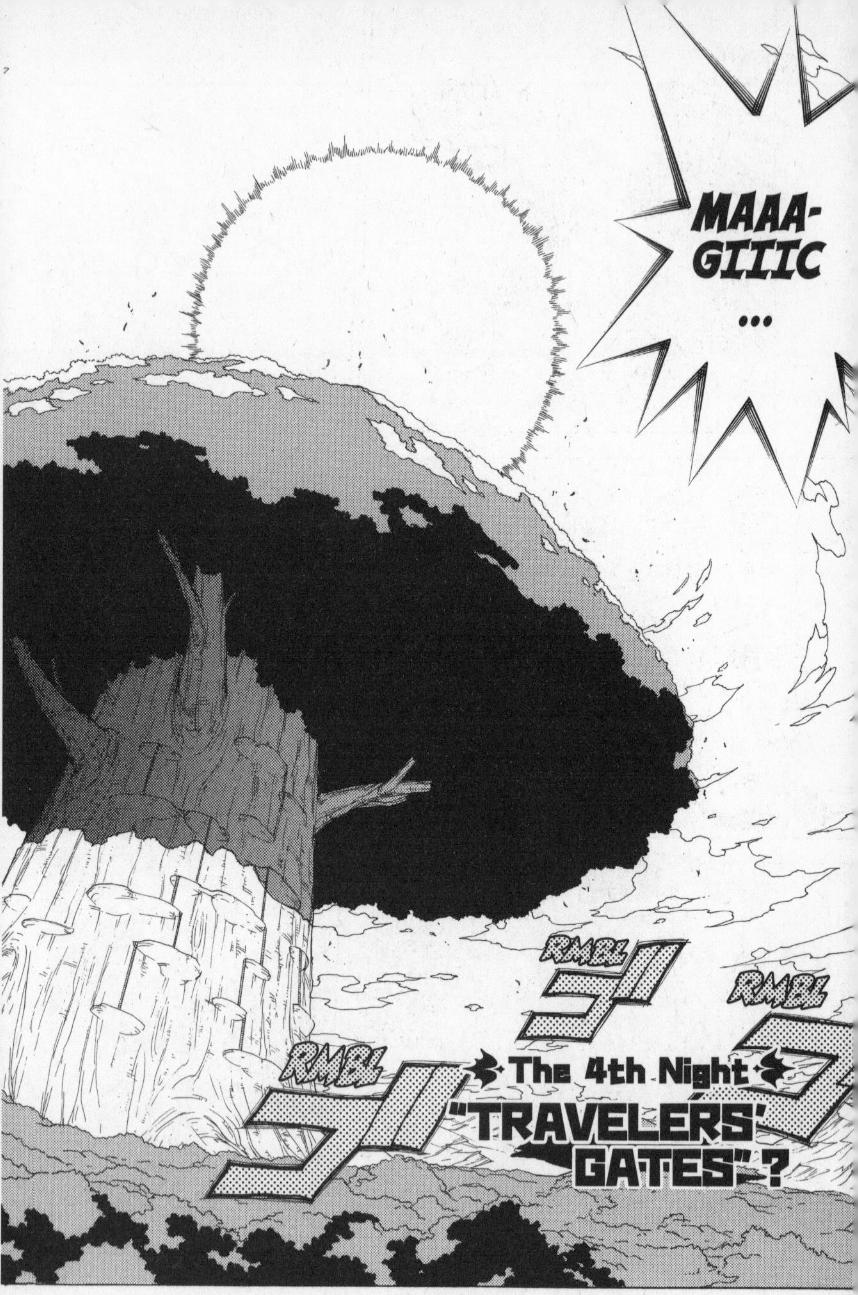
MAAA-GIIIC ...
RMBL
RMBL
RMBL
The 4th Night
"TRAVELERS' GATES"?

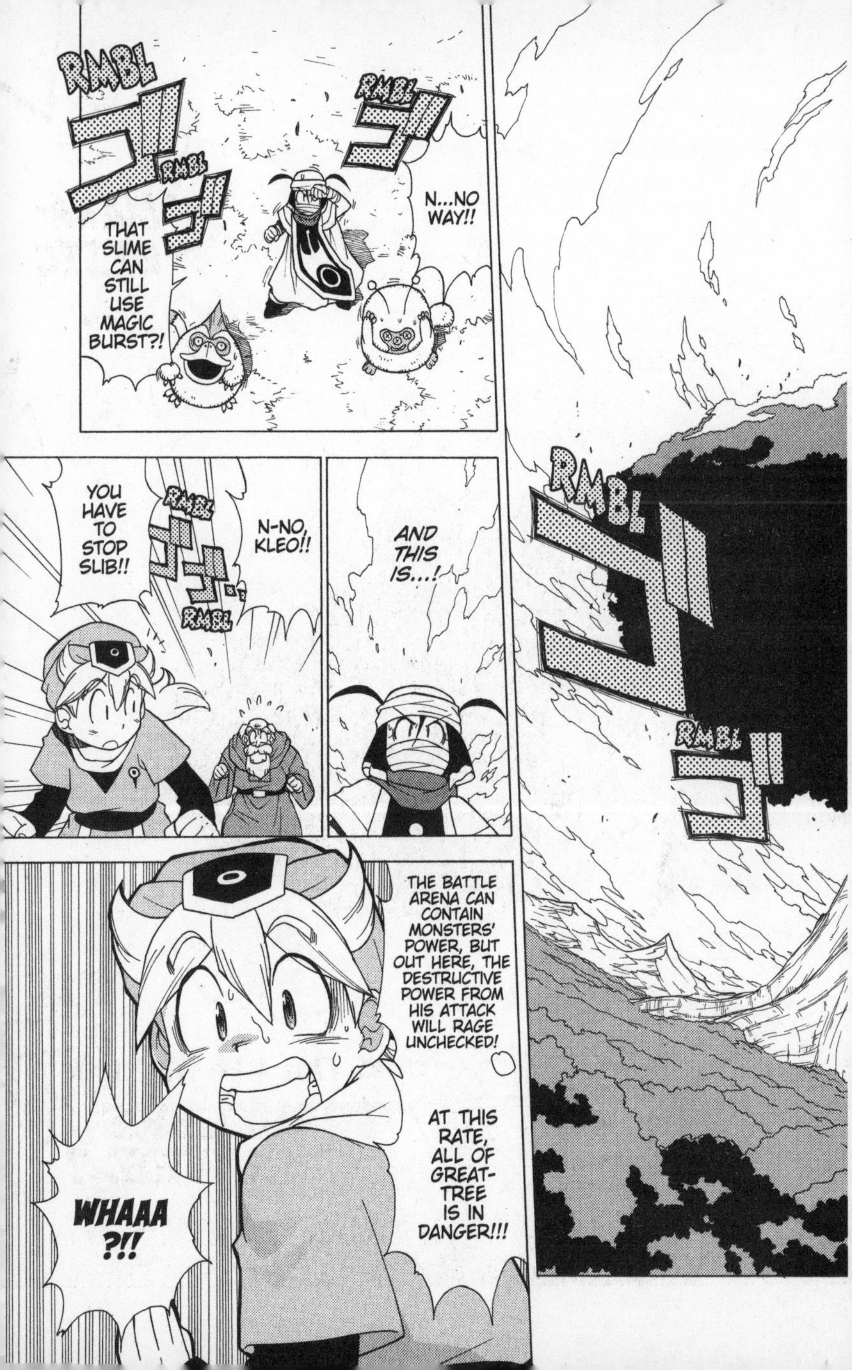
RMBL
RMBL
RMBL
N...NO WAY!!
RMBL
RMBL
THAT SLIME CAN STILL USE MAGIC BURST?!
AND THIS IS...!
N-NO, KLEO!!
RMBL
RMBL
YOU HAVE TO STOP SLIB!!
THE BATTLE ARENA CAN CONTAIN MONSTERS' POWER, BUT OUT HERE, THE DESTRUCTIVE POWER FROM HIS ATTACK WILL RAGE UNCHECKED!
AT THIS RATE, ALL OF GREAT-TREE IS IN DANGER!!!
WHAAA ?!!

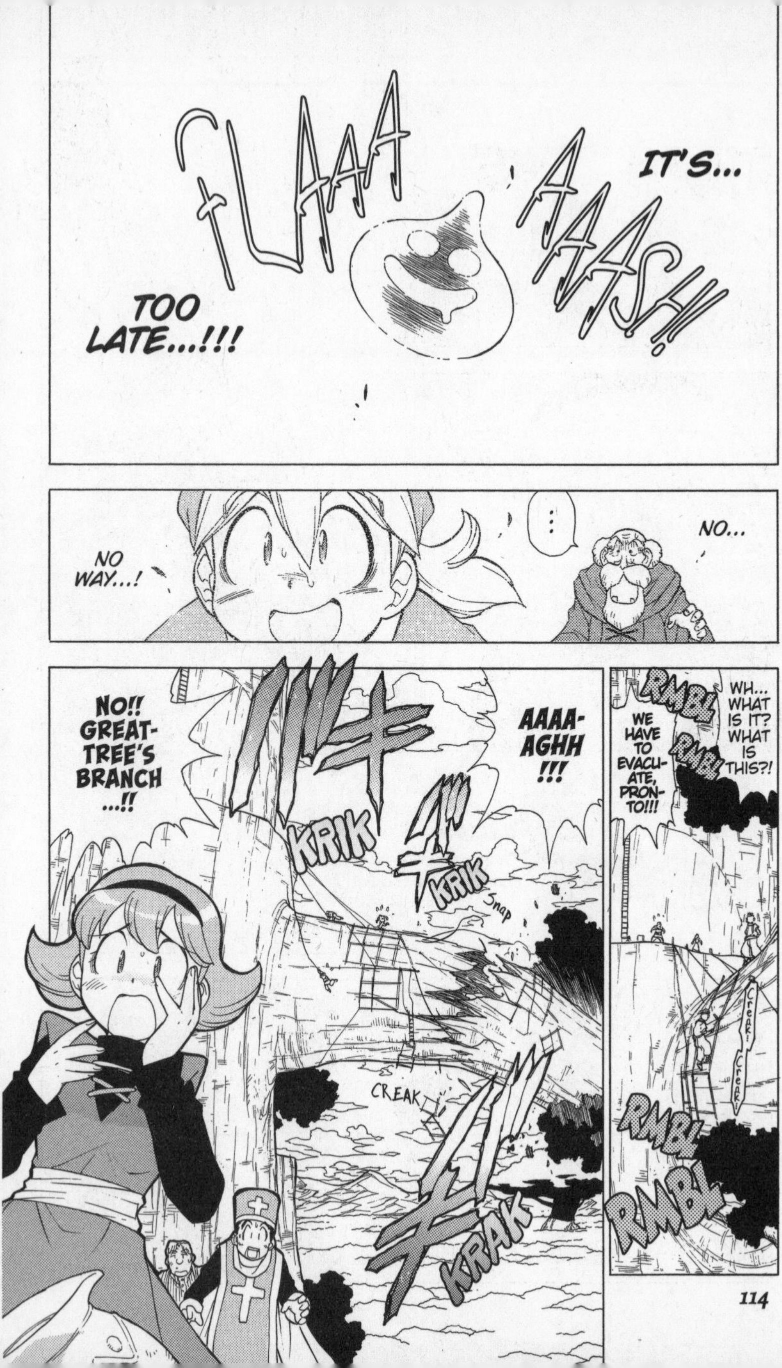
IT'S...
FLAAAAAASH!!
TOO LATE...!!!
NO...
...
NO WAY...!
WH... WHAT IS IT? WHAT IS THIS?!
RMBL RMBL
WE HAVE TO EVACUATE, PRONTO!!!
Creak Creak
RMBL RMBL
AAAA-AGHH!!!
KRIK
KRIK
Snap
NO!! GREAT-TREE'S BRANCH...!!
CREAK
KRAK

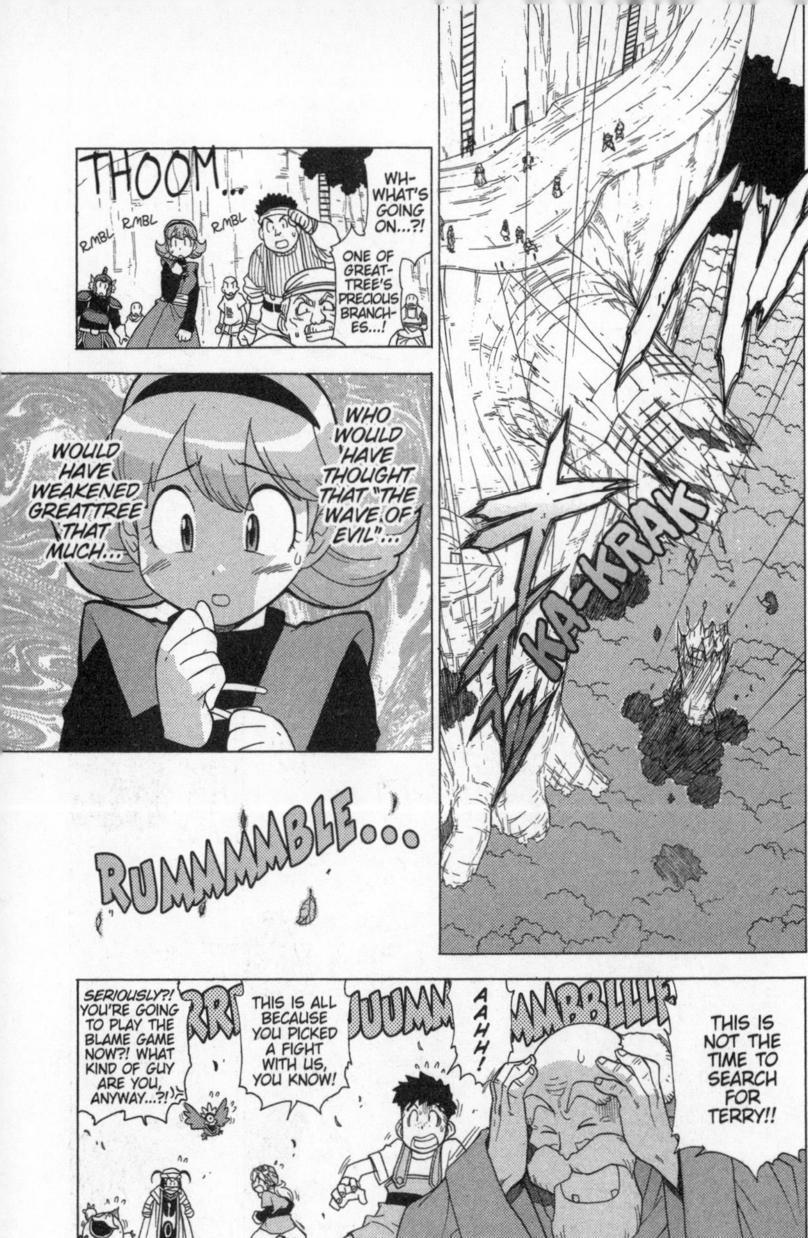
KA-KRAK
WH-WHAT'S GOING ON...?!
ONE OF GREAT-TREE'S PRECIOUS BRANCH-ES...!
THOOM...
RMBL
RMBL
RMBL
WHO WOULD HAVE THOUGHT THAT "THE WAVE OF EVIL"...
WOULD HAVE WEAKENED GREATTREE THAT MUCH...
RUMMMMBLE...
THIS IS NOT THE TIME TO SEARCH FOR TERRY!!
AAHH!
THIS IS ALL BECAUSE YOU PICKED A FIGHT WITH US, YOU KNOW!
SERIOUSLY?! YOU'RE GOING TO PLAY THE BLAME GAME NOW?! WHAT KIND OF GUY ARE YOU, ANYWAY...?!

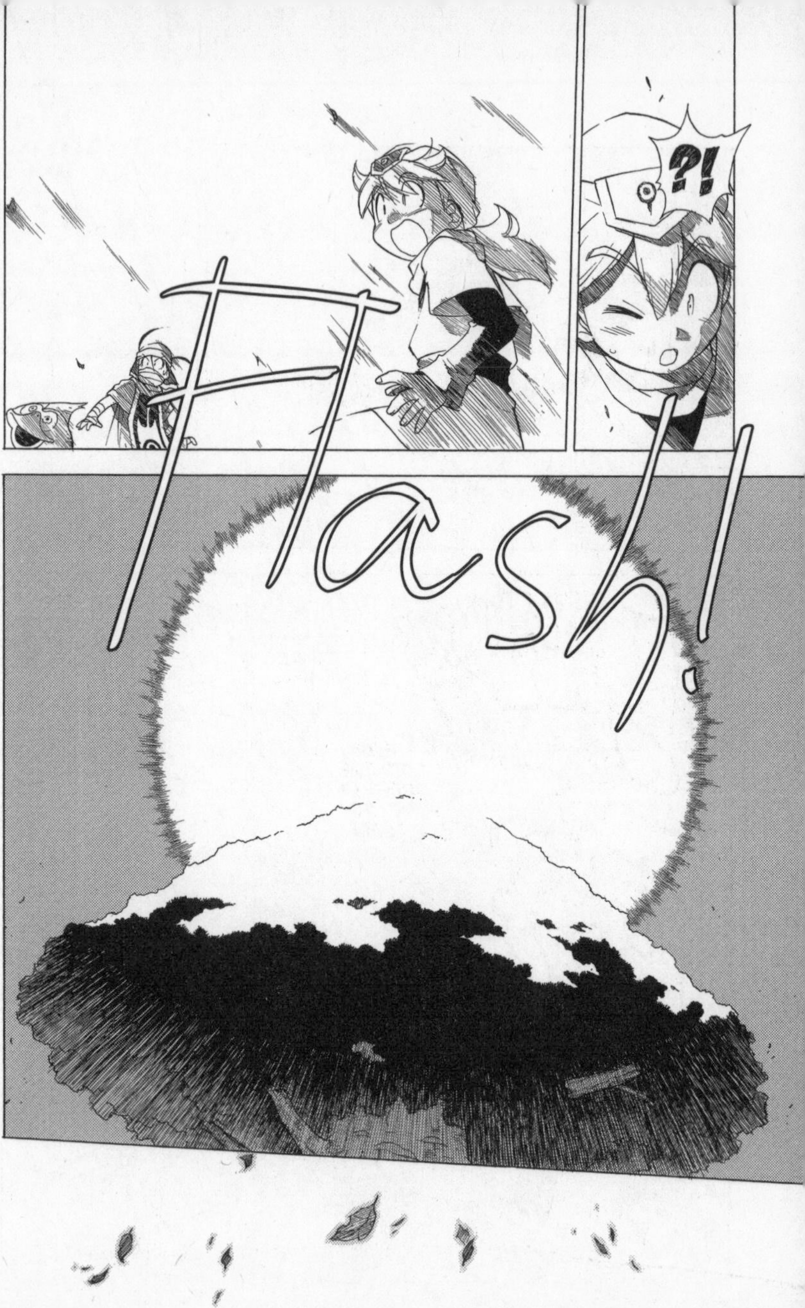
?!
Flash!

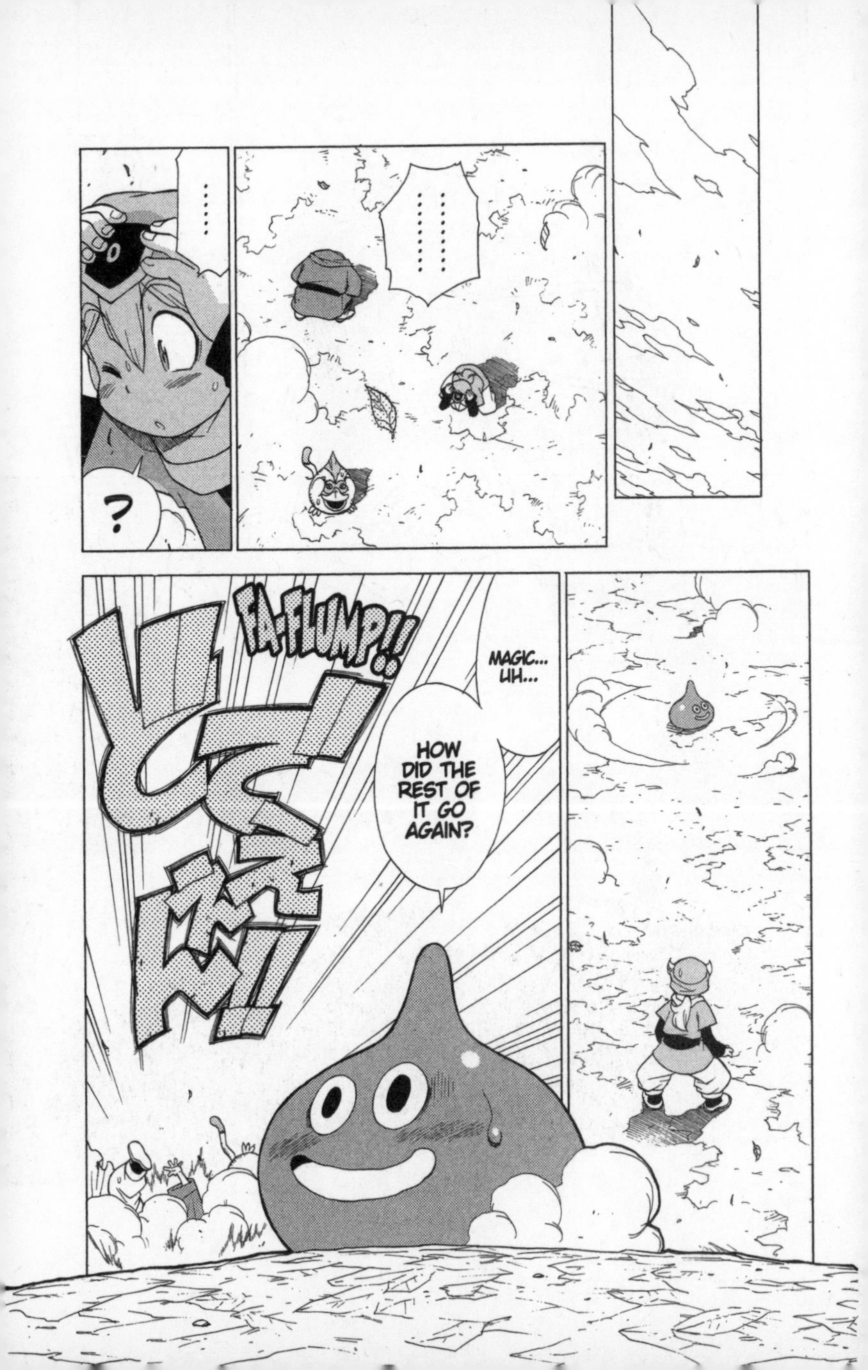
......
......
?
MAGIC... UH...
HOW DID THE REST OF IT GO AGAIN?
FA-FLUMP!!

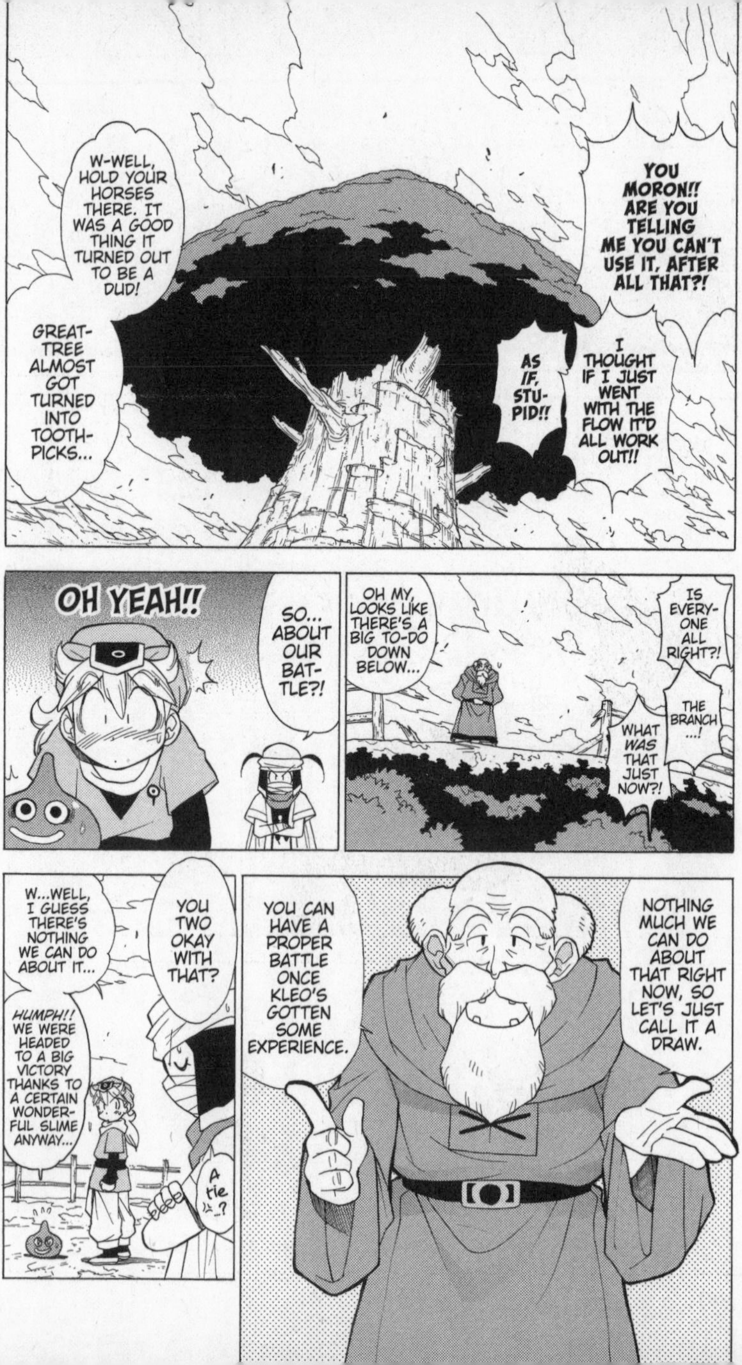
YOU MORON!! ARE YOU TELLING ME YOU CAN'T USE IT, AFTER ALL THAT?!
I THOUGHT IF I JUST WENT WITH THE FLOW IT'D ALL WORK OUT!!
AS IF, STUPID!!
W-WELL, HOLD YOUR HORSES THERE. IT WAS A GOOD THING IT TURNED OUT TO BE A DUD!
GREAT-TREE ALMOST GOT TURNED INTO TOOTH-PICKS...
IS EVERY-ONE ALL RIGHT?!
THE BRANCH...!
WHAT *WAS* THAT JUST NOW?!
OH MY, LOOKS LIKE THERE'S A BIG TO-DO DOWN BELOW...
SO... ABOUT OUR BATTLE?!
OH YEAH!!
NOTHING MUCH WE CAN DO ABOUT THAT RIGHT NOW, SO LET'S JUST CALL IT A DRAW.
YOU CAN HAVE A PROPER BATTLE ONCE KLEO'S GOTTEN SOME EXPERIENCE.
YOU TWO OKAY WITH THAT?
W...WELL, I GUESS THERE'S NOTHING WE CAN DO ABOUT IT...
A tie...?
HUMPH!! WE WERE HEADED TO A BIG VICTORY THANKS TO A CERTAIN WONDERFUL SLIME ANYWAY...

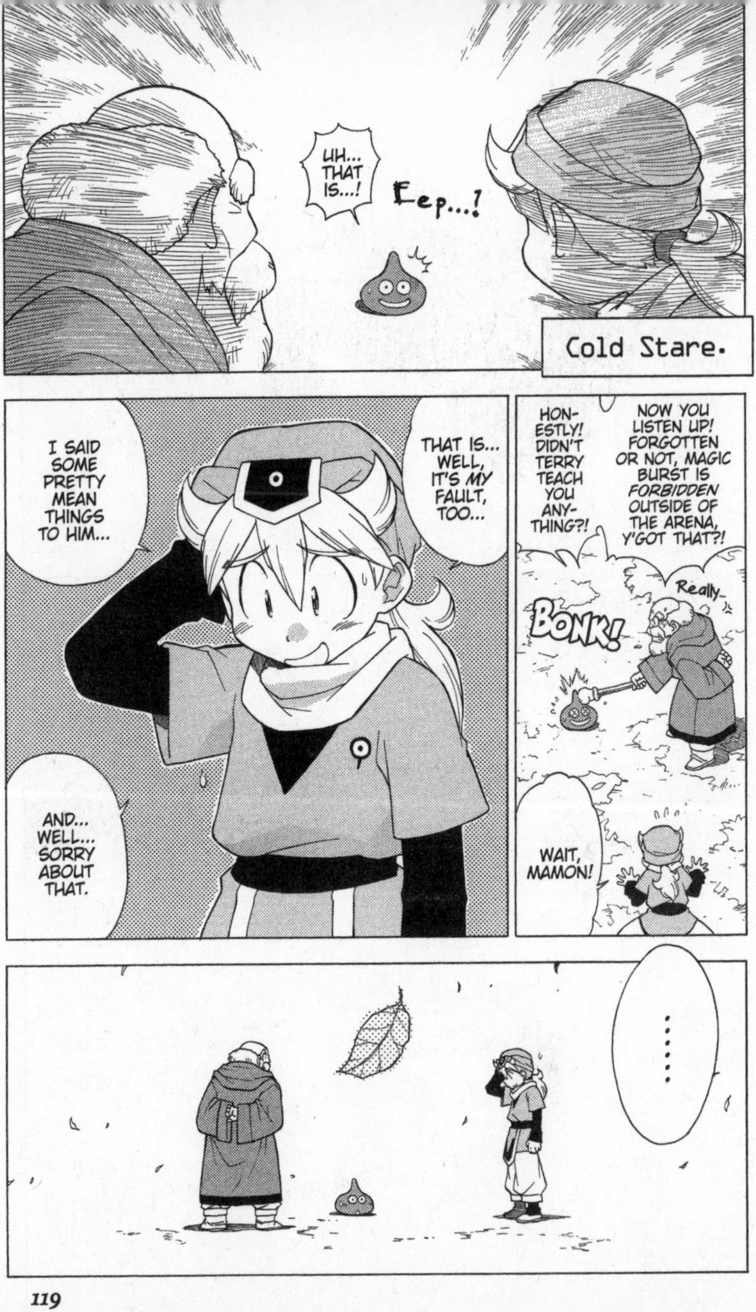
UH... THAT IS...!
Eep...!
Cold Stare.
NOW YOU LISTEN UP! FORGOTTEN OR NOT, MAGIC BURST IS *FORBIDDEN* OUTSIDE OF THE ARENA, Y'GOT THAT?!
HON-ESTLY! DIDN'T TERRY TEACH YOU ANY-THING?!
Really..
BONK!
WAIT, MAMON!
THAT IS... WELL, IT'S *MY* FAULT, TOO...
I SAID SOME PRETTY MEAN THINGS TO HIM...
AND... WELL... SORRY ABOUT THAT.
......

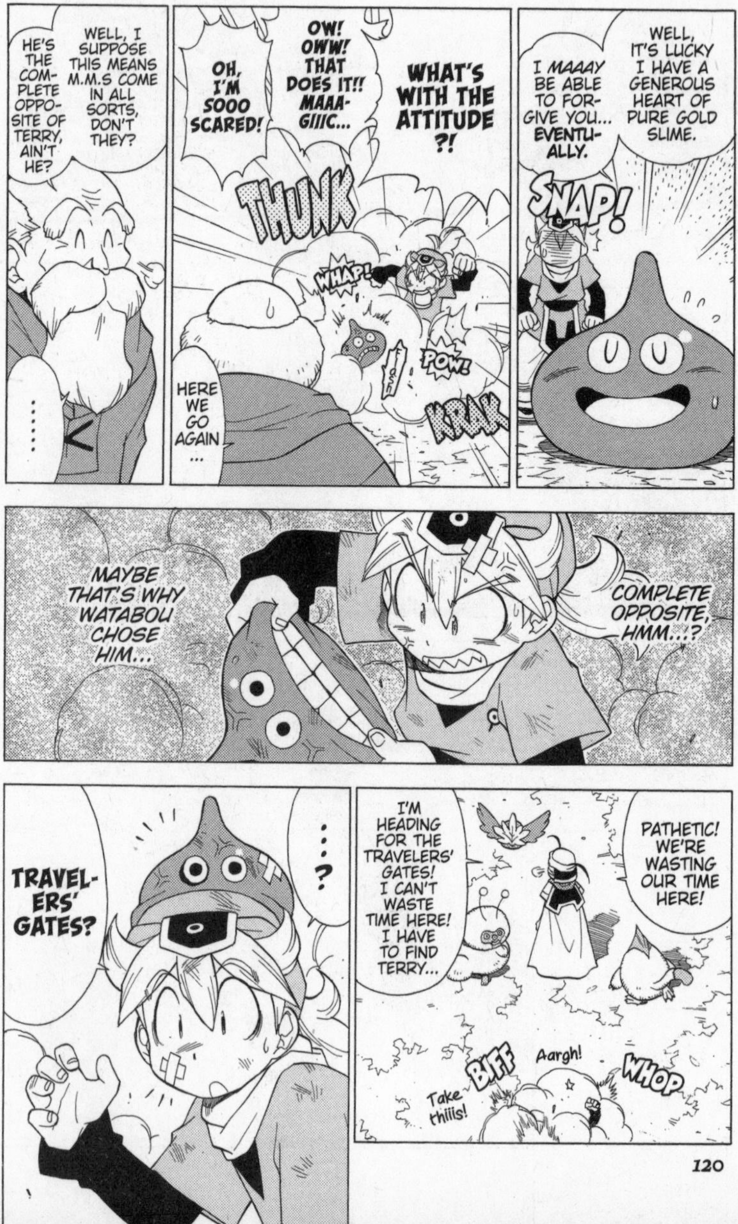
WELL, IT'S LUCKY I HAVE A GENEROUS HEART OF PURE GOLD SLIME.
I *MAAAY* BE ABLE TO FOR-GIVE YOU... EVENTU-ALLY.
SNAP!
WHAT'S WITH THE ATTITUDE?!
OW! OWW! THAT DOES IT!! MAAA-GIIIC...
OH, I'M SOOO SCARED!
THUNK
WHAP!
POW!
KRAK
HERE WE GO AGAIN...
WELL, I SUPPOSE THIS MEANS M.M.S COME IN ALL SORTS, DON'T THEY?
HE'S THE COM-PLETE OPPO-SITE OF TERRY, AIN'T HE?
......
COMPLETE OPPOSITE, HMM...?
MAYBE THAT'S WHY WATABOU CHOSE HIM...
PATHETIC! WE'RE WASTING OUR TIME HERE!
I'M HEADING FOR THE TRAVELERS' GATES! I CAN'T WASTE TIME HERE! I HAVE TO FIND TERRY...
WHOP
Aargh!
BIFF
Take thiiis!
...?
TRAVEL-ERS' GATES?

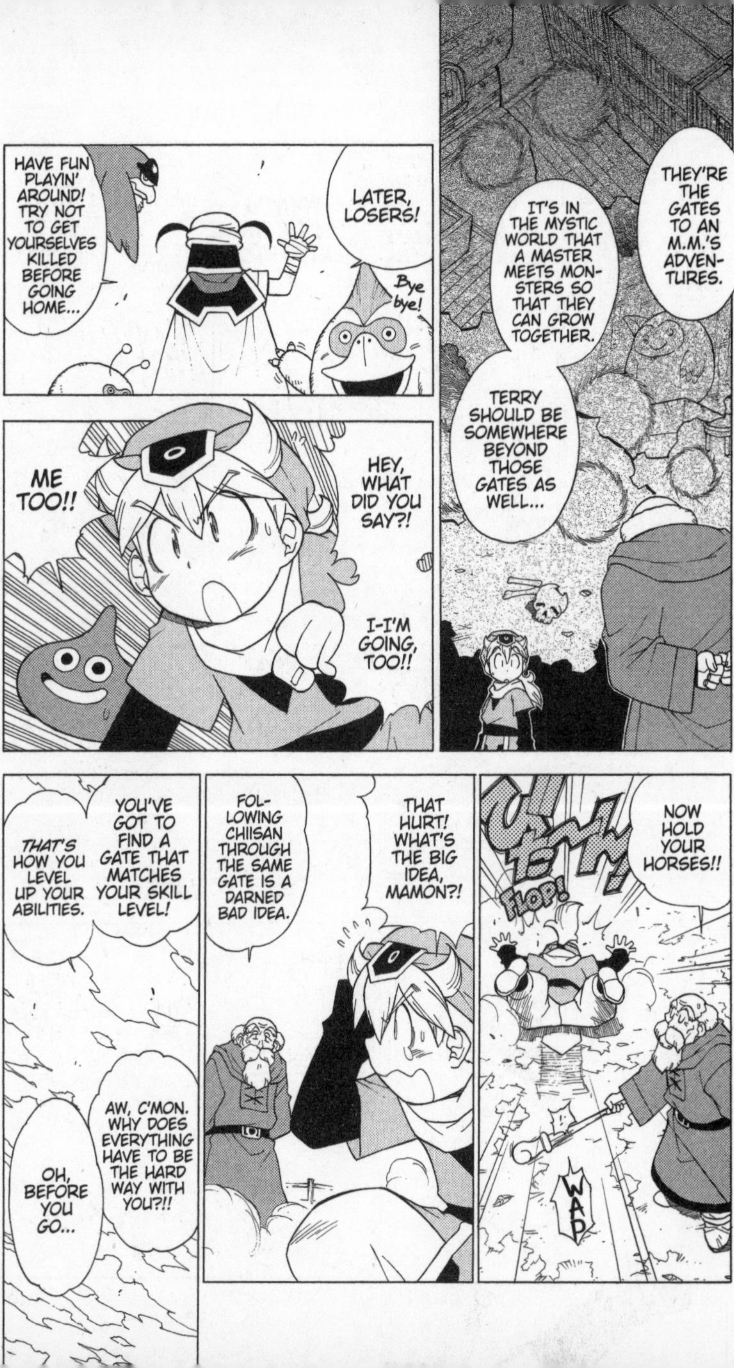

THEY'RE THE GATES TO AN M.M.'S ADVENTURES.
IT'S IN THE MYSTIC WORLD THAT A MASTER MEETS MONSTERS SO THAT THEY CAN GROW TOGETHER.
TERRY SHOULD BE SOMEWHERE BEYOND THOSE GATES AS WELL...
LATER, LOSERS!
Bye bye!
HAVE FUN PLAYIN' AROUND! TRY NOT TO GET YOURSELVES KILLED BEFORE GOING HOME...
HEY, WHAT DID YOU SAY?!
I-I'M GOING, TOO!!
ME TOO!!
NOW HOLD YOUR HORSES!!
FLOP!
WAP
THAT HURT! WHAT'S THE BIG IDEA, MAMON?!
FOLLOWING CHIISAN THROUGH THE SAME GATE IS A DARNED BAD IDEA.
YOU'VE GOT TO FIND A GATE THAT MATCHES YOUR SKILL LEVEL!
THAT'S HOW YOU LEVEL UP YOUR ABILITIES.
AW, C'MON. WHY DOES EVERYTHING HAVE TO BE THE HARD WAY WITH YOU?!!
OH, BEFORE YOU GO...

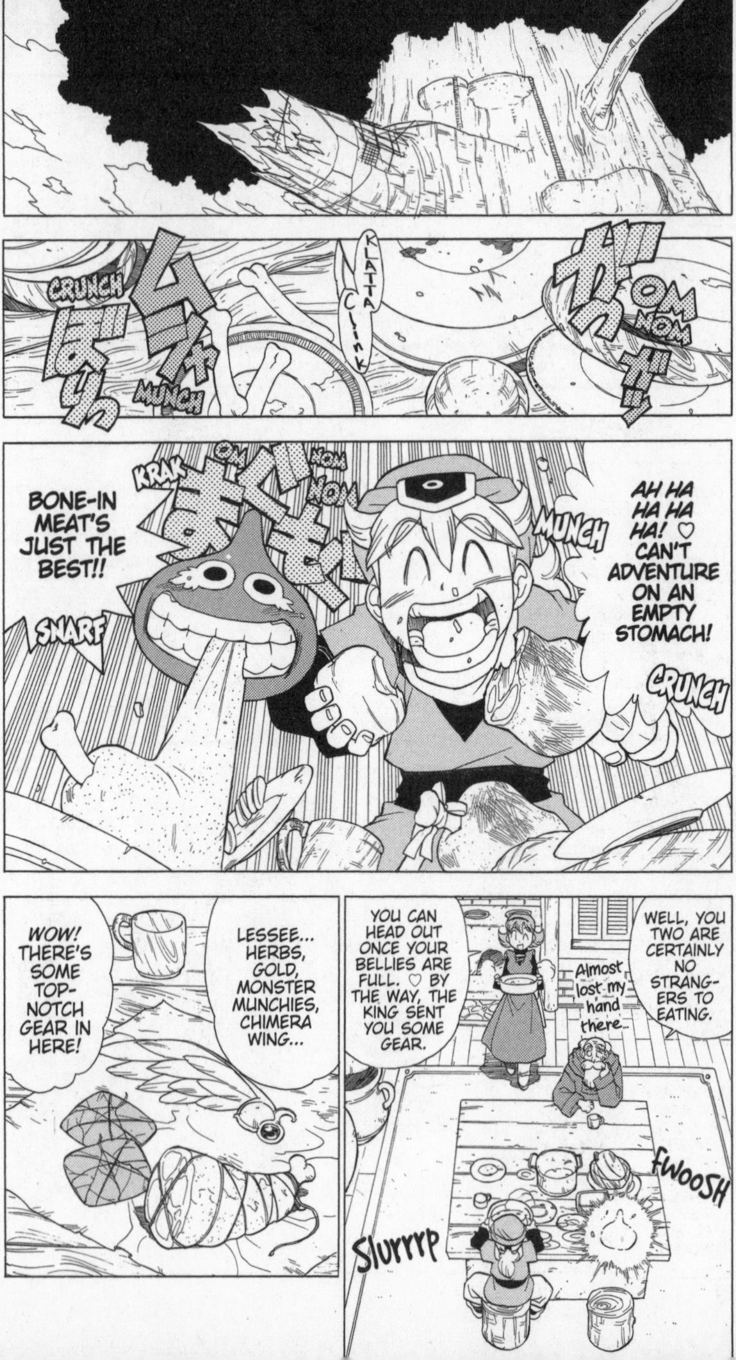OM NOM
KLATTA CLink
CRUNCH
MUNCH
AH HA HA HA HA! ♡ CAN'T ADVENTURE ON AN EMPTY STOMACH!
MUNCH
CRUNCH
OM NOM NOM
KRAK
BONE-IN MEAT'S JUST THE BEST!!
SNARF
WELL, YOU TWO ARE CERTAINLY NO STRANGERS TO EATING.
Almost lost my hand there...
YOU CAN HEAD OUT ONCE YOUR BELLIES ARE FULL. ♡ BY THE WAY, THE KING SENT YOU SOME GEAR.
FWOOSH
Slurrrp
LESSEE... HERBS, GOLD, MONSTER MUNCHIES, CHIMERA WING...
WOW! THERE'S SOME TOP-NOTCH GEAR IN HERE!

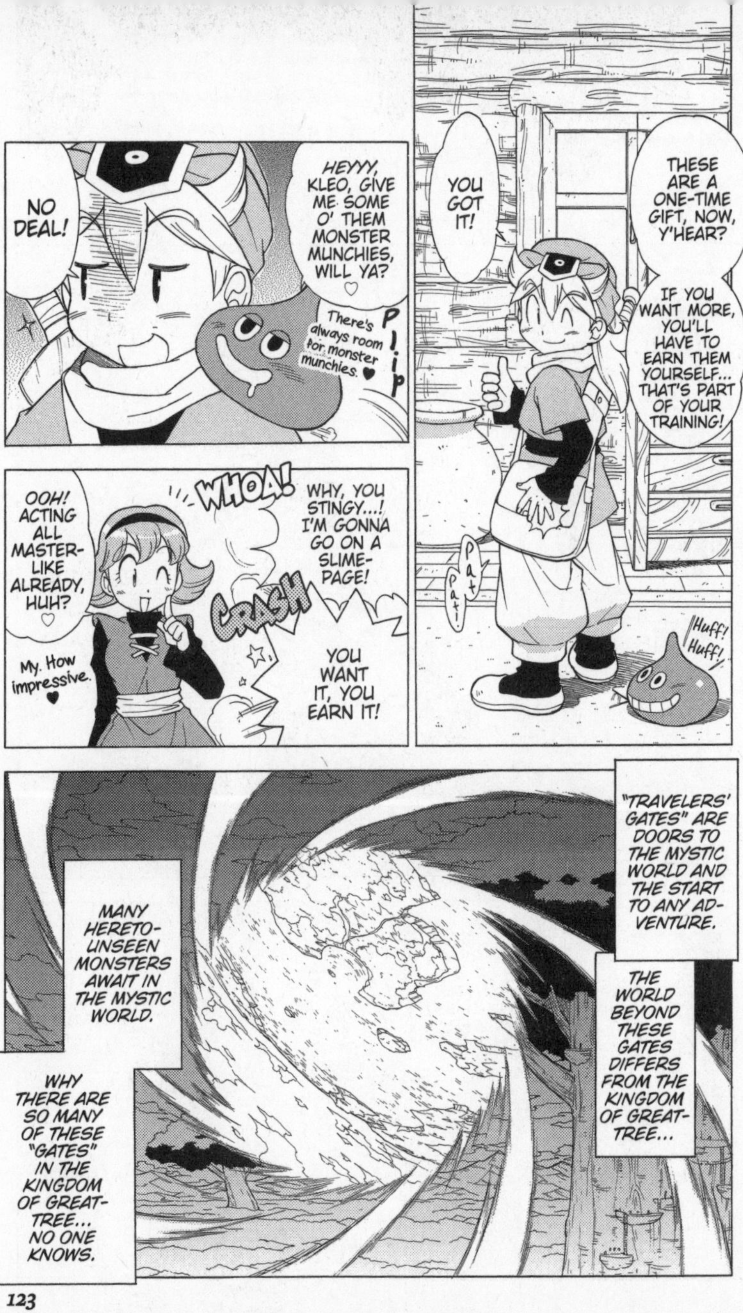

THESE ARE A ONE-TIME GIFT, NOW, Y'HEAR?
IF YOU WANT MORE, YOU'LL HAVE TO EARN THEM YOURSELF... THAT'S PART OF YOUR TRAINING!
YOU GOT IT!
Pat
Pat
Huff! Huff!
HEYYY, KLEO, GIVE ME SOME O' THEM MONSTER MUNCHIES, WILL YA? ♡
There's always room for monster munchies. ♥
Plip
NO DEAL!
WHY, YOU STINGY...! I'M GONNA GO ON A SLIME-PAGE!
WHOA!
YOU WANT IT, YOU EARN IT!
CRASH
OOH! ACTING ALL MASTER-LIKE ALREADY, HUH? ♡
My. How impressive. ♥
"TRAVELERS' GATES" ARE DOORS TO THE MYSTIC WORLD AND THE START TO ANY AD-VENTURE.
THE WORLD BEYOND THESE GATES DIFFERS FROM THE KINGDOM OF GREAT-TREE...
MANY HERETO-UNSEEN MONSTERS AWAIT IN THE MYSTIC WORLD.
WHY THERE ARE SO MANY OF THESE "GATES" IN THE KINGDOM OF GREAT-TREE... NO ONE KNOWS.

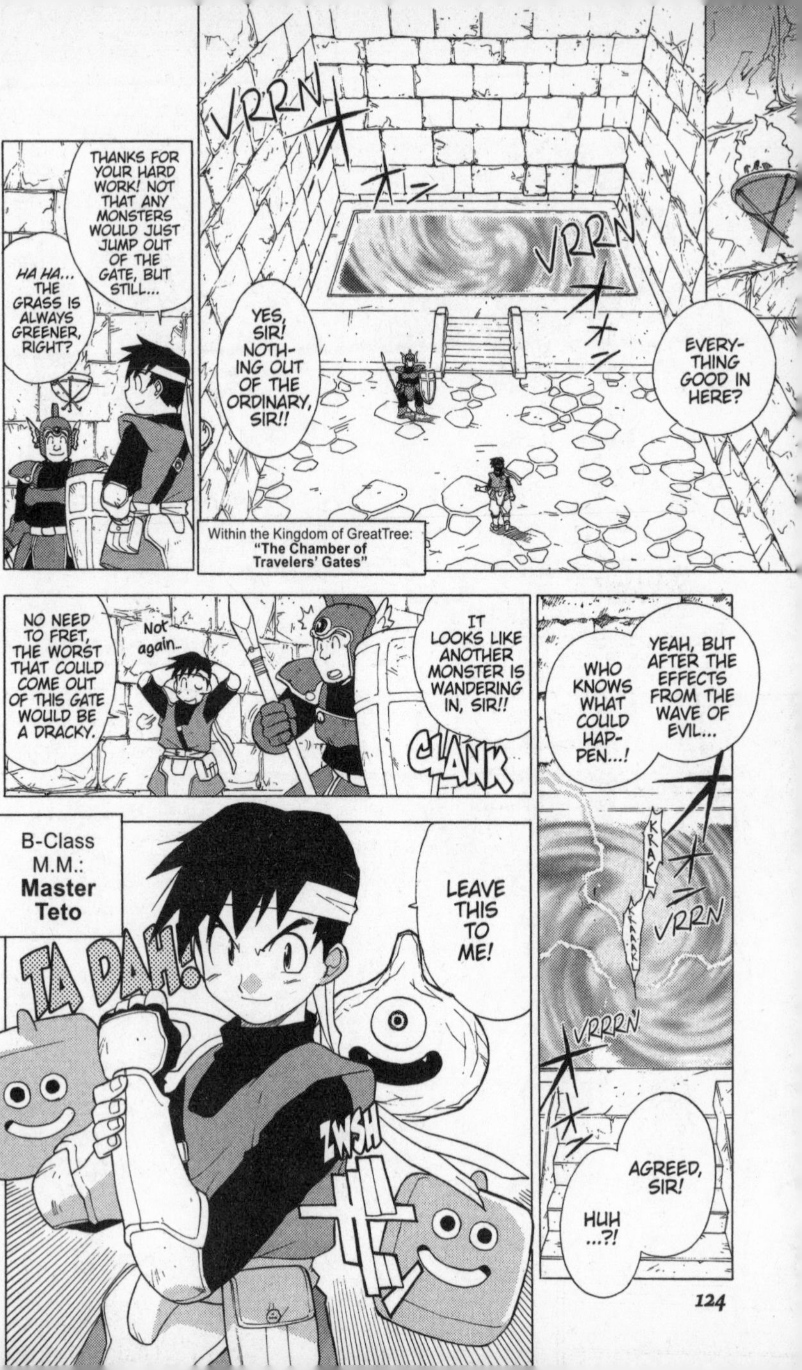
VRRN
EVERY-THING GOOD IN HERE?
VRRN
YES, SIR! NOTH-ING OUT OF THE ORDINARY, SIR!!
Within the Kingdom of GreatTree: "The Chamber of Travelers' Gates"
THANKS FOR YOUR HARD WORK! NOT THAT ANY MONSTERS WOULD JUST JUMP OUT OF THE GATE, BUT STILL...
HA HA... THE GRASS IS ALWAYS GREENER, RIGHT?
YEAH, BUT AFTER THE EFFECTS FROM THE WAVE OF EVIL...
WHO KNOWS WHAT COULD HAP-PEN...!
KRAKL
VRRN
KRAAKL
VRRRN
AGREED, SIR!
HUH ...?!
IT LOOKS LIKE ANOTHER MONSTER IS WANDERING IN, SIR!!
CLANK
Not again..
NO NEED TO FRET, THE WORST THAT COULD COME OUT OF THIS GATE WOULD BE A DRACKY.
LEAVE THIS TO ME!
B-Class M.M.: Master Teto
TA DAH!
ZWSH

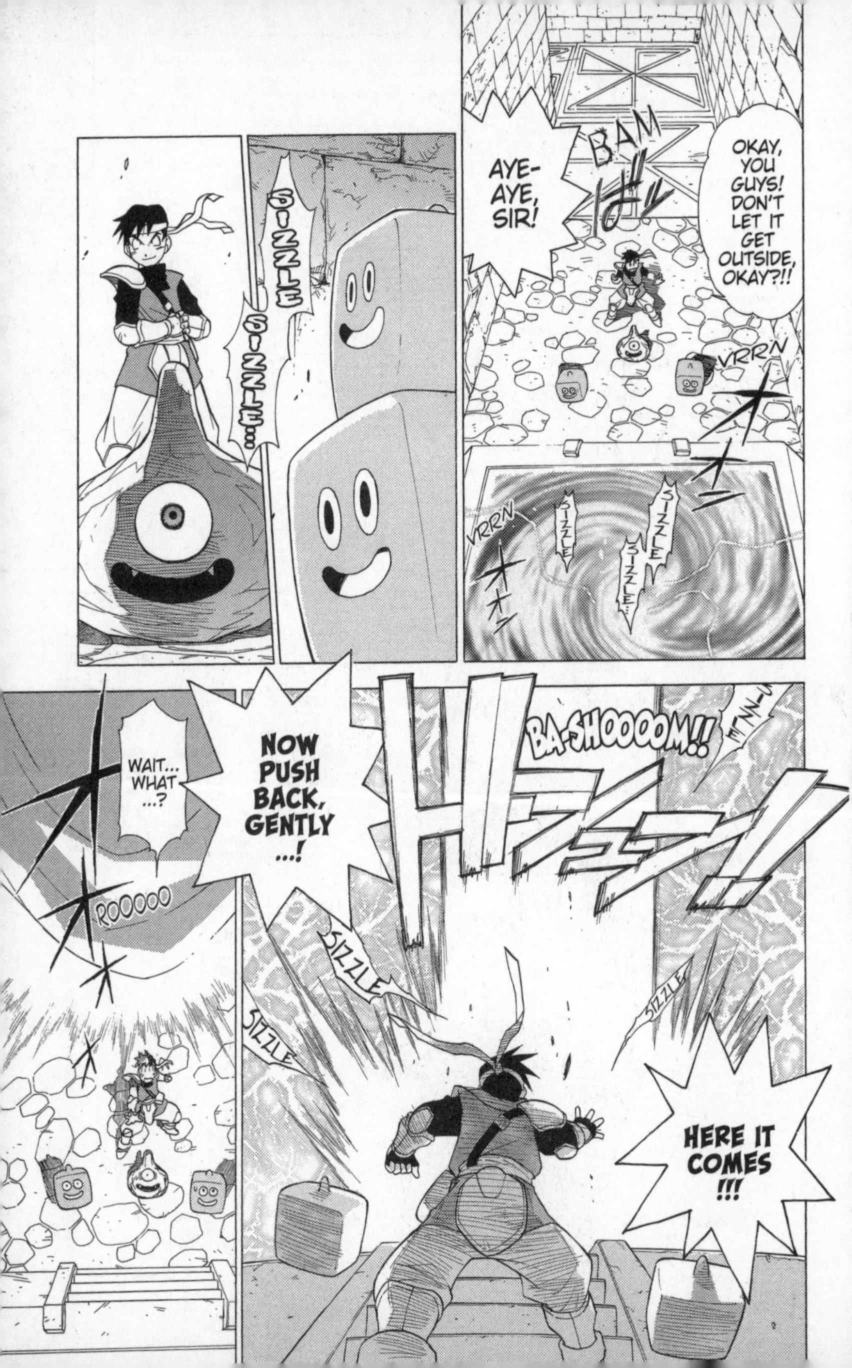
OKAY, YOU GUYS! DON'T LET IT GET OUTSIDE, OKAY?!!
BAM
AYE-AYE, SIR!
VRRN
SIZZLE
SIZZLE
SIZZLE...
VRRN
SIZZLE
SIZZLE...
BA-SHOOOOM!!
SIZZLE
SIZZLE
SIZZLE
HERE IT COMES!!!
NOW PUSH BACK, GENTLY...!
WAIT... WHAT...?
ROOOOO

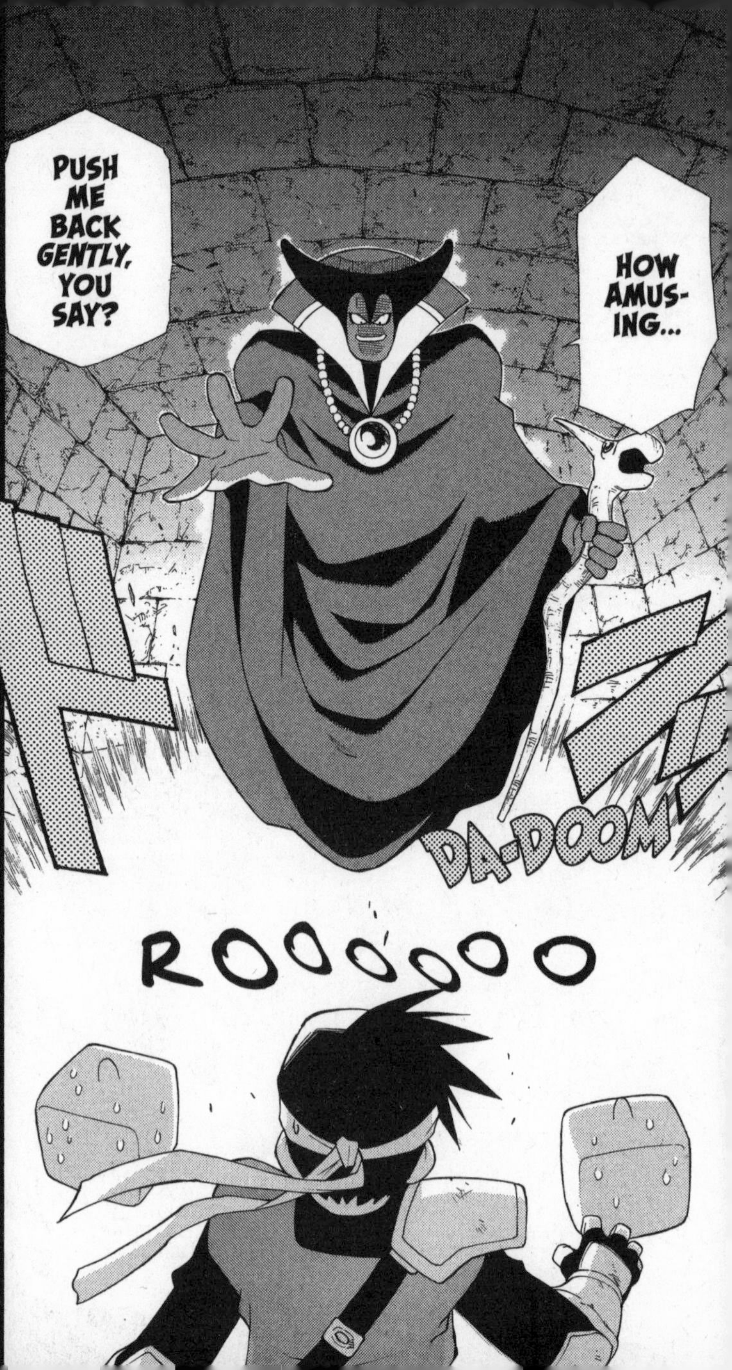
PUSH ME BACK GENTLY, YOU SAY?
HOW AMUS-ING...
DA-DOOM
ROOOOOO

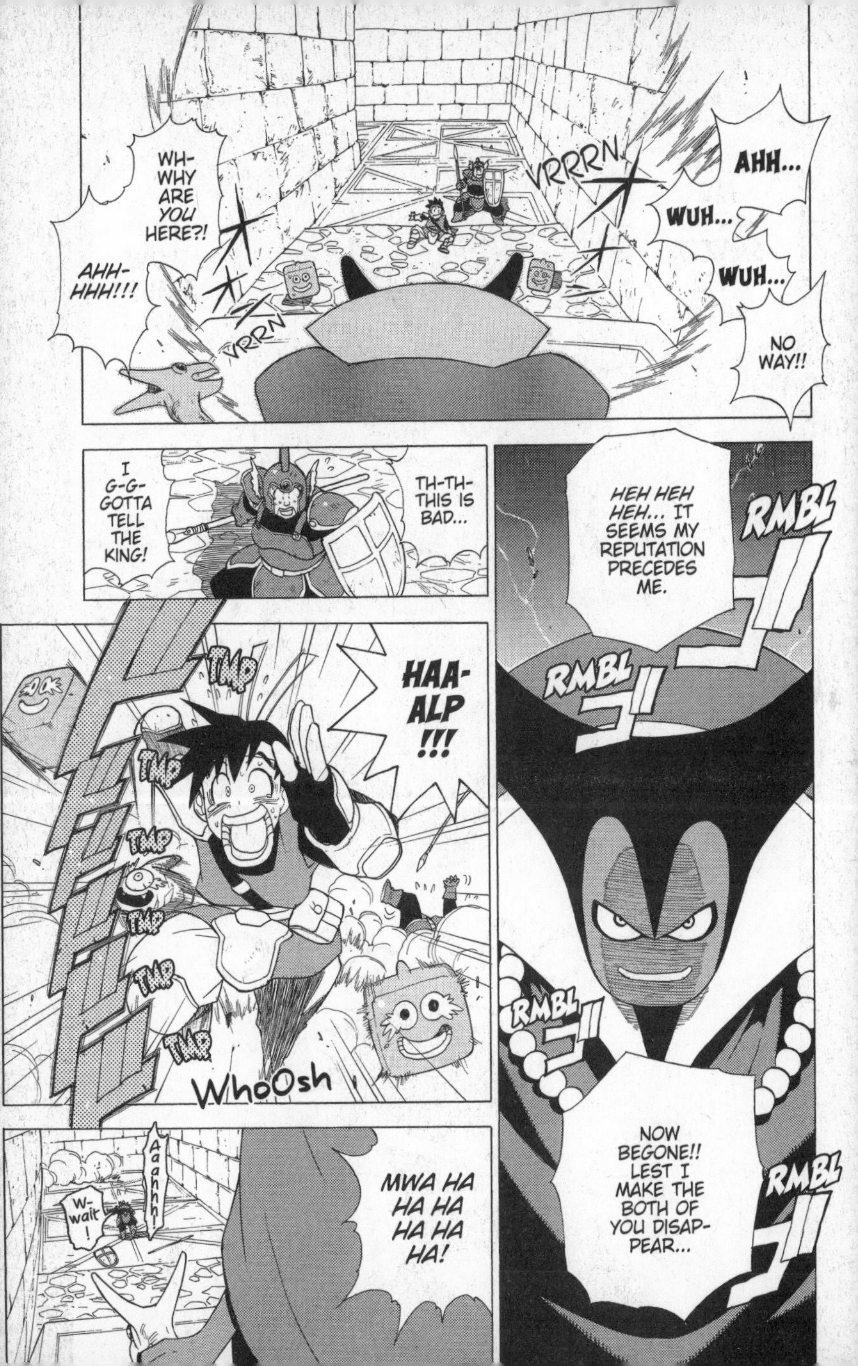
AHH...
VRRRN
WUH...
WUH...
WH-WHY ARE YOU HERE?!
NO WAY!!
AHH-HHH!!!
VRRN
HEH HEH HEH... IT SEEMS MY REPUTATION PRECEDES ME.
RMBL
RMBL
RMBL
NOW BEGONE!! LEST I MAKE THE BOTH OF YOU DISAP-PEAR...
RMBL
TH-TH-THIS IS BAD...
I G-G-GOTTA TELL THE KING!
HAA-ALP!!!
TMP
TMP
TMP
TMP
TMP
TMP
WhoOsh
MWA HA HA HA HA HA HA!
Aaahhh!
W-wait!

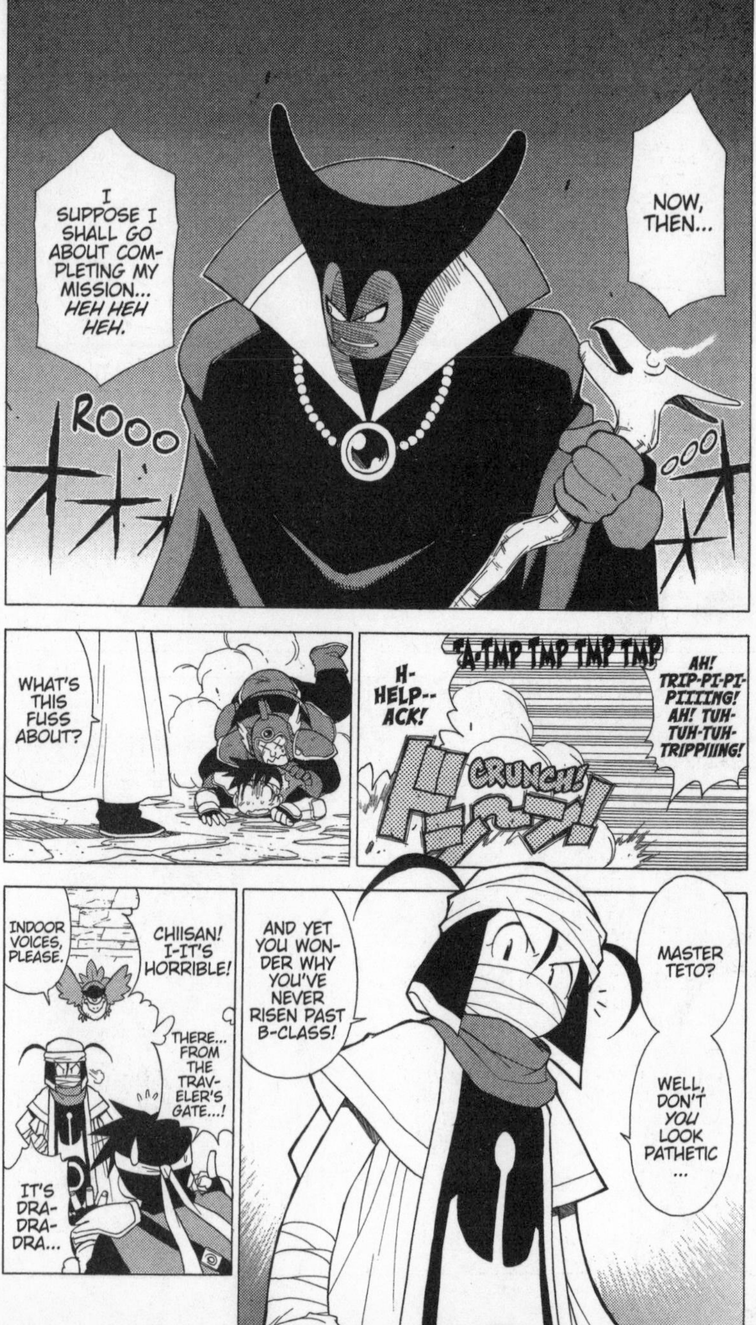
NOW, THEN...
I SUPPOSE I SHALL GO ABOUT COMPLETING MY MISSION... HEH HEH HEH.
ROOOOOO
*A-TMP TMP TMP TMP
AH! TRIP-PI-PI-PIIIING! AH! TUH-TUH-TUH-TRIPPIIING!
H-HELP--ACK!
CRUNCH!
WHAT'S THIS FUSS ABOUT?
MASTER TETO?
WELL, DON'T YOU LOOK PATHETIC ...
AND YET YOU WONDER WHY YOU'VE NEVER RISEN PAST B-CLASS!
CHIISAN! I-IT'S HORRIBLE!
INDOOR VOICES, PLEASE.
THERE... FROM THE TRAVELER'S GATE...!
IT'S DRA-DRA-DRA...

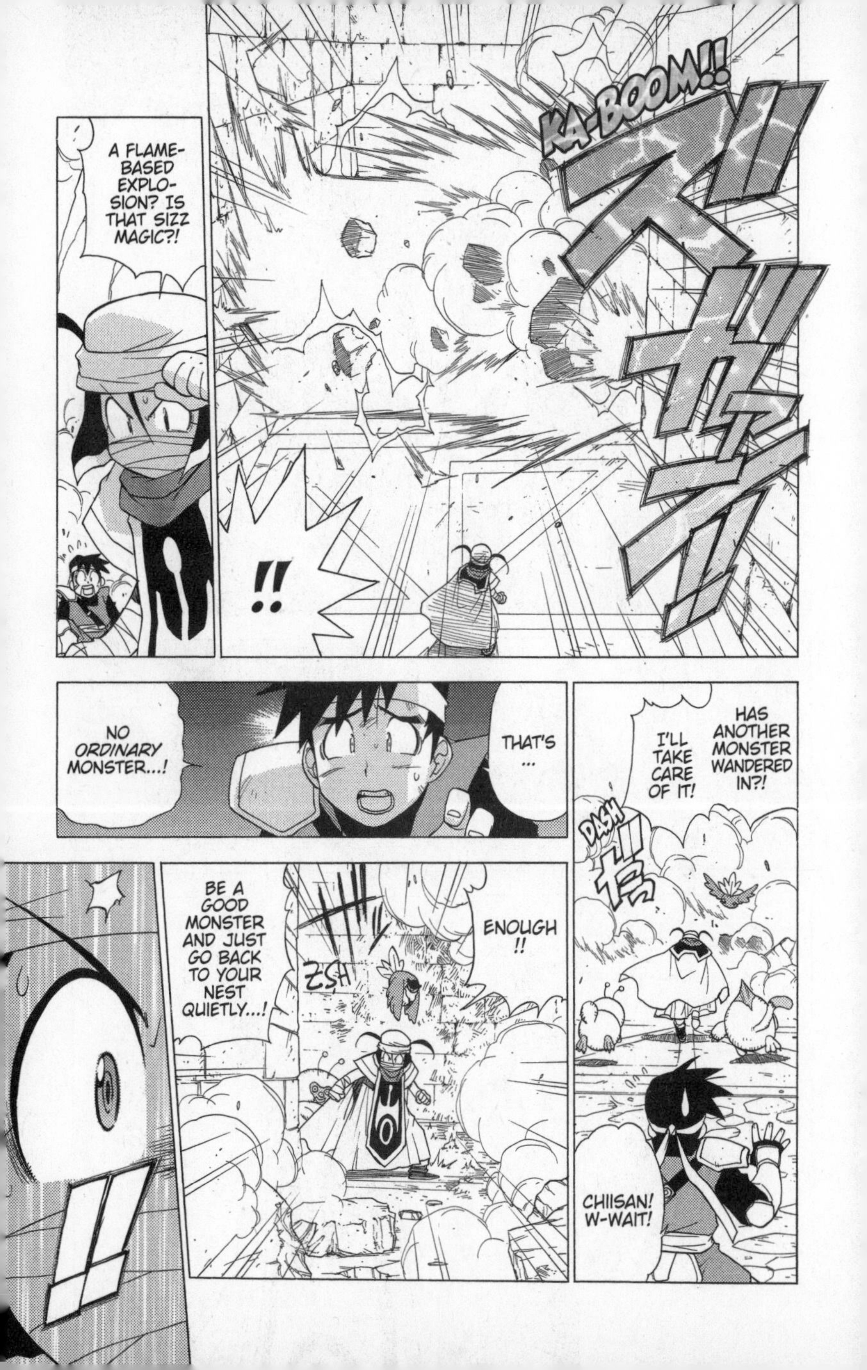
KA-BOOM!!
!!
A FLAME-BASED EXPLOSION? IS THAT SIZZ MAGIC?!
HAS ANOTHER MONSTER WANDERED IN?!
I'LL TAKE CARE OF IT!
DASH
CHIISAN! W-WAIT!
THAT'S...
NO ORDINARY MONSTER...!
ENOUGH!!
ZSH
BE A GOOD MONSTER AND JUST GO BACK TO YOUR NEST QUIETLY...!
!!

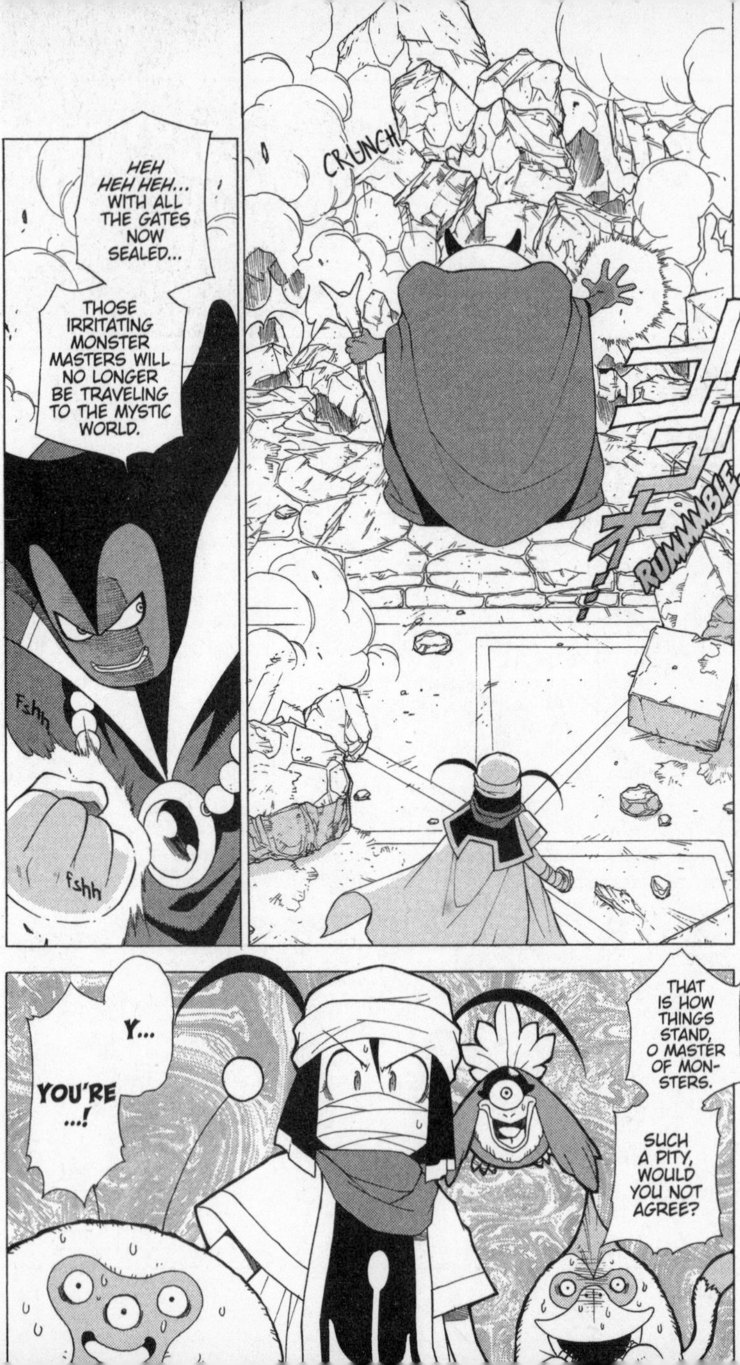
CRUNCH!
RUMMMBLE OOO
HEH HEH HEH... WITH ALL THE GATES NOW SEALED...
THOSE IRRITATING MONSTER MASTERS WILL NO LONGER BE TRAVELING TO THE MYSTIC WORLD.
fshh
fshh
THAT IS HOW THINGS STAND, O MASTER OF MON-STERS.
SUCH A PITY, WOULD YOU NOT AGREE?
Y...
YOU'RE ...!

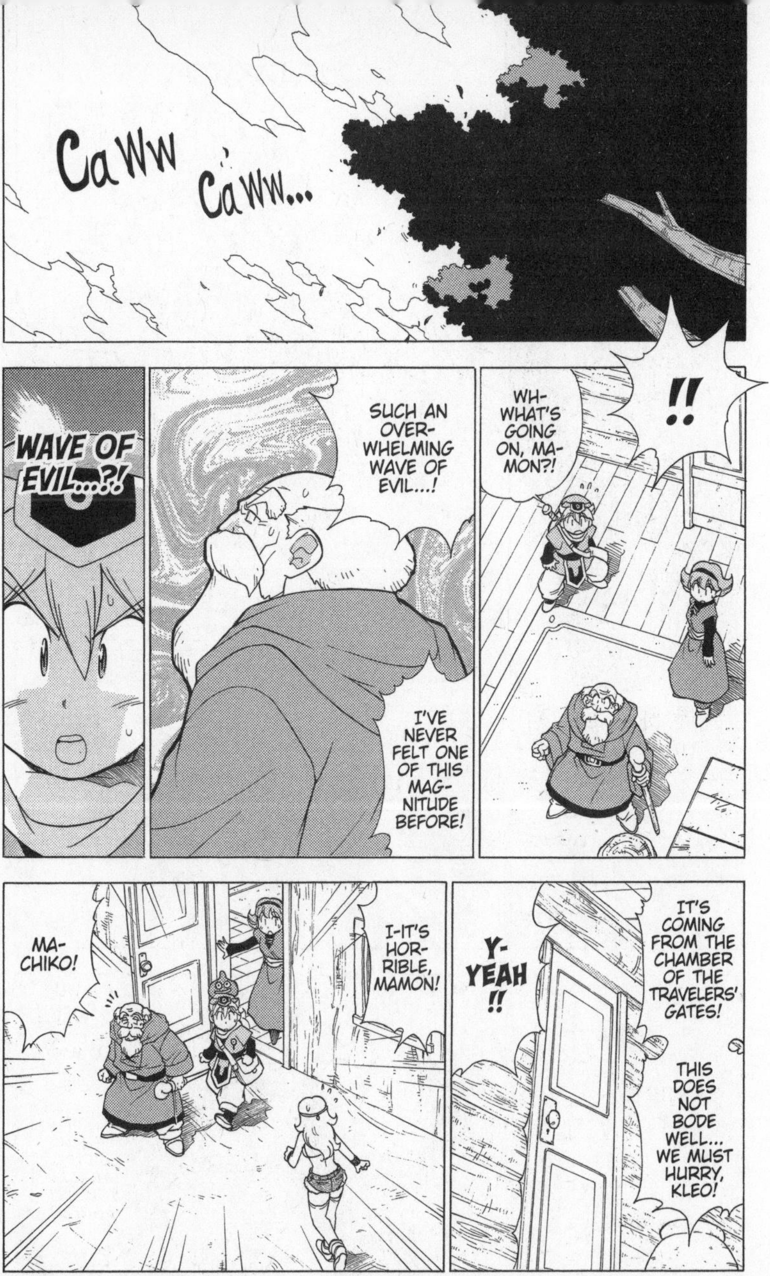
CAWW CAWW...
!!
WH-WHAT'S GOING ON, MAMON?!
SUCH AN OVERWHELMING WAVE OF EVIL...!
I'VE NEVER FELT ONE OF THIS MAGNITUDE BEFORE!
WAVE OF EVIL...?!
IT'S COMING FROM THE CHAMBER OF THE TRAVELERS' GATES!
THIS DOES NOT BODE WELL... WE MUST HURRY, KLEO!
Y-YEAH!!
I-IT'S HORRIBLE, MAMON!
MACHIKO!

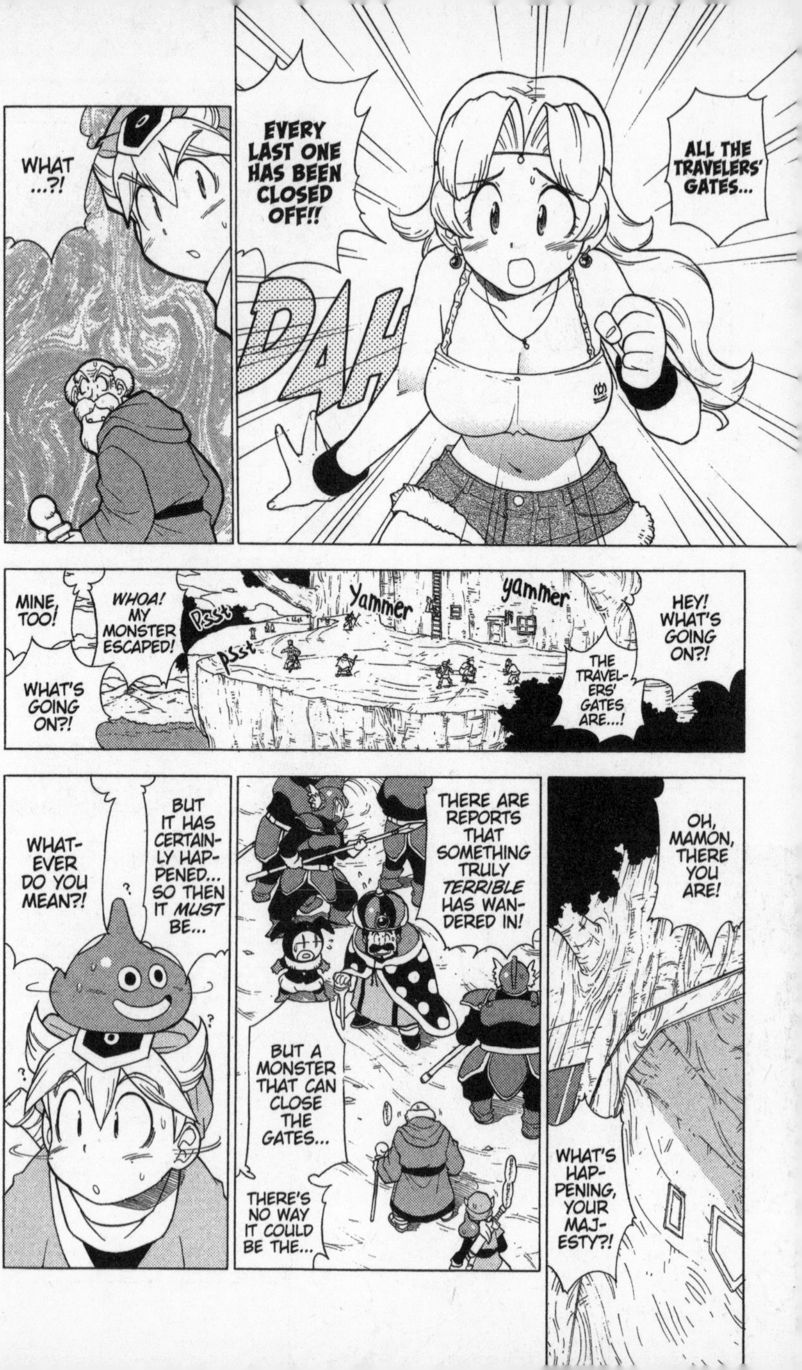
ALL THE TRAVELERS' GATES...
EVERY LAST ONE HAS BEEN CLOSED OFF!!
DAH
WHAT ...?!
HEY! WHAT'S GOING ON?!
THE TRAVELERS' GATES ARE...!
yammer
yammer
psst
psst
WHOA! MY MONSTER ESCAPED!
MINE, TOO!
WHAT'S GOING ON?!
OH, MAMON, THERE YOU ARE!
WHAT'S HAPPENING, YOUR MAJESTY?!
THERE ARE REPORTS THAT SOMETHING TRULY *TERRIBLE* HAS WANDERED IN!
BUT A MONSTER THAT CAN CLOSE THE GATES...
THERE'S NO WAY IT COULD BE THE...
BUT IT HAS CERTAINLY HAPPENED... SO THEN IT *MUST* BE...
WHATEVER DO YOU MEAN?!

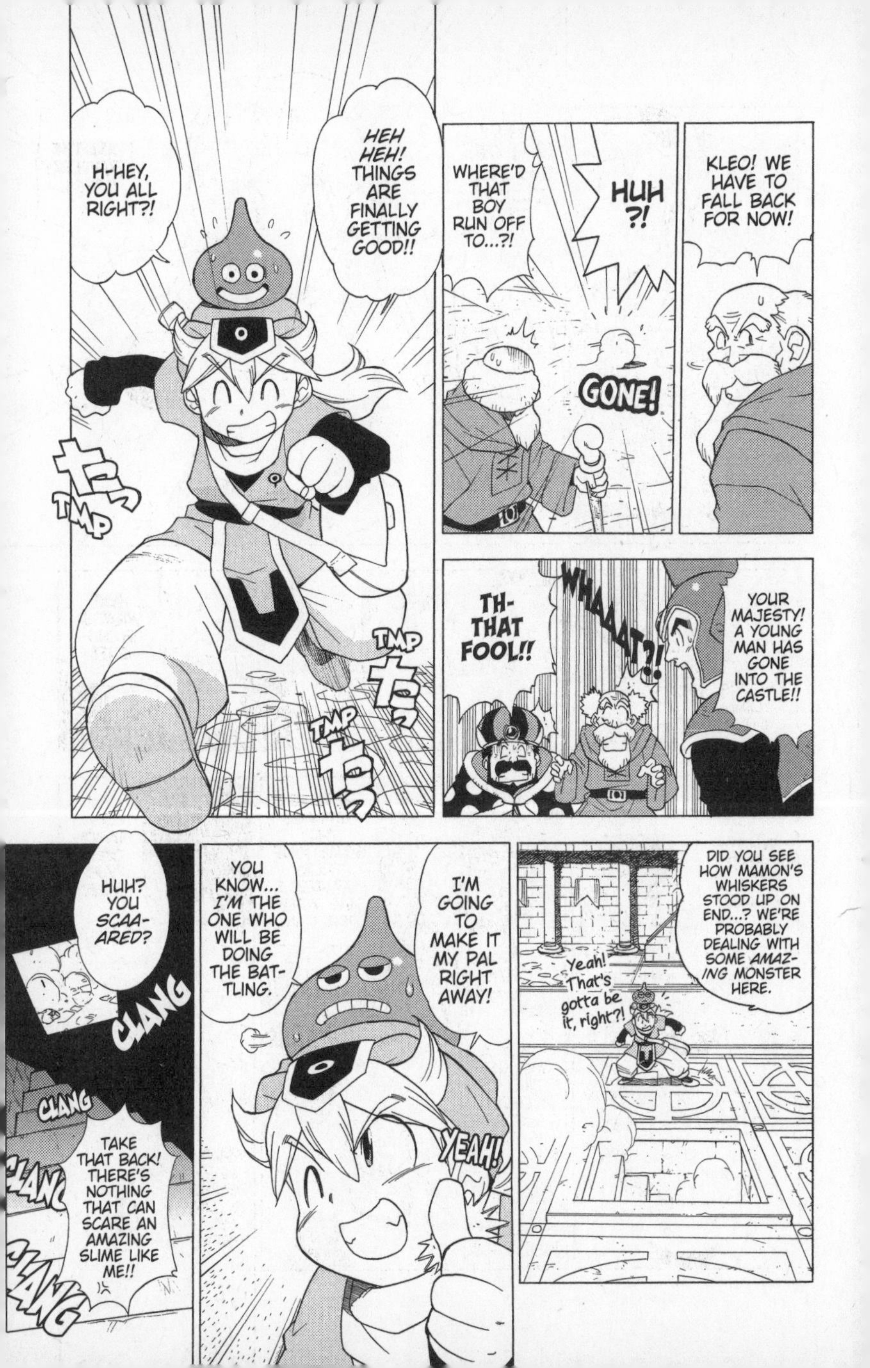
KLEO! WE HAVE TO FALL BACK FOR NOW!
WHERE'D THAT BOY RUN OFF TO...?!
HUH ?!
GONE!
YOUR MAJESTY! A YOUNG MAN HAS GONE INTO THE CASTLE!!
WHAAAT?!
TH-THAT FOOL!!
HEH HEH! THINGS ARE FINALLY GETTING GOOD!!
H-HEY, YOU ALL RIGHT?!
TMP
TMP
TMP
DID YOU SEE HOW MAMON'S WHISKERS STOOD UP ON END...? WE'RE PROBABLY DEALING WITH SOME *AMAZING* MONSTER HERE.
Yeah! That's gotta be it, right?!
I'M GOING TO MAKE IT MY PAL RIGHT AWAY!
YOU KNOW... *I'M* THE ONE WHO WILL BE DOING THE BATTLING.
YEAH!
HUH? YOU *SCAA-ARED*?
CLANG
CLANG
TAKE THAT BACK! THERE'S NOTHING THAT CAN SCARE AN AMAZING SLIME LIKE ME!!
CLANG
CLANG

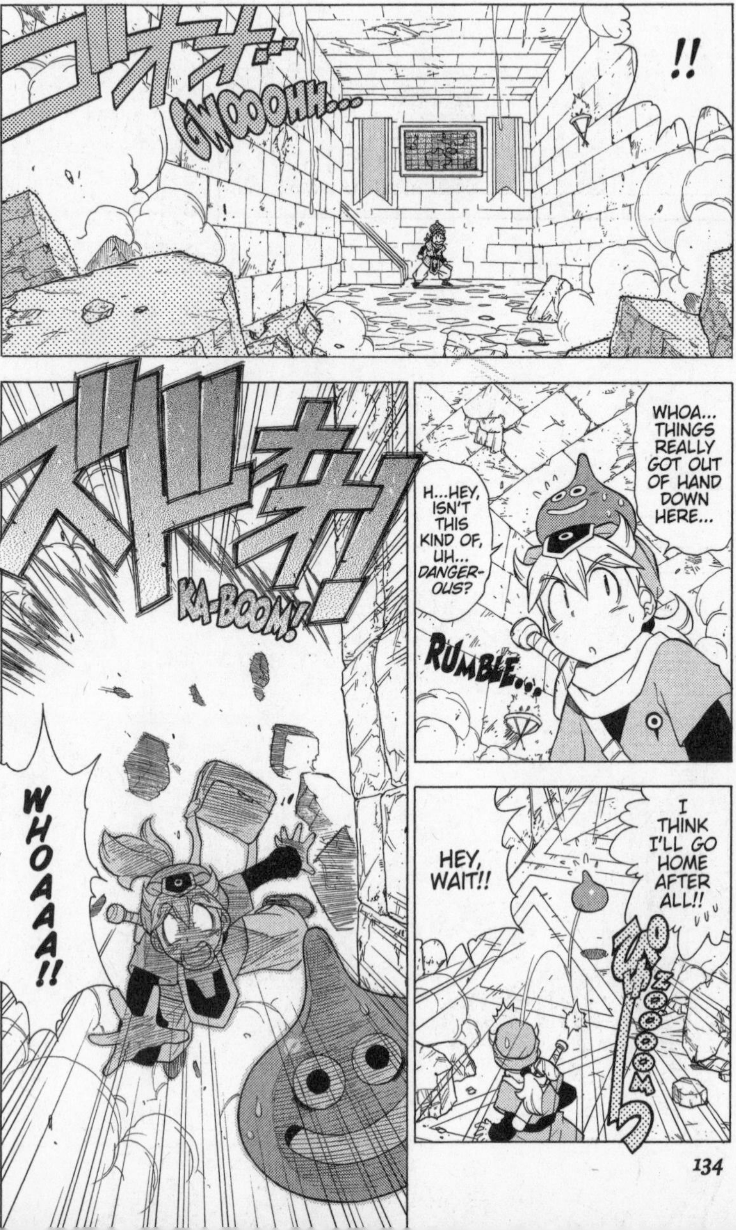
GWOOOHH...
!!
WHOA... THINGS REALLY GOT OUT OF HAND DOWN HERE...
H...HEY, ISN'T THIS KIND OF, UH... DANGER-OUS?
RUMBLE...
I THINK I'LL GO HOME AFTER ALL!!
HEY, WAIT!!
ZOOOOOM
KA-BOOM!
WHOAAAA!!

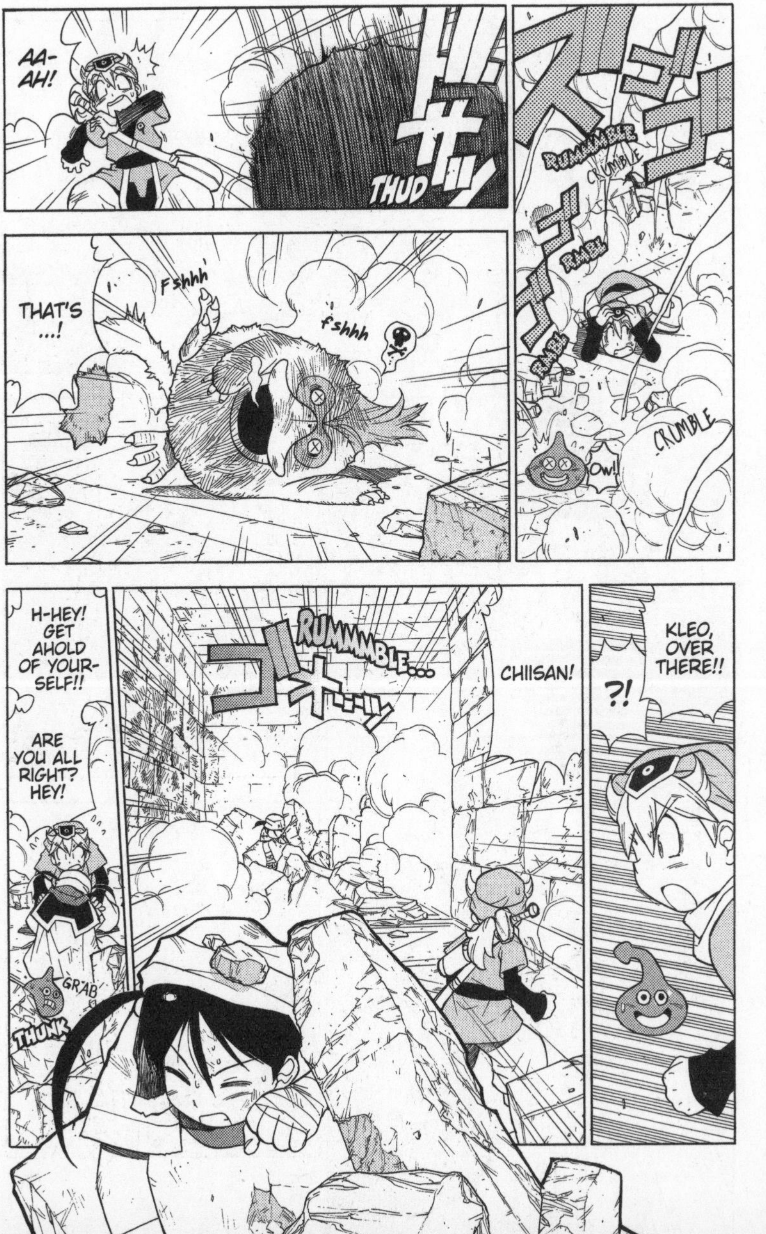
RUMMMMBLE
CRUMBLE
RMBL
RMBL
CRUMBLE
OW!
THUD
AA-AH!
fshhh
fshhh
THAT'S ...!
KLEO, OVER THERE!!
?!
RUMMMBLE...
CHIISAN!
H-HEY! GET AHOLD OF YOURSELF!!
ARE YOU ALL RIGHT? HEY!
GRAB
THUNK

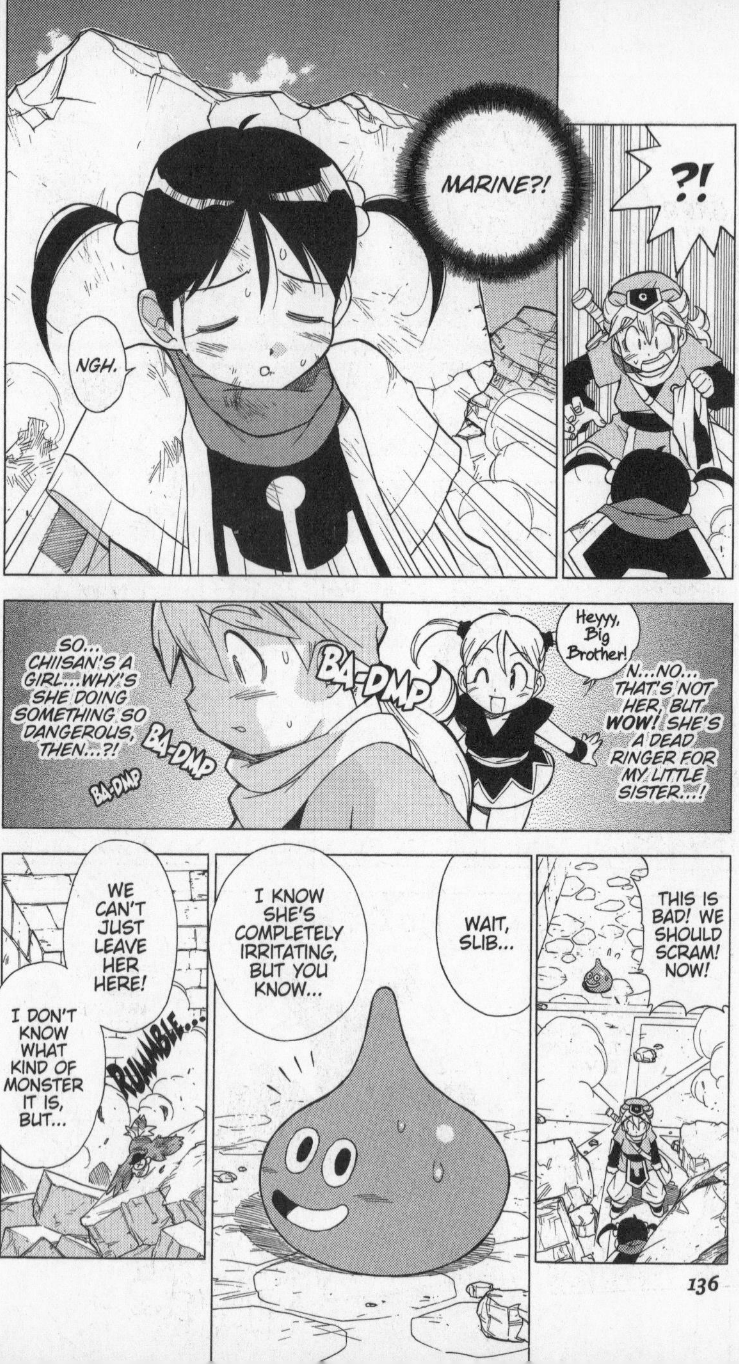
?!
MARINE?!
NGH.
Heyyy, Big Brother!
N...NO... THAT'S NOT HER, BUT WOW! SHE'S A DEAD RINGER FOR MY LITTLE SISTER...!
BA-DMP
BA-DMP
SO... CHIISAN'S A GIRL...WHY'S SHE DOING SOMETHING SO DANGEROUS, THEN...?!
BA-DMP
THIS IS BAD! WE SHOULD SCRAM! NOW!
WAIT, SLIB...
I KNOW SHE'S COMPLETELY IRRITATING, BUT YOU KNOW...
WE CAN'T JUST LEAVE HER HERE!
RUMMBLE...
I DON'T KNOW WHAT KIND OF MONSTER IT IS, BUT...

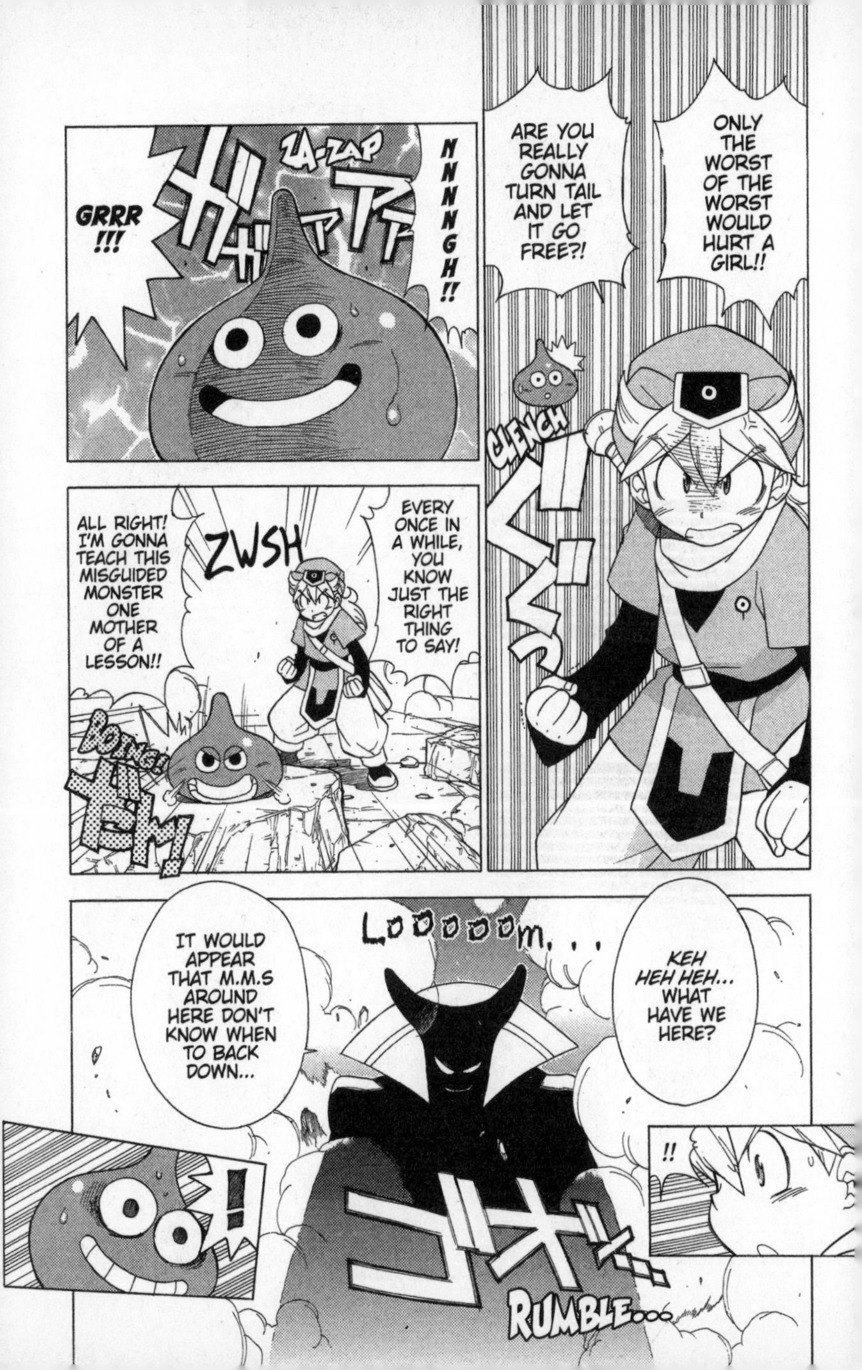
ONLY THE WORST OF THE WORST WOULD HURT A GIRL!!
ARE YOU REALLY GONNA TURN TAIL AND LET IT GO FREE?!
CLENCH
NNNNNGH!!
ZA-ZAP
GRRR!!!
EVERY ONCE IN A WHILE, YOU KNOW JUST THE RIGHT THING TO SAY!
ZWSH
ALL RIGHT! I'M GONNA TEACH THIS MISGUIDED MONSTER ONE MOTHER OF A LESSON!!
BOING!
KEH HEH HEH... WHAT HAVE WE HERE?
LOOOOOOM...
IT WOULD APPEAR THAT M.M.S AROUND HERE DON'T KNOW WHEN TO BACK DOWN...
!!
RUMBLE...

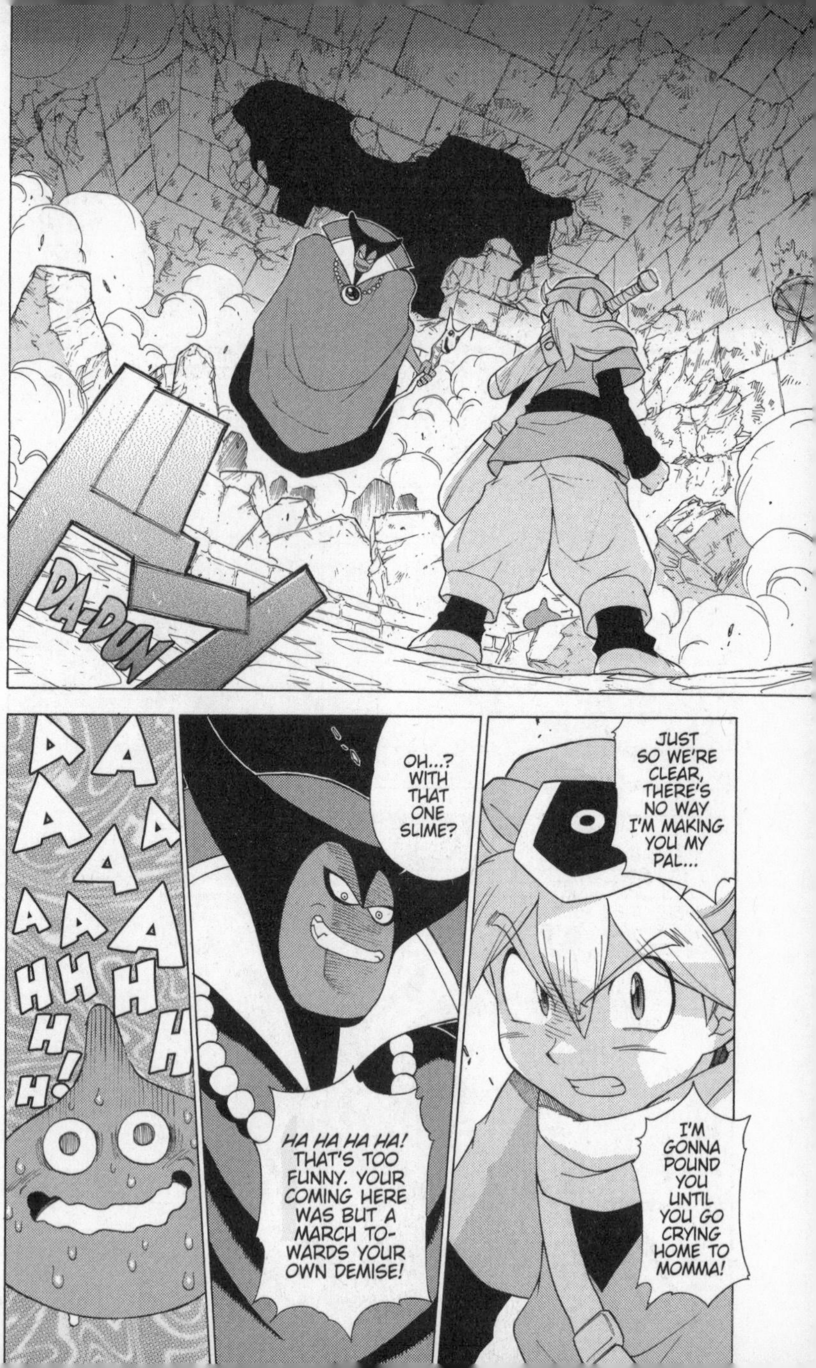
DA-DUN
JUST SO WE'RE CLEAR, THERE'S NO WAY I'M MAKING YOU MY PAL...
I'M GONNA POUND YOU UNTIL YOU GO CRYING HOME TO MOMMA!
OH...? WITH THAT ONE SLIME?
HA HA HA HA! THAT'S TOO FUNNY. YOUR COMING HERE WAS BUT A MARCH TO-WARDS YOUR OWN DEMISE!
AAAAAAAAHHHHHH!

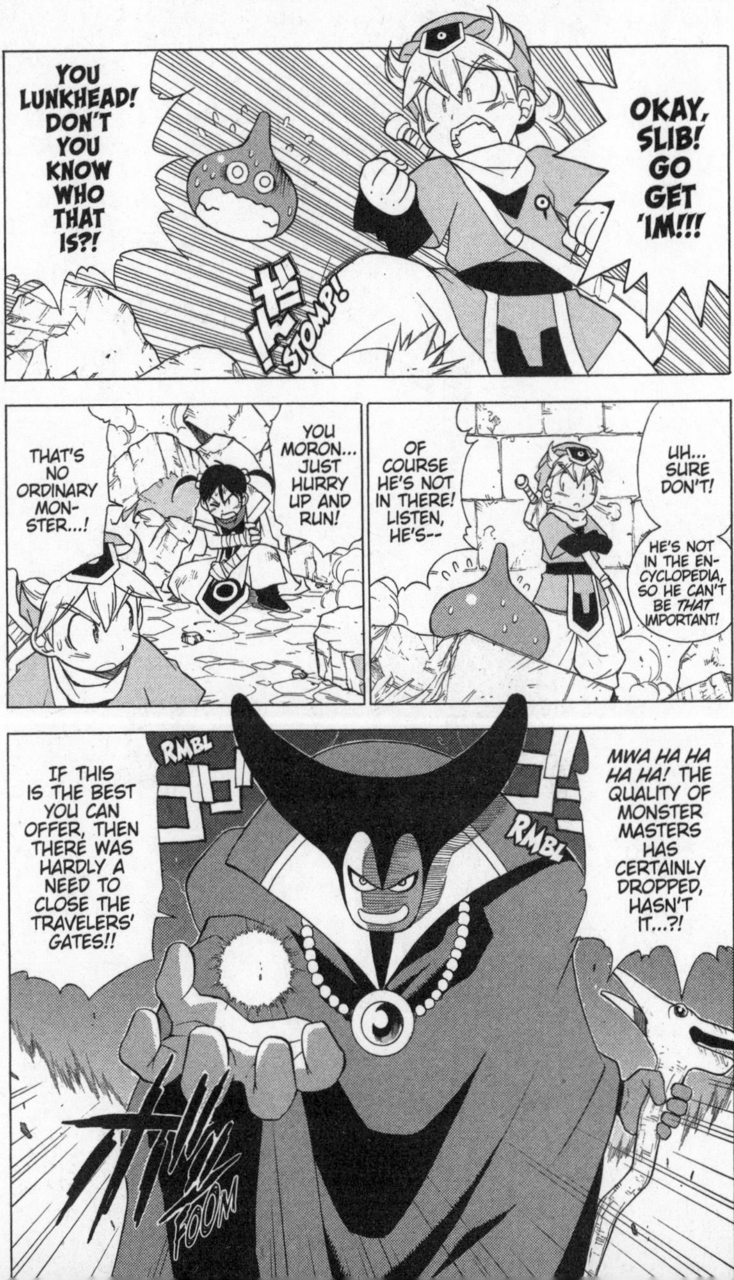
OKAY, SLIB! GO GET 'IM!!!
YOU LUNKHEAD! DON'T YOU KNOW WHO THAT IS?!
だん
STOMP!
UH... SURE DON'T!
HE'S NOT IN THE ENCYCLOPEDIA, SO HE CAN'T BE *THAT* IMPORTANT!
OF COURSE HE'S NOT IN THERE! LISTEN, HE'S--
YOU MORON... JUST HURRY UP AND RUN!
THAT'S NO ORDINARY MONSTER...!
RMBL
RMBL
MWA HA HA HA HA! THE QUALITY OF MONSTER MASTERS HAS CERTAINLY DROPPED, HASN'T IT...?!
IF THIS IS THE BEST YOU CAN OFFER, THEN THERE WAS HARDLY A NEED TO CLOSE THE TRAVELERS' GATES!!
FOOM

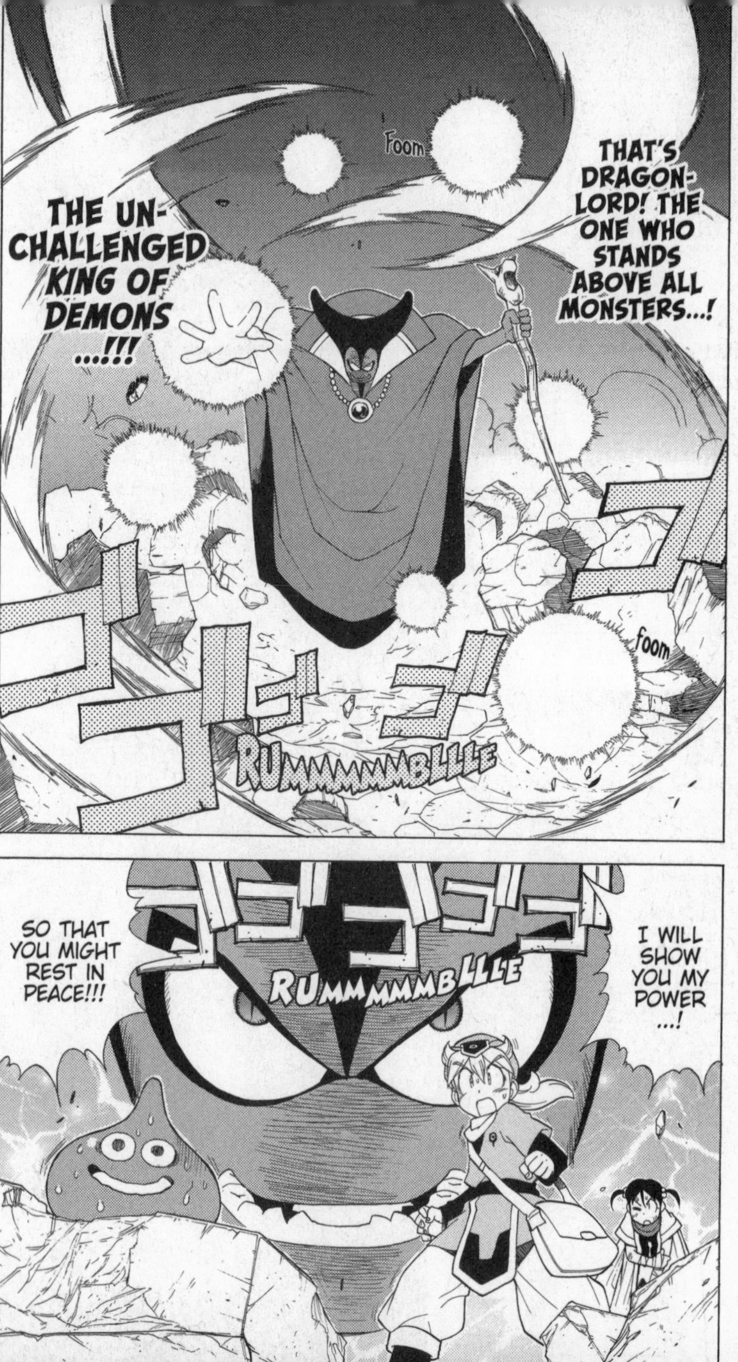
THAT'S DRAGON-LORD! THE ONE WHO STANDS ABOVE ALL MONSTERS...!
Foom
THE UN-CHALLENGED KING OF DEMONS ...!!!
foom
RUMMMMMMBLLLE
I WILL SHOW YOU MY POWER ...!
RUMMMMMMBLLLE
SO THAT YOU MIGHT REST IN PEACE!!!

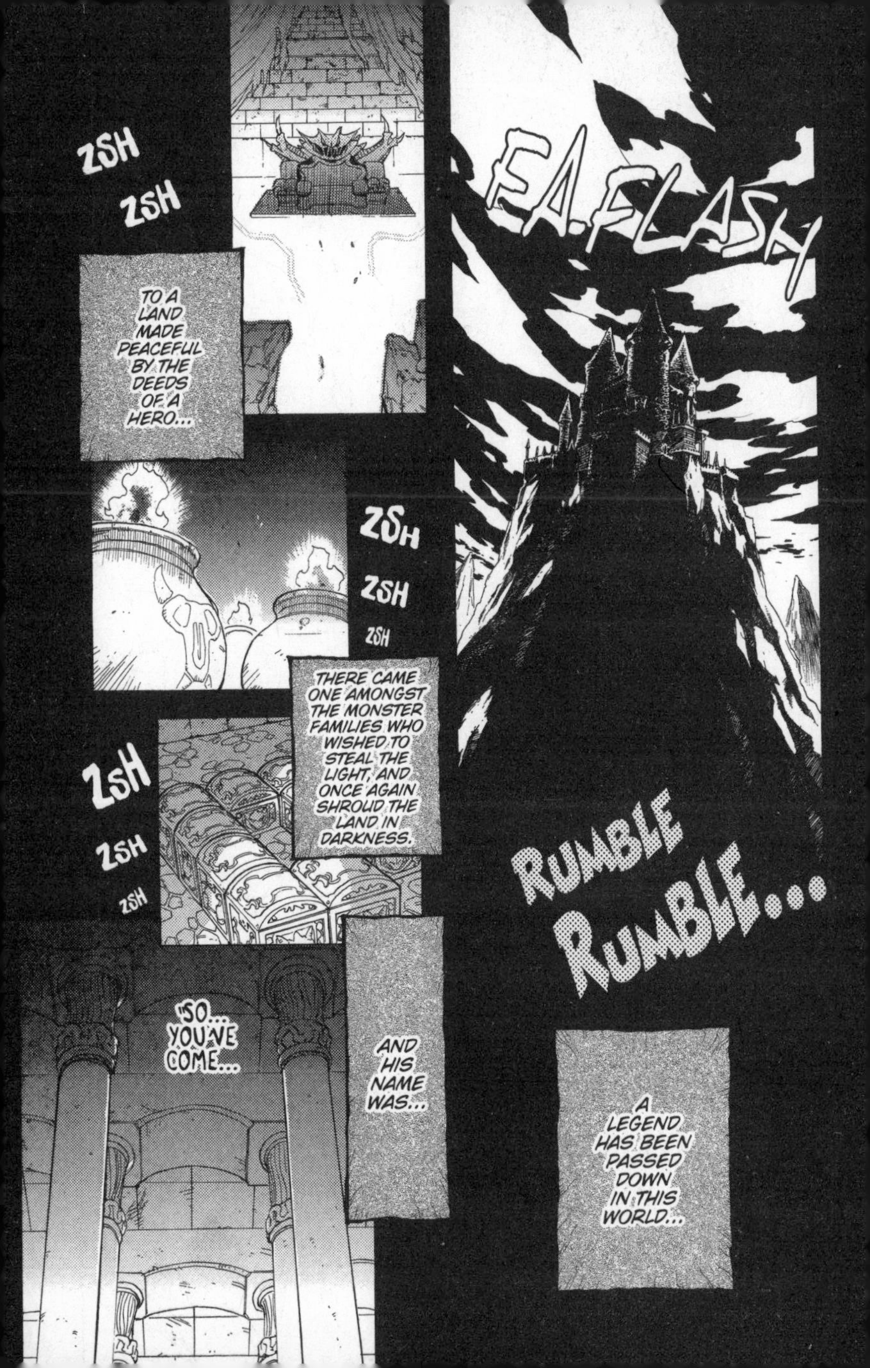
F.A.FLASH
RUMBLE RUMBLE...
A LEGEND HAS BEEN PASSED DOWN IN THIS WORLD...
ZSH
ZSH
TO A LAND MADE PEACEFUL BY THE DEEDS OF A HERO...
ZSH
ZSH
ZSH
THERE CAME ONE AMONGST THE MONSTER FAMILIES WHO WISHED TO STEAL THE LIGHT, AND ONCE AGAIN SHROUD THE LAND IN DARKNESS.
ZSH
ZSH
ZSH
AND HIS NAME WAS...
"SO... YOU'VE COME...

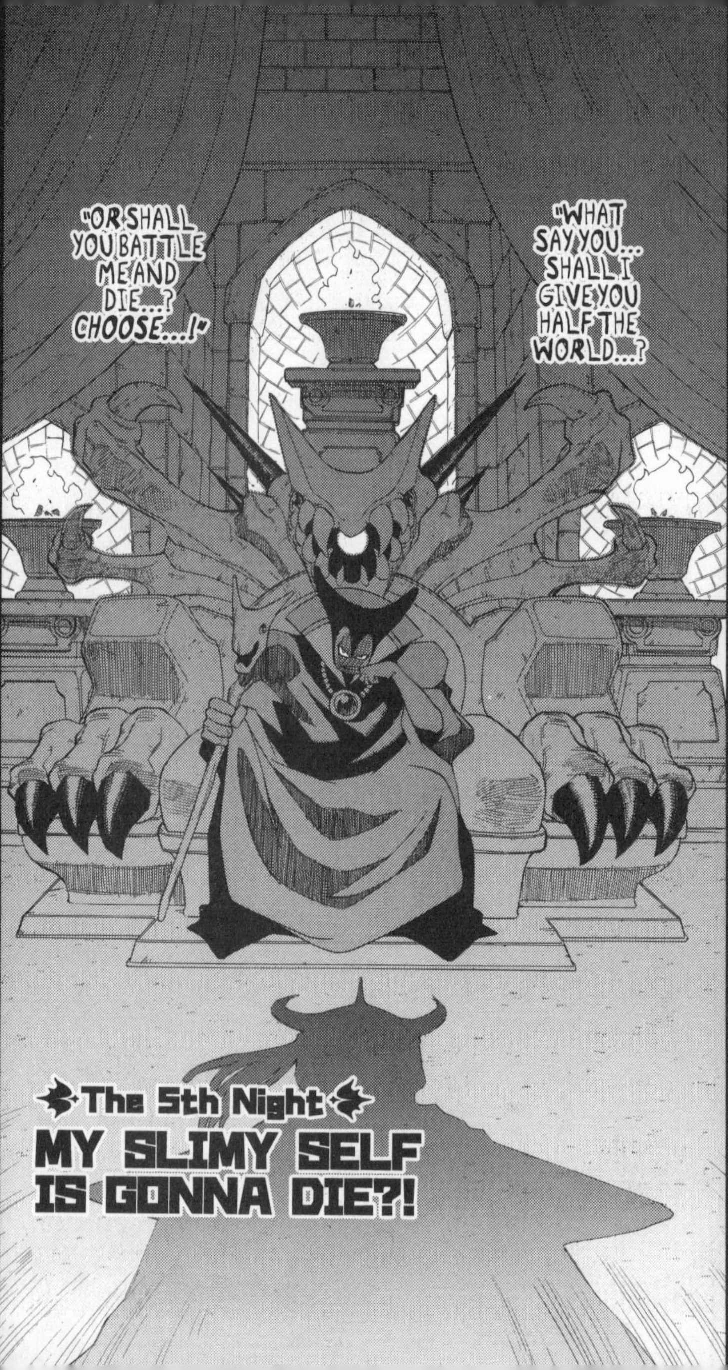
"WHAT SAY YOU... SHALL I GIVE YOU HALF THE WORLD...?
"OR SHALL YOU BATTLE ME AND DIE...? CHOOSE...!"
The 5th Night
MY SLIMY SELF IS GONNA DIE?!

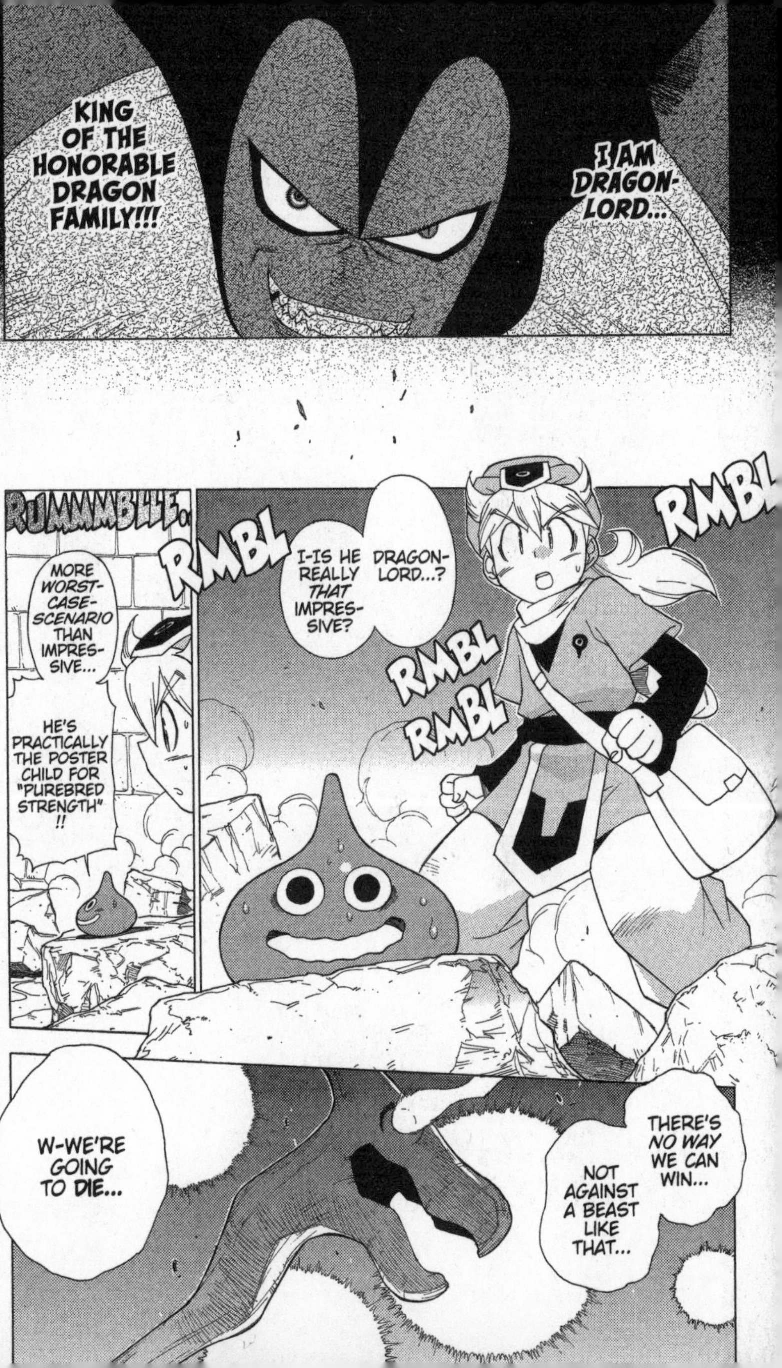
I AM DRAGON-LORD...
KING OF THE HONORABLE DRAGON FAMILY!!!
RMBL
DRAGON-LORD...?
I-IS HE REALLY *THAT* IMPRESSIVE?
RMBL
RMBL
RMBL
RMBL
RUMMMBLLLE
MORE WORST-CASE-SCENARIO THAN IMPRESSIVE...
HE'S PRACTICALLY THE POSTER CHILD FOR "PUREBRED STRENGTH"!!
THERE'S NO WAY WE CAN WIN...
NOT AGAINST A BEAST LIKE THAT...
W-WE'RE GOING TO DIE...

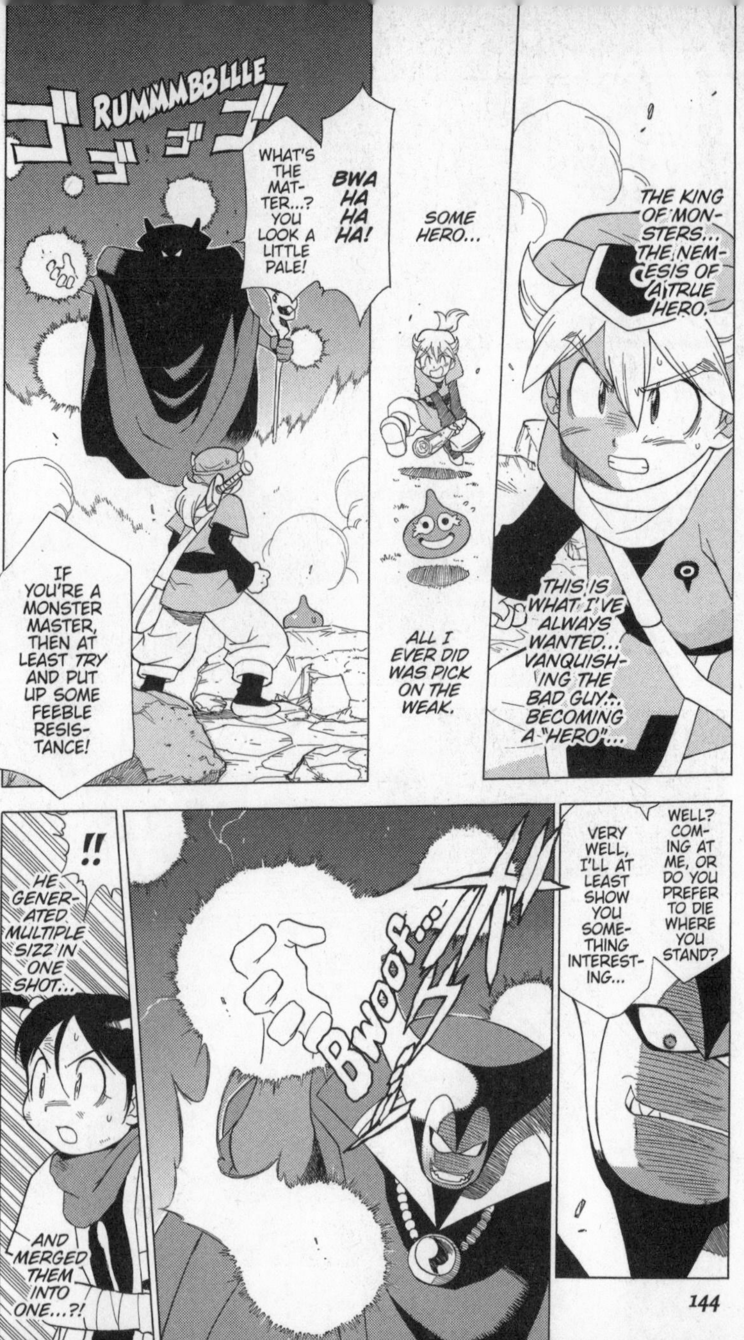
THE KING OF MONSTERS... THE NEMESIS OF A TRUE HERO.
THIS IS WHAT I'VE ALWAYS WANTED... VANQUISHING THE BAD GUY... BECOMING A "HERO"...
SOME HERO...
ALL I EVER DID WAS PICK ON THE WEAK.
RUMMMBBLLLE
WHAT'S THE MATTER...? YOU LOOK A LITTLE PALE!
BWA HA HA HA!
IF YOU'RE A MONSTER MASTER, THEN AT LEAST TRY AND PUT UP SOME FEEBLE RESISTANCE!
WELL? COMING AT ME, OR DO YOU PREFER TO DIE WHERE YOU STAND?
VERY WELL, I'LL AT LEAST SHOW YOU SOMETHING INTERESTING...
BWOOF...
!!
HE GENERATED MULTIPLE SIZZ IN ONE SHOT...
AND MERGED THEM INTO ONE...?!

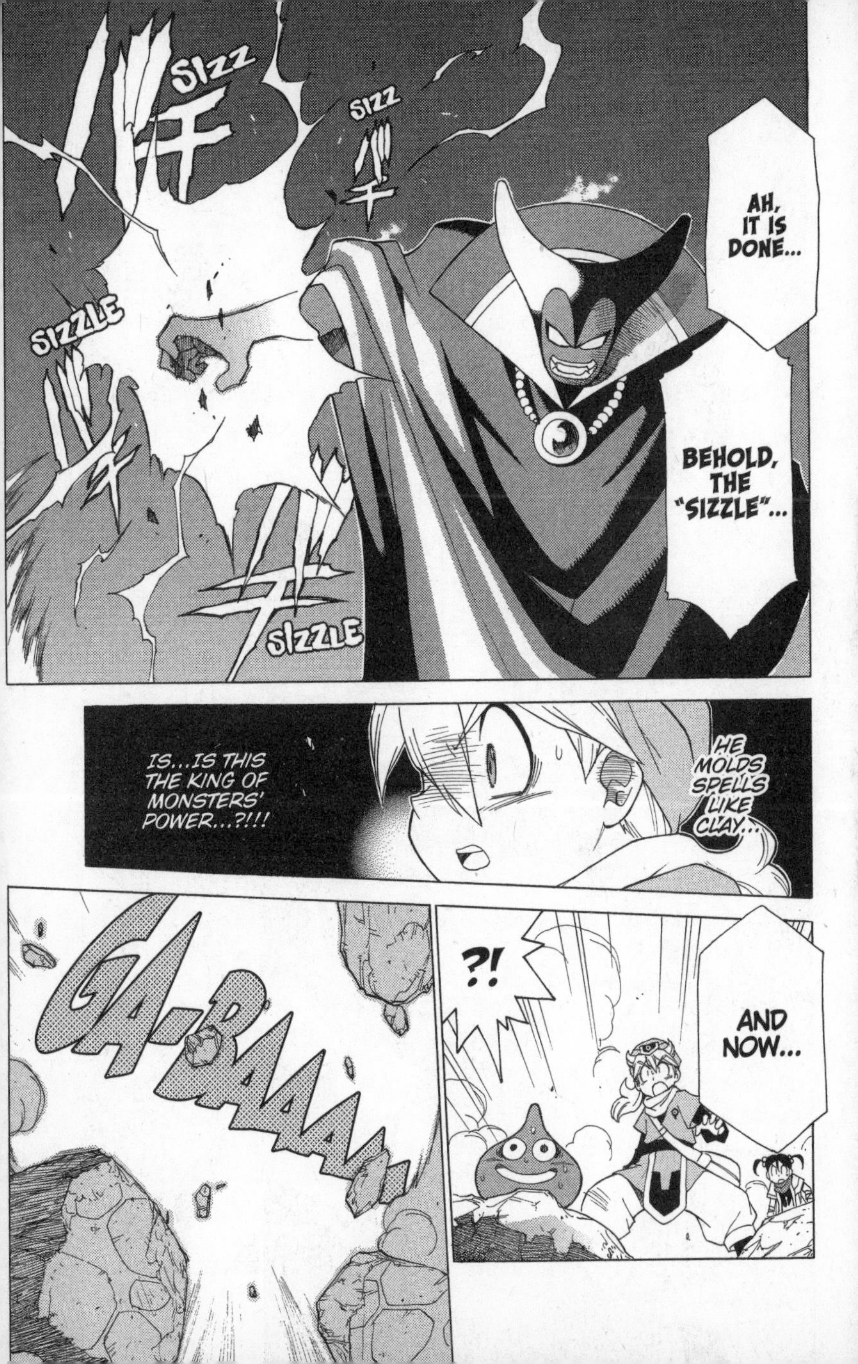
AH, IT IS DONE...
BEHOLD, THE "SIZZLE"...
SIZZ
SIZZ
SIZZLE
SIZZLE
HE MOLDS SPELLS LIKE CLAY...
IS...IS THIS THE KING OF MONSTERS' POWER...?!!!
AND NOW...
?!
GA-RAAAA

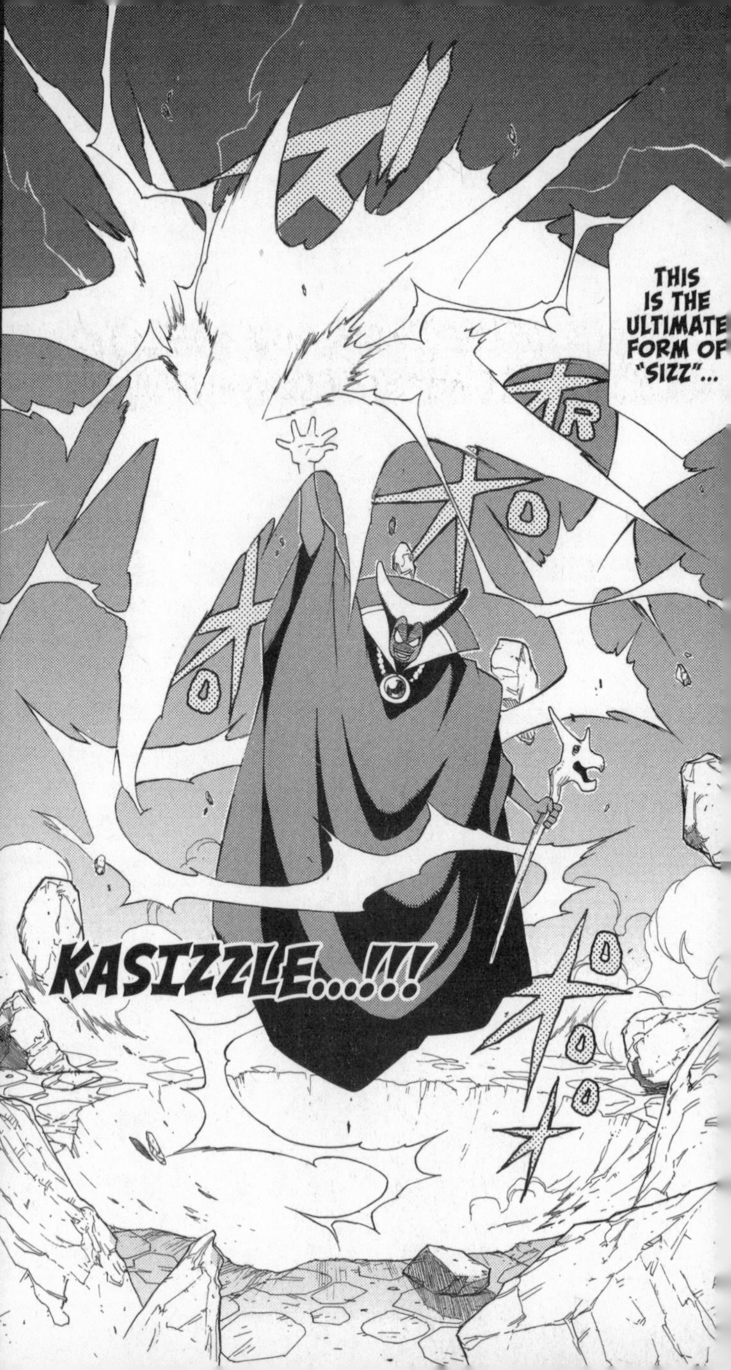
THIS IS THE ULTIMATE FORM OF "SIZZ"...
KASIZZLE...!!!

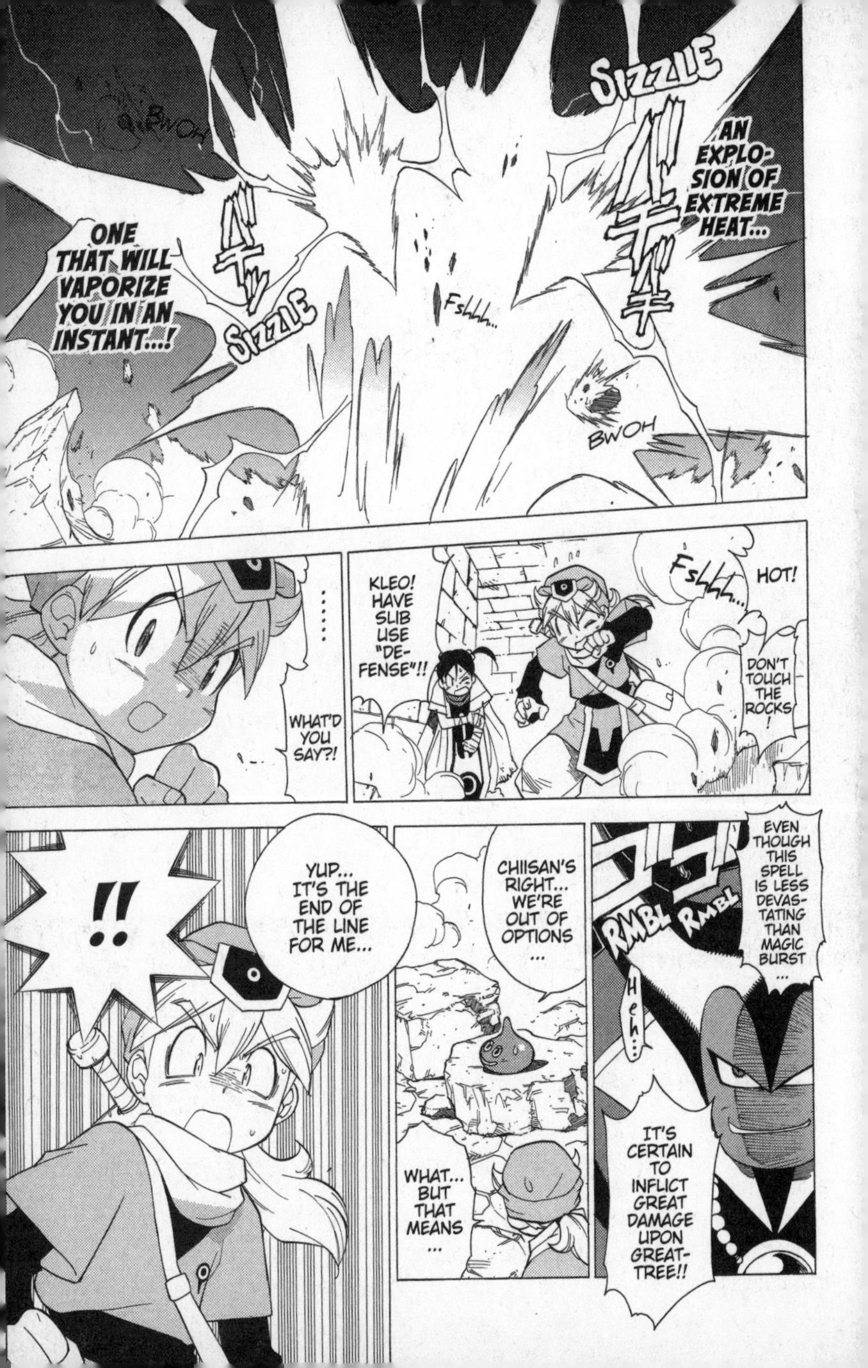
SIZZLE
AN EXPLOSION OF EXTREME HEAT...
ONE THAT WILL VAPORIZE YOU IN AN INSTANT...!
BWOH
SIZZLE
Fshhh...
BWOH
HOT!
Fshhh...
DON'T TOUCH THE ROCKS!
KLEO! HAVE SLIB USE "DE-FENSE"!!
......
WHAT'D YOU SAY?!
EVEN THOUGH THIS SPELL IS LESS DEVAS-TATING THAN MAGIC BURST...
RMBL RMBL
Heh...
IT'S CERTAIN TO INFLICT GREAT DAMAGE UPON GREAT-TREE!!
CHIISAN'S RIGHT... WE'RE OUT OF OPTIONS...
WHAT... BUT THAT MEANS...
YUP... IT'S THE END OF THE LINE FOR ME...
!!

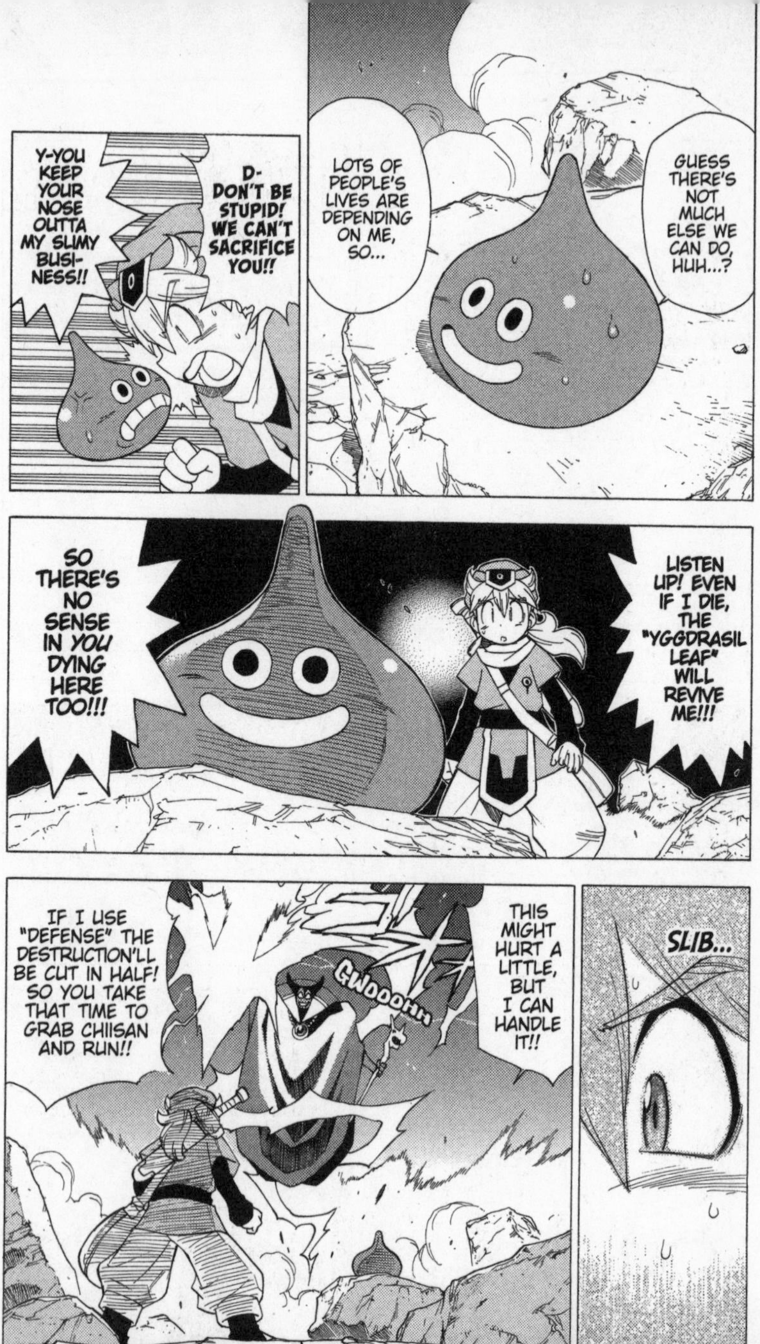
GUESS THERE'S NOT MUCH ELSE WE CAN DO, HUH...?
LOTS OF PEOPLE'S LIVES ARE DEPENDING ON ME, SO...
D-DON'T BE STUPID! WE CAN'T SACRIFICE YOU!!
Y-YOU KEEP YOUR NOSE OUTTA MY SLIMY BUSINESS!!
LISTEN UP! EVEN IF I DIE, THE "YGGDRASIL LEAF" WILL REVIVE ME!!!
SO THERE'S NO SENSE IN *YOU* DYING HERE TOO!!!
SLIB...
THIS MIGHT HURT A LITTLE, BUT I CAN HANDLE IT!!
GWOOOHH
IF I USE "DEFENSE" THE DESTRUCTION'LL BE CUT IN HALF! SO YOU TAKE THAT TIME TO GRAB CHIISAN AND RUN!!

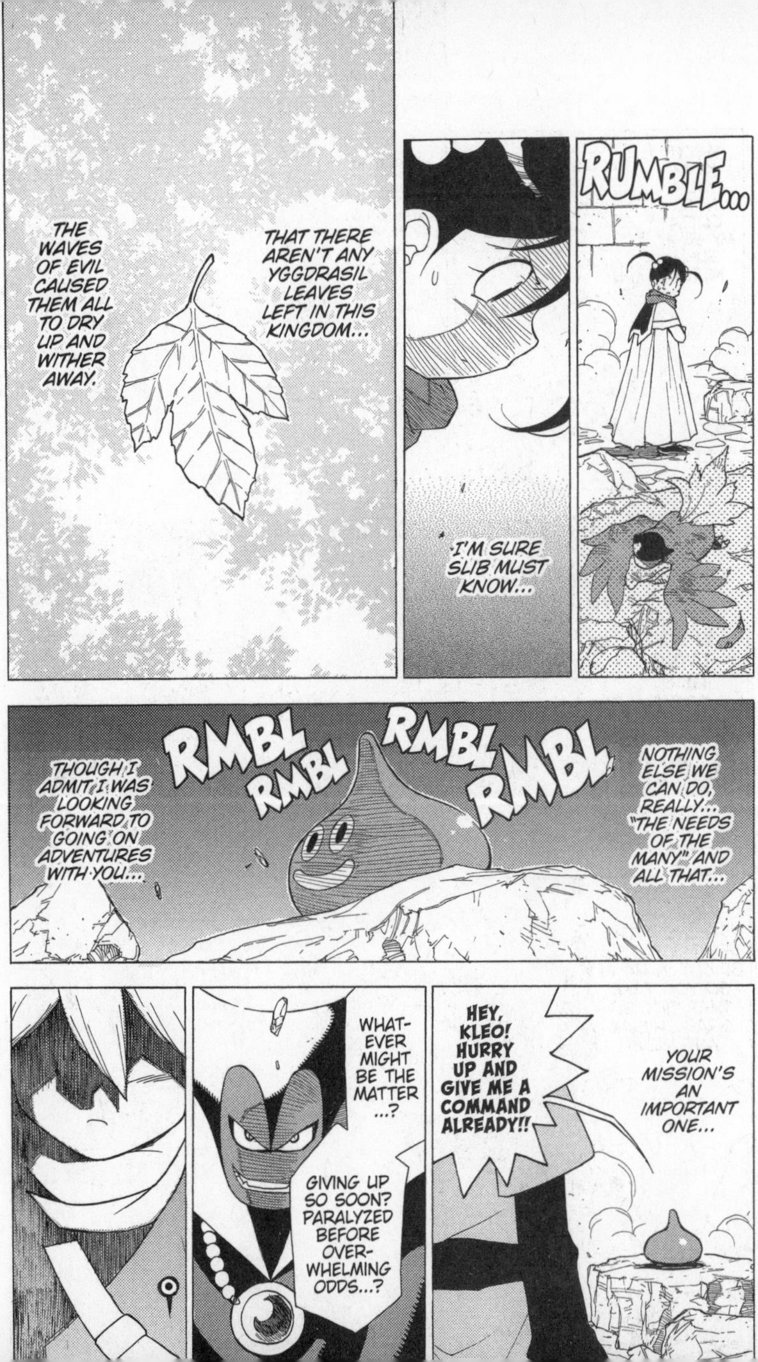
RUMBLE...
I'M SURE SLIB MUST KNOW...
THAT THERE AREN'T ANY YGGDRASIL LEAVES LEFT IN THIS KINGDOM...
THE WAVES OF EVIL CAUSED THEM ALL TO DRY UP AND WITHER AWAY.
NOTHING ELSE WE CAN DO, REALLY... "THE NEEDS OF THE MANY" AND ALL THAT...
RMBL RMBL RMBL RMBL
THOUGH I ADMIT I WAS LOOKING FORWARD TO GOING ON ADVENTURES WITH YOU...
YOUR MISSION'S AN IMPORTANT ONE...
HEY, KLEO! HURRY UP AND GIVE ME A COMMAND ALREADY!!
WHAT-EVER MIGHT BE THE MATTER ...?
GIVING UP SO SOON? PARALYZED BEFORE OVER-WHELMING ODDS...?

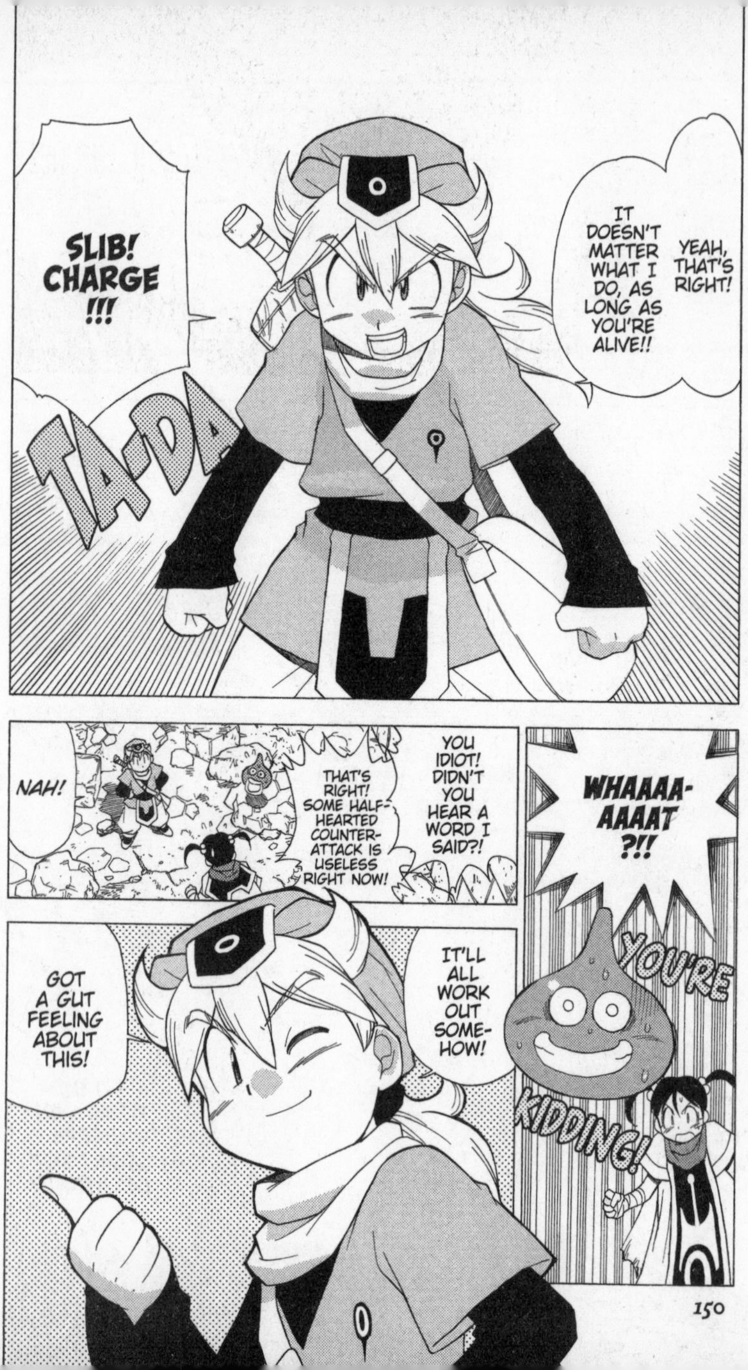
YEAH, THAT'S RIGHT!
IT DOESN'T MATTER WHAT I DO, AS LONG AS YOU'RE ALIVE!!
SLIB! CHARGE!!!
TA-DA
WHAAAA-AAAAT?!!
YOU'RE KIDDING!
YOU IDIOT! DIDN'T YOU HEAR A WORD I SAID?!
THAT'S RIGHT! SOME HALF-HEARTED COUNTER-ATTACK IS USELESS RIGHT NOW!
NAH!
IT'LL ALL WORK OUT SOME-HOW!
GOT A GUT FEELING ABOUT THIS!

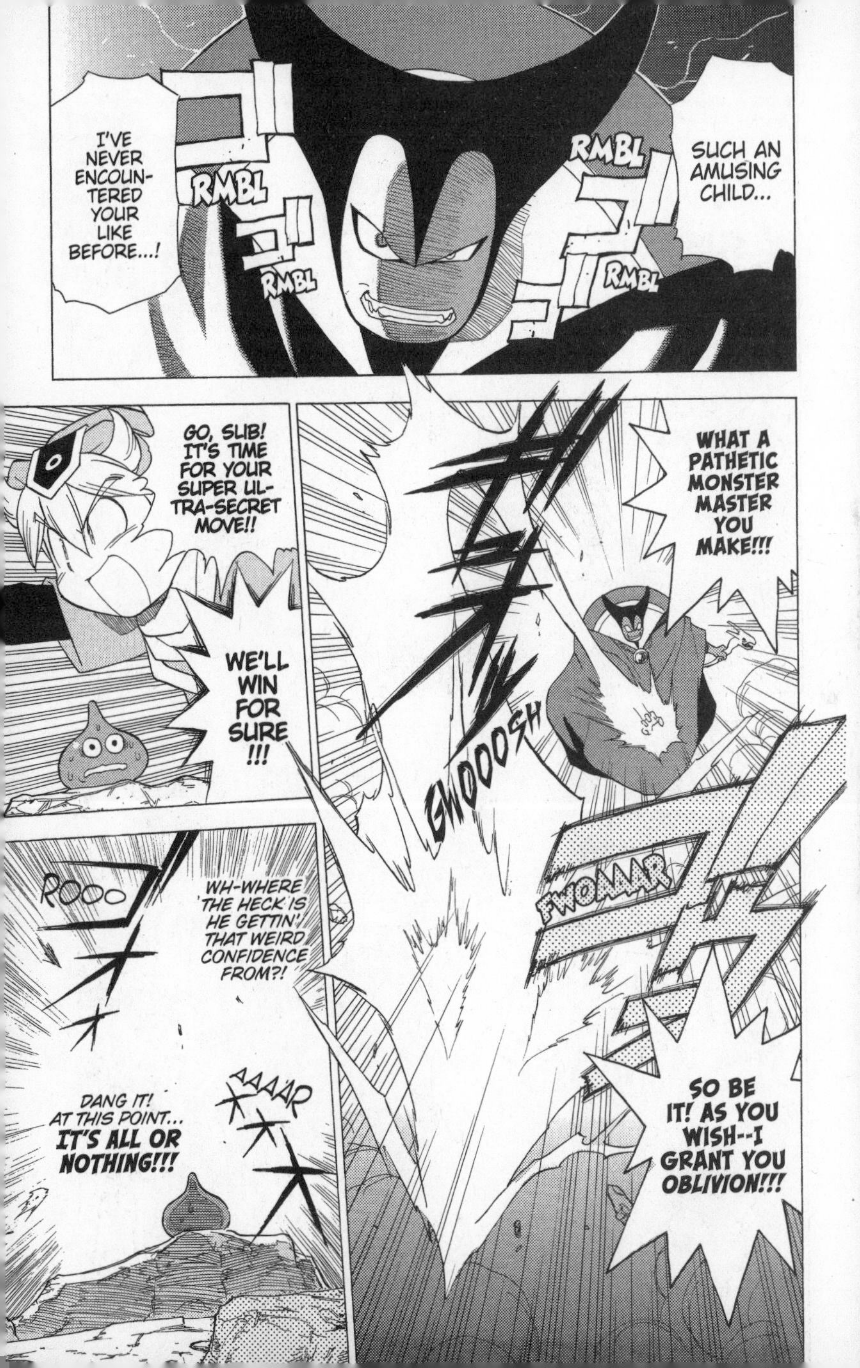
SUCH AN AMUSING CHILD...
RMBL
RMBL
I'VE NEVER ENCOUN-TERED YOUR LIKE BEFORE...!
RMBL
RMBL
WHAT A PATHETIC MONSTER MASTER YOU MAKE!!!
GWOOOSH
FWOAAAR
SO BE IT! AS YOU WISH--I GRANT YOU OBLIVION!!!
GO, SLIB! IT'S TIME FOR YOUR SUPER ULTRA-SECRET MOVE!!
WE'LL WIN FOR SURE!!!
WH-WHERE THE HECK IS HE GETTIN' THAT WEIRD CONFIDENCE FROM?!
ROOO
DANG IT! AT THIS POINT... IT'S ALL OR NOTHING!!!
AAAAR

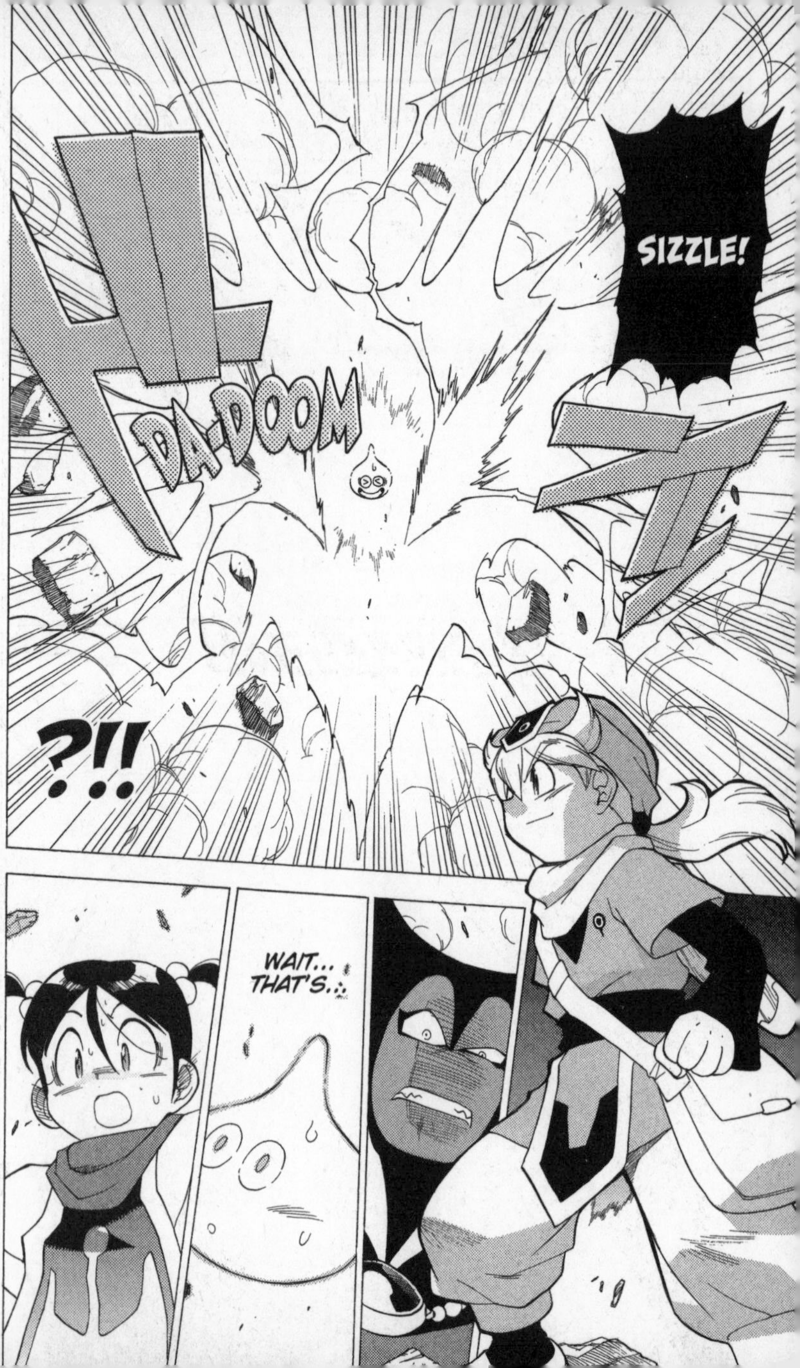
SIZZLE!
DA-DOOM
?!!
WAIT... THAT'S...

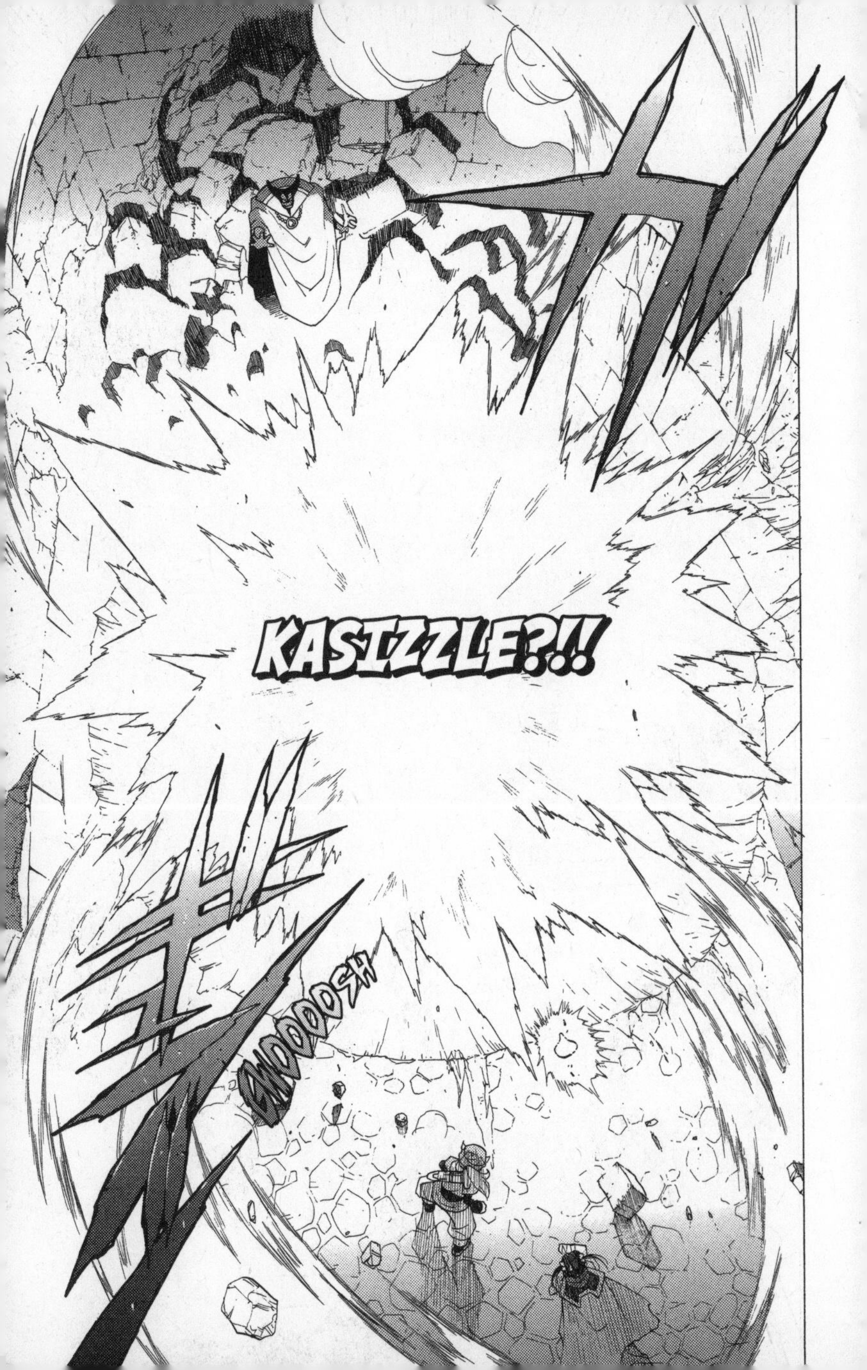
KASIZZLE?!!
SHWOOOSH

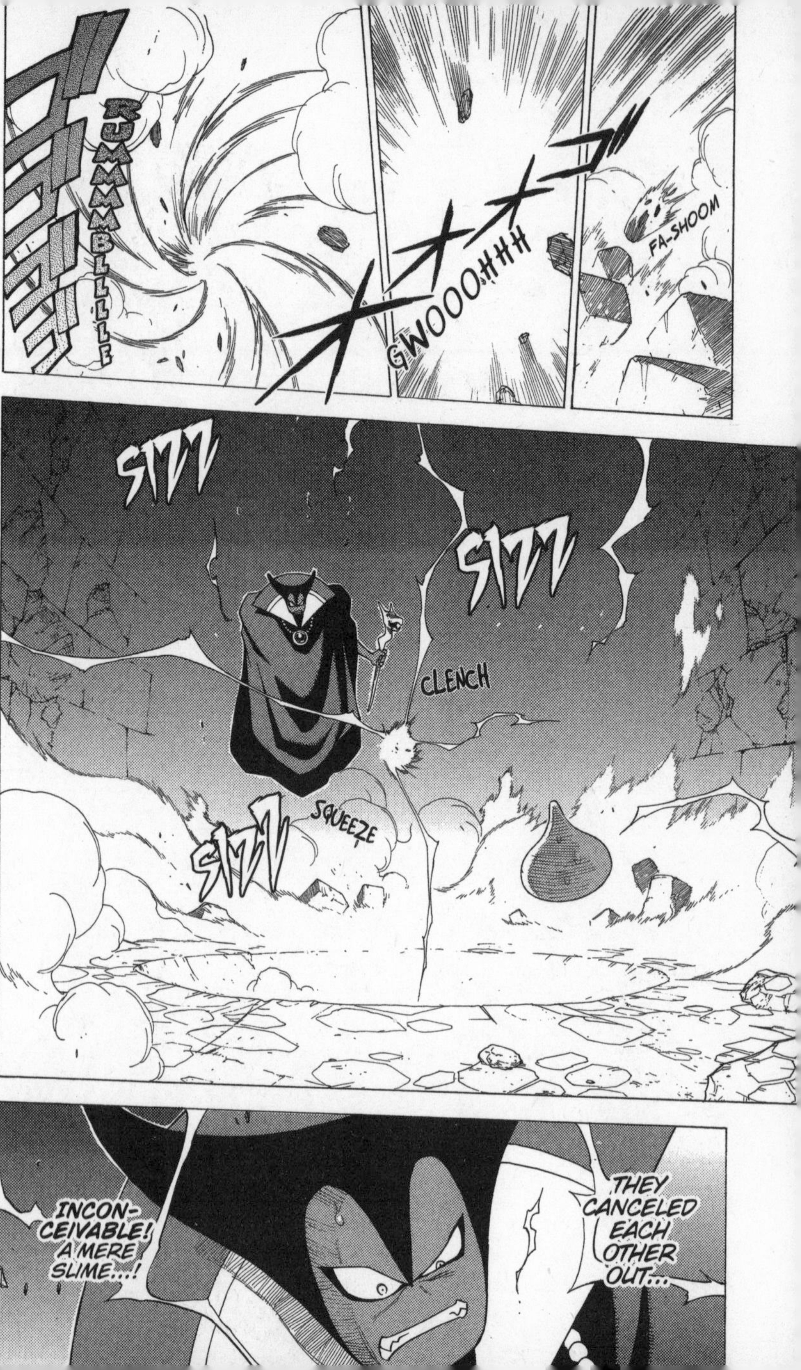
FA-SHOOM
GWOOOHHH
RUMMMBLLLLE
SIZZ
CLENCH
SIZZ
SQUEEZE
SIZZ
THEY CANCELED EACH OTHER OUT...
INCON-CEIVABLE! A MERE SLIME...!

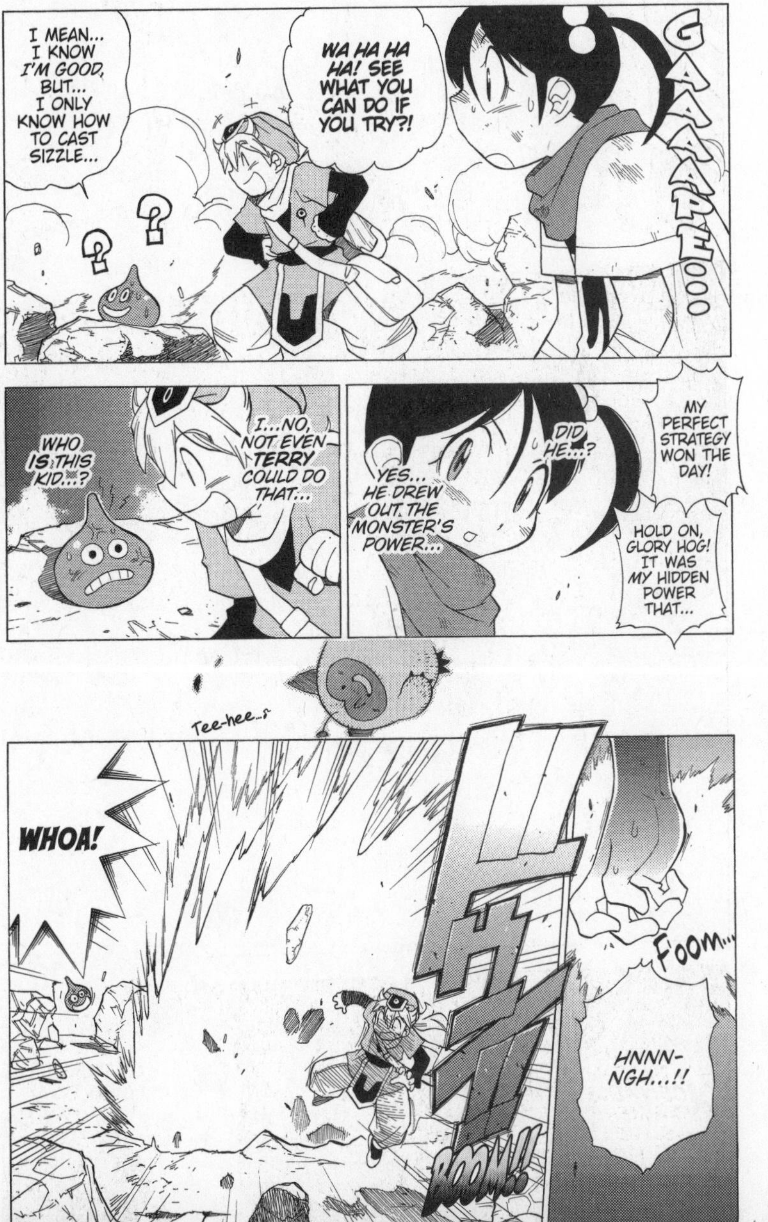
GAAAAPEOOO
WA HA HA! SEE WHAT YOU CAN DO IF YOU TRY?!
I MEAN... I KNOW I'M GOOD, BUT... I ONLY KNOW HOW TO CAST SIZZLE...
MY PERFECT STRATEGY WON THE DAY!
HOLD ON, GLORY HOG! IT WAS MY HIDDEN POWER THAT...
DID HE...?
YES... HE DREW OUT THE MONSTER'S POWER...
I...NO, NOT EVEN TERRY COULD DO THAT...
WHO IS THIS KID...?
Tee-hee...
Foom...
HNNN-NGH...!!
BOOM!!
WHOA!

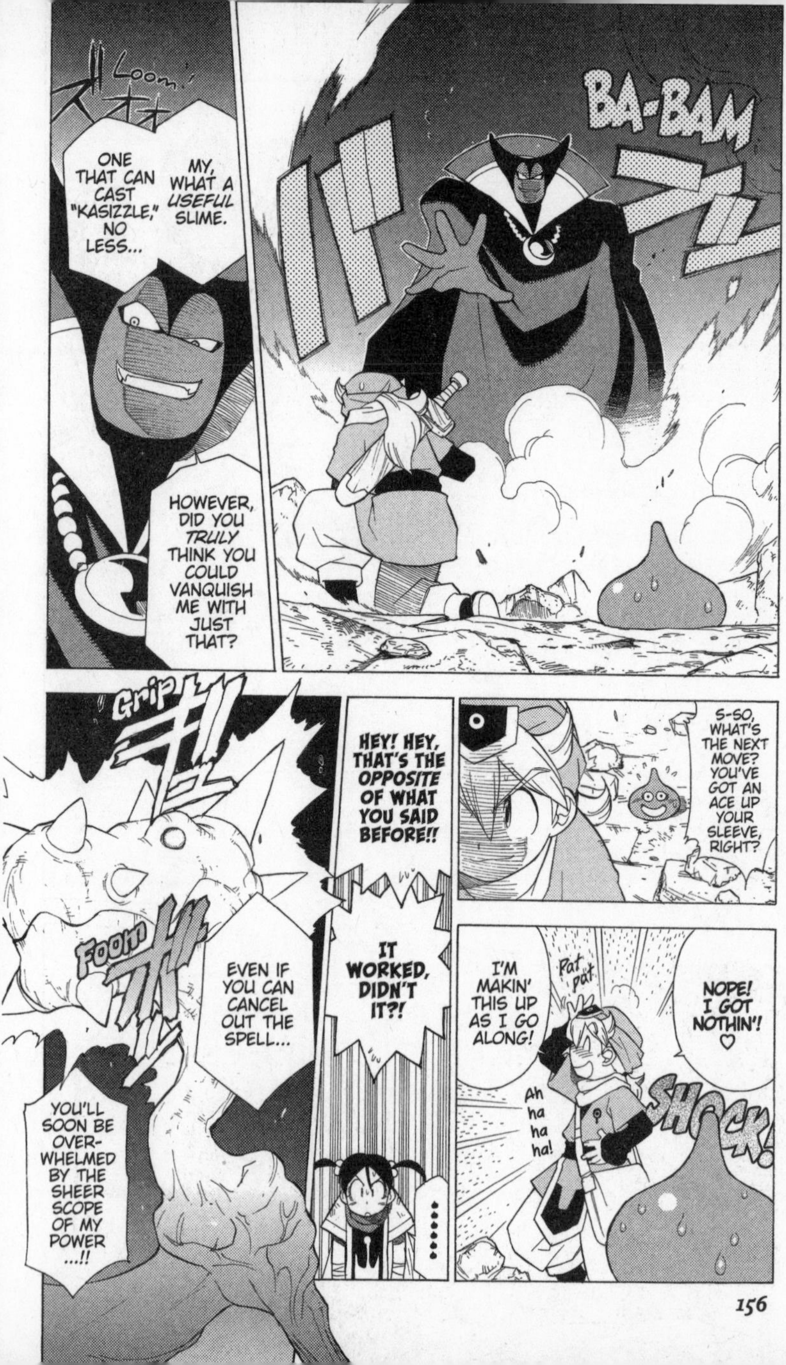
BA-BAM
Loom!
MY, WHAT A USEFUL SLIME.
ONE THAT CAN CAST "KASIZZLE," NO LESS...
HOWEVER, DID YOU TRULY THINK YOU COULD VANQUISH ME WITH JUST THAT?
S-SO, WHAT'S THE NEXT MOVE? YOU'VE GOT AN ACE UP YOUR SLEEVE, RIGHT?
NOPE! I GOT NOTHIN'! ♡
SHOCK!
I'M MAKIN' THIS UP AS I GO ALONG!
Pat pat
Ah ha ha ha!
HEY! HEY, THAT'S THE OPPOSITE OF WHAT YOU SAID BEFORE!!
IT WORKED, DIDN'T IT?!
Grip
Foom
EVEN IF YOU CAN CANCEL OUT THE SPELL...
YOU'LL SOON BE OVER-WHELMED BY THE SHEER SCOPE OF MY POWER ...!!

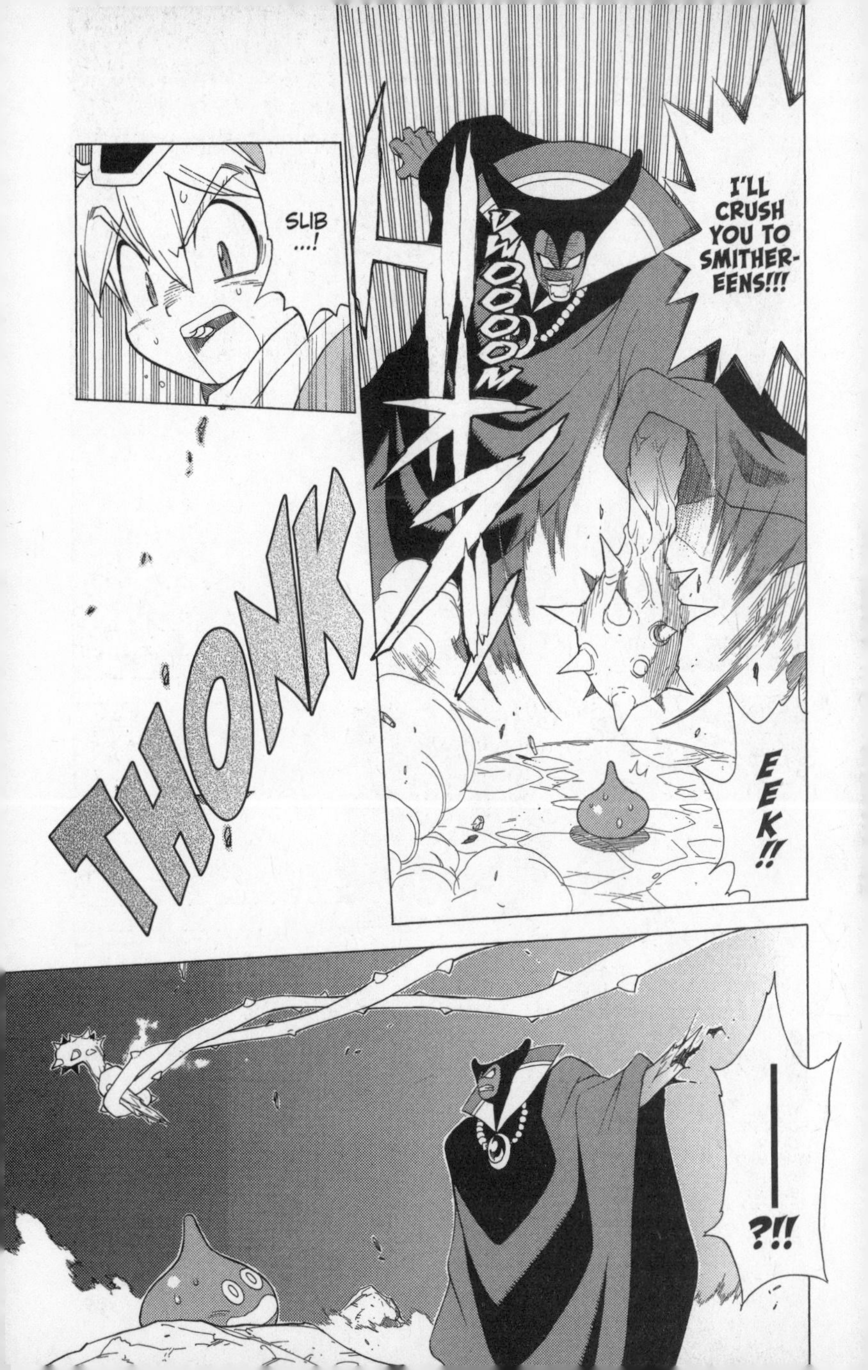
I'LL CRUSH YOU TO SMITHER-EENS!!!
DWOOOOOOM
EEK!!
SLIB ...!
THONK
——?!!

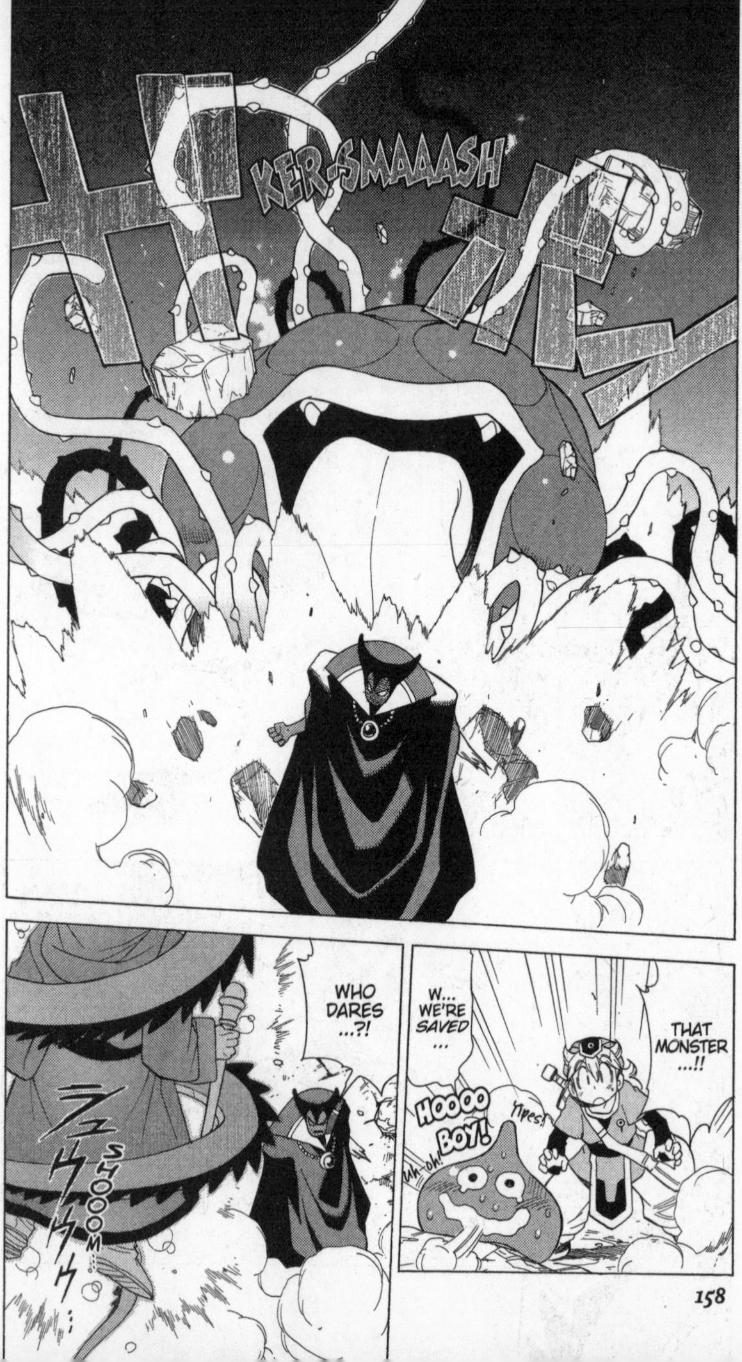
KER-SMAAASH
THAT MONSTER ...!!
W... WE'RE SAVED ...
Yipes!
HOOOO BOY!
Uh-oh!
WHO DARES ...?!
SHOOOM...

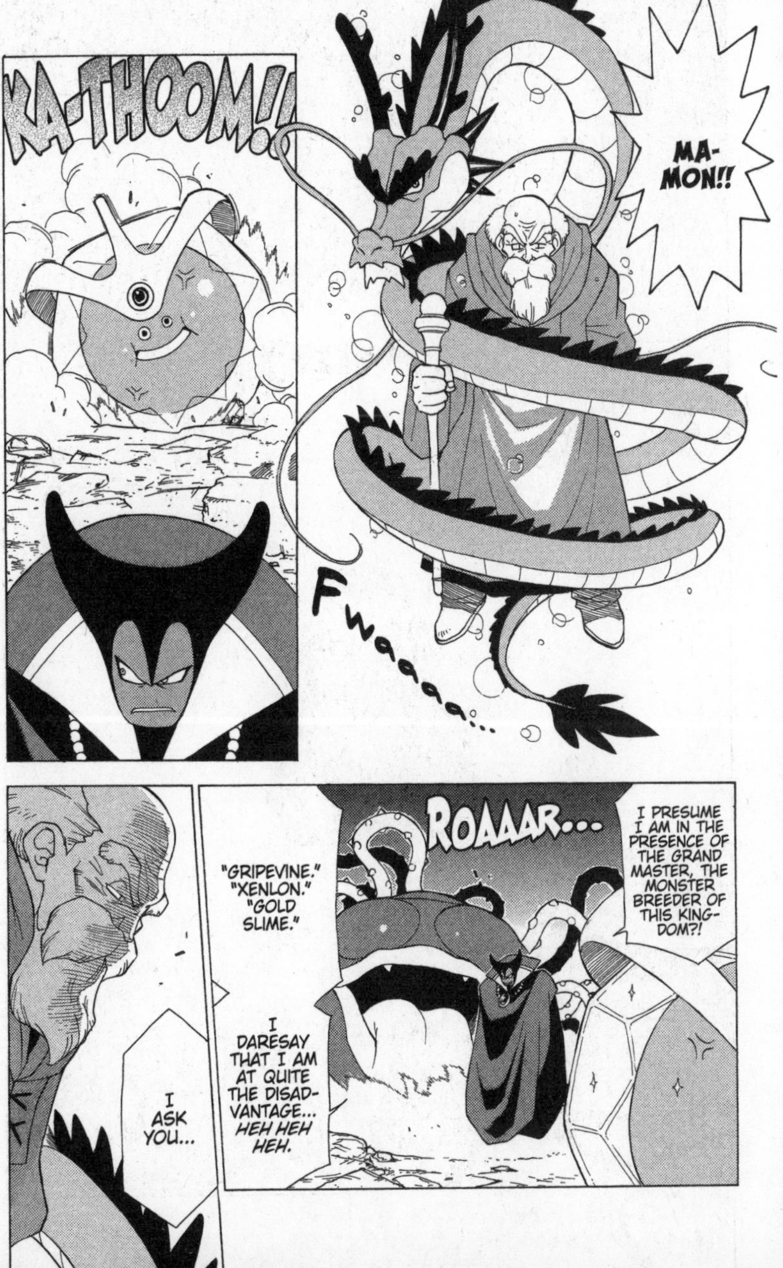
MA-MON!!
Fwaaaa...
KA-THOOM!!
I PRESUME I AM IN THE PRESENCE OF THE GRAND MASTER, THE MONSTER BREEDER OF THIS KING-DOM?!
ROAAAR...
"GRIPEVINE." "XENLON." "GOLD SLIME."
I DARESAY THAT I AM AT QUITE THE DISAD-VANTAGE... HEH HEH HEH.
I ASK YOU...

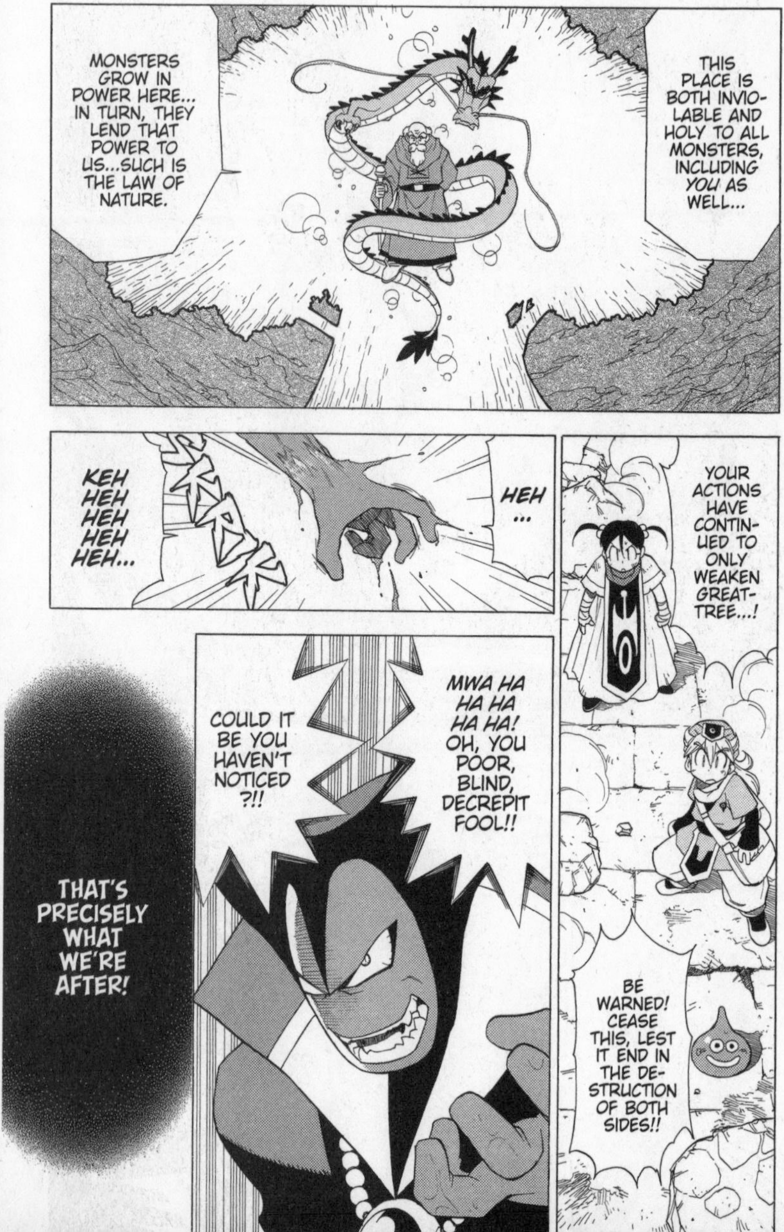
THIS PLACE IS BOTH INVIO-LABLE AND HOLY TO ALL MONSTERS, INCLUDING *YOU* AS WELL...
MONSTERS GROW IN POWER HERE... IN TURN, THEY LEND THAT POWER TO US...SUCH IS THE LAW OF NATURE.
YOUR ACTIONS HAVE CONTIN-UED TO ONLY WEAKEN GREAT-TREE...!
HEH ...
KEH HEH HEH HEH HEH...
BE WARNED! CEASE THIS, LEST IT END IN THE DE-STRUCTION OF BOTH SIDES!!
MWA HA HA HA HA HA! OH, YOU POOR, BLIND, DECREPIT FOOL!!
COULD IT BE YOU HAVEN'T NOTICED ?!!
THAT'S PRECISELY WHAT WE'RE AFTER!

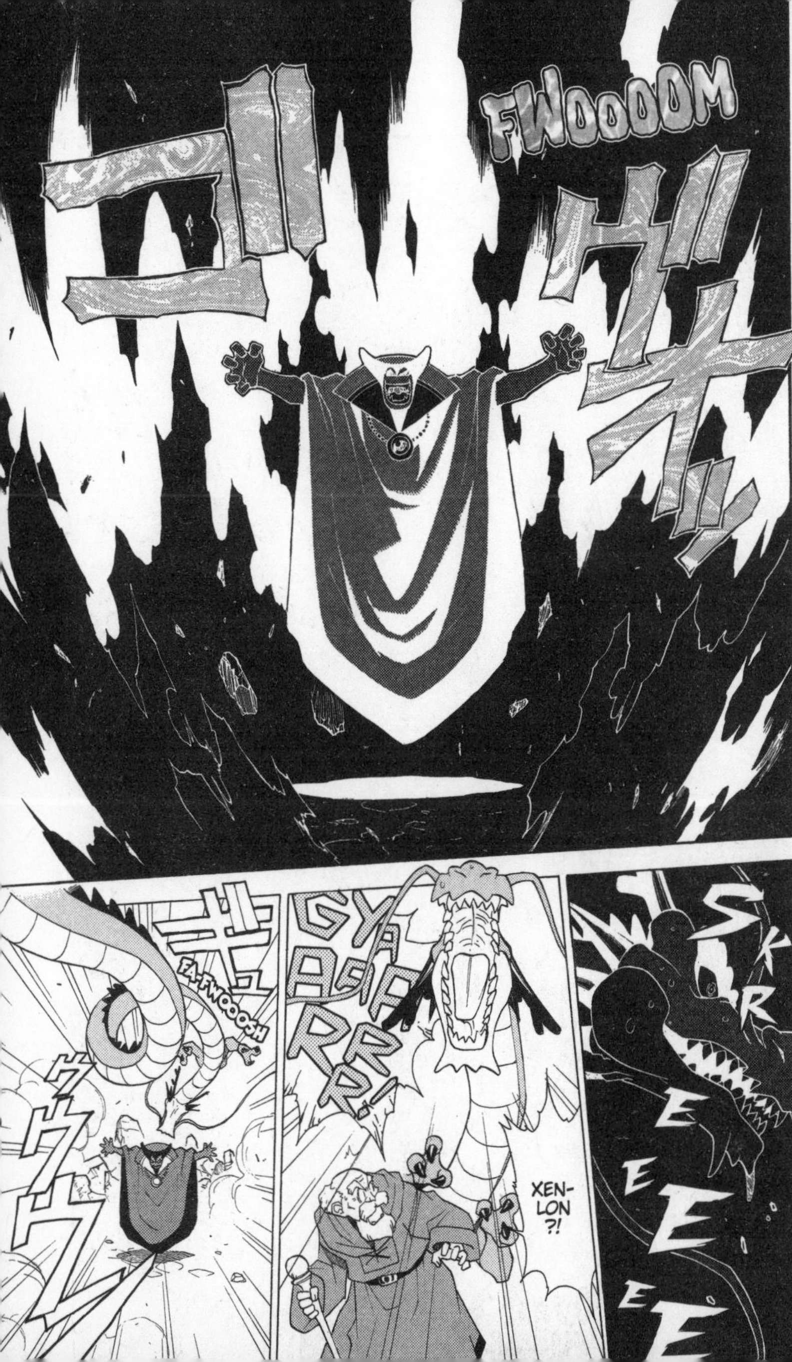
ゴヴォッ
FWOOOOM
SKREEEEEE
GYAAARRRR!
XEN-LON ?!
FA-FWOOOSH

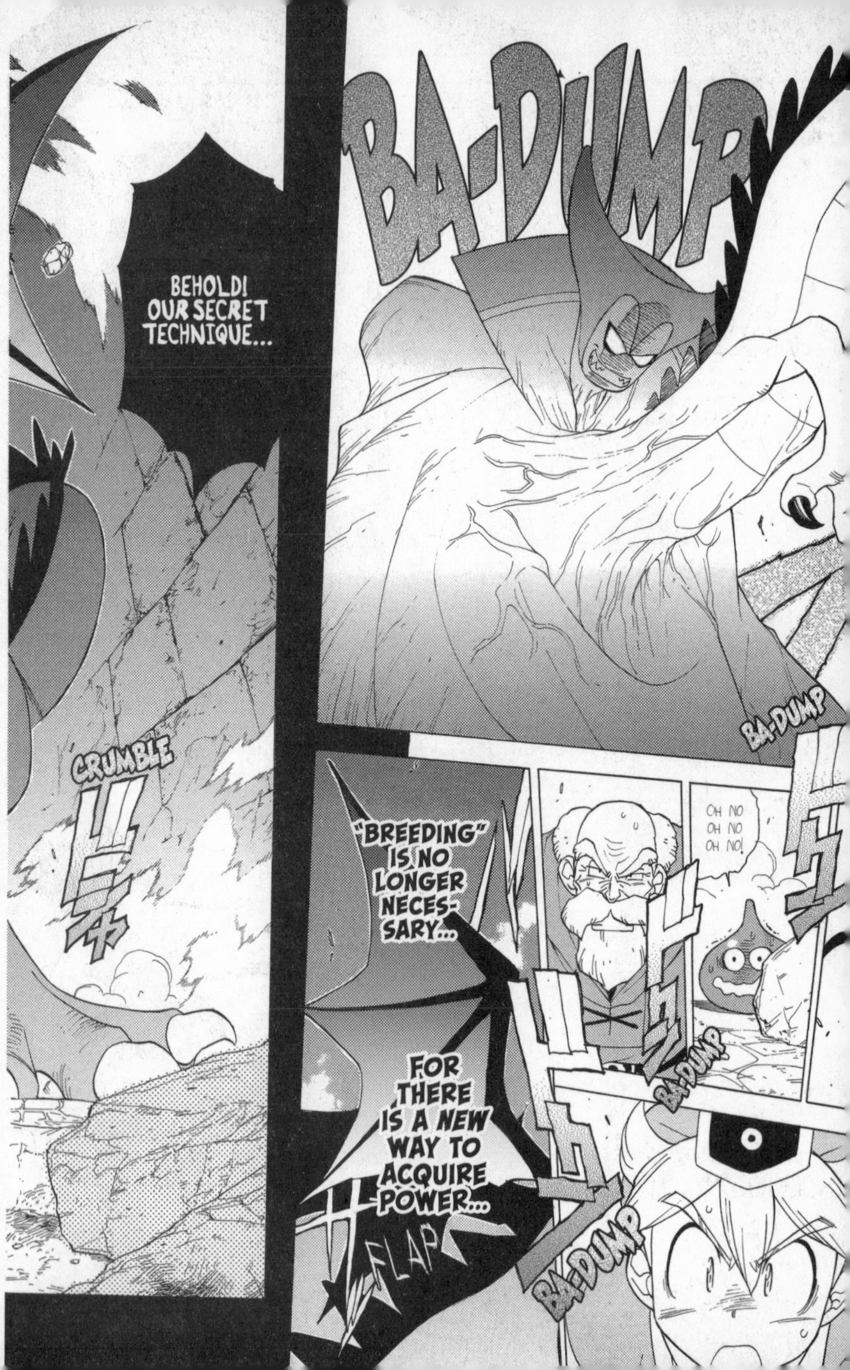
BA-DUMP
BA-DUMP
OH NO
OH NO
OH NO!
BA-DUMP
BA-DUMP
"BREEDING" IS NO LONGER NECES-SARY...
FOR THERE IS A *NEW* WAY TO ACQUIRE POWER...
FLAP
BEHOLD! OUR SECRET TECHNIQUE...
CRUMBLE

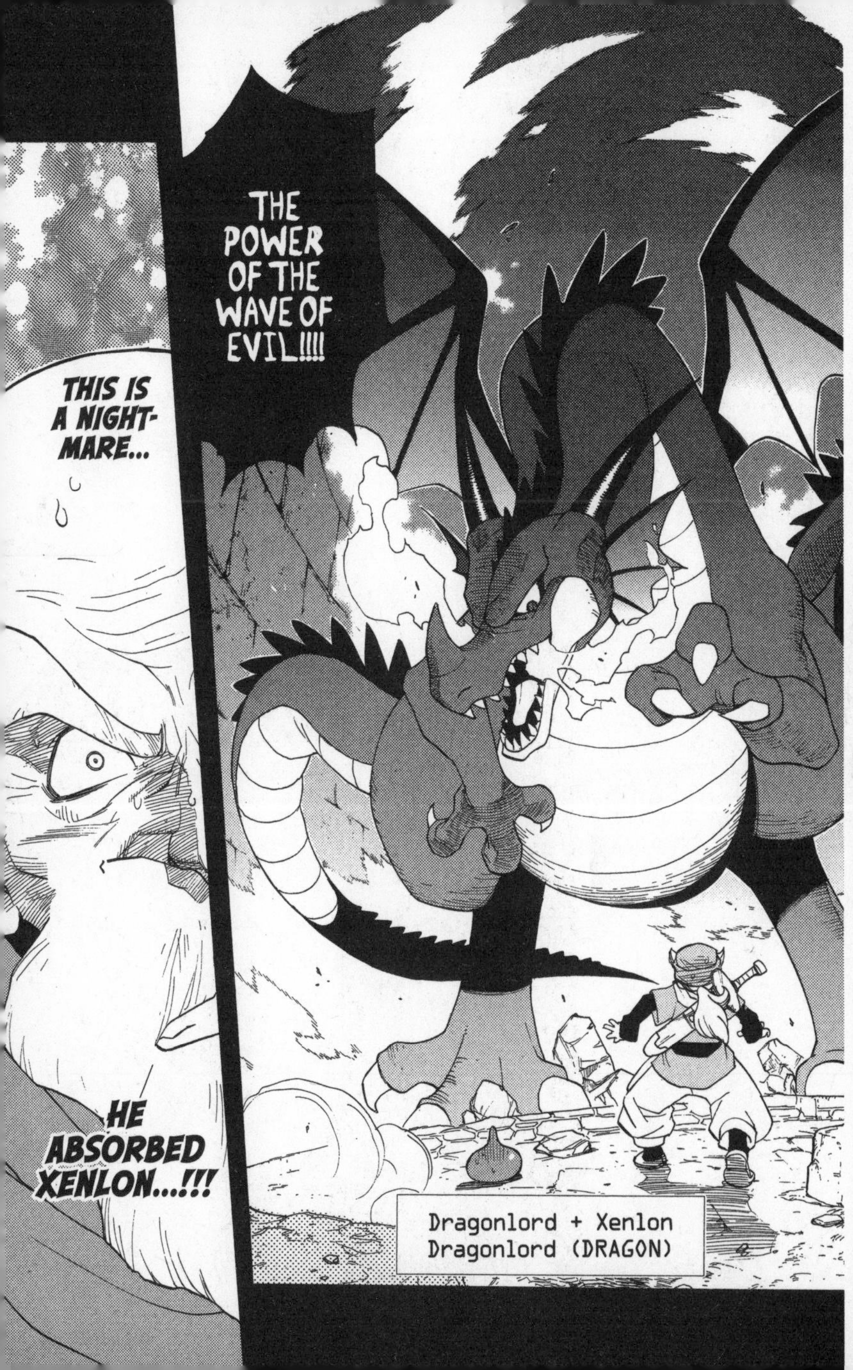
THE POWER OF THE WAVE OF EVIL!!!!
Dragonlord + Xenlon
Dragonlord (DRAGON)
THIS IS A NIGHT-MARE...
HE ABSORBED XENLON...!?!

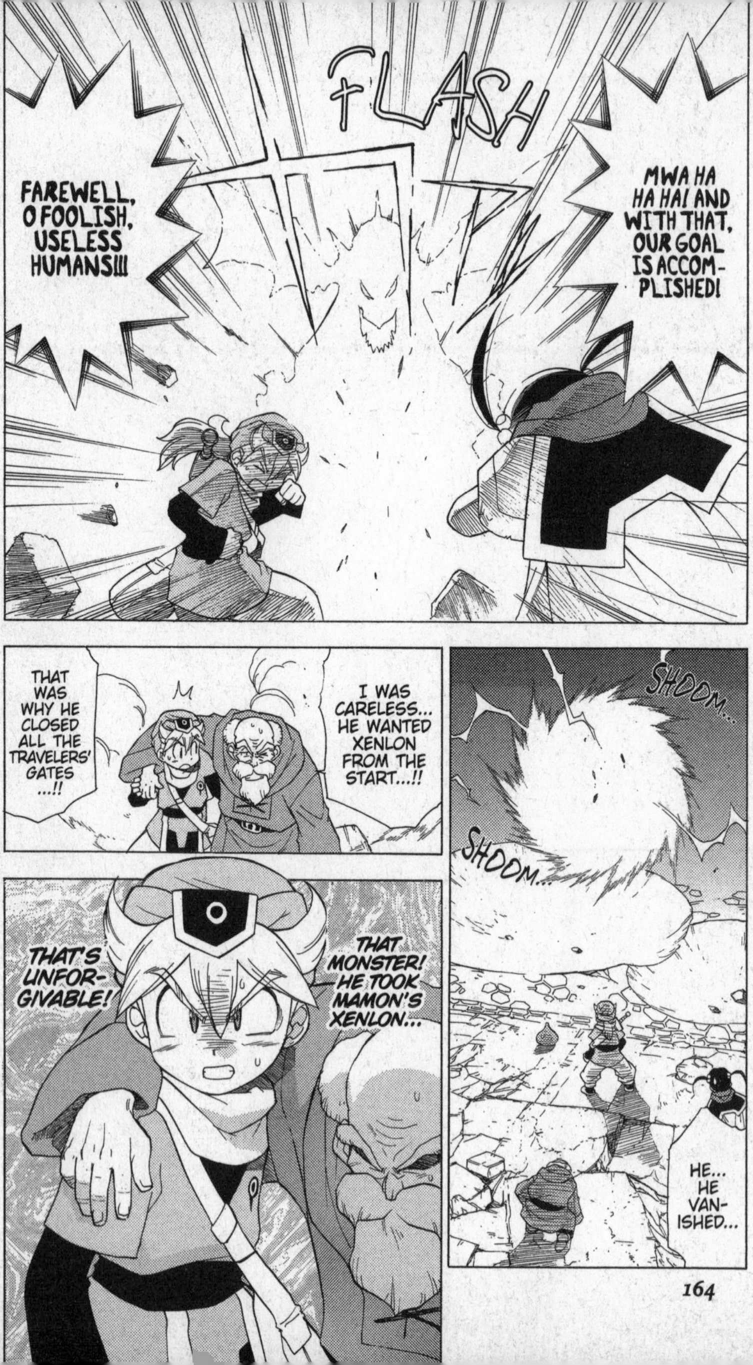
FLASH
MWA HA HA HA! AND WITH THAT, OUR GOAL IS ACCOM-PLISHED!
FAREWELL, O FOOLISH, USELESS HUMANS!!!
SHOOM...
SHOOM...
HE... HE VAN-ISHED...
I WAS CARELESS... HE WANTED XENLON FROM THE START...!!
THAT WAS WHY HE CLOSED ALL THE TRAVELERS' GATES ...!!
THAT MONSTER! HE TOOK MAMON'S XENLON...
THAT'S UNFOR-GIVABLE!

DRAGON
QUEST
MONSTERS +

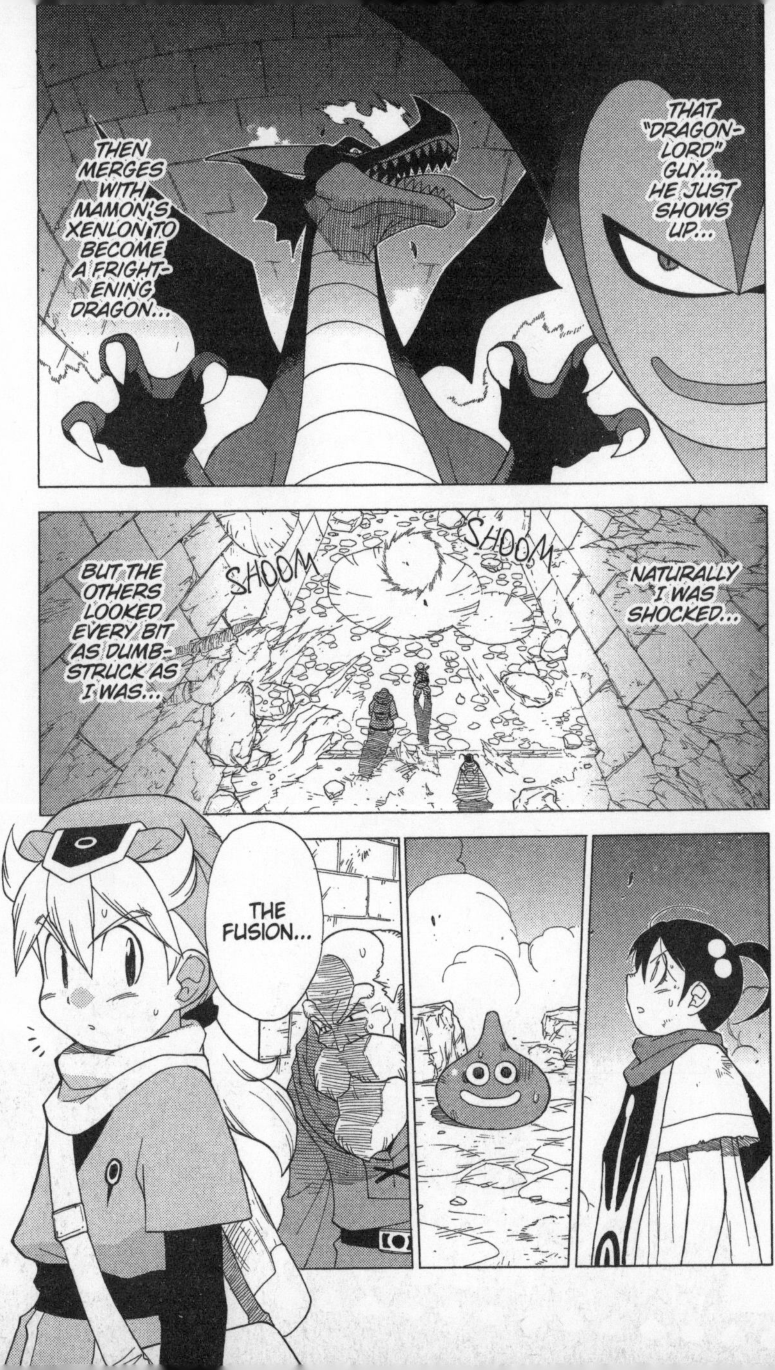
THAT "DRAGON-LORD" GUY... HE JUST SHOWS UP...
THEN MERGES WITH MAMON'S XENLON TO BECOME A FRIGHT-ENING DRAGON...
SHOOM
NATURALLY I WAS SHOCKED...
SHOOM
BUT THE OTHERS LOOKED EVERY BIT AS DUMB-STRUCK AS I WAS...
THE FUSION...

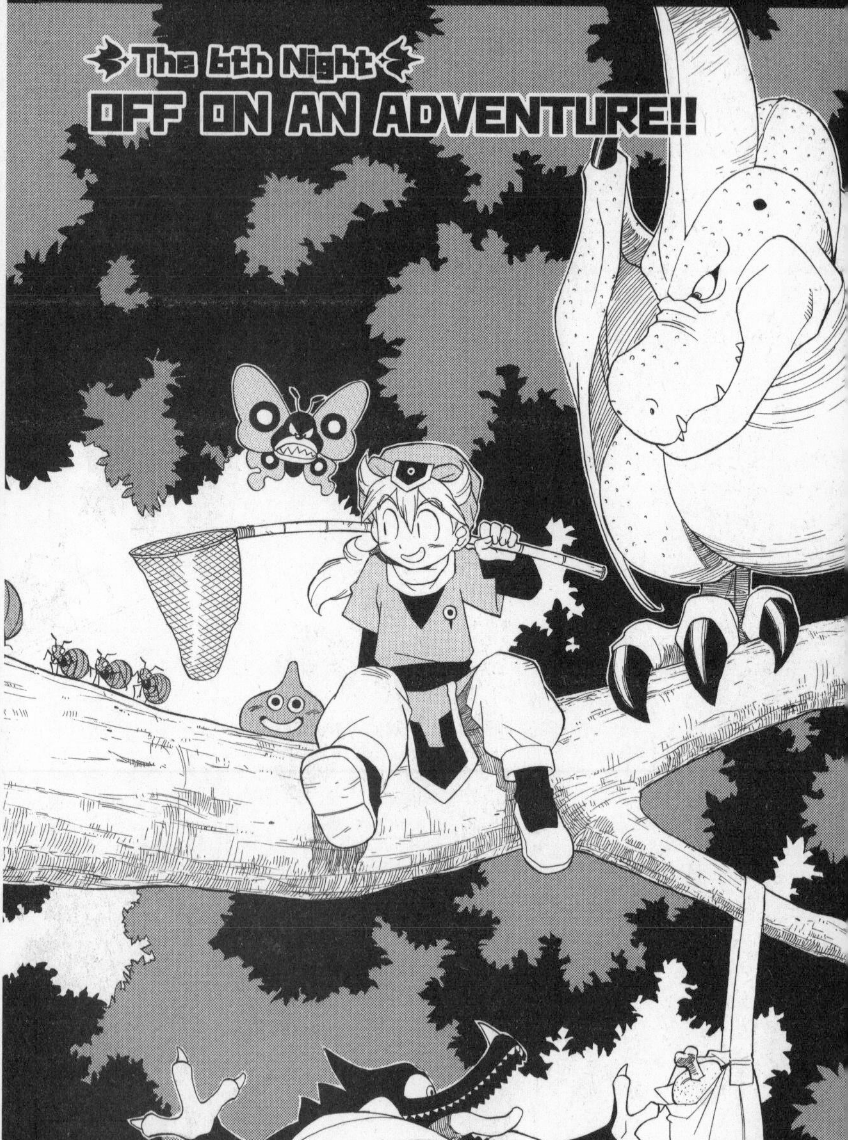
The 6th Night
OFF ON AN ADVENTURE!!

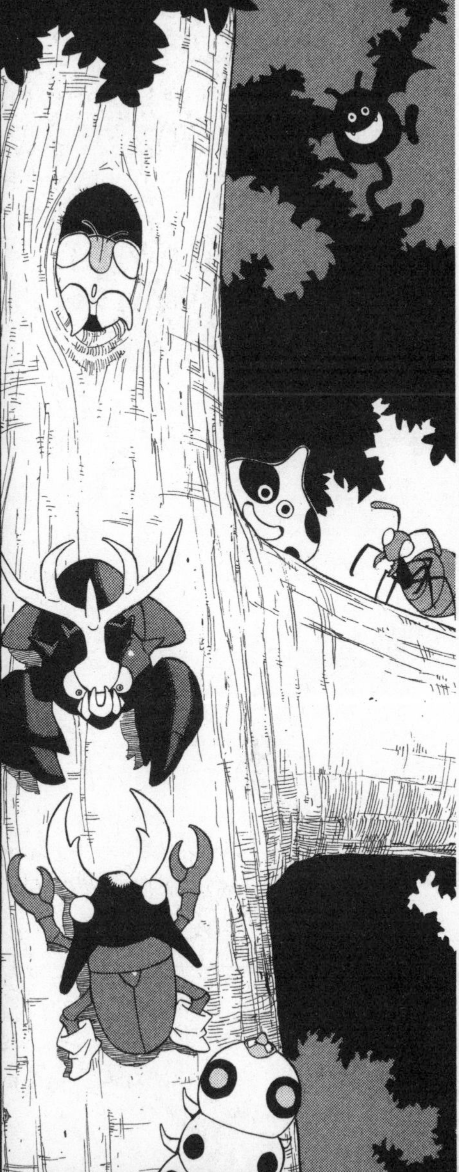

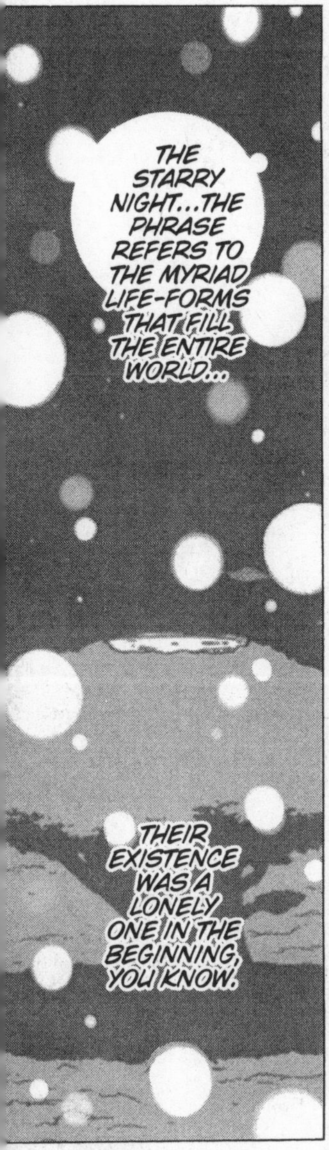
THE STARRY NIGHT...THE PHRASE REFERS TO THE MYRIAD LIFE-FORMS THAT FILL THE ENTIRE WORLD...
THEIR EXISTENCE WAS A LONELY ONE IN THE BEGINNING, YOU KNOW.

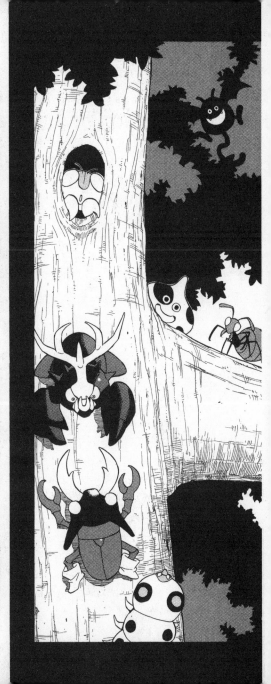

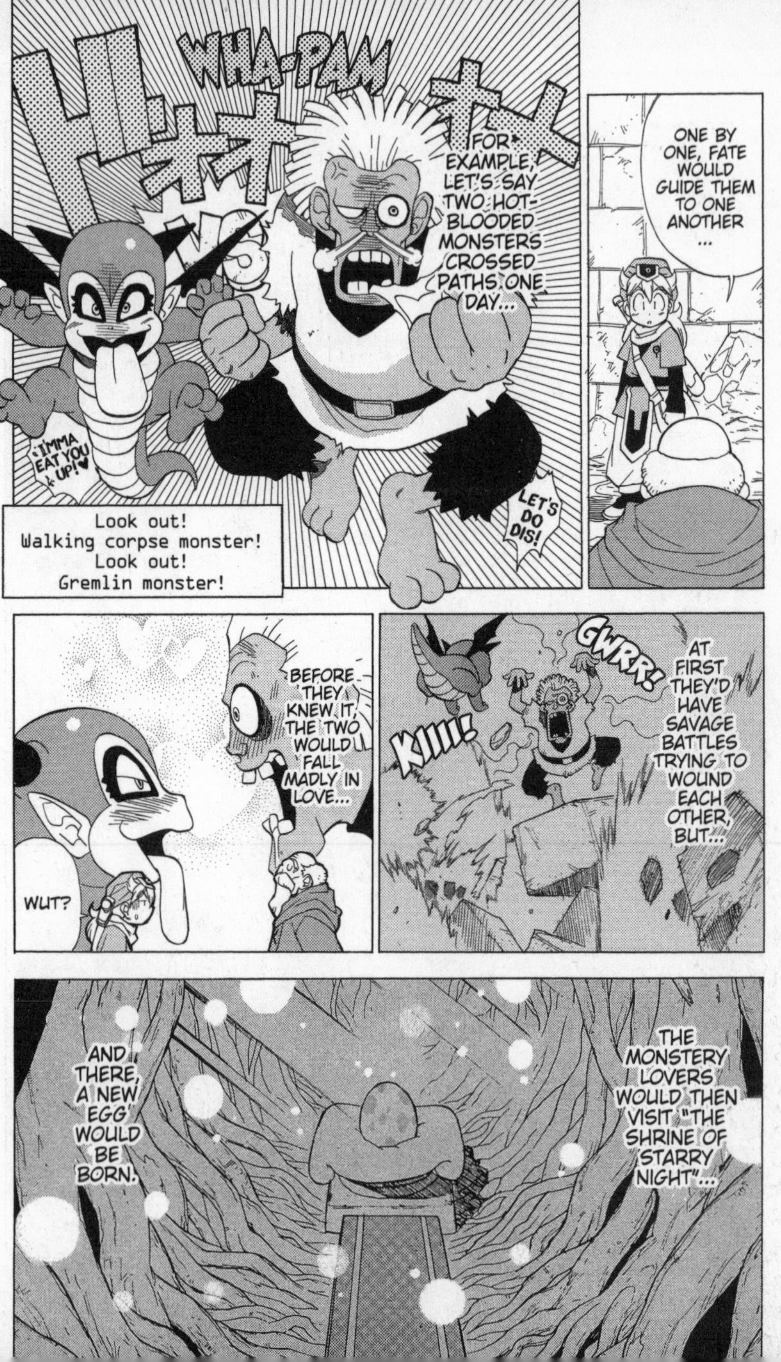
ONE BY ONE, FATE WOULD GUIDE THEM TO ONE ANOTHER ...
WHA-PAM
FOR EXAMPLE, LET'S SAY TWO HOT-BLOODED MONSTERS CROSSED PATHS ONE DAY...
LET'S DO DIS!
I'MMA EAT YOU UP!♥
Look out!
Walking corpse monster!
Look out!
Gremlin monster!
GWRR!
AT FIRST THEY'D HAVE SAVAGE BATTLES TRYING TO WOUND EACH OTHER, BUT...
KIIII!
BEFORE THEY KNEW IT, THE TWO WOULD FALL MADLY IN LOVE...
WUT?
THE MONSTERY LOVERS WOULD THEN VISIT "THE SHRINE OF STARRY NIGHT"...
AND THERE, A NEW EGG WOULD BE BORN.

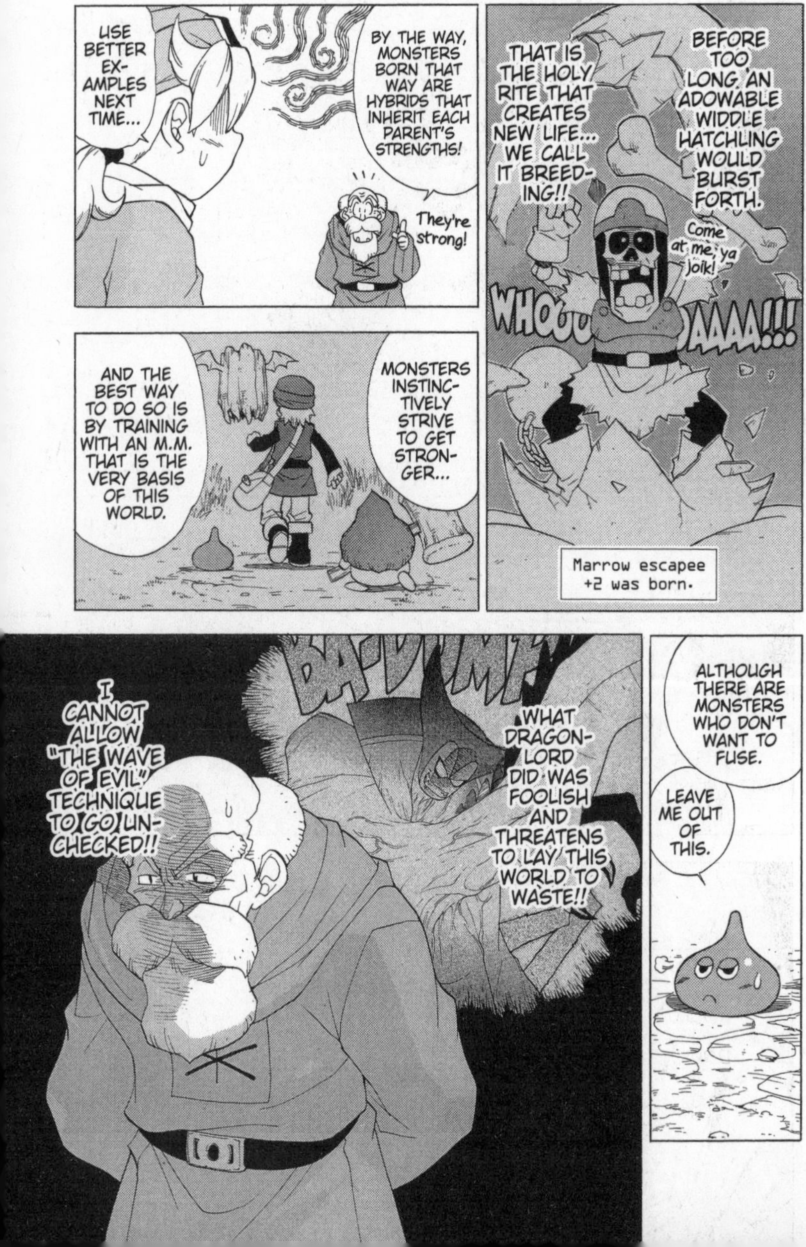
BEFORE TOO LONG, AN ADOWABLE WIDDLE HATCHLING WOULD BURST FORTH.
THAT IS THE HOLY RITE THAT CREATES NEW LIFE... WE CALL IT BREEDING!!
Come at me, ya joik!
WHOO AAAA!!!
Marrow escapee +2 was born.
BY THE WAY, MONSTERS BORN THAT WAY ARE HYBRIDS THAT INHERIT EACH PARENT'S STRENGTHS!
They're strong!
USE BETTER EX-AMPLES NEXT TIME...
MONSTERS INSTINCTIVELY STRIVE TO GET STRONGER...
AND THE BEST WAY TO DO SO IS BY TRAINING WITH AN M.M. THAT IS THE VERY BASIS OF THIS WORLD.
ALTHOUGH THERE ARE MONSTERS WHO DON'T WANT TO FUSE.
LEAVE ME OUT OF THIS.
BA-DUM
WHAT DRAGONLORD DID WAS FOOLISH AND THREATENS TO LAY THIS WORLD TO WASTE!!
I CANNOT ALLOW "THE WAVE OF EVIL" TECHNIQUE TO GO UNCHECKED!!

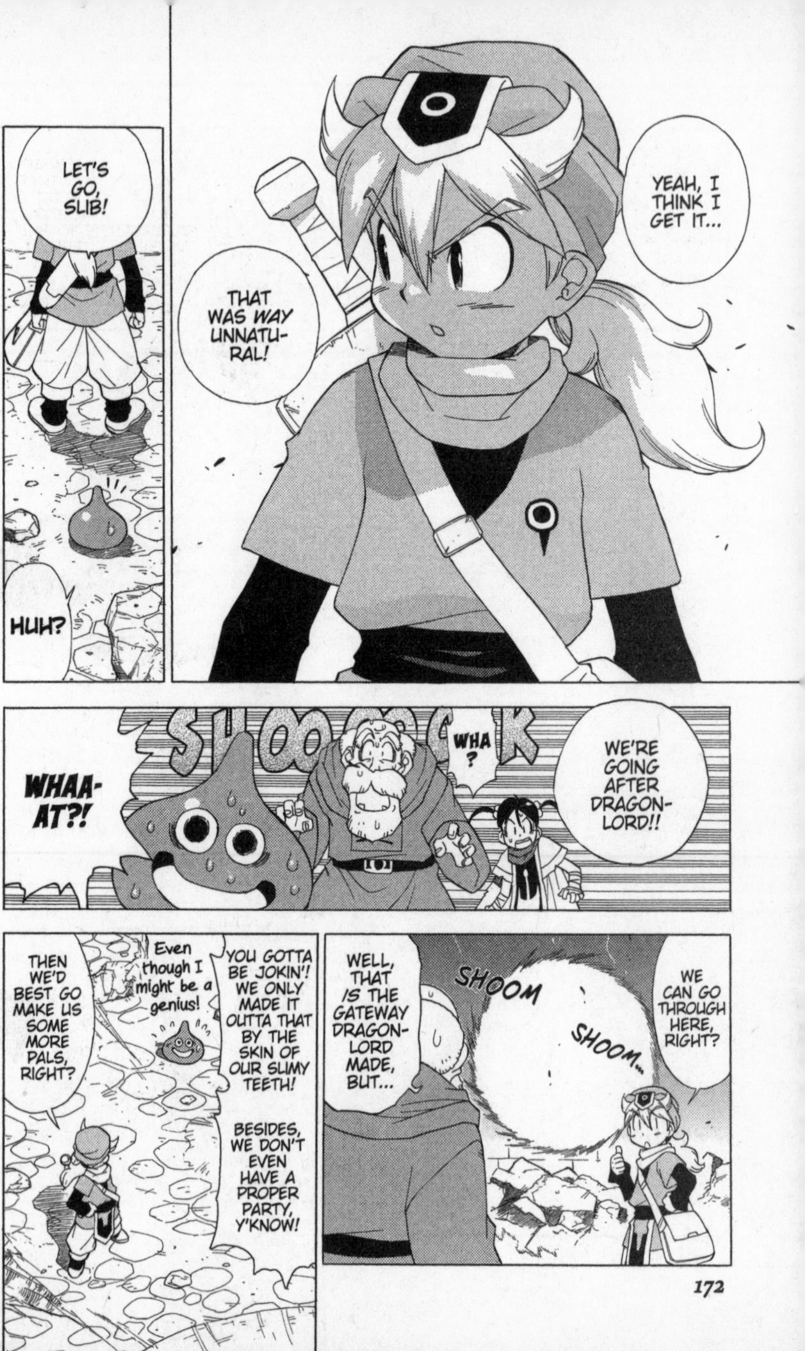
YEAH, I THINK I GET IT...
THAT WAS *WAY* UNNATURAL!
LET'S GO, SLIB!
HUH?
WE'RE GOING AFTER DRAGONLORD!!
WHA?
WHAAAT?!
WE CAN GO THROUGH HERE, RIGHT?
SHOOM
SHOOM...
WELL, THAT *IS* THE GATEWAY DRAGONLORD MADE, BUT...
YOU GOTTA BE JOKIN'! WE ONLY MADE IT OUTTA THAT BY THE SKIN OF OUR SLIMY TEETH!
BESIDES, WE DON'T EVEN HAVE A PROPER PARTY, Y'KNOW!
Even though I might be a genius!
THEN WE'D BEST GO MAKE US SOME MORE PALS, RIGHT?

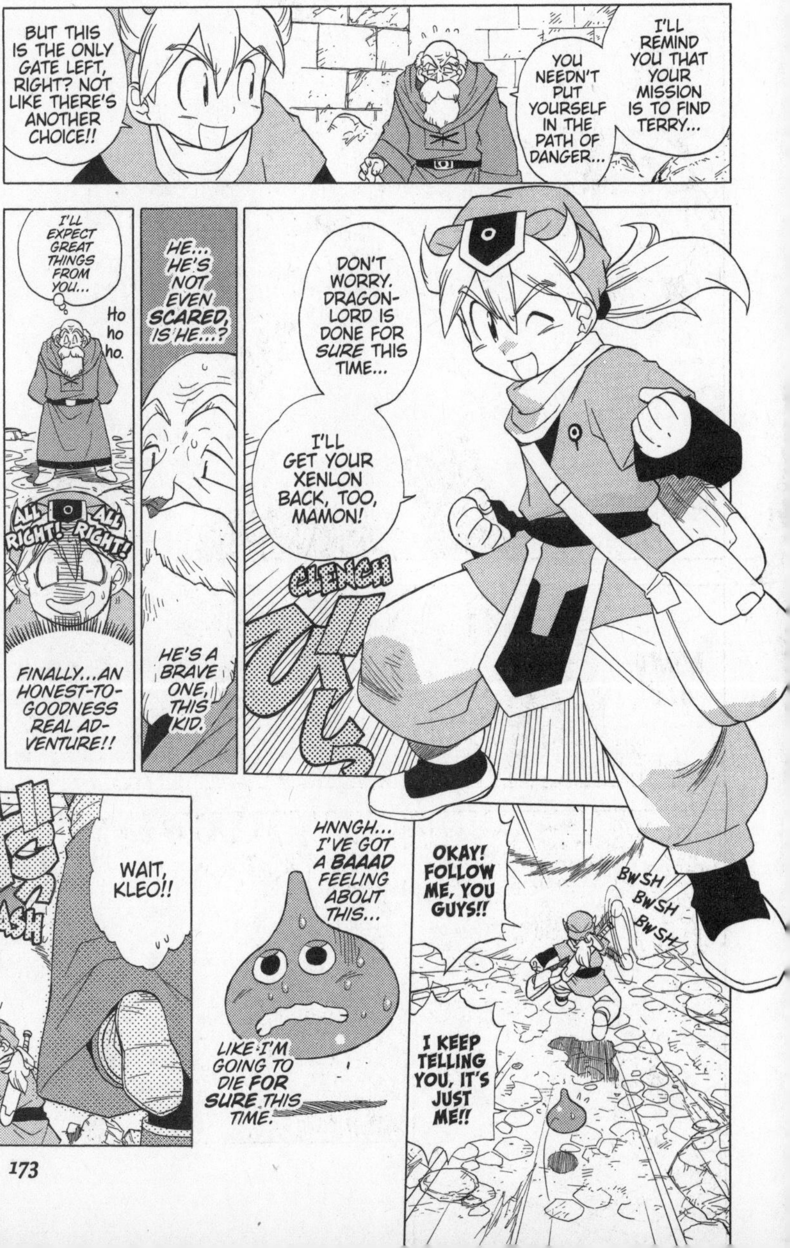
I'LL REMIND YOU THAT YOUR MISSION IS TO FIND TERRY...
YOU NEEDN'T PUT YOURSELF IN THE PATH OF DANGER...
BUT THIS IS THE ONLY GATE LEFT, RIGHT? NOT LIKE THERE'S ANOTHER CHOICE!!
DON'T WORRY. DRAGON-LORD IS DONE FOR SURE THIS TIME...
I'LL GET YOUR XENLON BACK, TOO, MAMON!
CLENCH
HE... HE'S NOT EVEN SCARED, IS HE...?
HE'S A BRAVE ONE, THIS KID.
I'LL EXPECT GREAT THINGS FROM YOU...
Ho ho ho.
ALL RIGHT! ALL RIGHT!
FINALLY...AN HONEST-TO-GOODNESS REAL AD-VENTURE!!
OKAY! FOLLOW ME, YOU GUYS!!
BWSH BWSH BWSH
I KEEP TELLING YOU, IT'S JUST ME!!
HNNGH... I'VE GOT A BAAAD FEELING ABOUT THIS...
LIKE I'M GOING TO DIE FOR SURE THIS TIME.
WAIT, KLEO!!
DASH

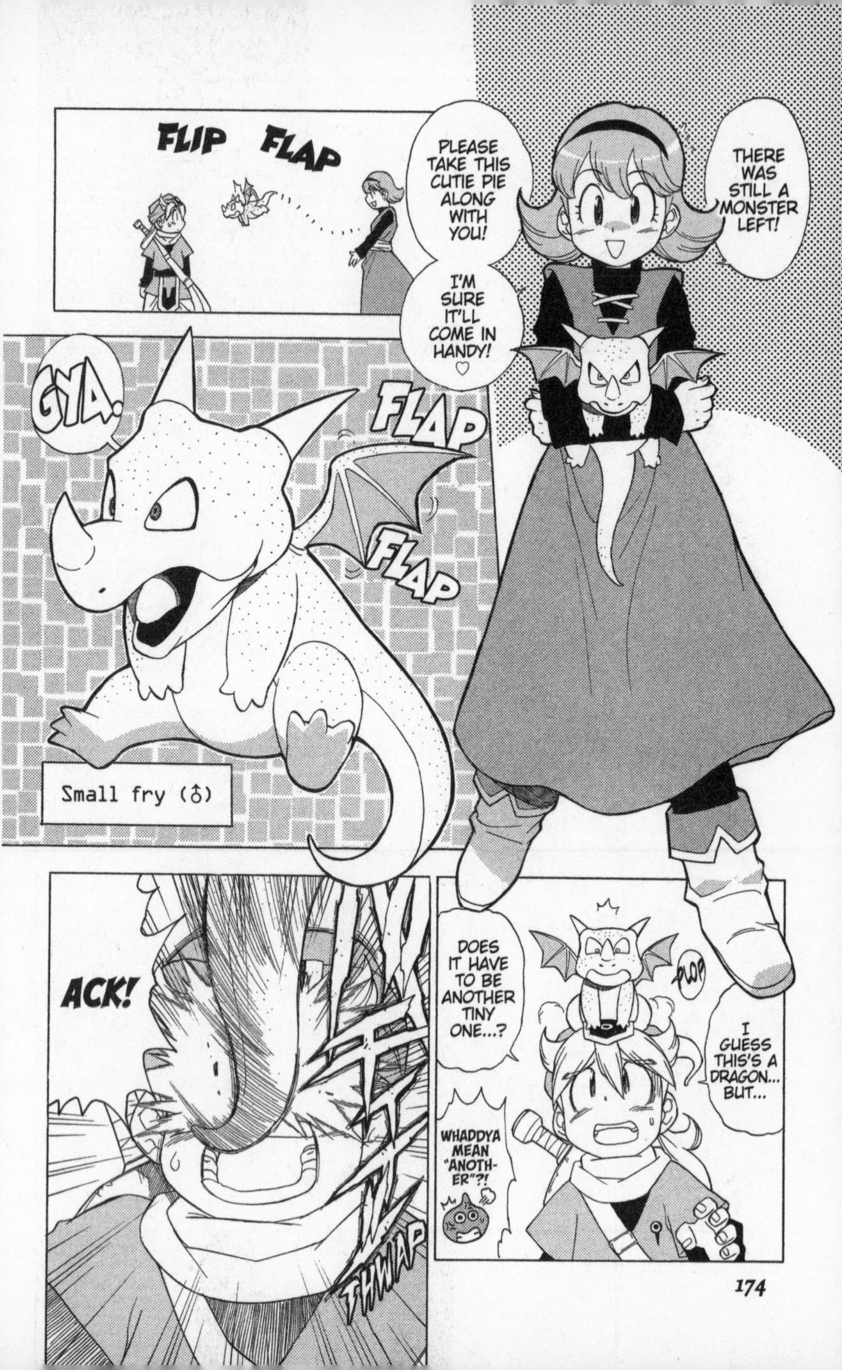
THERE WAS STILL A MONSTER LEFT!
PLEASE TAKE THIS CUTIE PIE ALONG WITH YOU!
I'M SURE IT'LL COME IN HANDY! ♡
FLIP FLAP
GYA.
FLAP
FLAP
Small fry (♂)
PLOP
I GUESS THIS'S A DRAGON... BUT...
DOES IT HAVE TO BE ANOTHER TINY ONE...?
WHADDYA MEAN "ANOTHER"?!
ACK!
THWAP

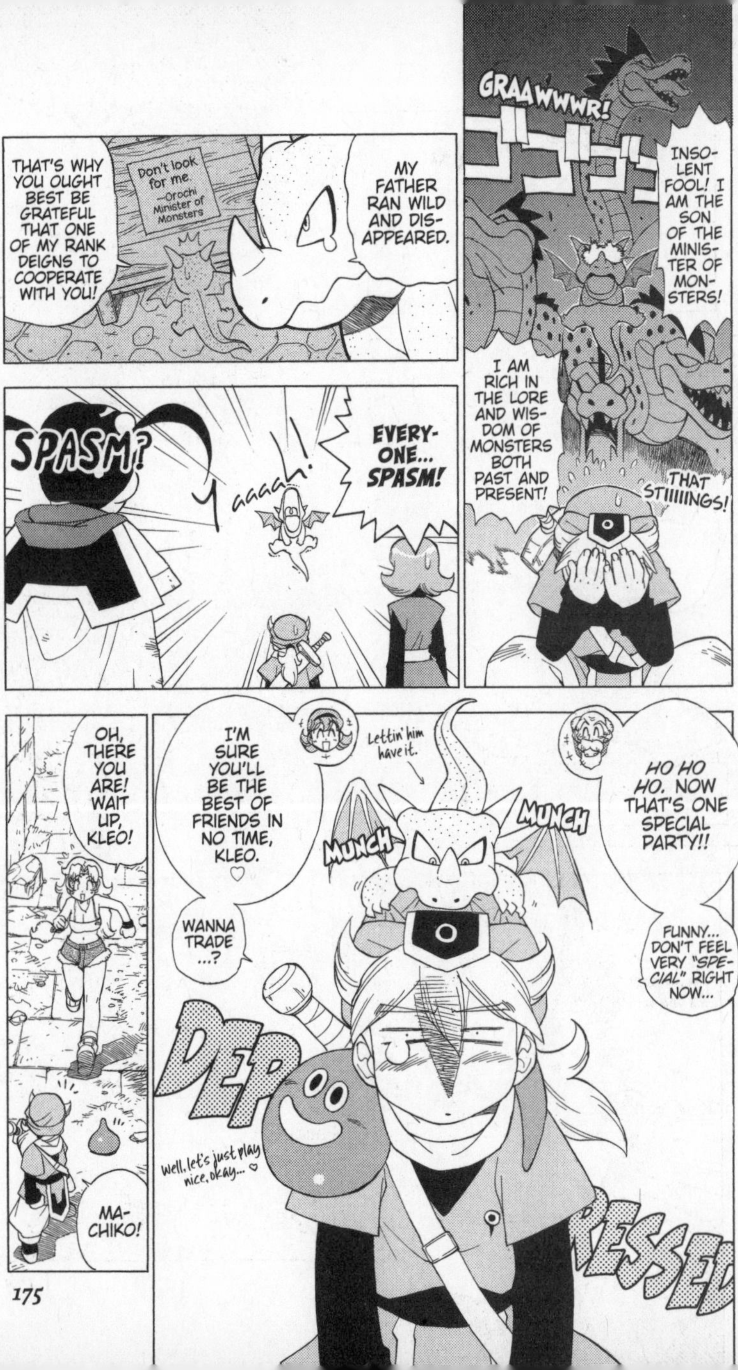
GRAAWWWR!
INSOLENT FOOL! I AM THE SON OF THE MINISTER OF MONSTERS!
I AM RICH IN THE LORE AND WISDOM OF MONSTERS BOTH PAST AND PRESENT!
THAT STIIIINGS!
MY FATHER RAN WILD AND DISAPPEARED.
Don't look for me. —Orochi Minister of Monsters
THAT'S WHY YOU OUGHT BEST BE GRATEFUL THAT ONE OF MY RANK DEIGNS TO COOPERATE WITH YOU!
EVERYONE... SPASM!
Yaaaah!
SPASM?
HO HO HO. NOW THAT'S ONE SPECIAL PARTY!!
Lettin' him have it.
I'M SURE YOU'LL BE THE BEST OF FRIENDS IN NO TIME, KLEO. ♡
MUNCH
MUNCH
FUNNY... DON'T FEEL VERY "SPECIAL" RIGHT NOW...
WANNA TRADE ...?
DEPRESSED
Well, let's just play nice, okay... ♡
OH, THERE YOU ARE! WAIT UP, KLEO!
MACHIKO!

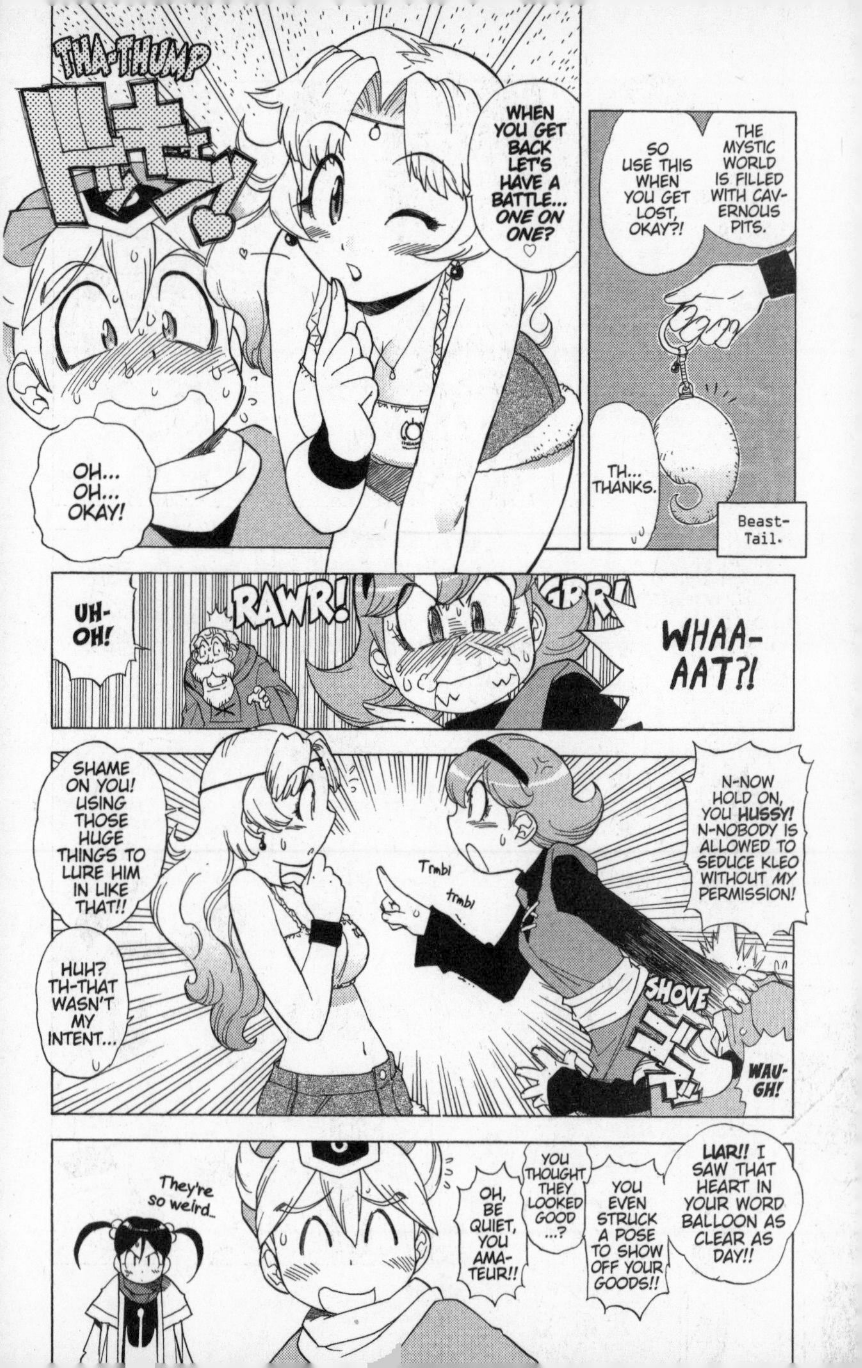
THE MYSTIC WORLD IS FILLED WITH CAVERNOUS PITS.
SO USE THIS WHEN YOU GET LOST, OKAY?!
TH... THANKS.
Beast-Tail.
THA-THUMP
WHEN YOU GET BACK LET'S HAVE A BATTLE... ONE ON ONE? ♡
OH... OH... OKAY!
WHAA-AAT?!
GRR!
RAWR!
UH-OH!
N-NOW HOLD ON, YOU HUSSY! N-NOBODY IS ALLOWED TO SEDUCE KLEO WITHOUT MY PERMISSION!
Trmbl
trmbl
SHAME ON YOU! USING THOSE HUGE THINGS TO LURE HIM IN LIKE THAT!!
HUH? TH-THAT WASN'T MY INTENT...
WAU-GH!
SHOVE
LIAR!! I SAW THAT HEART IN YOUR WORD BALLOON AS CLEAR AS DAY!!
YOU EVEN STRUCK A POSE TO SHOW OFF YOUR GOODS!!
YOU THOUGHT THEY LOOKED GOOD ...?
OH, BE QUIET, YOU AMATEUR!!
They're so weird...

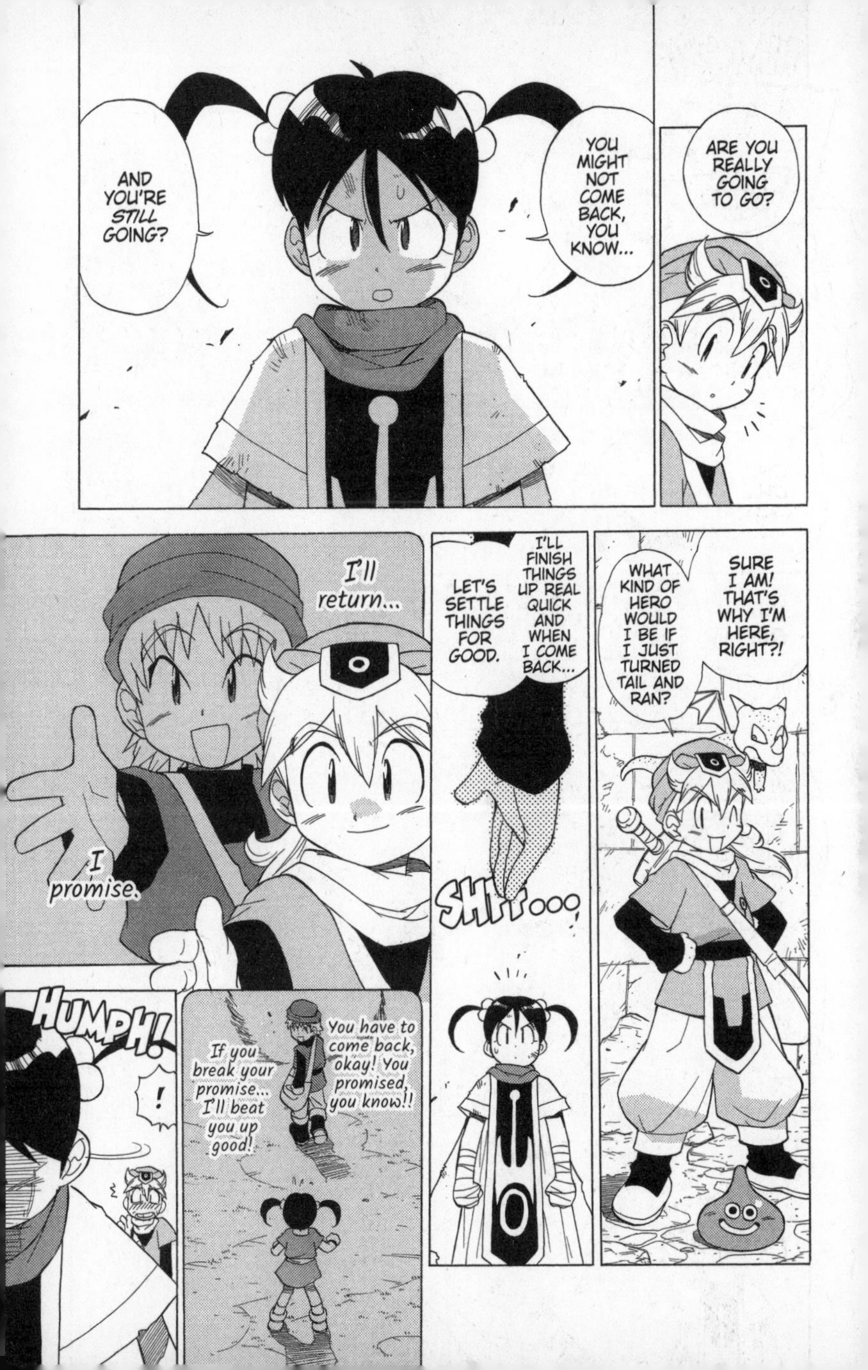
ARE YOU REALLY GOING TO GO?
YOU MIGHT NOT COME BACK, YOU KNOW...
AND YOU'RE STILL GOING?
SURE I AM! THAT'S WHY I'M HERE, RIGHT?!
WHAT KIND OF HERO WOULD I BE IF I JUST TURNED TAIL AND RAN?
I'LL FINISH THINGS UP REAL QUICK AND WHEN I COME BACK...
LET'S SETTLE THINGS FOR GOOD.
SHFFooo
I'll return...
I promise.
You have to come back, okay! You promised, you know!!
If you break your promise... I'll beat you up good!
HUMPH!
!

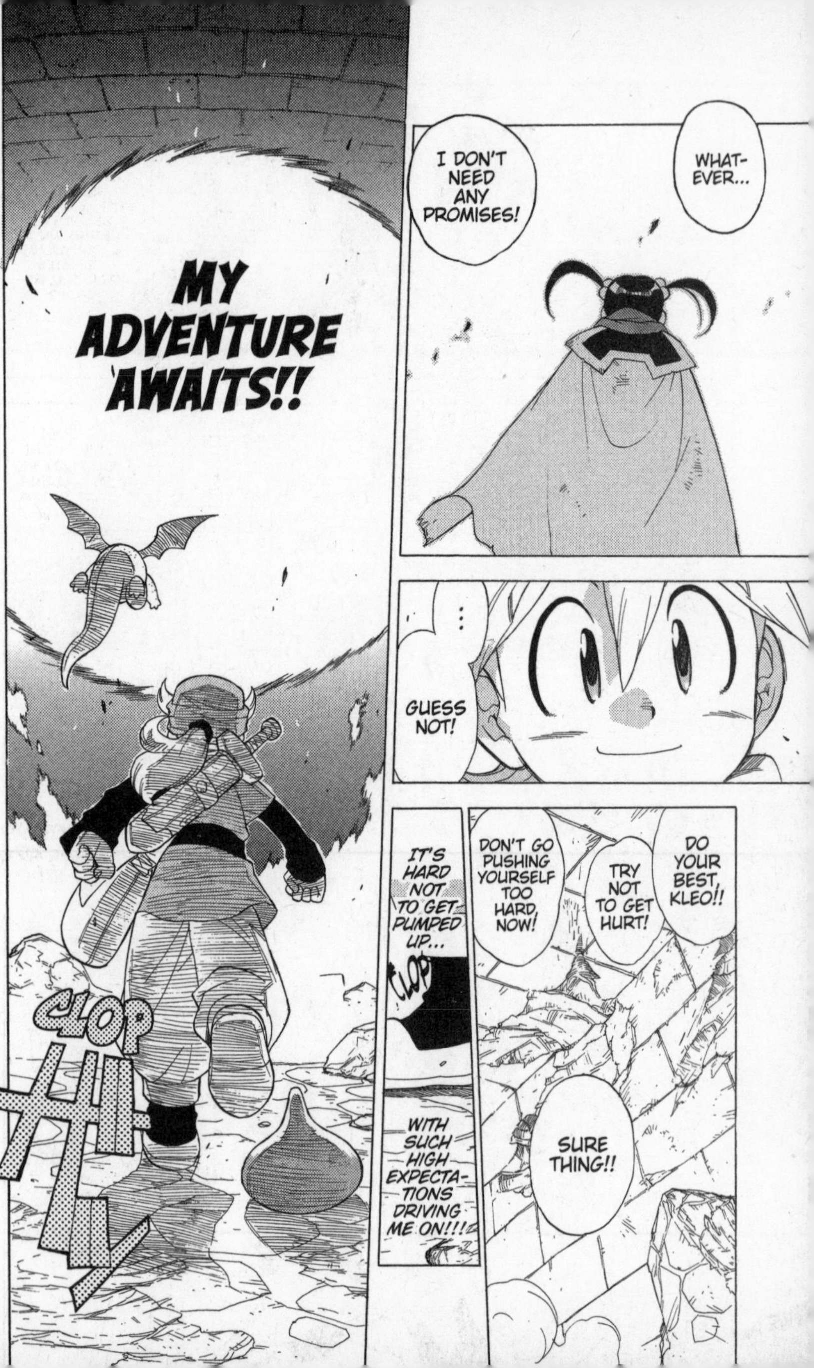
WHAT-EVER...
I DON'T NEED ANY PROMISES!
...
GUESS NOT!
DO YOUR BEST, KLEO!!
TRY NOT TO GET HURT!
DON'T GO PUSHING YOURSELF TOO HARD, NOW!
SURE THING!!
IT'S HARD NOT TO GET PUMPED UP...
CLOP
WITH SUCH HIGH EXPECTATIONS DRIVING ME ON!!!
MY ADVENTURE AWAITS!!
CLOP

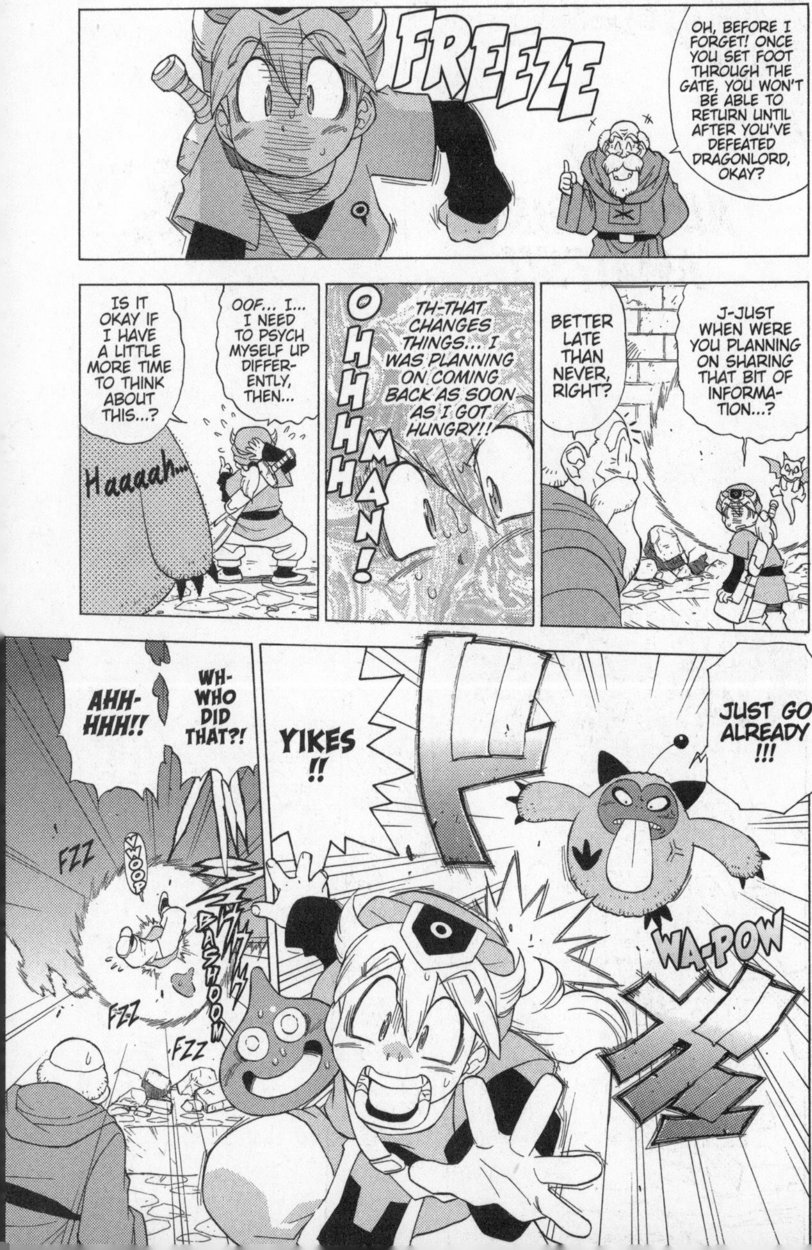
OH, BEFORE I FORGET! ONCE YOU SET FOOT THROUGH THE GATE, YOU WON'T BE ABLE TO RETURN UNTIL AFTER YOU'VE DEFEATED DRAGONLORD, OKAY?
FREEZE
J-JUST WHEN WERE YOU PLANNING ON SHARING THAT BIT OF INFORMATION...?
BETTER LATE THAN NEVER, RIGHT?
TH-THAT CHANGES THINGS... I WAS PLANNING ON COMING BACK AS SOON AS I GOT HUNGRY!!
OHHHHHH
MAN!
OOF... I... I NEED TO PSYCH MYSELF UP DIFFERENTLY, THEN...
IS IT OKAY IF I HAVE A LITTLE MORE TIME TO THINK ABOUT THIS...?
Haaaah...
JUST GO ALREADY !!!
WA-POW
YIKES !!
WH-WHO DID THAT?!
AHH-HHH!!
FZZ
VWOOP
BASHOOM
FZZ
FZZ

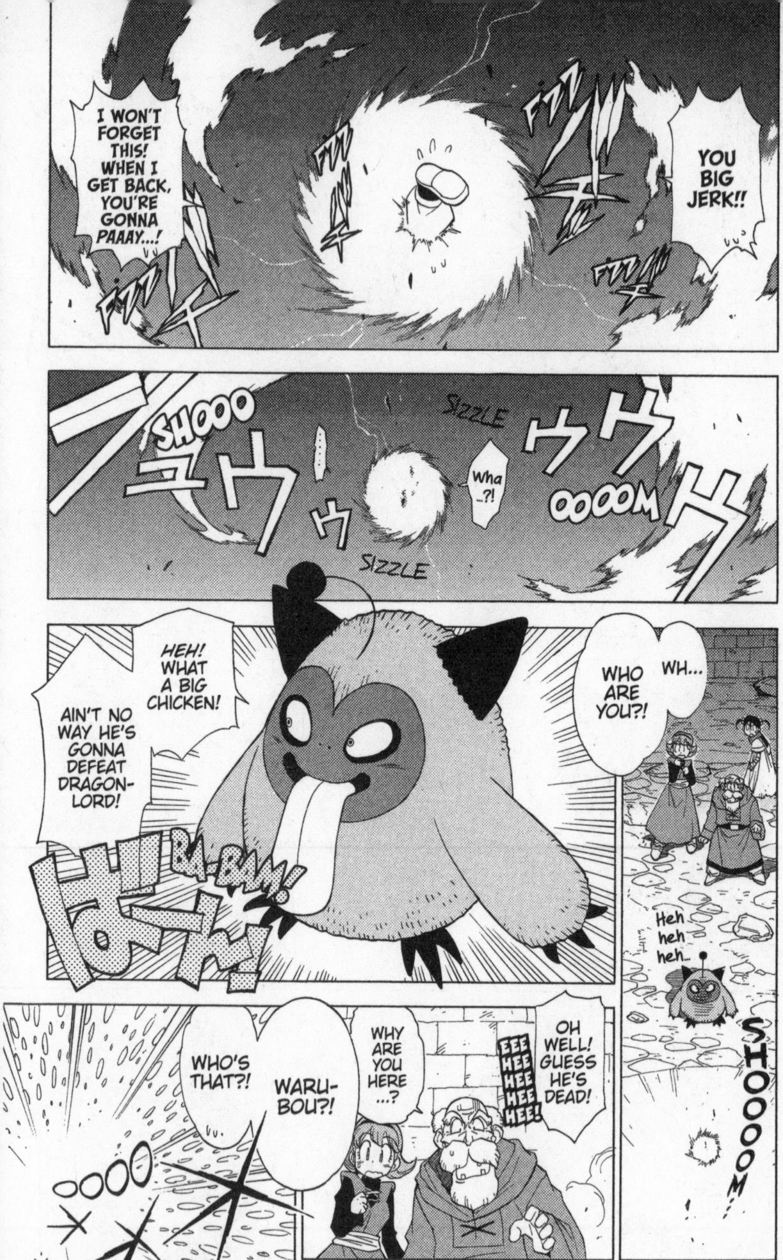
YOU BIG JERK!!
I WON'T FORGET THIS! WHEN I GET BACK, YOU'RE GONNA PAAAY...!
OOOOM
SIZZLE
Wha ...?!
SHOOO
SIZZLE
WH...
WHO ARE YOU?!
Heh heh heh...
SHOOOOOM!
HEH! WHAT A BIG CHICKEN!
AIN'T NO WAY HE'S GONNA DEFEAT DRAGON-LORD!
BA-BAM!
OH WELL! GUESS HE'S DEAD!
EEE HEE HEE HEE HEE!
WHY ARE YOU HERE ...?
WARU-BOU?!
WHO'S THAT?!
OOOO

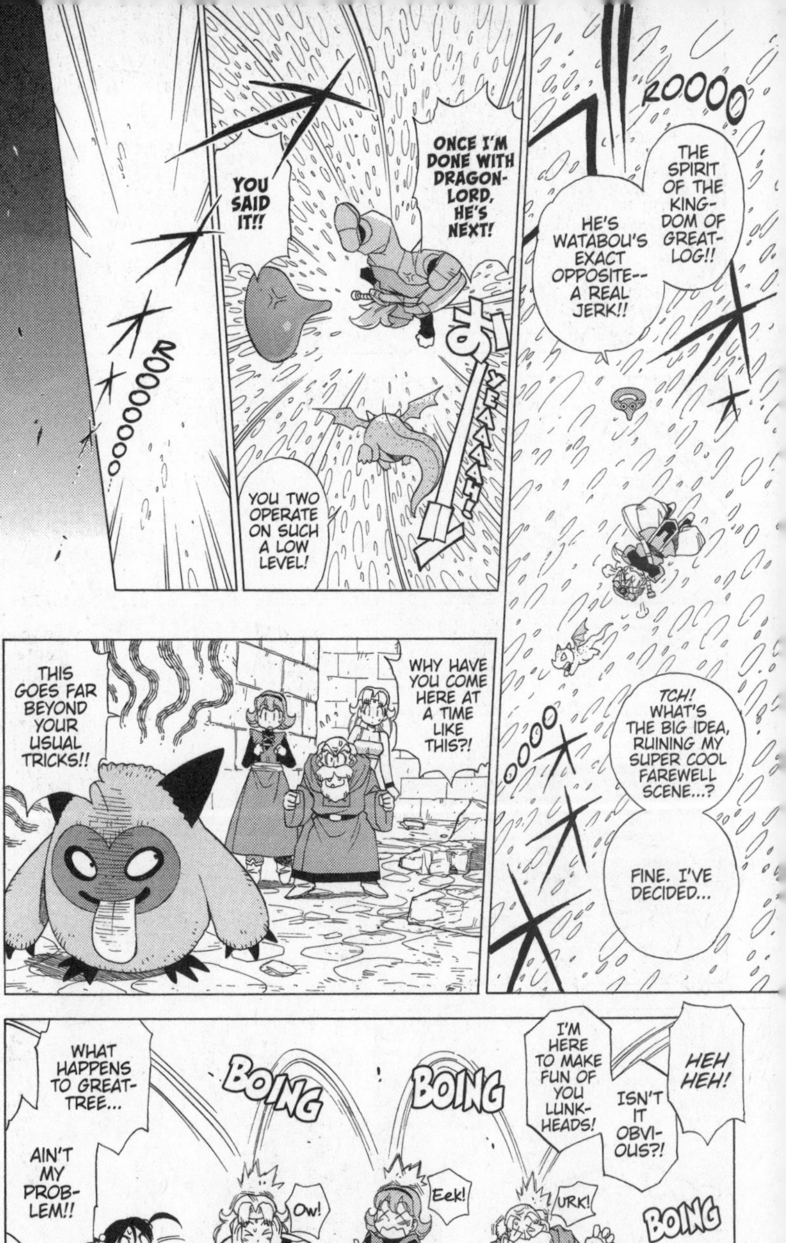
ROOOO
THE SPIRIT OF THE KING-DOM OF GREAT-LOG!!
HE'S WATABOU'S EXACT OPPOSITE-- A REAL JERK!!
OOOO
TCH! WHAT'S THE BIG IDEA, RUINING MY SUPER COOL FAREWELL SCENE...?
FINE. I'VE DECIDED...
ONCE I'M DONE WITH DRAGON-LORD, HE'S NEXT!
YOU SAID IT!!
お
YEAAAAH!
YOU TWO OPERATE ON SUCH A LOW LEVEL!
ROOOOOOOO
WHY HAVE YOU COME HERE AT A TIME LIKE THIS?!
THIS GOES FAR BEYOND YOUR USUAL TRICKS!!
HEH HEH!
ISN'T IT OBVI-OUS?!
I'M HERE TO MAKE FUN OF YOU LUNK-HEADS!
BOING
BOING
BOING
URK!
Eek!
Ow!
WHAT HAPPENS TO GREAT-TREE...
AIN'T MY PROB-LEM!!

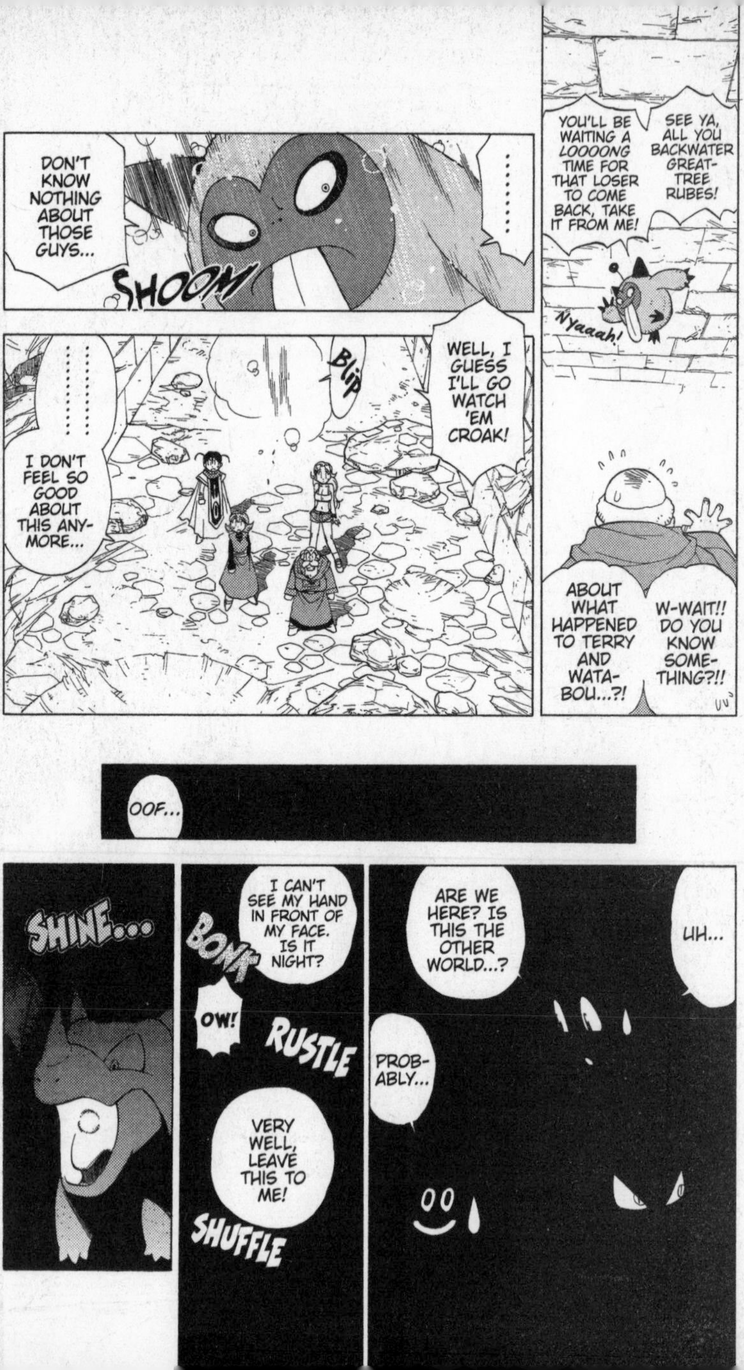
SEE YA, ALL YOU BACKWATER GREAT-TREE RUBES!
YOU'LL BE WAITING A LOOOONG TIME FOR THAT LOSER TO COME BACK, TAKE IT FROM ME!
Nyaaah!
W-WAIT!! DO YOU KNOW SOME-THING?!!
ABOUT WHAT HAPPENED TO TERRY AND WATA-BOU...?!
......
DON'T KNOW NOTHING ABOUT THOSE GUYS...
SHOOM
WELL, I GUESS I'LL GO WATCH 'EM CROAK!
Blip
......
I DON'T FEEL SO GOOD ABOUT THIS ANY-MORE...
OOF...
UH...
ARE WE HERE? IS THIS THE OTHER WORLD...?
PROB-ABLY...
I CAN'T SEE MY HAND IN FRONT OF MY FACE. IS IT NIGHT?
BONK
OW!
RUSTLE
VERY WELL, LEAVE THIS TO ME!
SHUFFLE
SHINE...

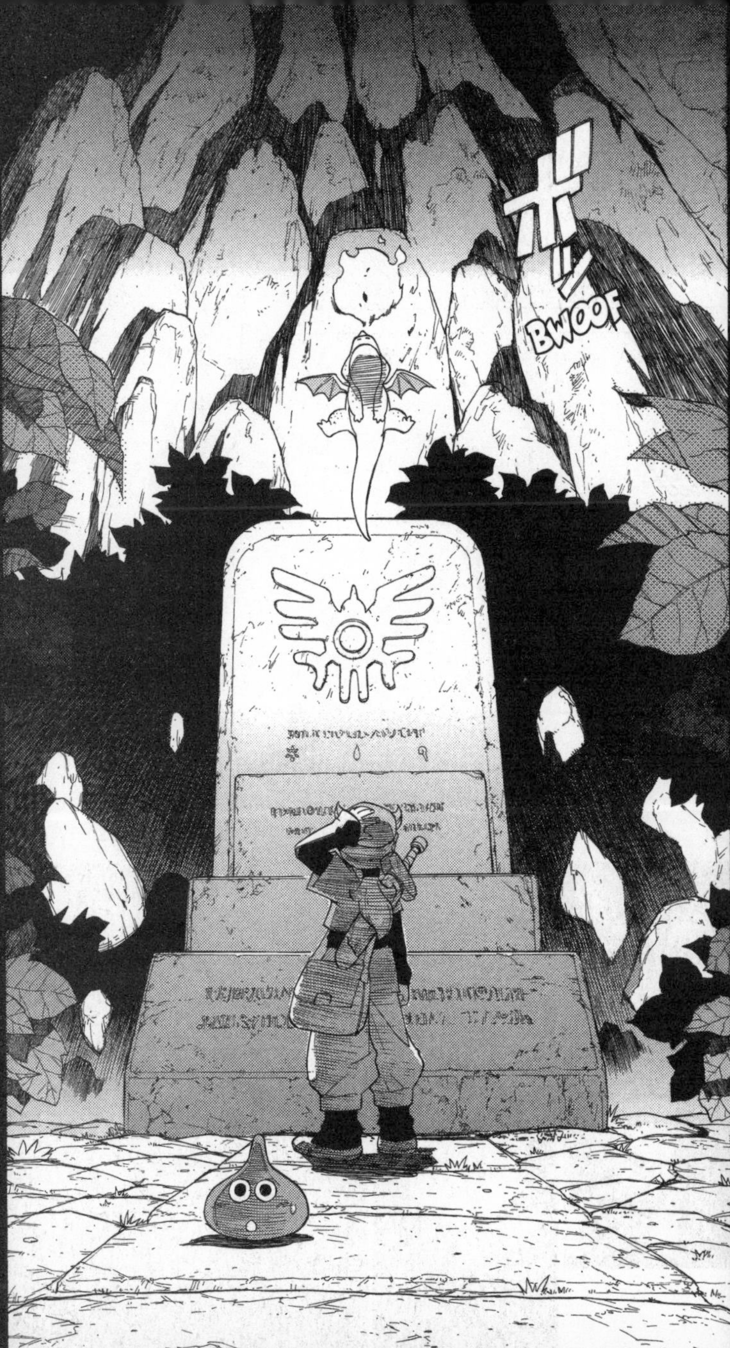
ボッ
BWOOF

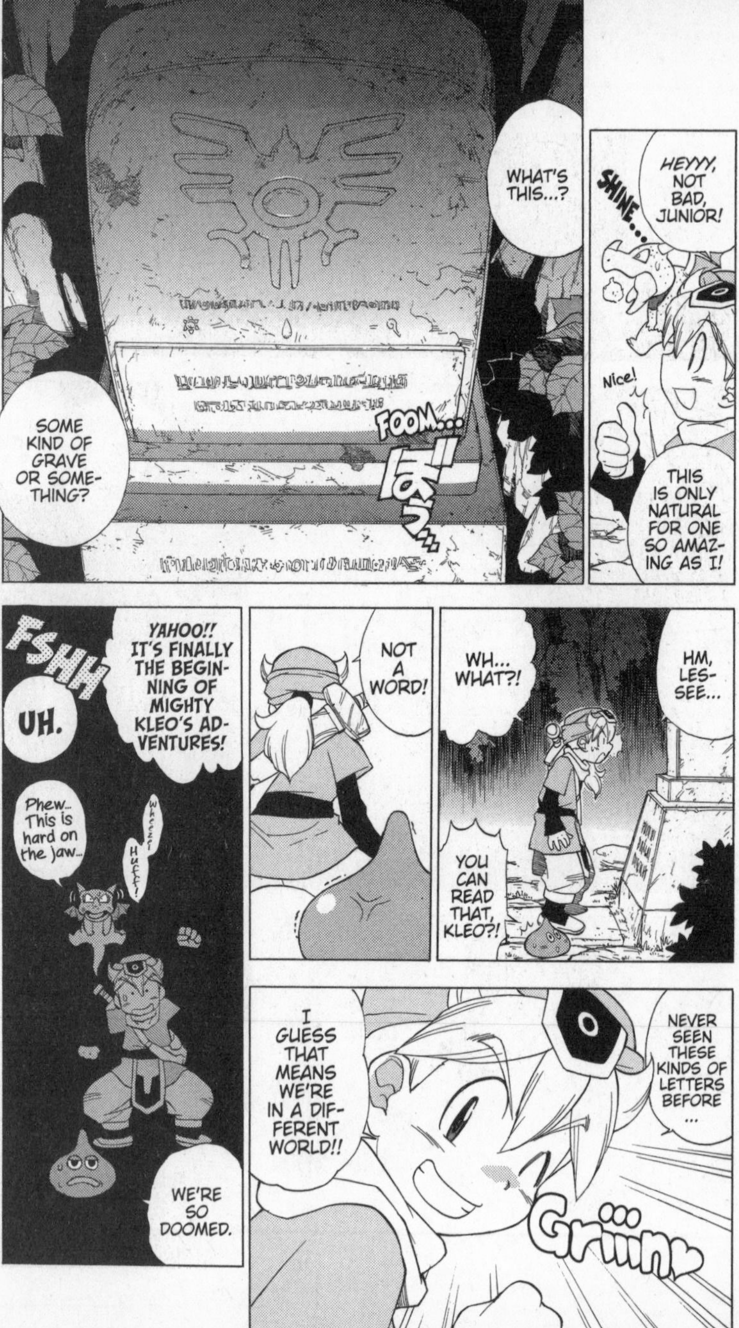
HEYYY, NOT BAD, JUNIOR!
SHINE...
Nice!
THIS IS ONLY NATURAL FOR ONE SO AMAZING AS I!
WHAT'S THIS...?
FOOM...
ぼう...
SOME KIND OF GRAVE OR SOMETHING?
HM, LESSEE...
WH... WHAT?!
YOU CAN READ THAT, KLEO?!
NOT A WORD!
NEVER SEEN THESE KINDS OF LETTERS BEFORE...
I GUESS THAT MEANS WE'RE IN A DIFFERENT WORLD!!
...Griiin♥
YAHOO!! IT'S FINALLY THE BEGINNING OF MIGHTY KLEO'S ADVENTURES!
FSHH
UH.
Wheeze!
Huff!
Phew... This is hard on the jaw...
WE'RE SO DOOMED.

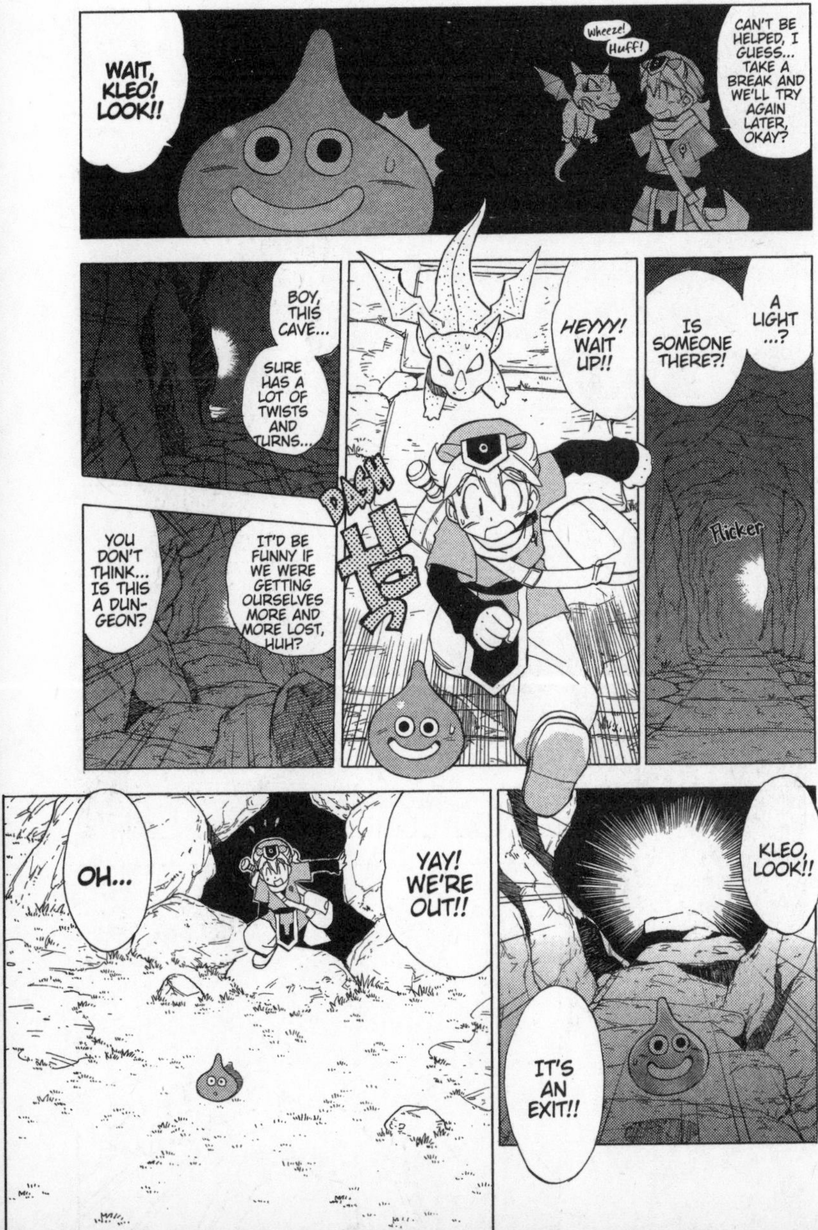
Wheeze!
Huff!
CAN'T BE HELPED, I GUESS... TAKE A BREAK AND WE'LL TRY AGAIN LATER, OKAY?
WAIT, KLEO! LOOK!!
A LIGHT ...?
IS SOMEONE THERE?!
Flicker
HEYYY! WAIT UP!!
DASH
BOY, THIS CAVE...
SURE HAS A LOT OF TWISTS AND TURNS...
IT'D BE FUNNY IF WE WERE GETTING OURSELVES MORE AND MORE LOST, HUH?
YOU DON'T THINK... IS THIS A DUN-GEON?
KLEO, LOOK!!
IT'S AN EXIT!!
YAY! WE'RE OUT!!
OH...

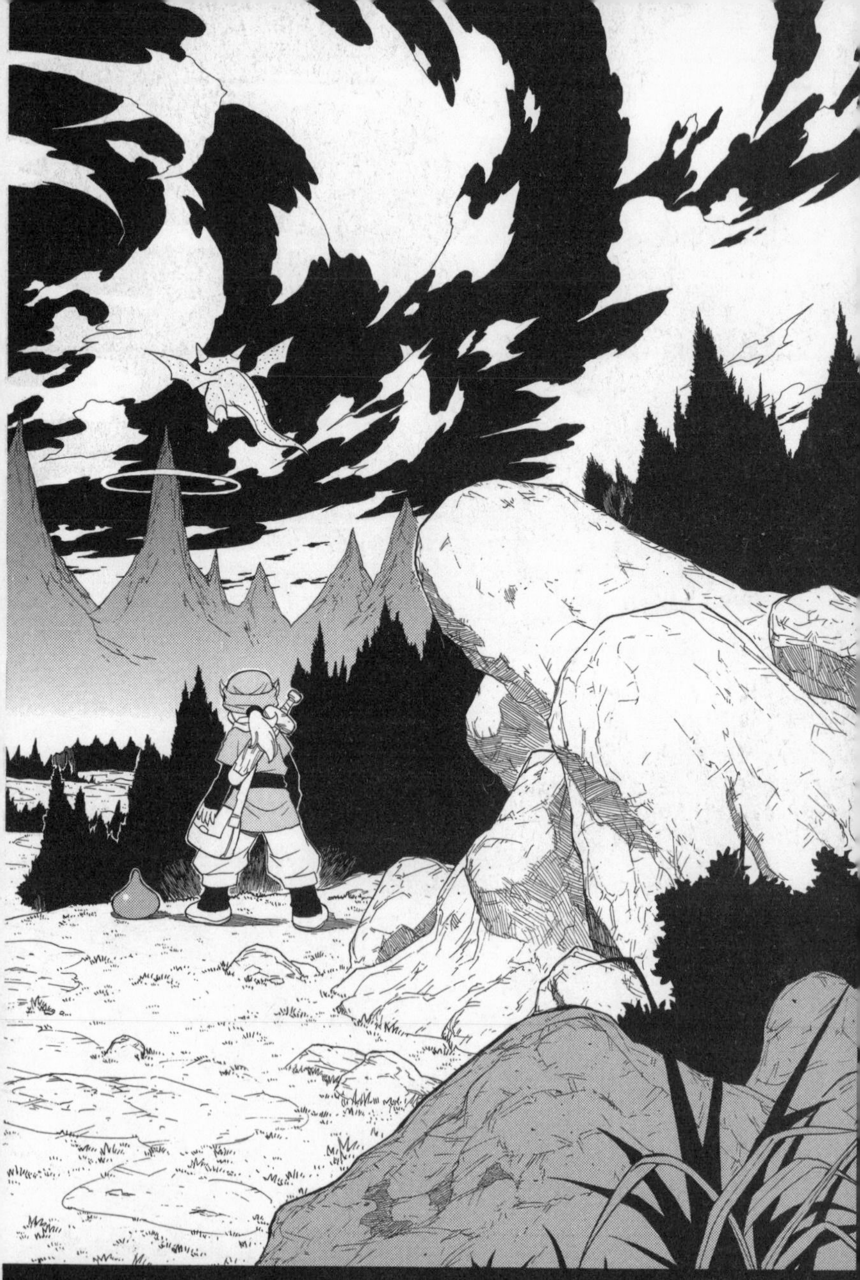

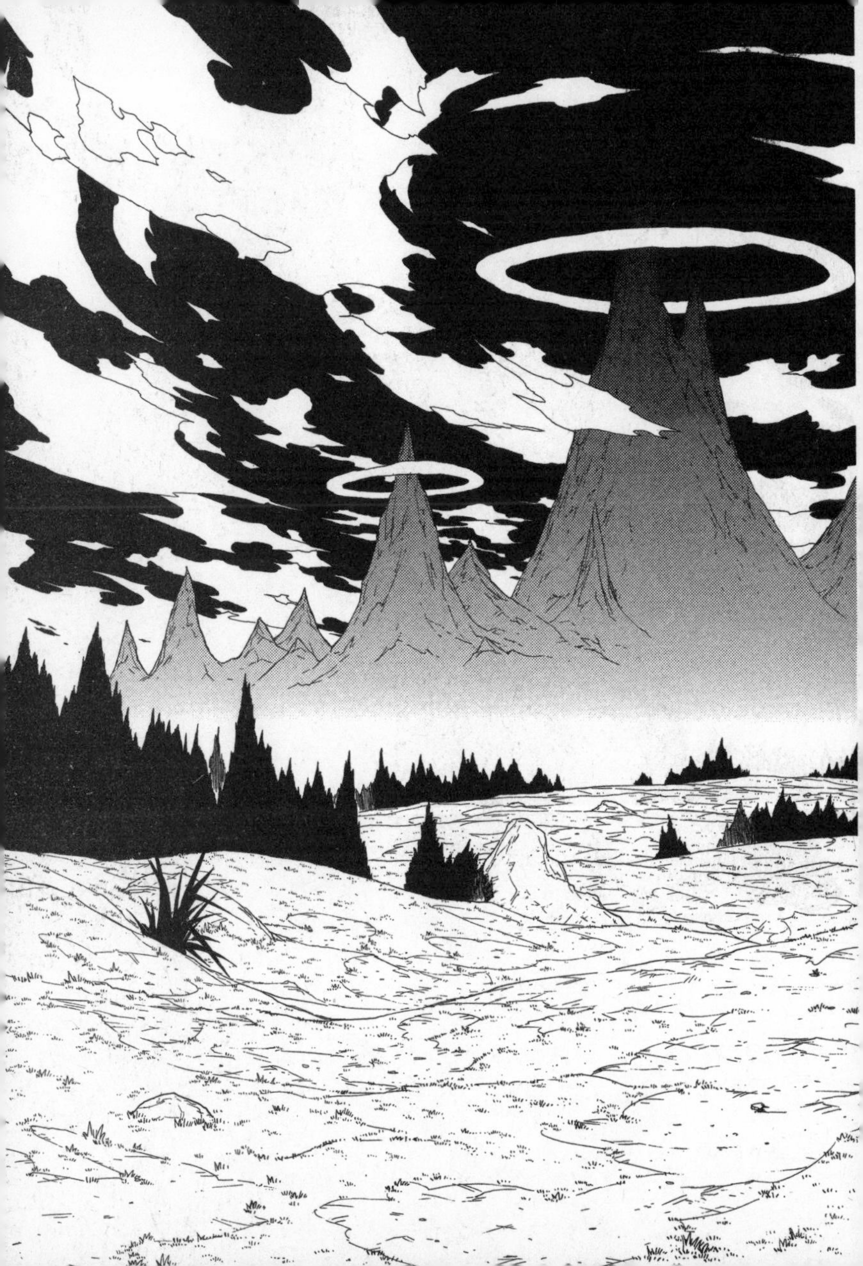

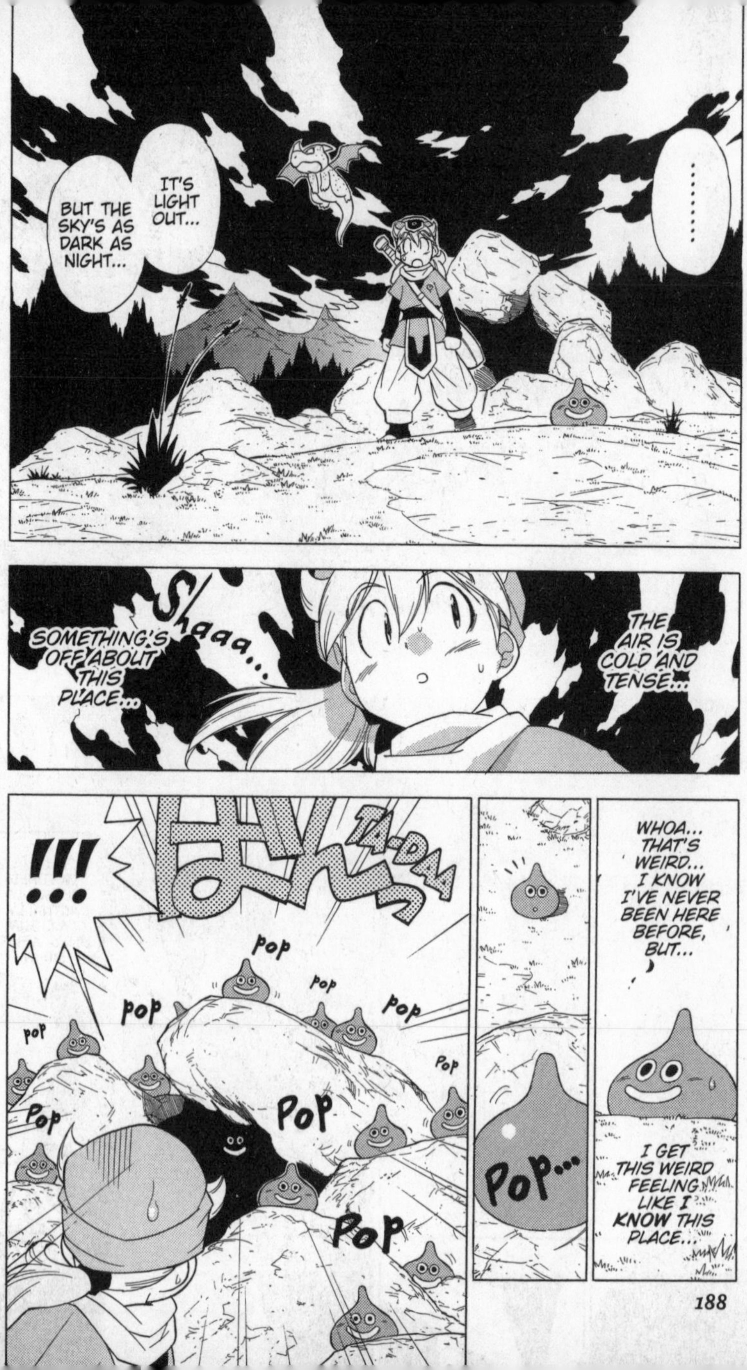

......
IT'S LIGHT OUT...
BUT THE SKY'S AS DARK AS NIGHT...
THE AIR IS COLD AND TENSE...
Shaaa...
SOMETHING'S OFF ABOUT THIS PLACE...
WHOA... THAT'S WEIRD... I KNOW I'VE NEVER BEEN HERE BEFORE, BUT...
I GET THIS WEIRD FEELING LIKE I KNOW THIS PLACE...
POP...
TA-DAA
!!!
pop
pop
pop
pop
pop
Pop
POP
POP

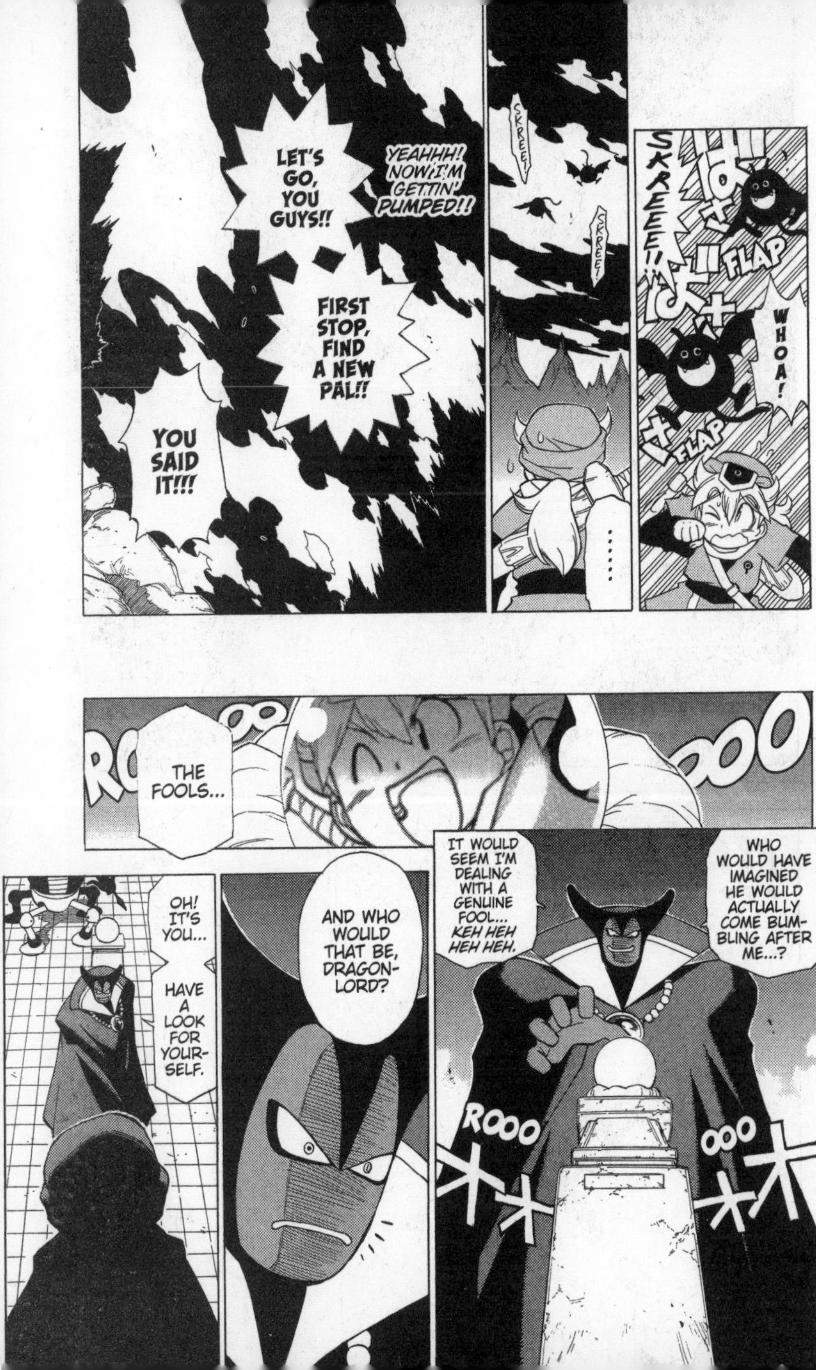
SKREEE!!
FLAP
FLAP
WHOA!
SKREE!
SKREE!
......
YEAHHH! NOW I'M GETTIN' PUMPED!!
LET'S GO, YOU GUYS!!
FIRST STOP, FIND A NEW PAL!!
YOU SAID IT!!!
ROOOOOO
THE FOOLS...
WHO WOULD HAVE IMAGINED HE WOULD ACTUALLY COME BUMBLING AFTER ME...?
IT WOULD SEEM I'M DEALING WITH A GENUINE FOOL... KEH HEH HEH HEH.
ROOO
OOO
AND WHO WOULD THAT BE, DRAGONLORD?
OH! IT'S YOU...
HAVE A LOOK FOR YOURSELF.

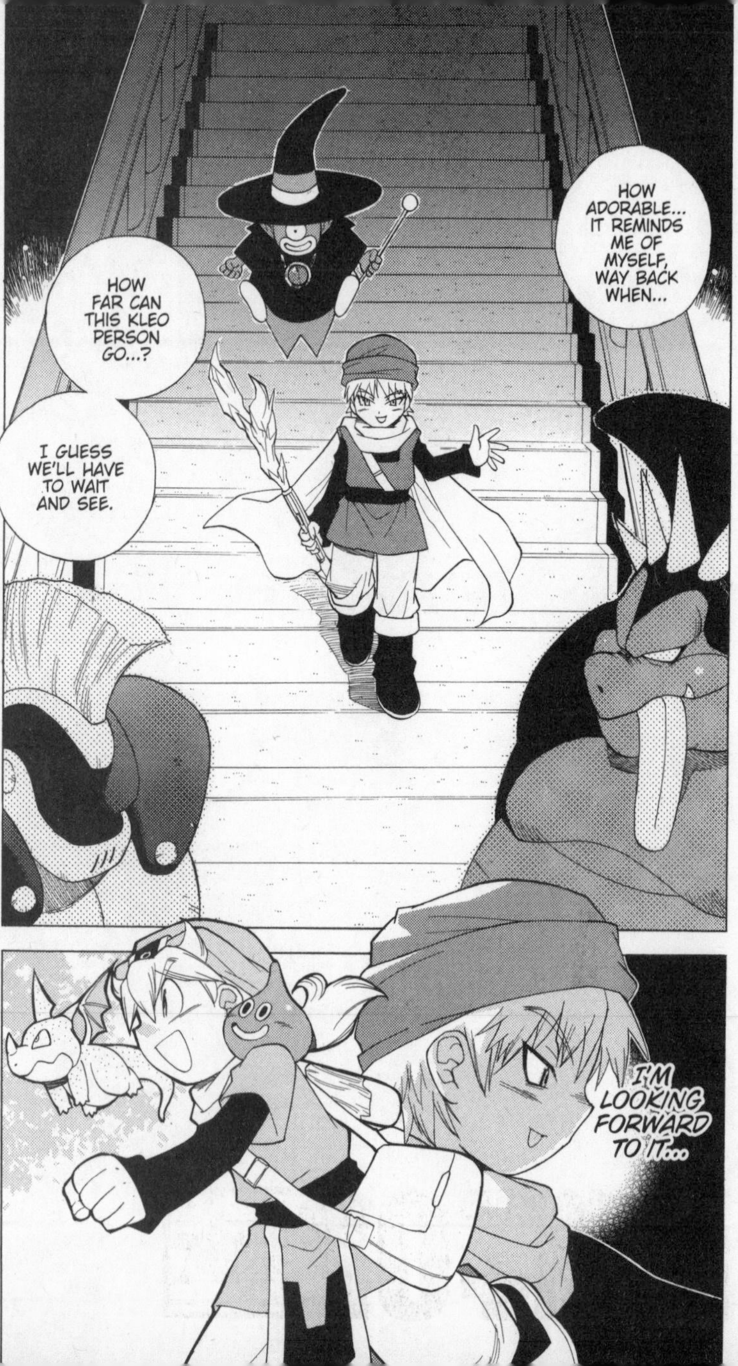
HOW ADORABLE... IT REMINDS ME OF MYSELF, WAY BACK WHEN...
HOW FAR CAN THIS KLEO PERSON GO...?
I GUESS WE'LL HAVE TO WAIT AND SEE.
I'M LOOKING FORWARD TO IT...

TO BE CONTINUED

DQM+02

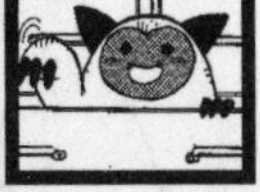

Monster Encyclopedia Vol.1

Here's a list of the quirky monsters that appear in this manga!

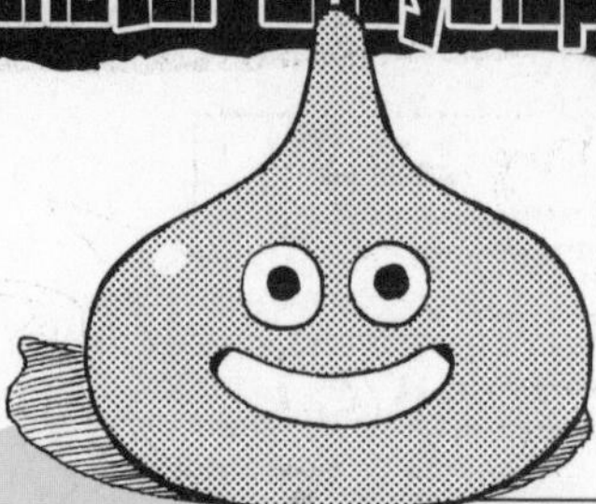

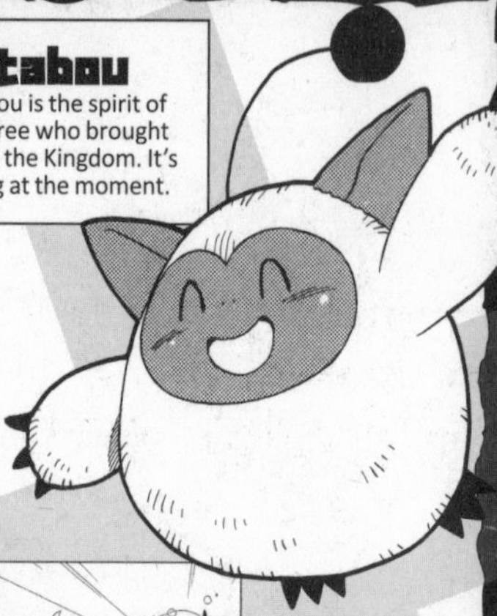

Watabou

Watabou is the spirit of GreatTree who brought Kleo to the Kingdom. It's missing at the moment.

Slime [Slib]

This purebred slime had accompanied Terry while training at one time. Slib believed in Terry and waited for his return even after Terry went missing.

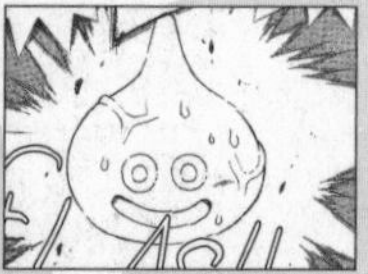
FLASH

▶ Though Slib got in a ton of training with Terry, his current abilities are unknown.

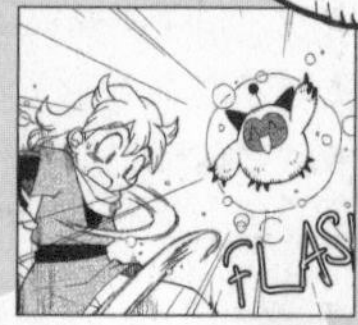
FLASH

◀ Watabou opened a Gate to another world and called Kleo over to become a new monster master.

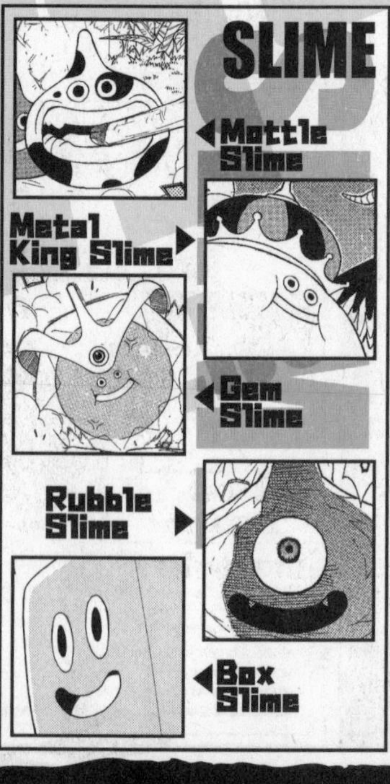
SLIME
◀ Mottle Slime
Metal King Slime ▶
◀ Gem Slime
Rubble Slime ▶
◀ Box Slime

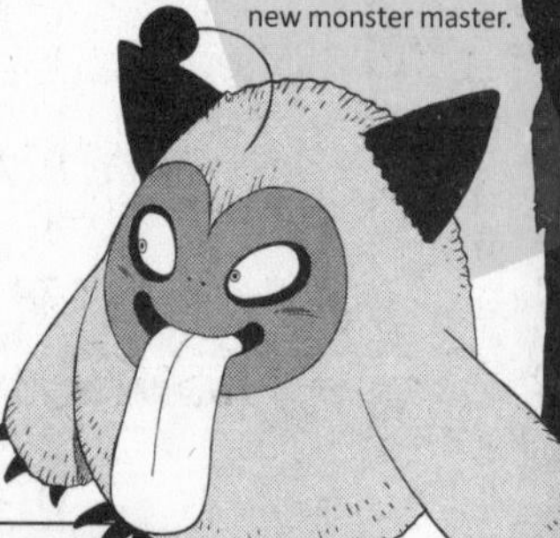

Warubou

It's the spirit of GreatLog, and has a horrible personality. It seems it's not too popular with the people of GreatTree, either.

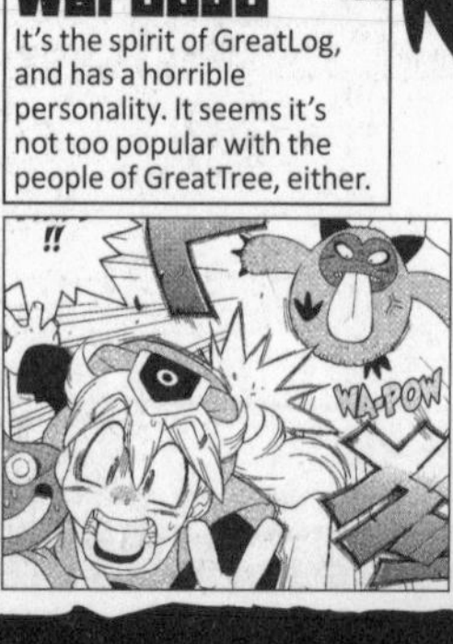
!!
WA-POW

◀ It looks like Warubou is following Kleo on his adventures, but what's its real goal?!

Dragon Quest Monsters +

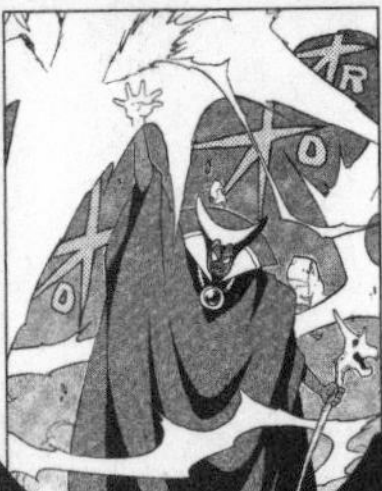

Dragonlord can use the ultimate Sizz fire spell, Kasizzle.

Small Fry [Jr.]

Jr. was one of the few monsters left in the Kingdom of Great-Tree. Jr. is justified in showing off his smarts because he knows a lot about monsters.

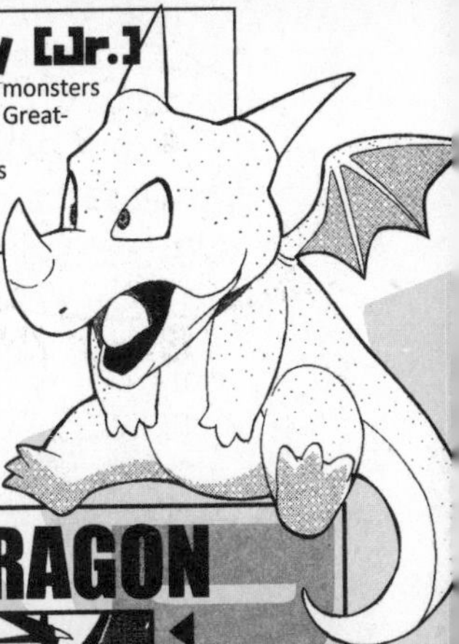

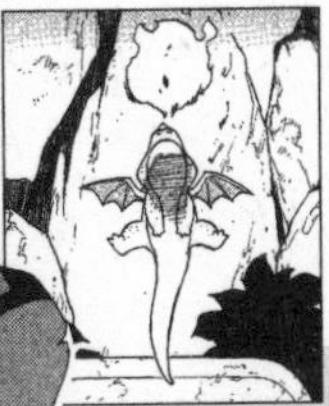

Jr. looks small, but he can use "Fire Breath."

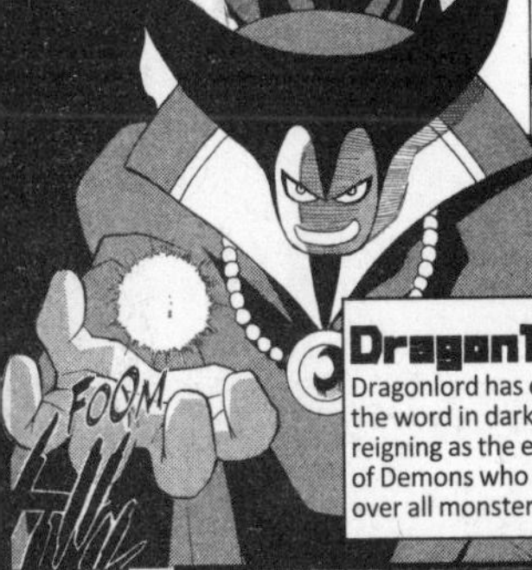

FOOM

Dragonlord

Dragonlord has enveloped the word in darkness, reigning as the evil King of Demons who lords over all monsters.

DRAGON

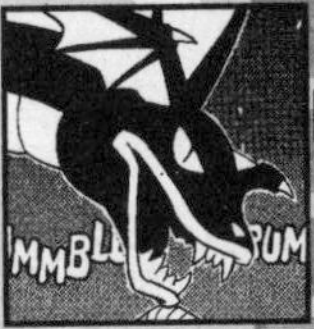

MMBL
RUM

▲Coatol

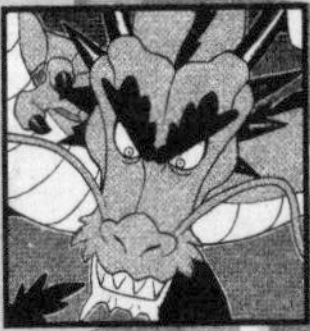

◀Xenlon

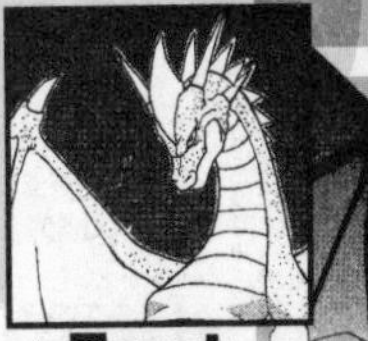

▲Great Dragon

Dragonlord (Dragon) ↴

The form Dragonlord took after he ate a xenlon. He evolved by the power of the "evil waves" that threaten to destroy the world.

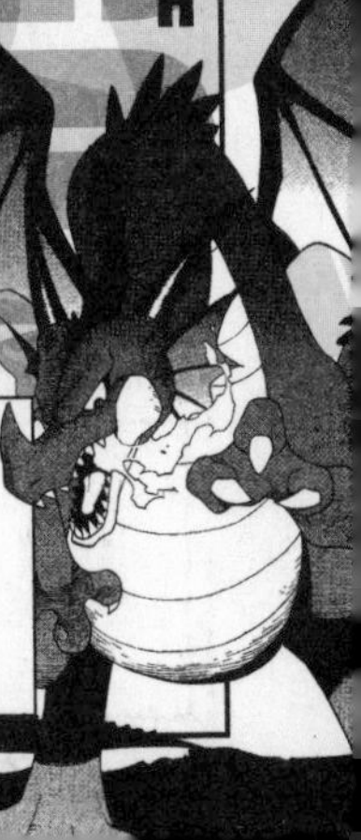

AND OTHER MONSTERS

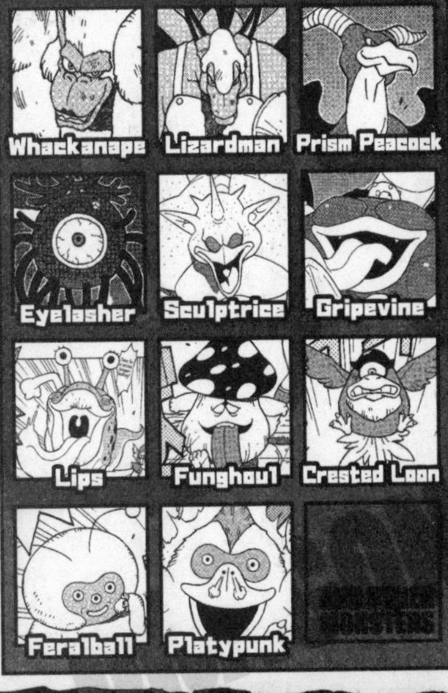

Whackanape
Lizardman
Prism Peacock
Eyelasher
Sculptrice
Gripevine
Lips
Funghoul
Crested Loon
Feralball
Platypunk

SEVEN SEAS ENTERTAINMENT PRESENTS

DRAGON QUEST MONSTERS+

story and art by MINE YOSHIZAKI

VOL. 1

TRANSLATION
Beni Axia Conrad

ADAPTATION
Danielle King

LETTERING AND RETOUCH
Carolina Hernández Mendoza

COVER DESIGN
Nicky Lim

PROOFREADER
Brett Hallahan

EDITOR
J. P. Sullivan

PRODUCTION MANAGER
Lissa Pattillo

MANAGING EDITOR
Julie Davis

EDITOR-IN-CHIEF
Adam Arnold

PUBLISHER
Jason DeAngelis

DRAGON QUEST MONSTERS+ SHINSOBAN vol.1
©2000, 2012 Mine Yoshizaki/SQUARE EXNI CO., LTD.
©1998, 2012 ARMOR PROJECT/BIRD STUDIO/SQUARE ENIX
All Rights Reserved.
First published in Japan in 2012 by SQUARE ENIX CO., LTD.
English translation rights arranged with SQUARE ENIX CO., LTD. and
SEVEN SEAS ENTERTAINMENT, LLC. through Tuttle-Mori Agency, Inc.

Seven Seas books may be purchased in bulk for promotional, educational, or
business use. Please contact your local bookseller or the Macmillan Corporate
and Premium Sales Department at 1-800-221-7945, extension 5442, or by
e-mail at MacmillanSpecialMarkets@macmillan.com.

Seven Seas and the Seven Seas logo are trademarks of
Seven Seas Entertainment, LLC. All rights reserved.

ISBN: 978-1-642750-47-8

Printed in Canada

First Printing: January 2019

10 9 8 7 6 5 4 3 2 1

FOLLOW US ONLINE: **www.sevenseasentertainment.com**

READING DIRECTIONS

This book reads from *right to left*, Japanese style.
If this is your first time reading manga, you start
reading from the top right panel on each page and
take it from there. If you get lost, just follow the
numbered diagram here. It may seem backwards at
first, but you'll get the hang of it! Have fun!!

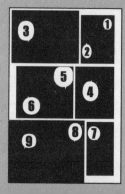